INTRODUCTION TO PHILOSOPHY

INTRODUCTION TO PHILOSOPHY

A Christian Perspective

NORMAN L. GEISLER
AND
PAUL D. FEINBERG

BAKER BOOK HOUSE
Grand Rapids, Michigan

Copyright 1980 by
Baker Book House Company
ISBN: 0-8010-3735-2

Library of Congress Catalog Card Number: 79-54188

PRINTED IN THE UNITED STATES OF AMERICA

Preface

Throughout history, philosophy has had a love-hate relationship with Christianity and Christian theology. Some have considered philosophy the handmaiden of theology, seeing its task as the formulation of arguments for the defense of Christianity. Others have regarded philosophy as the tool of the devil, echoing Tertullian's question: "What have Athens and Jerusalem to say to one another?" After all, the god of the philosophers is not the God of the Bible, the God of Abraham, Isaac, and Jacob.

We do not feel the urge to either glorify or vilify philosophy. Its continued existence among the humanities is sufficient testimony to its importance. Quite apart from its relationship to Christianity, we believe that philosophical debate has merit. Its questions are significant and of fundamental and enduring value. It is true that philosophical thought can significantly contribute to theological understanding.

However, the errors of philosophy must be recognized and refuted, to confirm the reasonableness of Christianity.

This text is unashamedly written from a Christian perspective. Thus, in the discussion of various positions we have tried to refute only those views that are anti-Christian. At the same time, we have attempted to present every position as fairly as possible. Among the several Christian perspectives, we have presented argument and counterargument, leaving the teacher or student to judge which view is most adequate.

It is our firm conviction that philosophy should be studied with exposure to primary sources. Therefore, we have provided suggested readings at the end of each chapter. We have also supplied a glossary at the end of the book, to define for the beginning student important philosophical terms.

We would like to express appreciation to our families and particularly to our wives, Barbara Geisler and Iris Feinberg, who have patiently supported us in this endeavor. Also, we are grateful for the pleasant and efficient way in which Renae Grams, Patty Light, and Karen Sich have typed the manuscript for this book.

We hope that this text will lead many to a lifelong study of philosophy on behalf of Christ's kingdom.

Contents

PART THREE
What Is Reality?

PART FOUR
What Is the Ultimate?

PART FIVE
What Is Good or Right?

PART ONE

Introduction to Philosophy

1 What Is Philosophy?

Welcome to the study of philosophy. Many students are not quite sure what philosophy is; indeed, most people know very little about the subject. Some think that it is an abstruse, even dangerous combination of astrology, psychology, and theology. Others think that philosophers are among the intellectual elite, people of great wisdom. This exalted view of philosophy is due at least in part to the fact that it is seldom studied before college. Elementary and secondary school students study math, literature, science, and history, but not philosophy. When students enter college, they often seek to avoid philosophy because of its alleged difficulty.

Those who do take philosophy in college find themselves discussing technical questions of little or no evident practical value. This apparent impracticality seems reason enough for rejecting the study of philosophy out of hand. However, this chapter will attempt to show that many initial fears and reservations about this discipline are unfounded. It is true that in many ways the study of philosophy is unlike the study of any other subject. One is not asked to memorize dates, formulas, or rules (at least these are not the most important aspects of the study). There is no field work or laboratory experiments, and no need to purchase any technical equipment such as a slide rule or microscope.

What is needed to be a good philosopher? At various times everyone philosophizes. This means that a course in philosophy is not an attempt to teach some unusual set of facts or to provide a totally new skill. It is, rather, an effort to help the student improve an ability that he already possesses and at times exercises on his own. This philosophizing takes place whenever one reflects upon either the fundamental presuppositions of thought and action, or the ends to which the conduct of human life should be directed.

Suppose you and a friend are discussing nutrition. You both express concern that the widespread use of pesticides and additives in the production of food has serious and damaging effects on the human body. You remark that the increased instances of cancer in modern society are directly related to the expanded use of chemicals. To this point your discussion has not been philosophical; it has been biological. But then your friend remarks that the government has a responsibility to ban such agents from foods, since all persons are *obligated* to preserve life. You disagree, asserting that the highest good is *not* the preservation of life. Furthermore, you contend, the government has no obligation to its people except non-interference in their private affairs. Your discussion has now turned to philosophical issues. You are raising the issues of "obligation" and the "end" or "meaning of life."

What, then, do you need to be a good philosopher? More will be said later about the tools of the philosopher. Briefly, however, the indispensable ingredient possessed by a good philosopher is an *inquiring* or *questioning* mind. You have the necessary equipment.

The Nature of Philosophical Inquiry

The Problem of Definition

The logical place to begin the study of philosophy is with a definition of the discipline. In other disciplines, defining the nature of the subject is usually easy and noncontroversial. Such is not the case with philosophy. Some philosophers have argued that the central and most fundamental philosophical question is the nature of philosophy itself. Definitions and expositions of philosophy have differed radically, even among practicing philosophers. Often one group of philosophers has thought that another has badly mistaken the task of philosophy. Some have said that philosophy is the "queen of the sciences," the most general and universal science as opposed to the particular sciences such as physics or biology. Others have denied that philosophy is a science at all. Some have argued that philosophy tells us about the ultimate constituents of the world, while other philosophers have rejected even the possibility of such an inquiry. Some have said that philosophy is basically a rational activity, centering in argument and the critical evaluation of evidence. But still others have denied that the use of reason is essential or that there are *any* convincing arguments in philosophy. Hence, a simple, comprehensive, and accurate account of philosophy would have to include a host of apparently inconsistent views and practices.

A possible solution might be to ask someone outside of philosophy—say, a historian of ideas—to simply observe those activities that various philosophers consider to be philosophical, mark their common characteristics and construct a neutral definition based on these characteristics. Such a request certainly would not be impossible for a well-trained historian who was also philosophically astute. However, this assumes that there is some set of characteristics or properties common to everything that has usually been called "philosophy." Besides, such a definition would only describe those activities that have traditionally been called philosophy, and we are asking for more when we inquire into the nature of philosophy. We are looking for a definition that will *prescribe* what philosophy is, and good philosophy at that.

Another place that we might start in our quest for a definition of philosophy is the dictionary. There we would learn that the word *philosophy* comes from two Greek words which mean "loving wisdom." This idea of wisdom was central in the thought of the ancients. In this view of philosophy, the primary role of philosophy was ethical education. That is, philosophy was to teach the good life. Even the more abstract aspects of philosophy played their part in achieving this goal, because knowledge and understanding were a part of the good life. According to the Greek philosophers, the ignorant man cannot be genuinely happy. Socrates, whose maxim, "The unexamined life is not worth living" is often quoted, was the embodiment of the ideal philosopher, or lover of wisdom. The classic conception of philosophy ("to know the good is to do it") was also central in the writings of the two greatest Greek philosophers, Plato and Aristotle. Yet this philosophical approach has been less and less influential in recent centuries. If you were to read the philosophical journals today, you would see that they do not play much of a role in ethical education.

So then, is a definition of philosophy impossible? We think not, for it is possible to point to the root difficulty that leads to such diverse conceptions of the discipline of philosophy. Having done this, we can give a definition that, while admittedly reflecting a particular view of that root difficulty, will be useful generally.

Analytic and/or Speculative Philosophy

What, then, is the root difficulty in defining philosophy? Simply put, it is the disagreement among philosophers whether philosophy is solely concerned with the analysis of concepts and presuppositions, or whether it is something more. Most philosophers working in the field today would agree that philosophy is something more, but would disagree about the exact nature of the something more. Let us examine this dispute more closely.

Philosophical inquiry began in a systematic way in the Greek colony of Miletus, roughly about 600 B.C. In examining the history of philosophy, it is possible to distinguish two different (though related) approaches to philosophy. We shall call these approaches *analytical philosophy* or *conceptual analysis,* and *speculative philosophy.*

Analytic philosophy or conceptual analysis.   Conceptual analysis is the belief that the sole or at least a central concern of philosophy is the analytic study of concepts. Philosophy's job is to define philosophic and scientific terms, and clarify the language of ideas. The philosopher is an analyst, but not in the same sense as a scientist. The scientist attempts to systematically explain the world in which we live. In order to carry out his task he must use carefully controlled observation and experimentation. The aim of the analytic philosopher, on the other hand, is quite different. He examines the basic presuppositions and concepts that the scientist, moralist, and theologian use. The philosopher tries to clarify the methodological concepts and principles that those in the special disciplines employ uncritically. Analytic philosophy is not only concerned with the scientist, moralist, and theologian. Each of the major areas of inquiry has basic terms and principles that need clarification. Often such inquiries are called *metaphilosophical*.

All great philosophers have at times engaged in this kind of inquiry to some degree. For instance, in Plato's *Gorgias,* Socrates goes about asking for the definition of "good." However, it was not until the beginning of the twentieth century that this kind of philosophy took on its distinctive identity and could be characterized as a movement or school of philosophy. Analytic philosophy has exerted considerable influence on the development of contemporary thought through the writings of its leading adherents, George Edward Moore (1873–1958), Bertrand Russell (1872–1970), and Ludwig Wittgenstein (1889–1951).

Objections to analytic philosophy. While analytic philosophy is in vogue today in English-speaking countries, not all philosophers are equally happy with it. Some feel that analytic philosophy overemphasizes questions of meaning and underemphasizes questions of truth. Morever, there is a large body of opinion which holds that the verification principle, a key concept in analytic philosophy, is an unreliable test of meaning or meaningfulness.

According to the verification principle, a statement is meaningful only if it is either purely definitional or else verifiable by one or more of the five senses. All other statements, including ethical, theological, and metaphysical ones, are meaningless (see p. 50 for a discussion of the verification principle). But we know on independent grounds that many propositions deemed meaningless according to verificationist criteria are in fact meaningful. Even analytic philosophers have noted the problems of the verification principle, and have worked to revise it.

Analysis and clarification of propositions, then, is admittedly a vital task for philosophy. But some thinkers point out that the preoccupation with clarification of philosophical propositions can overshadow other important concerns of philosophy. We can spend so much time defining the terms in a statement that we lose sight of the truth of the statement.

Speculative philosophy. Speculative philosophy is the second branch of philosophical inquiry. It too has a long and noble history, though recently it has come into disfavor, particularly in the Anglo-American tradition of philosophy. In fact, to brand some piece of philosophical argument today "speculative philosophy" is to stigmatize it.

Speculative philosophy moves in a quite different direction from analytical philosophy. While analytical philosophy is interested in *analyzing the foundations* of knowledge, speculative philosophy, at least in its more extreme forms, is concerned with *synthesizing the results* of the conceptual inquiry into a comprehensive and integrated view of reality. The final goal of some speculative philosophy is to systematically explain the ultimate constituents of the world and reality, and define the proper place of man and his activities in this world. Thus, speculative philosophy in some of its forms goes beyond the mere description of how the world is and how men act, to how the world *ought* to be and how men *ought* to act. Therefore, at least some speculative philosophy has two concerns which are foreign to the more severe analytical philosophy. First, there is an attempt to integrate all knowledge into a single, all-encompassing view of reality. Second, there is an effort to formulate a unified system of religious, moral, and aesthetic values.

Analytic and speculative philosophy are not necessarily opposed to one another. The various fields which compose philosophy contain *both* conceptual and speculative questions. For instance, in ethics we have conceptual questions that deal with the analysis of such key terms as "good," "wrong," "responsibility," "freedom," and "praise." On the other hand, there are the speculative questions of the highest good, man's ability to act altruistically, and whether a lie is ever "right." However, critical or analytical philosophy must come before speculative philosophy in the sense that one must understand the concepts before one can formulate ultimate principles of knowledge, action, and destiny.

Objections to speculative philosophy. Regardless of the possible complimentary nature of analytical and speculative philosophy, speculative philosophy has recently come under severe and consistent attack, most notably in the Anglo-American tradition. Why should this be? In many respects the questions of speculative philosophy are far more interesting and significant than those of analytic philosophy. The questions of speculative philosophy are the "big questions," the questions that are of importance to us all, such as: What are the aims of education? What is the role of the arts in a democratic society? What is the correct standard of morality? These questions touch everyone. But the questions of analytical philosophy often seem dry and unimportant. Why, then, would philosophers reject the genuinely interesting matters in their discipline?

There are a number of reasons that speculative philosophy has been under attack. First, there are a number of philosophers who believe that the integration of all knowledge and values is an impossibility. Such a task demands an omniscient and infallible mind, and asks too much of philosophy. Second, a good number of philosophers hold that speculative philosophy is not only impossible but is *nonsense*—a pseudo-science without a real subject matter. This claim is stronger than the first, and is usually based on the assertion that these speculative questions can never be decided based on man's experience.

Where then does that leave modern philosophers? At least two things can be concluded. First, regardless of how one decides the speculative issue, philosophy is concerned with the systematic analysis of fundamental concepts. Second, speculative philosophy includes questions that traditionally have been called *normative* as well as genuinely speculative. Normative questions ask for both prescriptive and descriptive answers—what ought to be as well as what is. For example, when someone asks if abortion is right, he or she does not simply want to know what most of the people faced with this situation are doing. He or she wants an answer that includes an "ought," regardless of what others are doing. Many philosophers would admit normative questions, while rejecting the more speculative and all-embracing questions. For the purpose of this book we will follow this middle course, recognizing that there are good philosophers who are either more analytic or more speculative.

Philosophy is, then, the critical analysis of fundamental concepts of human inquiry, and the normative discussion of how human thought and action ought to function, as well as the description of the nature of reality.

Characteristics of Philosophical Inquiry

Before ending the discussion on definition, it will be helpful to state some of the characteristics of philosophical inquiry.

1. *Philosophical disputes are not caused by a lack of factual information.* In general, philosophical arguments arise even when all the facts are agreed upon by the parties in conflict. The disputes are, rather, disagreements of interpretation, or of *value*. To illustrate, let us suppose that two people are arguing over the respective merits of two cars. They are agreed on such items as the cost of the cars, miles per gallon, and acceleration speed. Yet they cannot agree on which car is *best*. Thus, the problem is not directly, at least, a factual problem.

2. *Philosophical problems are seldom solved by an appeal to facts.* While it is always possible that some fact or set of facts might resolve a philosophical dispute, it is highly unlikely. Let us return to our car disagreement. Suppose that some new factual study comparing a number of different aspects of the two cars were released. Further, assume that the first car out-performed the second in *every* area. The second-car backer might find it difficult to continue his support of the car, thus changing allegiance to the first car.

However, such a turn of events is unlikely for two reasons. First, it is improbable that such one-sided information would become available. As a rule, evidence is more ambiguous, favoring one side here and the other side there. Second, since the dispute arose due to considerations other than purely factual ones, the second-car backer might still maintain the superiority of his car in spite of the findings. We can imagine the argument going something like this. "My family has always driven Chevrolets, and they have always served us well. One doesn't desert an old friend. I'm not going to change my allegiance now."

Both of the characteristics discussed to this point demonstrate that philosophy does not merely deal with simple empirical description.

3. *Philosophy is often more concerned with method than with theoretical content.* A number of philosophers have argued that philosophy has no distinct subject matter of its own. Thus, it is not primarily concerned with theoretical content. Rather, it is a second-order discipline, examining method and concepts of first-order disciplines such as biology, history, and education. In this sense philosophy is the development of a *skill* rather than the acquisition of a body of knowledge.

4. *One of philosophy's chief goals is clarification.* A distinctive mark of philosophical inquiry is rigorous thinking in pursuit of intellectual

clarity. Some contemporary analytic philosophers have endeavored to show that a good many philosophical puzzles are caused by unclear wording or by misinterpretation, and thus are *dissolved* rather than *solved* when properly analyzed. For instance, J. L. Austin has argued that many epistemological problems (*epistemology* is the branch of philosophy that investigates the nature and origin of knowledge) arise from a misunderstanding of such words as *real* and *illusion*. Gilbert Ryle has claimed that the ongoing philosophical debate on the relationship between mind and body (see chap. 12) is at least in part the result of a "category mistake." According to Ryle, philosophers err when they put the mental in one category and the physical in another. In other words, the "mind-body problem" is rooted in philosophical discussion, not in reality. These analytical philosophers assert that philosophical problems are caused only when one has misconceived the situation.

5. *Philosophy is concerned with the critical reflection on justification and evidence.* Philosophy evaluates arguments and assesses presuppositions and truth claims. This is why the student with a head for argument will usually do well in philosophy.

6. *Philosophical inquiry centers on a quest for truth about crucial issues that are perennially discussed by thoughtful men.* These issues are crucial in two respects. First, they are fundamental or foundational issues, such as, Is man free? or, On what principle do we act? Second, the issues apply to more than one field of inquiry. For instance, when we ask about the nature of knowledge, we are interested in the relationship between scientific knowledge, mathematical knowledge, and religious knowledge. Do these kinds of knowledge need the same sort of justification, or are there important differences in the requirements of evidence and certainty for the various fields?

7. *Philosophical analysis and explanation involves appeals to systems of principles.* This characteristic gives philosophy both its depth and its breadth. A philosophical answer is designed to be consistent with a set of principles which are regarded as true and which apply to the phenomena in question. The philosopher attempts to provide answers which appeal to a system of principles, by the light of which the case in question may be explained. A clear example of this is the nomological, or "covering law," explanation in science. The botanist explains pink

carnations as a *particular* instance of the *general* genetic laws governing the offspring of red and white carnations.

8. *Some philosophy is concerned with the nature of "being," or reality.* Philosophy studies not only *how* we know (epistemology) but *what* we know about reality (metaphysics). Although some philosophers hold that the quest for ultimate reality is beyond the domain of philosophy, others insist it is an important, if not essential, philosophical pursuit.

The Value of Philosophy

Before we close this chapter we need to answer the question, Why study philosophy? Some philosophers would consider such a question unworthy of an answer, and indicative of the American pragmatic mentality that wants to know, "What's it worth to me?" and "What will it do for me?" Such philosophers would say that philosophy has its own inherent justification; it needs no instrumental or external justification. If a non-philosopher does not understand and appreciate the issues that interest the philosopher, that is his problem. The non-philosopher's questions indicate his or her ignorance and lack of appreciation for the sophistication of the human mind.

Such condescending condemnation is hasty and harsh. It is possible to enumerate some good reasons for pursuing the study of philosophy.

Understanding Society

An understanding and appreciation of philosophy will help one understand his society. Philosophy has had a profound influence on the formation and development of institutions and values. We should not underestimate the importance of ideas in shaping society. For example, regard for the individual and freedom are in no small measure the product of Western thought. Philosophy helps us see what is involved in the "big questions" that individuals and societies must ask.

Liberation from Prejudice and Provincialism

The critical and evaluative elements of philosophy can help liberate one from the grip of prejudice, provincialism, and poor reasoning. In philosophical reflection we can gain distance from our own beliefs and those of others, and view them with some skepticism. We will read newspapers and magazines more critically, leaving us less susceptible to propaganda. Philosophy can help us to see through the evasions and omissions of political and advertising techniques. In a democracy there is the need to develop a healthy skepticism about our beliefs and those of others, as well as an ability to recognize good argumentation and evidence. This does not mean that we should become total skeptics or agnostics. Quite the contrary, those beliefs that pass the scrutiny of rational evaluation should be held with the utmost confidence. Wholesale and abiding doubt is absurd and unnecessary.

Practical Value

In spite of the abstract nature of much of philosophy, it can be a help in daily life. Surely, the ancients' emphasis of "wisdom" as the philosophical quest was correct. It would be pointless to seek clarity in all our fundamental concepts if this clarity were of no help in our lives, or did not contribute to the attainment of the wisdom we have talked about. For instance, ethical discussions dealing with principles of action may seem removed from the arena of real life, but they are not. Suppose that you are considering an abortion. Your decision will be greatly influenced by whether you believe action should be guided by *expediency* or by *duty*. Even where God has given us direct commands, we can examine God's justification of these commands. Since God is both moral and rational, His commands are not the result of arbitrary will. Moreover, since Scripture does not prescribe *all* action in specific terms, we need guidance concerning the application of biblical and moral principles to action. Indeed, philosophy is intensely practical.

The Christian Challenge

A Christian has a specific interest in and responsibility to study philosophy. Philosophy will both challenge and contribute to the understanding of his faith. Some Christians are suspicious of philosophy because they have heard stories of others who have lost their faith through the study of philosophy. They have been advised to avoid philosophy like the plague. Upon serious reflection it is clear that this is not wise advice. Christianity *can* stand up to the intellectual challenge mounted against it. The result of such a challenge should not be the loss of faith, but the priceless possession of a well-reasoned and mature faith. Furthermore, there are serious consequences of a failure to be aware of contemporary thought patterns. Rather than being exempt from their influence, one becomes their *unwitting* prey. Unfortunately, too many Christians hold beliefs that are inimical to the Christian faith, and are unaware of that fact.

Since all truth is God's truth, and since philosophy is a quest for truth, then philosophy will contribute to our understanding of God and His world. Furthermore, history shows that philosophical arguments and concepts have played a large and important role in the development of Christian theology. While not all theologians agree on the value or appropriateness of these arguments, all admit that some knowledge of philosophical roots is necessary to the understanding of Christian theology.

Suggested Readings

Ayer, A. J. *The Problem of Knowledge*
Holmes, Arthur. *Philosophy: A Christian Perspective*
Plato *Apology*
Plato *Meno*
Wittgenstein, Ludwig. *Philosophical Investigations,* paragraphs
    109–133

2 Disciplines Within Philosophy

As we saw in chapter 1, a definition of philosophy is both difficult and controversial. Even those who are "professionals" in the field disagree about the exact nature of philosophy. However, the situation is quite different when we turn to specifying the divisions or areas within philosophy. Here philosophers are generally agreed. In this chapter we will survey these major areas, to give an idea of the kinds of questions that will fall within each domain. As we noted, there are two approaches to philosophy, analytical and speculative. Because not all philosophers agree on the validity of certain speculative questions, a number of the problems mentioned below are seen by some as pseudo-problems.

Before we turn to a discussion of each area of philosophy, let us note that we have included some of the newer areas of inquiry, such as action theory. Although this book does not develop them, the questions of action theory are significant for a number of other philosophical areas. It is hoped that as the student becomes interested in philosophy, he will pursue these questions and problems beyond the discussions contained here.

Ethics

Probably the best known area of philosophy is the study of ethics. Hardly a day goes by that we are not faced with questions of morality. Will I cheat on my income tax? Is abortion right? While philosophy generally deals with the abstract, this is certainly not true of ethics. The issues of ethical theory are practical questions, problems that touch everyday life.

While the philosopher's use of the term *ethics* in many respects resembles the ordinary use of the word, there are also differences. When the man on the street speaks of ethics, he usually refers to a set of rules or principles by which he is either permitted or forbidden certain kinds of conduct. For instance, when we speak of "ministerial ethics," we generally mean rules or principles that govern a minister's behavior toward his parishioners or other ministers. Or, if we speak of the need for "business ethics," we mean a code that regulates, or better ought to regulate, the actions of businessmen toward their customers, employees, and competitors.

Philosophers also use the word *ethics* in this sense. For example, when the philosopher speaks of "Christian ethics," he commonly means those principles which guide the actions of Christians, principles such as those set down in the Ten Commandments and the Sermon on the Mount. The philosopher, however, also uses the word in a broader sense. More generally, he employs the term to denote a branch of philosophy. Here *ethics* is a theoretical subject. It can be distinguished from the other divisions of philosophy primarily by what it theorizes about. Whereas the epistemologist theorizes about knowledge and the aestheticist about beauty, the moral philosopher is interested in the nature of the good life, in ultimate worth, and in the propriety of certain actions and courses of life.

Ethics is partly an analytic or meta-ethical activity. *Meta-ethics* denotes the search for the meanings of certain key terms that appear in ethical statements, statements that ascribe praise or blame for actions.

A partial list of these terms would include, "good," "wrong," "right," "responsible," "ought," and "should."

On the other hand, there are many philosophers who hold that ethics is also a normative inquiry. These philosophers claim that ethical theories recommend, appraise, and *justify* the choice of certain actions. They evaluate goals and, ultimately, courses of life as morally valuable. The ethicist is concerned to do more than merely describe how people act. He wants to prescribe. That is, he is interested in ascribing courses of action which *ought* to be followed or praised.

Having noted the theoretical character of ethics, we do not mean to suggest that it has no relevance to the practical difficulties that face the ordinary man. Quite the contrary. Ethical theorizing almost always has its roots in human efforts to solve practical and immediate problems. As a matter of fact, the final test of any ethical theory is its ability to resolve the practical problems which give rise to the inquiry. The moral philosopher puts himself in the place of a man or woman caught in a moral dilemma and seeks principles to guide appropriate action. What makes the philosopher's task different from that of the common man is that he seeks to probe the problem more deeply. He is not only concerned with the right action; he is interested in the *principle* which justifies that action. While the ordinary man or woman desires a personal solution, the philosopher works for a solution that will be universally, or at least generally, applicable in similar situations.

Recently it has been argued that universal or absolute principles of action are impossible. Ethical rules at best are situation- or culture-dependent. This view of ethics is called moral or ethical *relativism*. Joseph Fletcher's *Situation Ethics* is a good example of this type of moral philosophy. According to Fletcher, "anything and everything is right or wrong, according to the situation," depending on whether one acts on the basis of love (*agape*).[1]

The search for universal rules of action has been attacked from another direction as well. A group of philosophers, generally within the analytic school of logical positivism (see p. 405), claims that statements of moral principle are not prescriptive, at least not in any straightforward sense. Rather, they express personal approval or disapproval. So to say, "Killing is wrong," is merely to express one's

---

1. Joseph Fletcher, *Situation Ethics: The New Morality* (Philadelphia: Westminster Press, 1966), p. 124.

own distaste for murder. It is true that the statement advises a similar policy for others, but they are under no obligation to comply. This form of ethical theory is known as *emotivism,* and is expounded by A. J. Ayer and C. L. Stevenson (see Part Five for a more complete discussion of various ethical theories).

Social and Political Philosophy

Social and political philosophy is closely related to ethics. Whereas ethics is concerned with actions of individuals, social and political philosophy is interested in actions as they relate to a group or society.

Roughly speaking, philosophical reflections concerning society fall into two distinct but closely related classes. The first class attempts to examine why society is the way it is. Why do war, crime, and poverty exist? If these reflections are pursued and classified, they are found to be a part of the disciplines of psychology, anthropology, political science, and economics. The second class of philosophical reflections probes the goals of society and the part that the state may play in achieving those goals. This second kind of inquiry is called social or political philosophy.

It should be noted that while the two types of inquiry distinguished above are logically independent of each other, in practice it is quite difficult to be concerned with one and not the other. One can be a sociologist without engaging in social and political philosophy, or do political philosophy without being an economist or political scientist. But generally it is difficult to separate the disciplines so neatly.

The social and political philosopher will analyze such concepts as authority, power, justice, and individual rights. Obviously, such analysis is closely related to ethical theory. But social and political philosophy is interested in more than just theory. It deals with questions such as, Who should govern society? Is political obligation comparable to other kinds of obligation? Are freedom and organization compatible? What is the meaning of democracy, and is it a justifiable form of government? What should be the place of the state in a properly run community? Again, though these questions are theoretical, they have enormous practical importance.

Aesthetics

Aesthetics is an essential part of value theory, or *axiology*. At some points it touches on ethical or social and political issues as well. The analysis of such ideas as beauty, taste, and art, and how we use these terms is fundamental to this branch of philosophy.

As with the other areas of philosophy, there are questions that go beyond the mere analysis of aesthetic concepts. Questions of style, the intention of the creator, and the nature of creativity in art are a part of aesthetics. One of the more interesting issues in aesthetics is related to the criticism of works of art. What makes a good poem? A beautiful painting? A moving symphony? How are interpretation and evaluation distinguished? Some philosophers have sought to examine the place of art in a stable society or its role in changing a corrupt society. Unfortunately, most beginning philosophy students get little or no exposure to this division within philosophy, although it is one of the most interesting.

Logic

In some ways the most fundamental area of philosophy is logic, since philosophy is a rational inquiry and since logic systematically sets forth the laws of thought and argument.

Most people do not use logical, deductive arguments with structured premises and conclusions. This is not to say that their arguments could not be so summarized; but in ordinary discussion such formalization is unnecessary. Therefore, there is need for logical principles whereby we can evaluate informal arguments. Most logic courses begin with a discussion of informal fallacies, that is, errors of argumentation in ordinary discourse.

Some of the most common fallacies are the appeal to authority rather than to evidence in support of one's position, and the attack on the man (called *argumentum ad hominem*) rather than countering his justification or evidence. For example, to appeal to my father's testimony in support of my belief in the rotation of the earth or the existence of Santa Claus is an example of an appeal to authority. Such an appeal is invalid when the "authority" is not qualified to evaluate the question at hand: my father is not an astronomer, nor has he seen Santa Claus.

The *ad hominem* fallacy can be observed commonly in courts of law. Suppose a witness testifies that he saw the defendant murder Mr. Brown. He recites the gory details in full. The defense lawyer gets up to cross-examine. Rather than questioning the particulars of the testimony or presenting counter evidence, the lawyer points out that the witness is a habitual liar and was having an affair with Mrs. Brown, making his testimony false. Obviously, these points brought out by the defense lawyer, if true, have some bearing on the case, but they in no way show that the testimony of the witness is false. They are an attack on the witness, not his testimony. They may lead us to suspect the witness's testimony, but they do not in any way prove his testimony false.

Logic, however, is most concerned with cases of formalized argument. These formalized arguments are of two basic kinds, deductive and inductive (see pp. 57–60). Rules for the validity of arguments in the form of deductive syllogisms, consisting of a major premise, a minor premise, and a conclusion, were first systematically set down by Aristotle (383–322 B.C.). More recently, Aristotelian logic has been modified and given a symbolic formalization. This formalization looks very much like a sort of mathematics, as a perusal of any modern logic text will reveal. The men most responsible for *symbolic logic*, as it is called, are Gottlob Frege (1848–1925), Bertrand Russell (1872–1970), and Alfred North Whitehead (1861–1947). Inductive logic, on the other hand, received its impetus from the writings and thought of Francis Bacon (1561–1626) and John Stuart Mill (1806–1873).

In many ways the twentieth century, at least in Anglo-American circles, has been the century of logic. This can be seen in the development of numerous logics. Though the kinds of questions and issues the new logics have raised were discussed previously in the history of philosophy, philosophers saw a tool in the formalization of logic that would allow more careful and objective analysis. There are at least three such logics that deserve mention.

The first is *modal* logic. Modal logic deals with the three principal philosophical modalities: impossibility, contingency, and necessity. Some philosophers interpret these modalities in terms of possible worlds. "Impossibility" means that a statement is false in every possible world. "Necessity" means that a statement is true in every possible world. "Contingency" means that a proposition is true in *at least one* possible world.

Deontic and *doxastic* logics are two other logics. *Deontic* logic is related to ethics, as it is an attempt to put in formal structure the functioning of the word "ought" in moral contexts, particularly in moral commands. *Doxastic* logic deals with statements that begin with "I think," "I believe," "he thinks," or "he believes." It is not hard to show that these propositional attitudes, as they are sometimes called, affect the truth value of statements. For example, it is true that "Walter Scott wrote *Ivanhoe*," but it could be false that "John Grey believes that Walter Scott wrote *Ivanhoe*." Doxastic logic is interested in these differences and the consequences that these differences have in logical derivations.

Finally, in the twentieth century, interest has developed in what has come to be called the *philosophy of logic*. Two widely-discussed issues have to do with whether negative existentials (for example, no inhabited stars exist) can be stated at all, and the difference between a logically proper name (Socrates, Descartes, or Kant) and a definite description (the bard of Avon or the present king of France). These issues may not seem important to the ordinary man, but when the logician wants to translate into a formalized language and make derivations, these questions become significant.

Philosophy of Religion

The characteristic questions of philosophy of religion grow out of intensive, intellectual scrutiny of living religions. It is necessary to distinguish the philosopher of religion from the historian of religion, the comparative religionist, and the theologian. The historian of religion attempts to trace the origin and development of religions. If a certain religion grew out of fears related to an eclipse of the sun, the historian of religion would document this and the effects of this fear on the entire body of belief. He would chart the group's religious history, noting that originally the worshipers recognized ten deities, but as time went on the ritual centered on a single, supreme god.

The comparative religionist is interested in the similarities between religions. He finds it noteworthy that all or most religions have a belief in a supreme power, principle, or being. Information gained from the historian of religion and the comparative religionist often is significant to the inquiries of the philosopher of religion. Yet the philosopher of religion generally begins his task where these activities end. The philosopher is interested in analyzing and evaluating the information, to discover what it means and whether it is true.

The activity of the philosopher of religion also differs from that of the theologian. The theologian is interested in philosophical questions that touch on his discipline, and is concerned with historical, textual, and exegetical matters. When the theologian deals with the general nature of religion and religious knowledge, the interests of the theologian and philosopher of religion are identical. But when the theologian studies the development of a doctrine or the interpretation of a text, the two diverge.

What kinds of questions are the stock and trade of the philosopher of religion? (A more complete discussion can be found in chaps. 17–22.) The first question examined in philosophy of religion is usually the nature of religion itself. Is there some defining characteristic or core of beliefs which is found in all religions, and which is the distinguishing mark of religion?

A second subject that the philosopher of religion critically evaluates is the arguments for God's existence. In the eighteenth century, Immanuel Kant said that there were three and only three rational arguments for God's existence. They are the ontological, cosmological, and teleological arguments. Subsequent philosophers of religion have added a fourth, the moral argument (these arguments receive fuller treatment in chap. 19, "Does God Exist?"). Interestingly enough, a group of philosophers of religion, known as "atheologians," have developed several atheistic proofs, arguments that attempt to prove that God does not exist.

A third subject of the philosopher of religion is the discussion of the attributes of God. For example, are infinite mercy and justice compatible? Is divine omniscience compatible with voluntary human action? Does the eternality of God mean that He exists outside of time, or does He exist in time for ever and ever? And finally, does the omnipotence of God mean that He can invent a task which is too difficult for Himself? Can He create a stone which He cannot lift? These are some of the most interesting problems in philosophy of religion. There is much work yet to be done in this area.

A fourth area in which the philosopher of religion has some interest is that of religious language. Indeed, though the subject has always generated controversy (Aquinas had much to say on the matter), in the last half century some philosophers have argued that religious language or talk about God is meaningless. In fact, truth and falsity cannot be attributed to statements about God at all, since they have no meaning (for a more complete discussion see chap. 20).

Finally a perennial question for the philosopher of religion is the problem of evil. While this problem can be considered on the purely conceptual level, most of us are acquainted with it *existentially,* that is, in our experience. The difficulty arises from the biblical teaching that God exists and that he is all-powerful, all-wise, and perfectly good. At the same time, evil, possibly even massive evil, exists. The philosopher of religion asks, Is the presence of evil consistent with the biblical view of God and the world, or must we deny one of the constituent elements of the problem? This leads to an examination of reasons that God might have for allowing evil in the world. The "justification of the ways of God to man" is called a *theodicy,* and is discussed in detail in chapter 21.

History of Philosophy

Unfortunately, philosophy is often studied without regard to the influences that led to the formulation of ideas, or the effect of those ideas on society, the course of history, or the person who wrote them. The twofold task of the philosopher is to explain what a man means, and to decide whether what he said is true. The history of philosophy, however, is an attempt to show how ideological influences led to certain philosophies; to observe how, in turn, these philosophies influenced societies and institutions; and to learn about the men behind the philosophies. Furthermore, the historian of philosophy tries to show the formulation and development of schools of thought, such as rationalism and empiricism.

To illustrate, the philosophy of René Descartes (1596–1650) is a part of the history of philosophy. We not only want to know what Descartes said and whether it was true, but some things about him and subsequent Cartesian thought. Did Descartes' time exalt reason and depreciate experience? Did Descartes' knowledge of mathematics influence his philosophical thought? How? Was Descartes' training at La

Flèche (the Jesuit school he entered at age 10) important in his philosophical development? In what ways did Descartes influence subsequent rationalists such as Spinoza, Leibniz, and Kant? Has Descartes' thought been an important factor in the development of contemporary philosophy? These are all questions that the historian of philosophy tries to answer.

Philosophy of History

While "philosophy of history" sounds like "history of philosophy," the two are quite different. Philosophy of history is critical reflection about the discipline of history, and it includes both analytic and speculative elements. The philosopher of history must first distinguish between the use of words such as *history* and *chronicle*. Then he can turn to problems of historical method, which are a central and important part of the philosophy of history.

Does the historian have a method unique to his discipline, or does he use the scientific method? Is the goal of historical explanation prediction, or merely understanding? Since the writing of history involves selection of material by the historian, should a historical document be considered objective? Are historical statements of the same nature as scientific ones, though about different subject matter, or are they *sui generis* (unique)? Can history be supra-historical? Anyone who has studied the development of Protestant theology over the past century realizes that these questions are enormously significant to the Christian. Christianity is a religion deeply rooted in history, which is why Christians have a large stake in these discussions.

There are also highly speculative questions related to history. Are there concepts that unite the data of history? Is history linear or cyclical? Is there such a thing as "universal history"? These latter questions receive their most profound treatment in the very difficult thought of Georg F. Hegel (1770–1831).

Philosophy of Science

The relationship of science to philosophy of science is much like that of history to the philosophy of history. Science itself is both observational and experimental. For instance, the biologist observes the structure and function of life, human and otherwise. On the basis of certain observations, the scientist can perform experiments to support his conclusions. Thus, biology is sometimes called a *first-order discipline*. On the other hand, the philosopher of science is not so much interested in observation and experiment, at least not in any primary sense, as he is in the critical examination and evaluation of key scientific concepts and scientific methodology. For this reason, philosophy of science has been called by some a *second-order discipline*.

Some questions within the philosophy of science are as follows. How should scientific theories be constructed and evaluated? What justification and criteria are necessary for scientific theories? What is the structure of scientific explanation? Can induction be successfully defended?

Philosophy of ...

Philosophy of religion, philosophy of history, and philosophy of science teach us about philosophical inquiry. It is possible, even desirable, to critically examine the primary terms and methodology of *any* discipline. For this reason, there is a philosophy of law, mathematics, education, and many other disciplines. Students in Christian colleges may well be asked to take a course in the philosophy of Christian education or the philosophy of evangelistic preaching. All this is evidence of the breadth of philosophy.

Epistemology

Epistemology, or the investigation of the origin and nature of knowledge, is one of the principal branches of philosophy. How do we know something? When is a claim to know justified? Is indubitable (certain) knowledge about anything possible? Does sensory perception give us reliable information about a world of physical objects? Are we directly aware of the physical world? Are our perceptions of objects identical with those objects?

The questions of epistemology are not the questions of psychology or natural science, although again certain results of these two sciences may be relevant to the epistemologist (for a more complete treatment of these issues see Part Two).

Metaphysics

To the novice in philosophy, metaphysics at first seems the most mysterious and foreboding of all the branches of philosophy. The name alone elicits images of abstract and difficult doctrines. In ordinary language we use the term of fanciful or mystical theories, which reinforces the idea that the subject matter of metaphysics is pure speculation with little practical importance.

Metaphysics actually received its name in a very simple way. The name comes from a Greek word which means "after physics." The term was introduced in the first century B.C. by Andronicus of Rhodes to designate the unnamed books which appeared after Aristotle's *Physics* in the original collection of his works. Thus, the subject matter of metaphysics was generally set by the sorts of problems that Aristotle dealt with in the sections which appeared after his *Physics*. Through usage the term has come to mean "beyond" the physical. Hence, metaphysics, at least for some philosophers, is the study of being or reality.

The Greek word for nature is *physis,* from which we get our English word *physics. Metaphysics* is an appropriate name for the material in the collection of Aristotle's writings, because for some time before Plato, Greek philosophers were writing works titled *About Nature.* In these treatises there was much which one today would categorize as natural science. However, they also contained speculations about the ultimate elements of the world which explained or caused all visible phenomena. For example, it was claimed that the ultimate elements of reality could be reduced to air, fire, water, and earth. According to early philosophers, these four elements in combination and interaction accounted for all reality. The Greeks did not distinguish between what we today call natural science and the more speculative enterprise; we tend to restrict the term *metaphysics* to explanations of reality that go beyond scientific accounts to investigate the *nature* of reality.

There is a subtle but significant shift of emphasis in metaphysics as compared to epistemology. Epistemology is concerned with the abilities and limitations of the knower, while metaphysics deals with the existence and nature of the known. In other words, the theory of knowledge considers the possibility and conditions of knowledge, while metaphysics considers the qualities and relations of the things known, that is, reality.

Some examples from the stock of traditional metaphysical questions are as follows. What are the ultimate, objective constituents of reality? What is the nature of space and time? Must every event have a cause? Are there such things as universals, and, if so, what are they? And finally, is there some substance or entity which always remains constant?

In recent times the group of philosophers called logical positivists have argued that a good deal of what had traditionally been a part of metaphysics was pseudoscience. Thus, they talked about the elimination of metaphysics, since they branded it as nonsense or meaningless. In spite of this attack, there has been a resurgence of interest in metaphysics today, though for many philosophers it is a more limited and modest branch of philosophy. Many of the questions today are more closely related to the nature and lives of human beings, questions such as, Does man have a free will? Do intentions cause anything?

Philosophy of Mind

As just noted, metaphysics has changed and developed in the last fifty to seventy-five years. The problems which occupy the attention of the contemporary philosopher are not new, but they have taken a more prominent place in philosophical discussion. One of the outgrowths of this development is the greater importance of philosophy of mind. This area of philosophy had traditionally been a part of metaphysics, and is still sometimes considered so. However, with our increased knowledge of the human brain and physics, philosophy of mind has received greater attention.

Some of the central questions are as follows. Is there in fact a level of reality we can call *mental?* If so, what are the distinguishing marks of the mental? If not, is consciousness merely associated with brain states? How do the body and mind relate? In what ways are machines like men? Can we construct artificial intelligences which function like minds?

Action Theory

One of the newest areas of concentration is that of action theory. Its emergence and prominence on the contemporary philosophical scene is intimately tied up with the other branches of philosophy. One does not go very far in philosophy of mind, philosophy of language, ethics, or many other fields without being faced with the crucial questions of action theory. Before it is possible to elucidate the nature of mind, it is necessary to understand the relationship of mental states to actions. Distinctions between various kinds of speech acts, and their relationships to one another is invaluable in language investigation. But it is probably ethics which profits most from the study and analysis of action. Questions of responsibility cannot adequately be dealt with apart from a discussion of ability and inability, and an analysis of the difference between intentional and unintentional acts. For instance, an ethical theory such as utilitarianism (the right act is the one that produces the most pleasure and least pain for the most people) cannot be properly evaluated without an understanding of the relationship between acts, consequences, circumstances, and motives.

The problems of action theory are fascinating. What is an act, and how is it related to an agent? What is the connection between act and desire? These questions are intrinsically interesting, quite apart from any importance that they have to other fields of inquiry. Thus, while action theory is not directly discussed in this book, we hope that the reader will pursue its study on his own.

Conclusion

In this chapter we have attempted to sketch the major branches of philosophy. The most prominent are ethics, philosophy of religion, philosophy of science, logic, epistemology, and metaphysics. Ethics studies the nature of obligation and the rules that govern right action. Philosophy of religion and philosophy of science seek to critically evaluate the concepts and methodologies of their respective disciplines. Logic, on the other hand, deals with the correct rules of argumentation. Theory of knowledge is another name for epistemology, while metaphysics is the study of reality or being.

It is evident that the questions and problems which make up

philosophical inquiry cover a wide spectrum. While the findings of a special science (such as biology or psychology) may have relevance for philosophy, the two are at least logically independent of one another.

Suggested Readings

Aquinas, Thomas. *On the Methods and Divisions of Philosophy*
Aristotle *Categories*
Ayer, A. J. "The Elimination of All Future Metaphysics"
Heidegger, Martin. *What Is Metaphysics?*

3 Methodology in Philosophy

Traditionally, philosophy has been the love of wisdom or the pursuit of truth. While the goal has been constant, the methods of reaching this goal have varied greatly. It is our purpose here to survey the main methodologies of philosophy and to approach them from a Christian perspective.

Some Methods from the Ancient World

Socrates' Method: Interrogation

There are numerous approaches to truth taken by ancient philosophers. Several of them stand out because of their enduring attraction. Perhaps the most famous method of deriving truth in the

39

ancient world was that of Socrates (469–399 B.C.). According to his most famous pupil, Plato (427–347 B.C.), Socrates used the question-and-answer method in his philosophical pursuit. In Plato's *Meno* the truths of Euclidian geometry are all freely elicited from an uneducated slave simply by asking questions. In this regard Socrates viewed himself as a sort of "midwife" who helped the individual give birth to ideas within his own mind. The presupposition of this method is that truth is inborn, or native to the human mind. Indeed, it was Socrates's belief (or at least Plato's) that these truths are innate; men knew them in a previous existence (preexistence). Hence, when the proper question is asked, one's memory is jogged to "recall" what he already knows. The philosophical method of interrogation, then, is simply an occasioning stimulus for the individual to remember truths latent in his soul.

Sometimes the question method can be very helpful. Indeed, clear questions often aid in their own answer. In addition the interrogative mood in human grammar is the natural method for gaining information. However, most contemporary philosophers are not nearly as optimistic as Socrates about man's native abilities. Indeed, the real success of the method seems to lie more with the asker's ability to load the question. Further, most philosophers today reject the doctrine of innate ideas. Many believe with Locke that man's mind begins as a *tabula rasa* (a blank slate) and that ideas are learned from experience in this life, not from prior exposure in a previous life. The Christian doctrine of creation definitely rejects any pre-incarnation implications of the Socratic method. Nonetheless, Christian or non-Christian, no thinking person ought to either stop asking questions or seeking answers. In this respect there is an indispensable and enduring usefulness of the Socratic method.

Zeno's Method: Reductio ad Absurdum

Even before Socrates, Zeno (c. 475 B.C.), the famous pupil of Parmenides, developed a method for determining truth by reducing alternative positions to the absurd. He began with Parmenides's teaching that the ultimate reality in the universe was one, not many. Zeno proceeded to prove this monism by showing that the view of reality as many led to contradictions. For example, if we assume there are many points between point A and point B, then we must conclude that there is an infinite number, since there could always be points between the points, and so on. But if there was an infinite number of points, then the distance would be infinite and untraversable. Yet we can travel from point A to point B; hence, it is traversable. So we conclude with the contradiction that the distance is both finite and infinite, traversible and intraversible.

Zeno's method is of enduring value for philosophy, for no position that generates contradictions can be considered true. The law of non-contradiction is one of the fundamental principles of logical thought. Further, the *reductio ad absurdum* argument is a "knock-down" argument, since something that is (or generates) a contradiction cannot be true. The method is helpful in argument, for one can assume the premises of an opponent and prove them to be false by reducing them to a contradiction.

On the other hand, there are serious problems with Zeno's method. First, Zeno implied highly questionable premises (for example, that matter or space is infinitely divisible). Second, not all arguments can be neatly divided into two and only two alternatives (reality is either one or it is many). With those arguments that can be so divided, there is often no successful way to show one position contradictory. At best, the *reductio ad absurdum* method is a negative test for truth. It may demonstrate that some positions are false, but cannot thereby determine which ones are true.

Aristotle's Method: Deduction

Aristotle (384–322 B.C.) actually accepted both inductive and deductive forms of reasoning. However, since he was the first Western philosopher to elaborate the rules for deductive reasoning, his name is generally associated with deduction.

Simply put, deductive reasoning is arguing from the general to the particular. If all horses are four-legged animals (the general), and Black Beauty is a horse (the particular), then it follows that Black Beauty is also a four-legged animal. This series of propositions is called a *syllogism,* the standard form of deductive argument. The traditional method of stating a syllogism is as follows:

All horses are four-legged animals.	(premise)
Black Beauty is a horse.	(premise)
Black Beauty is a four-legged animal.	(conclusion)

Inductive reasoning is just the reverse, that is, arguing from the particular (for instance, all observable elements of a wall are stone) to the general (the whole wall is stone).

Aristotle's deductive method involves several rules of inference, which are the subject of formal logic and will be discussed in the next chapter.

The most obvious difficulty with the deductive method is the shortage of universally true premises. This may be illustrated as follows:

> All men are mortal.
> Socrates is a man.
> Socrates is mortal.

The conclusion follows logically and validly from these premises, provided that the first premise is universally true. But there is a difference between a valid and a sound argument (see chapter 4). The problem here is, how do we know for sure that all men are mortal? All we know is that all men we observe die sooner or later. But if we cannot be sure that all *un*observed men will also die, then the syllogism takes this form:

> Most men are mortal.
> Socrates is a man.
> Socrates is mortal.

In this form, however, the conclusion does not follow logically from the premise, since Socrates may be one of the men who is not mortal. And since there are very few premises that even most thinking men agree are universally true, the effectiveness of Aristotle's method for discovering truth is seriously reduced.

There is, however, a redeeming factor about the deductive method in that it can be modified to accommodate our uncertainty about the universality of the premises. We may restate it as follows:

> It is probably true that all men are mortal.
> Socrates is a man.
> It is probably true that Socrates is mortal.

We may say "probably true," since all observed cases of mankind reveal that men are mortal, and so we may reasonably assume the rest are also mortal, until it is proven otherwise. The form of Aristotle's deductive logic, then, has a permanent value. All that is necessary is that one hold the conclusion with less dogmatism since one or more of the premises is only "probably" true.

Some Methods in the Modern World

Although the ancients (cf. Aristotle's *Topics*) were familiar with and used inductive reasoning, it is more characteristic of the modern period since it is closely associated with scientific methodology. But deductive methods have been used in recent centuries. (Both Descartes and Spinoza introduced deductive methods of geometric rationalism whereby they began with "self-evident" axioms and deduced everything from their own existence to God's existence.)

The Inductive Method

Francis Bacon (1561–1626) is credited with the overthrow of the "old" deductive method of discovering scientific truth and its replacement with the "new" inductive method. In colorful metaphors Bacon urged modern men to cease being scholastic "spiders" who spin truth out of their own deductive reason. He advised them rather to become scientific "bees" who buzz throughout nature in order that they may inductively transform nature's nectar into the practical products that can benefit mankind. Bacon did not invent the inductive method; he simply stressed it as a tool of scientific discovery and urged that experimentation be combined with it. Aristotle had done observation and even inductive generalization based on the inductive method but was decidedly lacking in experimentation. With Bacon came the impetus for a new kind of inductive method that involved more extensive observation and systematic experimentation.

Mill's Canons of Induction

Bacon himself formulated the basic rules of induction (*New Organon*, 2.XI.f) which became the forerunner of *Cannons of Inductive*

Logic, by John Stuart Mill (1806–1873). Mills's inductive method can be summarized by these rules:

(1) *The Method of Agreement.*   The one factor common to all antecedent situations where an effect occurs is probably the cause of the effect.

(2) *The Method of Difference.*   Whenever an effect occurs when A is present but not when it is absent, then A is probably the cause of the effect.

(3) *The Joint Method.*   Combine the first two methods when one method alone does not yield a definite result.

(4) *The Method of Concomitant Variations.*   When an antecedent factor varies concomitantly with a consequent factor, then the former is probably the cause of the latter.

Some opponents argue that one can never be sure he has arrived at any truth through the inductive method unless he has complete or universal observation, which is impossible. But the proponents of induction content themselves with the tentative and progressive nature of science and consider absolute certainty (at least in science) a will-o-the-wisp. Having said this the inductivists attack the fruitlessness of the old deductive method and point proudly to the amazing progress of human scientific knowledge since the inductive method has been adopted.

The Scientific Method

Strictly speaking, the modern "scientific method" is neither deductive nor inductive, but a combination of both with an additional "adductive" element. The basic elements of the scientific method are as follows:

(1) *Situation which generates the problem.*   Concern for John getting sick after dinner.

(2) *Formulation of the problem.*   Why did John, who is very healthy, get sick after dinner?

(3) *Observation of relevant facts.* John ate anchovy pizza, drank milk, and had vanilla ice cream for dinner.

(4) *Use of previous knowledge.* (a) John often eats pizza without getting sick; (b) he usually drinks milk without problems; (c) ice cream is his favorite dessert, and (d) this is the first time John has had anchovies on his pizza.

(5) *Formalization of a hypothesis.* The anchovies were the cause of John's illness.

(6) *Deduction from the hypothesis.* If John eats anchovies again he will get sick.

(7) *Testing the hypothesis.* (a) John eats all the same food except anchovies the next night and does not get sick; (b) John eats all the same food with anchovies the third night and gets sick again.

(8) *Conclusion.* Anchovies make John sick.

In addition to the obvious success of the scientific method its proponents argue that it is self-corrective, while the deductive method is not. If one continually holds open his conclusions to further confirmation or refutation, then he need never fear stagnation or dogmatization that became so obvious in the ancient deductive methodology. However, conclusions must always be tentative since the evidence is only fragmentary. And the fact that there are scientific "dogmas" (such as the macro-evolutionary hypothesis) makes the method liable to the same criticism leveled at ancient scientific dogmas (such as the pre-Copernican belief in the geocentricity of the universe). Perhaps an even more pertinent reaction to the scientific method is that it is considered by many to have a monopoly on the truth market. That is, it is believed to be the *only* method for discovering truth. Perhaps this is one of the reasons that contemporary thinkers have sought other methods.

Some Contemporary Methods

Three methods of truth-seeking stand out in the contemporary world: existentialism, phenomenology, and the analytic method. The first is clearly a reaction against "scientism" or the absolutizing of the scientific method, as against rationalism.

The Existential Method

There are actually many existential methodologies, but most have a common denominator that is typified in the methodology of the father of existentialism, Sören Kierkegaard (1813-1855). Kierkegaard was primarily reacting against what he considered to be a dead Hegelian rationalism. His writing, however, and the actions of many of his existential successors, reveals the same disdain for scientism.

While not denying that there is such a thing as *objective* scientific truth, the existentialist does not consider that kind of truth important, at least not nearly as important as *subjective* truth. Indeed, Kierkegaard declared "truth is subjectivity." By that he did not mean that any subjective belief is true, but that unless one believes something subjectively and passionately he does not possess the truth. Truth is always personal and not merely propositional. One never gains truth by mere observation, but by obedience; never by being a spectator, but only by being a participator in life. Truth is found in the concrete, not in the abstract; in the existential, not in the rational. In fact, one places himself in the truth only by an act of his will, by a "leap of faith." It is not deliberation of the mind but a decision of the will by which one comes to know truth. Truth, says Kierkegaard, is not in the area of the rational but in the "paradoxical" (supra-rational). This is dramatized by his famous Abraham and Isaac illustration (in *Fear and Trembling*) in which, according to Kierkegaard, Abraham is asked to leave the rational, ethical, and universal realm of "Thou shall not kill" and move by faith into the religious realm. Abraham is asked to transcend the objective realm of reason and enter the subjective realm of faith. For, says Kierkegaard, the moral Lawgiver supersedes the moral law as religious truth transcends ethical or rational thought.

There are, of course, a number of non-Christian existentialists who reject Sören Kierkegaard's belief in God. But they, too, stress the subjective, the individual, and his freedom. Jean-Paul Sartre, for example, believes that "man is condemned to freedom" and that there are no values to be discovered in any factual or objective realm. Indeed, values are never discovered; they are *created* by our free choice. In summation, one might say that the existential method, in contrast to the scientific method, would consider the most important thing about the scientific process not what is in the test tube but who is standing outside the test tube looking in. That is, subjectivity is more important than objectivity, as value is superior to fact. Hence, any method, such as the traditional scientific method, that does not seek truth in the realm of subjective value is wrongheaded.

Perhaps one of the most valuable aspects of the existential methodology is the corrective balance it brings to the purely objective scientific approach to truth. To put it another way, there is more to truth than pure scientific facticity. Truth, particularly religious truth, is personal—and the existentialist is to be thanked for broadening the horizon to include this important dimension of truth. There is more to life than objects; there are subjects or persons. Further, it should be expected that the method of obtaining objective truth will not be the same as that for obtaining subjective truth, any more than one concludes the Pythagorean theorem from Euclid's axioms by the same method he discovers the cause of an emotional breakdown.

There are, however, some serious drawbacks and dangers in the existential method. For one, it leads easily to subjectivism. How is one to avoid making his own feelings the test for truth? How can he avoid deception and illusion? In response to Kierkegaard's illustration, how does one know it is God and not a devil or his own evil desires that are saying, "Kill your son?"

Phenomenological Method

Edmund Husserl (1859–1938) is the founder of the phenomenological method, although phenomenology springs from the distinction Immanuel Kant made between the real (*noumenal*) and apparent (*phenomenal*) worlds, and the development of a *phenomenology of Spirit* by Hegel.

In its most basic form, the phenomenological method is an attempt to get back to a pre-theoretical approach to one's primary awarenesses. It seeks to give a purely "neutral" description of one's awareness of the world, before he ever begins to think about it reflectively. In this sense the phenomenological method claims to be a presuppositionless method—letting the bare facts of one's primary experience "speak for themselves." It follows Descartes in an attempt to find absolutely certain foundation for knowledge.

The *phenomenological reduction* is an attempt to entirely avoid presuppositions by deferring all question of existence. Husserl believed that by an *eidetic reduction,* that is, reducing one's perception of the world to an intuitive apprehension, one could condense all mental activity to an essence or idea. Such a reduction would reveal the structure of the world. Questions concerning the existence of the world and any possible ultimate meaning must be deferred (by the phenomenological reduction). One must first concentrate on the pure data of unreflective consciousness.

Martin Heidegger (1889–1976) borrowed Husserl's phenomenological method and applied it to a study of man. His first conclusion was that man is the being-there *(Dasein).* That is, man is a being-in-time or a "being-unto-death," for time and death directly affect man's concrete existence. Man has a sense of dread *(Angst);* he is a being thrust into the world and headed for death (nothingness) with no explanation "why there is something rather than nothing at all." Man as a being-unto-nothingness, then, is the fundamental structure of reality discovered by the phenomenological method.

Using the same phenomenological starting point and method, Jean-Paul Sartre (1905–80) concluded that man is "a useless passion." All of life is an empty bubble on the sea of nothingness. In his book *Being and Nothingness,* Sartre concludes, "Thus it amounts to the same thing whether one gets drunk alone or is a leader of nations."[1] The titles of two other works, *No Exit* and *Nausea,* indicate something of Sartre's existential despair. Other phenomenologists come to similar though less radical conclusions about life by using the phenomenological method.

Another aspect of phenomenology originated by Husserl is the *transcendental reduction,* or the recognition that all human meaning implies a mean-er. That is, all affirmations imply an affirmer. There is an "I" behind every "I think." This ego transcends any objectification. In fact, as Sartre put it, we can only see the transcendental ego as it were "out of the corner of our eye." That is, there is no direct way to analyze the "I." Once one views the "I" (subject) directly, it becomes a "me" (object). Once I put myself in a test tube it is a "me," and there is always an "I" outside looking in. We can get at best an

---

1. Jean-Paul Sartre, *Being and Nothingness,* trans. Hazel E. Barnes (New York: Washington Square Press, 1965) p. 767.

indirect grasp of this subjective "I" or transcendental ego. We can see its projects or "what it is up to" in the world. But since consciousness is always consciousness of something, a phenomenologist can never get at pure consciousness itself, even though he knows it is there. Hence, for Sartre there is a radical disjunction, and the "I" (subject) can never become "me" (that is, it can never objectify itself). In Sartre's terminology, the "for-itself" (man) can never become the "in-itself" (God). This is why man's basic existence is meaningless and futile. Nonetheless, it is the task of phenomenology to recognize the transcendental subjectivity and to describe its fundamental projects or intentions.

One objection to the phenomenological method is that it is doubtful any purely presuppositionless ways of approaching the world exist. Indeed, is not the claim that one should approach the world without any presuppositions in itself a presupposition? Perhaps we cannot attempt to separate reflective thinking from prereflective consciousness. It is highly questionable that there is such a thing as a "purely neutral," presuppositionless approach to the world. This may, in fact, be undesirable as well as impossible. Perhaps everyone must, as Kant claimed, bring with him certain forms or categories of understanding for the proper understanding of the phenomena of the world.

The radical separation of the subject and object made by some phenomenologists also seems unjustified. It appears to be based on a questionable dichotomy between fact (object) and value (subject). Perhaps, as others have claimed, man is the fact (object) who has value (that is, who is subject).

Phenomenology is, however, valuable as far as it affirms that subjectivity is not to be excluded from the realm of truth. In addition, it attempts to be descriptive and objective about one's experiences of the world. It is often true that one rationalizes away or obscures the truth of experience by superimposing on it thoughts, categories, and concepts which are extraneous to the world he experiences.

Despite the advantages of the phenomenological method, however, it seems a bit naive, if not self-defeating, to presuppose that it alone is a presuppositionless method. Perhaps the most counterproductive presupposition one can make is that the best way to understand the world is to set aside all questions concerning its reality. Indeed, if truth has anything to do with reality, then the sooner one recognizes reality the better. Setting it aside will not help the truth-search. In short, the method actually ends in solipsism, for it never succeeds in transcending the realm of one's consciousness in which it begins.

The Analytic Method

There is no single analytic method, and we will examine two currents of this contemporary methodology. The first is concerned primarily with verification or confirmation and the other with clarification.

Verification Method. The Vienna Circle of the 1920s and the logical positivism movement in general, included men such as A. J. Ayer, (1910–1970), Moritz Schlick (1882–1936), and Rudolf Carnap (1891–1970). In *Language, Truth and Logic* Ayer attempts, as indicated in the title of the first chapter, "The Elimination of Metaphysics." This alleged elimination is based on his verification principle, that for a statement to be meaningful it must be either purely definitional (analytic) or else verifiable (synthetic) by one or more of the five senses. All other statements (ethical, theological, and metaphysical statements) are non-sense, or meaningless.

The principle of verification has gone through many revisions by Ayer and by others in attempts to save it from collapse. Some have broadened it to include experiences that are not strictly empirical and others prefer to speak of confirmation rather than verification. But the original form of the principle of verification is all but universally rejected, even by most members of the original Vienna Circle. One objection to the principle of empirical verifiability is that the principle itself is not empirically verifiable. Some have responded to this objection by claiming that the principle is merely a meta-language rule explaining how language is to be used. But if the principle is merely a rule about the use of language, then it cannot be used in a prescriptive way, say, to eliminate statements about God or ultimate reality. Perhaps the best way to describe the failure of the verification principle is to point out that in some forms it is too exclusive, and in others it is too inclusive.

There is also a negative side of verification, which Antony Flew in *Theology and Falsification* called the "falsification principle." According to this principle, any statement or proposition is meaningless unless it is subject to falsification. That is, unless one would allow some event or information to count *against* his statement, then nothing should be allowed to count *for* it, either. If nothing can count against a statement, then it cannot be meaningful, let alone true.

Clarification Method. The other current of analytic philosophy springs directly from Ludwig Wittgenstein, who believed that philosophical puzzles could be solved by the analysis (clarification) of language. Where a question can be asked, said Wittgenstein, it can be answered. But Wittgenstein cautioned that not all questions can be *meaningfully* asked. The proper job of the philosopher is to "show the fly the way out of the fly-bottle," that is, guide us out of our philosophical traps. This is to be accomplished by discovering the rules of the "language-game" that is being played with ordinary language expressions. Then we will not misinterpret linguistic meanings, and call our errors philosophical problems. Rather than attempting to *legis-late* what one must mean (as did A. J. Ayer), we must *listen* to what is meant. And since all language is communal—Wittgenstein insisted that there is no such thing as a private language—we must analyze the "forms of life" at the basis of each language game. In short, experience is the final court that judges meaning. What is meant is determined by how a word is used in that context. By an analysis of language, one can clarify the meaning of language as intended by its users.

Clarification is indeed a key element in any pursuit of truth, for ambiguity leads to confusion. Analytic thinking is as essential to good philosophy as good instruments and clean hands are to a surgical operation. On the other hand, some analytic philosophers seem to spend so much time on the tool-sharpening and hand-washing that they never get around to the operation! In their preoccupation with *meaning,* they forget about *truth.* It is insufficient to place meaning in experience as mediated through language. All experience in itself proves is that one has had experience. No matter how clearly he describes the experience, there are always subsequent questions concerning the meaning and implications of the experience. Experience as such is not self-verifying.

Those in the analytic tradition interested in verification or confirmation are moving in the right direction, providing they are using confirmation as a test for *truth,* and not merely as a criterion for meaning.

Truth claims need to be tested or confirmed, for there are many conflicting truth claims.

One further caution should be mentioned: "verification" or even
"confirmation" are often narrowly conceived by many analytic
philosophers. They limit the terms to merely empirical or experiential
confirmation. Wittgenstein's followers, for example, deny that one can
speak descriptively about God, not to mention having any rational
justification for believing in God's existence. In this sense the analytic
tradition reveals the need for some kind of *justification* of one's beliefs. Unjustified beliefs may be true, but there is no way one can *know*
that they are—one can simply maintain them as unjustified belief.

Conclusion

There is not just one method of doing philosophy; there are many. It
is obvious that some methods are better adapted to certain kinds of
truth-seeking, as other methods are to other kinds. For instance, empirical verification is appropriate to history, and the scientific method to a
study of the natural world. Neither of these, however, is adequate for
discovering valuational or personal truth. For this an existential or
phenomenological method is more fitting. In the same way, a strict
deductive method is only usable where one has access to mathematical,
theological, or philosophical premises from which he can make logical
deductions. It seems clearly wrong to insist that there is one and only
one method by which one can discover all truth.

Neither philosophers in general nor Christian philosophers in particular agree on which method(s) is to be used to justify religious
beliefs. Indeed, some Christian philosophers are *fideistic,* holding that
there is no rational way to justify a religious belief. What Christians do
insist on, however, is that no philosophical methodology can eliminate
the possibility of divine revelation. The existence of the God who has
revealed Himself in sacred Scripture is an essential belief of Christianity. How the Christian may justify this belief is an intramural
problem. But Christians assert that all philosophies which legislate the
impossibility of God's revelation are doomed to failure. In this regard
the challenge of Christian philosophy is to "destroy arguments and
every proud obstacle to the knowledge of God" (II Cor. 10:5).

Suggested Readings

Aquinas, Thomas. *Summa contra Gentiles,* book 1
Clark, Gordon H. *Reason, Religion and Revelation*
Feuerbach, Ludwig. *The Essence of Christianity*
Flew, Antony. *God and Philosophy*
Freud, Sigmund. *The Future of an Illusion*
Hume, David. *Dialogues Concerning Natural Religion*
Plantinga, Alvin. *God and Other Minds*

4 The Tools of Philosophy

It is relatively easy to assert a belief or opinion. It is quite another matter to defend that belief or opinion. Obviously, the mere assertion of a belief does not guarantee its truth.

We turn to the philosopher for help, since his trade is argumentation. However, we may be disappointed, for it appears that philosophers defend a number of more or less conflicting points of view about very abstract questions. It is difficult to learn who, if anyone, is right or wrong. Views often seem to be held simply because of how one *feels* about the point at issue. William James even claimed that our emotions finally determine what we consider right and wrong. Thus, the beginning philosophy student might get the impression that there is no right or wrong, just matters of opinion. The best that a student can do, so it seems, is to sympathetically explain each philosopher's writings, but critical evaluation, which was said earlier to be at the heart of philosophical inquiry, is impossible.

This assumption needs to be challenged. If it is true, then in philosophy all answers are equally adequate, or what comes to the same thing, equally inadequate. No idea can properly be called true or false. This assumption, however, is simply incorrect. Some philosophical problems have answers that are clearly true. Moreover, even in philosophical disputes where there is no single answer, one should not thereby assume that he can believe whatever he likes. Some answers can with certainty be ruled out. Others, though not perfectly satisfactory, are clearly more adequate or probable than others. Further, one can observe progress in the discussion of these most difficult problems. It could be that in the future an answer will emerge that, according to general consensus, is true or most adequate.

The tools with which philosophical problems are either answered or clarified fall within the province of logic, broadly defined.

The Nature of an Argument

Since philosophy is so concerned with argument, it is absolutely essential to clearly define what an argument is. An argument is any group of statements or propositions, one of which is claimed to follow from the others. These statements are regarded as providing the evidence or grounds for the conclusion. Thus, arguments have a certain structure—premises and conclusion. The premises are the evidence, or grounds, of an argument. The conclusion is the proposition that is claimed to follow from that evidence.

The structure of which we have just spoken may be formalized, as in the following argument:

> All men are mortal.
> Socrates is a man.
> _____
> Therefore, Socrates is mortal.

Or, the argument may be very informal, as in the following example. "Every college student should take at least three courses in philosophy (*conclusion*) because it frees the mind from prejudices and teaches principles for right action (*premises*)." Thus, even if a philosopher has not given us a formalized argument, we should be able to construct his argument in a more structured manner.

As you will see, there are no statements which are distinctively conclusions or premises. Any proposition may be either a conclusion or a premise. As a matter of fact, the conclusion of one argument might well be the premise of another.
Example:

> All millionaires are misers.
> All misers are unhappy.
> All millionaires are unhappy.

and:

> All millionaires are unhappy people.
> All unhappy people are hard to live with.
> All millionaires are hard to live with.

Kinds of Argument

Inductive Arguments

In inductive arguments the premises claim to give *some* evidence for the conclusion. A good inductive argument will have a *highly probable* conclusion. That is, there is a reasonable likelihood that the conclusion will come to pass or is true. Thus, inductive arguments are said to be either adequate or inadequate, not true or false. Or, the conclusion is said to be "probably true."

Let us give an example of an inductive argument. A large and varied number of college students have been observed. It has been noted that a good number of these students make appreciably better grades after a religious experience called conversion. It is also known on independent grounds that a religious experience sets one's mind at ease and increases motivation. John Woods has just been converted, and his grades have improved about one letter. Thus, it is natural to conclude that John's academic improvement is the result of his newly-found faith. However, note that while this is a reasonable induction, it is definitely not a deductively valid argument. Nor is the conclusion certain.

While the canons of inductive logic are not as rigid as those of deductive logic, John Stuart Mill laid down a number of rules which form the basis of inductive logic. These rules are the method of agreement, the method of difference, the joint method, and the method of concomitant variations (see chap. 3).

Deductive Arguments

For the rest of this chapter we will concern ourselves with deductive arguments. In a deductive argument, if valid, the premises guarantee the conclusion. That is, if the premises are true, then the conclusion follows with *logical necessity* and cannot be false. Deductively valid arguments hold, simply by virtue of their form.

It will be helpful at this point to explain some central concepts associated with deductively valid arguments. These concepts are validity, soundness, conclusive arguments, and reliable arguments.

Validity.   Validity has to do with the form or structure of the argument. The premises in a valid argument guarantee the conclusion. Example:

> All bachelors are unmarried males.
> Robert is a bachelor.
> _____
> Robert is an unmarried male.

and:

> If cows are animals, then the moon is made of cream cheese.
> Cows are animals.
> _____
> The moon is made of cream cheese.

Both of our examples are equally valid, although one is true and the other is ridiculous. Let us repeat, validity is only concerned with the *form* of an argument. Since it is common today to do logic symbolically, it will be helpful to translate the argument form into symbols. Form of the first argument:

$$\text{All } S \text{ is } P.$$
$$\underline{r \text{ is } S.\qquad}$$
$$r \text{ is } P.$$

and the second argument:

$$\text{If } p, \text{ then } q.$$
$$\underline{p.\qquad\qquad}$$
$$q.$$

Because validity has solely to do with the form of the argument, *any* argument that has either of the above structures will be valid. That means that no matter what is substituted for the S, P and r in the first argument or the p and q in the second argument, the conclusion will be logically necessary. On the other hand, any argument that does not have a valid structure or form is called an *invalid* argument.

It is crucial to understand that validity and truth are distinct notions. Arguments are valid or invalid. Statements, propositions or sentences are true or false. Arguments cannot be true or false, although their conclusions can be. Statements cannot, on the other hand, be either valid or invalid (*tautologies* are exceptions to this rule). Because the notions of truth and validity are distinct, it is possible to have a valid argument where both the premises and the conclusion are false. It is also possible to have a valid argument with a true conclusion and false premises. It is impossible, however, to have a valid argument with true premises and a false conclusion.

Invalidity and truth also relate in a number of different ways. For instance, an invalid argument can have true premises and a false conclusion. Or, an invalid argument might have false premises and a true conclusion.

Thus, it is important to see that the truth or falsehood of the premises and conclusion will not tell us anything about the validity of the argument. And conversely, the validity or invalidity of the argument will tell us nothing about the truth of the premises or conclusion. Logic alone cannot determine truth.

Soundness.   In real arguments we are interested in more than just validity, and so the idea of soundness becomes central. A sound argument is a valid argument with true premises. When the premises are true and the argument is valid, it follows that the conclusion *must* be true. A deductive argument which fails to establish the truth of its conclusion is called *unsound.* An argument may be unsound for either of two reasons. First, it may be invalid. Or, second, it may have one or more false premises.

We still need to distinguish between conclusive arguments and reliable arguments. An argument may be valid, but if we do not know the truth of our premises, we cannot know the truth of our conclusion.

Conclusive arguments.   G. E. Moore stressed the importance of not only sound arguments but of conclusive arguments, where they can be constructed. The difference between a sound argument and a conclusive one is that in a conclusive argument the premises are *known* to be true. In a merely sound argument the premises may or may not be known to be true. Since such an argument is appreciably weaker, conclusive arguments in philosophical discussion are highly desirable.

Reliable arguments.   Unfortunately, conclusive arguments are very hard to come by. Some philosophers have, in fact, argued that they do not exist. Thus, most philosophers speak of *reliable* arguments. A reliable argument is a valid argument in which we have *good evidence* for the truth of the premises. There are degrees of reliability, depending on the strength of the evidence for the premises' truth. In a reliable argument, if certain premises are true—or better, if we have good evidence for their truth—logic will be of help in determining the truth or reliability of conclusions that can be derived from these premises.

Thus we have seen that validity is not enough to guarantee the truth of any statement. By the same token, an invalid argument cannot possibly be sound, conclusive, or reliable. Hence, something more is needed for determining the truth of any premise.

Clarity

The first step in determining whether a proposition is true or false is to understand its meaning. This point may seem obvious, but in practice it cannot be overemphasized. A great number of disagreements are due at least in part to a failure to understand another's position. We often engage in argument before we know what we are arguing about. It is impossible to determine the truth or reliability of a statement without first having a clear idea of its meaning.

This brings us to a discussion of *definition* and the *analysis of concepts*. The two are not identical, for conceptual analysis is broader and is also concerned with use in context, but they do overlap.

Definitions

Definitions state the necessary and sufficient conditions for the use of words. For instance, a triangle is defined as an enclosed, three-sided figure. Thus, for any figure to be a triangle, it must have three sides. Conversely, any figure that does not have three sides is not a triangle. There are two types of definitions: nominal and real.

Nominal definitions. A nominal definition arbitrarily stipulates that a certain word will have a particular meaning. For example, we might invent a new word, "bemox" and stipulate that it is to mean "six feet tall." Many very important words in our scientific vocabularly have such an origin. "Neutron" and "einsteinium" are just two examples. We can also take a very common English word and stipulate a new meaning for it. For instance, we could decide that "good-bye" will from now on mean "hello." Of course, such a departure from common usage would be confusing and hinder communication, but it is not erroneous.

Usually, we do not take the time or effort to make our own language or define our own terms. Instead, we accept the nominal definitions that native speakers of a language accept. In English these definitions can be found in a good dictionary. Thus, when we talk of misusing a word, we mean that someone has departed from "ordinary" English usage.

Real definitions. Real definitions describe the set of properties possessed by all members of a certain class and not possessed by anything outside of that class.

It is crucial to note that real definitions can be true or false, while nominal definitions cannot. A nominal definition is bound only by the constraints of convention. Such a definition is neither true or false; it is either useful or inadequate. On the other hand, real definitions are concerned with factual considerations. If a real definition does not properly delineate the class of things it is formulated to define, it is false. If, on the other hand, it delimits that class adequately, it is true. For example, Aristotle thought that a real definition of man was "rational animal."

It should be noted that a fair body of contemporary philosophers disagree that real definitions are possible. They reject what they call *essentialism,* the doctrine that things, objects and people, have a set of characteristics or properties which are specific to that group.

Analysis of Concepts

Analysis of concepts, as has already been said, is closely related to the task of definition. Language analysis begins with examination of definitions, but it does not stop there. It seeks to observe the *usage* of these words, usually, although not always, in ordinary language. An outstanding practitioner of this method was J. L. Austin. In his famous little book, *How to Do Things with Words,* Austin sought to analyze words in the *total context* of what he called "the speech act."

The Scientific Method

Clarity is the first step in testing the truth or reliability of a statement, but something more is needed. We may understand what a sentence means, but we cannot from that know whether it is true.

In his famous essay, "The Fixation of Belief," Charles Saunders Peirce (1839–1914) examines the four basic methods of "fixing belief," or determining truth, which have been utilized by man through history. He calls these: the method of tenacity; the method of authority; the metaphysical or *a priori* method; and the scientific or pragmatic method. It is Peirce's view that only the last method is satisfactory, for the other three always break down in practice.

To see how this relates to the problem of the reliability of arguments, we need to begin by dividing statements into two classes, analytic and synthetic. Analytic statements are true by virtue of the meanings of their constituent parts. For example:

All bachelors are unmarried males.

$1 + 1 = 2$

Both of the sentences above are analytically true. The first sentence is true by virtue of the definitions of "bachelor" and "unmarried male," while the second statement is true because of the meaning of "1", "2", and the "+" and "=" signs. A number of further things have been claimed by some philosophers for analytic statements. They are true by definition. They are *a priori* (their truth is self-evident, "prior to" or independent of experience). Their denial is a contradiction. They are tautologies, necessarily true because of their logical form, and true in every possible world. And finally, they say nothing about the world. Sometimes this is expressed by saying that they are vacuous. The statement "all bachelors are unmarried males" does not indicate whether there are any bachelors in the world. Thus, philosophers claim that it lacks existential import or is vacuous.

Synthetic statements are quite another matter. They are *a posteriori*. That is, their truth is determined by appeal to factual evidence. It is here that Peirce's essay becomes important. The scientific method, as he calls it, requires that I treat all my beliefs as hypotheses. They all must be *open to public check*—to public confirmation or refutation. Only then is it possible for me to claim that a statement is true or justified. Moreover, since my beliefs are cast in the context of hypotheses, they will be subject to repeated testing or confirmation. The crucial point is that society's experience, not just an individual's experience, is the final court of appeal for a scientific theory or explanation.

The scientific method of determining whether a statement is true or reliable has four steps: (1) formulating the statement carefully and clearly; (2) predicting the implications of such a belief; (3) performing controlled experiments to confirm or refute these implications and observing the consequences; and (4) accepting or rejecting the statement as a result.

Some philosophers have claimed that the scientific method applies to all areas of inquiry that are a posteriori, including morality, aesthetics, and religion. Other contemporary philosophers reject the universal and absolute application of the scientific method, though they admit its importance in much of empirical inquiry.

Deductive Syllogisms

There are many ways in which a deductive argument or syllogism may fail to establish its conclusion. Thus, it is very helpful to have a set of rules that will facilitate the formulation of valid arguments. Such rules will make it easier for us to avoid fallacies which make conclusions invalid. Below are six rules for valid standard-form syllogisms.

1. A valid categorical syllogism must contain only three terms, no term being used in an equivocal sense.   The conclusion of an argument asserts a certain relationship between two terms. These two terms must be related to a third term found in the premises. Where this relationship is not true, then no valid relationship can be claimed in the conclusion.

Any syllogism that has more than three terms is invalid, and is said to commit the *Fallacy of Four Terms*. For example:

> Cows are brown.
> Animals have four legs.
>
> Therefore, cows have four legs.

The conclusion is true, but the argument is invalid. The reason is that we have four terms ("cows," "brown," "animals," and "four legs"). Nowhere do we state that cows are animals. Thus, the conclusion does not follow logically from the premises.

In our second example it *appears* that we have only three terms, but in this case one term is used in more than one sense, which is called *equivocation*. While this is a simple and clear example, equivocation can often be very sophisticated and difficult to detect.

> All sides of rivers are banks.
> All banks have money.
>
> All sides of rivers have money.

Here we have a false conclusion because of the four-term fallacy. While it may appear that we have used only three terms, "bank" is used in the premises of our argument in two quite different senses. Thus, the argument is invalid.

Rule 2. In a valid categorical syllogism the middle term must be distributed at least once in the premises. The middle term is easily identifiable in a categorical syllogism in that it is the term which is found *twice* in the premises. A term is distributed in a premise when it refers to all members of the class so designated. Simply, this generally means that the term will be preceded by either *all* or *no*, as in "all men" or "no women." Any syllogism which violates this rule is said to commit the *Fallacy of the Undistributed Middle*. For example:

> All dogs are mammals.
> All monkeys are mammals.
> Therefore, all dogs are monkeys.

Note that the middle term "mammals" is not distributed (not preceded by "all" or "no"). Thus the conclusion cannot describe the relationship of dogs to monkeys. Our example contains both an invalid argument and a false conclusion.

Rule 3. In a valid syllogism no term can be distributed in the conclusion which is not also distributed in the premises. The conclusion must not go beyond anything that is implicitly contained in the premises. When the conclusion does so, the argument is invalid. When the conclusion of a syllogism says something about a whole class (a distributed term) while the premise refers only to some of the class (an undistributed term), clearly the conclusion has gone beyond the premises.

This fallacy is of two types. When the undistributed term is in the first or major premise, the fallacy is the *Fallacy of the Illicit Major*. When the undistributed term is in the second or minor premise, the fallacy is the *Fallacy of the Illicit Minor*. For example:

> All dogs are mammals.
> No monkeys are dogs.
> Therefore, no monkeys are mammals.

The conclusion of this argument makes a claim about the *entire* class of mammals, asserting that all monkeys are excluded from the entire class of mammals. However, the premise only refers to a part of the class designated by the term mammals. Therefore, since the undistributed term is in the major premise, the fallacy is called the Illicit Major.

The same problem may relate to the minor premise, as in this argument:

> All dogs are animals.
> All dogs are four-legged beings.
> Therefore, all four-legged beings are animals.

In this argument "four-legged beings" is undistributed in the premise and distributed in the conclusion. Since it is in the minor premise, the fallacy is called Illicit Minor.

Rule 4. No categorical syllogism is valid which has two negative premises. The rationale of this rule is easy to see. Since negative propositions deny class inclusion (one term is not included in a second), no relationship is established through the third term. Any syllogism which breaks this rule is guilty of the *Fallacy of Exclusive Premises,* since both premises deny that the two terms of the conclusion are related to a third term. To illustrate:

> No dogs are mammals.
> No cats are mammals.
> Therefore, no dogs are cats.

We are unable to infer anything validly about the relationship between dogs and cats.

Rule 5. If one premise of a categorical syllogism is negative, then the conclusion must be negative. An affirmative conclusion claims that one class is either wholly or partially contained in a second. This relationship can only be guaranteed by premises that assert that there is some third term which contains the first term and is contained itself in the second term. In other words, for an affirmative conclusion to be valid *both* premises must affirm class inclusion. Class inclusion is only expressed by affirmative propositions. Therefore, if either premise is negative, the conclusion must be negative. A syllogism which violates this rule is said to commit the *Fallacy of Drawing an Affirmative Conclusion from a Negative Premise*.

Arguments which break this rule are indeed rare since they infer such implausible and, in some cases, impossible conclusions.

> No dogs are cats.
> All cats are animals.
> _____
> Therefore, all dogs are animals.

While our conclusion is true, the conclusion does not follow logically from the premises of the argument.

Rule 6. No valid categorical syllogism with a particular conclusion can have two universal premises. This rule prohibits moving from premises which have no existential import to a conclusion which does. Not all philosophers would agree that the rule is needed. It grows out of differing interpretations of the universal proposition. This rule will be better understood if we first illustrate it, then discuss the disagreement.

> All dogs are animals.
> No unicorns are animals.
> _____
> Therefore, some unicorns are not dogs.

As you will note, both of the premises of our syllogism are universal, one affirmative and one negative. Those philosophers who follow Aristotle's interpretation of universal propositions would consider this syllogism valid. As a matter of fact, the "stronger" conclusion, "no unicorns are dogs," could be inferred just as validly.

Other philosophers handle the question of existential import somewhat differently. They follow George Boole's (1815–1864) interpretation of universal propositions and assert that neither affirmative nor negative forms can make any claim about existence. For these philosophers only particular propositions make existential claims. Thus, according to Boolean interpretation, the example is invalid for the conclusion, being a particular proposition, asserts that unicorns exist (a false statement), while the premises do not say anything about the existence of unicorns (or of anything else). Because both premises are universal statements and because they are understood as having no existential import, a Boolean interpretation requires an additional premise, "There are unicorns," for validity. The resulting argument would be valid, but it would no longer be considered a syllogism since it would contain three premises.

Philosophers who would accept this rule call its violation the *Existential Fallacy*.

Conclusion

The primary tool of the philosopher is logic, which deals with the rules for proper argumentation. We have seen that the fundamental difference between inductive and deductive arguments is the relationship of the premises to the conclusion. In an inductive argument the premise only serves to make the conclusion probable. On the other hand, when the argument is valid and the premises are true, the premises guarantee the truth of the conclusion in a deductive argument.

While the philosopher is concerned with the form and truth of his arguments and thus may put them in syllogistic form, most of us are concerned with logic in a more informal sense.

Suggested Readings

Aristotle *Categories*
Bacon, Francis. *The New Organon*
Descartes, René. *Discourse on Method*
Mill, John Stuart. *A System of Logic*
Peirce, Charles S. "The Fixation of Belief"
Russell, Bertrand. *Principia Mathematica*

5 The Challenge of Philosophy

The Challenge of Philosophy in General

Socrates said, "The unexamined life is not worth living." Therein lies the basic and perennial challenge of philosophy. The philosopher continually examines life, its purposes and presuppositions. He is concerned with critical thinking, and with clear and correct thinking.

Philosophical Examination

Broadly speaking, philosophy deals with life as well as with thought. The philosopher seeks answers to basic questions about the purpose of life.

Examining the purposes of life. Aristotle said that philosophy "begins in wonder." Man can never stop asking questions or investigating his surroundings. The question of origin, "Where did I come from?" is as old as man himself. Not all philosophers believe there is a knowable answer to this question, but they recognize that thoughtful men will continue to ask it, nonetheless. The Christian philosopher will point to the Bible, and to the first chapters of Genesis in particular, as an answer to this question from the standpoint of God's revelation.

Men also ask, "Why am I here?" This question of purpose is answered differently by various philosophers. Some admit they have no answer at all, but even so they ask the question. As we noted, the existentialist Jean-Paul Sartre answered the question by contending that "all of life is an empty bubble on the sea of nothingness." Many Christians, on the other hand, speak of the "abundant life" in which we "glorify God and enjoy Him forever."

The final question is one of destiny, "Where am I going?" Martin Heidegger believes that man is a "being-unto-death." Others feel we are headed for a final "nothingness." Christians have a greater long-range optimism. They believe that God's kingdom will come, and His will shall be done "on earth as it is in heaven." Christians believe history is moving in a specific direction and will accomplish God's purposes. Bible-believing Christians believe "there is a heaven to gain and a hell to shun." They believe in what C. S. Lewis called "the great divorce" of heaven and hell, which will provide eternal bliss for those who say to God, "Thy will be done," and an eternal woe for those to whom God says, "*Thy* will be done."

Obviously, not all philosophers come to the same conclusion about life's meaning, but they do ask the same basic questions—and in this sense, they all fulfill the Socratic dictum by "examining" life's purposes.

Examining presuppositions of life.   It has been said that our most important characteristic is not what we think *about*, but rather what we think *with*. In short, our presuppositions are more fundamental than our preoccupations. Often we are unaware of the basic premises that guide our life and thought. This is due to the fact that they are imbibed almost unconsciously at an early age through our family and culture. One of the essential tasks of philosophy is to lay bare the fundamental presuppositions that lie behind the conclusions we come to in our thinking. Providing they are consistent with their own basic axioms of thought, men's conclusions are as radically different from each other as their suppositions. If one is dissatisfied with the conclusions to which a position comes, then he must examine the presuppositions on which they are based. For example, if one presupposes that "God is dead," then one must conclude, as did Nietzsche, that all absolute values died with Him. On the other hand, if one presupposes that "God is alive and well" and that He is not silent, but has declared in His Word how men should behave, then radically different consequences follow.

Clarification of Thought

Another basic task of philosophy is clarification. This is why logic is the essential tool for thinking. Reducing thoughts to their logical form is an important aid in eliminating ambiguity and fallacious thinking. Often the everyday ways of expressing things are more "colorful," but at the same time the metaphoric overtones conceal traps of ambiguity. The debates over whether or not "all men are created equal" are based on the ambiguity of the word "equal." Does it mean that all men are born physically or intellectually equal in ability? Obviously not. Does it mean they ought to be granted (under the U. S. Constitution) equal political and civil rights? We would say, definitely yes. Many thousands of hours of human effort have been wasted simply because men have not stopped to define their terms. Theoretical clarification of thought is a very practical procedure.

Argumentation

The word *argue* has both good and bad connotations. When the word is used to describe the petty disagreements between, say, brother and sister, it has a bad connotation. But when a client tells his lawyer, "You argued a good case," the word has a good connotation. The true philosopher is not interested in argument for the sake of arguing. He is, however, very much interested in argument for the sake of truth. If philosophy is the pursuit of truth, then argumentation is the strategy which directs that pursuit.

Some unnecessary distaste for philosophical debate is due to failure to distinguish between "being argumentative" and "argumentation." Philosophy specializes in the latter. In fact, philosophy is the only discipline *per se* which is dedicated to clear and correct argumentation.

In this sense, whether one is a scientist, a historian, or a lawyer, he needs to be a good arguer (or, reasoner), for in every discipline one gathers evidence and attempts to draw correct conclusions from it.

Systematization of Knowledge

Traditionally, philosophers have been—and many contemporary philosophers still are—concerned with correlating the various areas of knowledge into one comprehensive "system." There are several reasons this pursuit has come into disrepute. First, the term *system* implies to many a rigid, inflexible body of knowledge with a locked door to anyone who would intrude with new facts. Second, the idea of collecting and correlating all truths seems a much too ambitious a project, especially to the learned man who has been humbled by the realization of his ignorance.

However, we must understand the tentativeness of any human "system," and can compare that system to an organism, a growing body containing facts it has "ingested." In this sense, a philosophical "system" is an integrative unity of data it has absorbed while relating in balance to its environment. The apparent impossibility of any finite human mind gaining a comprehensive and coherent picture of all reality is no excuse for either laziness or futility, for the philosopher must attempt to be as complete and consistent as he can.

Relating and integrating all the various dimensions of human knowledge may be but a distant dream, but it is a goal that many philosophers consider worthy of pursuit. Peace and justice for all mankind seems just as unreachable, but it is still worth striving for. Since philosophy is not limited to any particular area of knowledge but embraces knowledge in general, it is in a unique position to work on the systematization of all knowledge.

As we have noted, there is a "philosophy" of many of the areas of human interest, such as philosophy of history, philosophy of science, philosophy of language, and so on. In view of this unique involvement of philosophy in non-philosophical disciplines, it is clear that philosophers are in a privileged position to attempt the systematization of knowledge. The basic elements of a complete philosophical system, which is sometimes called a *Weltanschauung* (world view), are: (1) internal consistency, (2) external comprehensiveness, and (3) correspondence. That is, a good philosophical system must, in a consistent or non-contradictory manner, account for all the facts of experience, as well as fit all the facts together. There are a number of philosophical systems that attempt to do this, such as theism, deism, pantheism, atheism, and so forth. (These will be discussed further in Part Four.)

The challenge of philosophy, then, is fourfold. The multiple challenge is to think critically (examination), to think clearly (clarification), to think correctly (argumentation), and to think comprehensively (systematization).

The Challenge of Philosophy for a Christian

Philosophy presents a particular challenge for the Christian, both positively and negatively. Philosophy serves in the construction of the Christian system and in the refutation of contrary views. There is a crucial text in the New Testament that corresponds to these two tasks. Paul said, "We destroy arguments and every proud obstacle to the knowledge of God [negative aspect], and take every thought captive to obey Christ [positive aspect]" (II Cor. 10:5). Without a thorough knowledge of philosophy the Christian is at the mercy of the non-Christian in the intellectual arena. The challenge, then, is for the Christian to "out-think" the non-Christian in both building a system of truth and in tearing down systems of error.

If this is the task of the Christian in philosophy then how does one explain the warning of the apostle Paul to "beware lest any man spoil you through philosophy" (Col. 2:8, KJV)? Unfortunately, some Christians have taken this verse to be an injunction against the study of philosophy. This is incorrect for several reasons. First, the verse is not a prohibition against philosophy as such, but against *false* philosophy, for Paul adds, "and [beware of] vain deceit, after the tradition of men." In fact, Paul is warning against a specific false philosophy, a kind of incipient gnosticism which had infiltrated the church at Colosse (the definite article "this" in Greek indicates a particular philosophy). Finally, one cannot really "beware" of false philosophy unless he is first aware of it. A Christian must recognize error before he can counter it, just as a doctor must study disease before he can knowledgeably treat it. The Christian church has on occasion been penetrated by false teaching precisely because Christians have not adequately been trained to detect the "disease" of error.

A good counterfeit will be as close to the truth as possible. This is why false, non-Christian philosophies that are dressed in Christian garb are particularly dangerous. Indeed, the Christian most likely to fall prey to false philosophy is the ignorant Christian.

The Biblical Basis for Christian Philosophy

God places no premium on ignorance. Christians do not receive a spiritual reward for an ignorant faith. Faith may be more *meritorious* than reason ("without faith it is impossible to please God," Heb. 11:6, NIV), but reason is more *noble* ("the Bereans were of more noble character than the Thessalonians, for they . . . examined the Scriptures every day to see if what Paul said was true," Acts 17:11, NIV). Indeed, the "great command" to the Christian is to "love the Lord your God with all your . . . *minds"* (Matt. 22:37, NIV). Peter says we are to be prepared "to give the *reason* for the hope that [we] have" (I Peter 3:15, NIV). Paul said we are set "in *defence* and confirmation of the gospel" (Phil. 1:7, KJV), and he himself "*reasoned . . .* out of the scriptures" (Acts 17:2, KJV).

It is true that we are warned against "the wisdom of this world" (I Cor. 1:20). But this too is part of the challenge of philosophy for a Christian. As C. S. Lewis correctly observed, "To be ignorant and simple now—not to be able to meet the enemies on their own ground—would be to throw down our weapons, and to betray our uneducated brethren who have, under God, no defense but us against the intellectual attacks of the heathen. Good philosophy must exist, if for no other reason, because bad philosophy needs to be answered."[1]

The Roles of Philosophy for a Christian

There are several functions of philosophy in the service of Christianity. Philosophy has been called "the handmaiden of theology"; it is a defense against heresy and is the crux of apologetics.

The function of philosophy in theology. One cannot do systematic theology without the aid of philosophy. The Bible provides the basic data for Christian theology, but theology is not systematic until it is

---

1. C. S. Lewis, *The Weight of Glory* (New York: Macmillan, 1949), p. 50.

"systematized." For example, orthodox Christians believe in one God who eternally exists in three persons—the Trinity. Yet this doctrine is the result of several philosophical procedures. First, there is an *inductive* study of the Scriptures. Second, there is a systematic *correlation* of all the biblical data that relates to God. This yields, among other things, two premises: (a) There is one God, and (b) there are three persons (Father, Son, and Holy Spirit) who are God. Third, there is a logical *deduction* that is drawn from these two premises, that is, the doctrine of the Trinity: there is one God who exists in three persons.

Beside this positive role of "constructing" Christian doctrine, philosophy has a negative role in systematic theology. Since no thinking person can be satisfied with what is logically contradictory, the Christian theologian must eliminate contradictions from the Christian "system." If the Bible says God has eyes (Heb. 4:13), and arms, and yet also claims that He is a spirit without a body (John 4:24), then the theologian must show that these are not logical contradictions. This is generally accomplished by reasoning that the references to eyes and arms are metaphorical, not literal. God is also described as having wings, but that illustrates His protective powers and does not mean He has feathers.

The philosopher-theologian has a more difficult task with some of the mysteries of the Christian faith, such as the two natures of Christ. Orthodox Christianity holds that Christ is both God and man; He is the God-man. But God is infinite and man is finite. How, then, can Christ be an infinite finite, which seems to be a clear contradiction? The philosopher-theologian answers: Christ is one person, but He has *two* natures. He is infinite in His divine nature and finite in His human nature, but one nature is not the other. The two natures are distinct but exist simultaneously in the same person. The mystery is *how* this can be so; it goes "beyond reason." But there is no contradiction in saying that Christ is one person (one sense) with two natures (another sense). Contradiction results only when one does not use two different senses, such as if one said God were one person and yet three persons *in the same sense*.

In short, without the aid of logic and philosophy Christian theology would not be possible. Coherent, consistent thinking about the Bible (which is a good, simple definition of theology) cannot take place without the aid of philosophy. The Christian theologian is in this sense a philosophical Bible student. He gives a *logos* (reason) about the *theos* (God) as known from Scripture.

The function of philosophy in apologetics.   The task of apologetics is to defend the Christian faith against attacks from the outside (I Peter 3:15). There are several ways in which philosophy is used to accomplish this task. There are both negative and positive apologetic tasks. The negative task is twofold: (1) Show that attacks on Christianity are false, that is, contrary to fact or contradictory; and (2) show that the non-Christian view is not necessarily true, that is, possible but not necessarily the case. Obviously, there is no way to effectively accomplish either of these tasks without using the philosophical tools of clear, consistent, and correct thinking.

The positive task of apologetics is also dependent on philosophy. It involves the construction of good arguments or the supplying of good evidence in justification of the basic truth of Christianity. Usually this involves arguments in support of God (theism) and evidence in support of the historical truth of Christianity. This task falls squarely on the shoulders of philosophy.

The function of philosophy in polemics.   The task of polemics is to argue against heresies within Christianity, in contrast to apologetics, which argues against errors from without. The same basic need for philosophy is manifest in polemics. One can argue no better for truth than when he is trained in philosophical argumentation. As a matter of fact, the Christian polemicist must understand both theology (which uses *systematic* philosophical thinking) and philosophy (which uses *logical* thinking). Heresies often arise from either false presuppositions or from fallacious conclusions from true premises. Philosophy specializes in recognizing both of these errors.

The function of philosophy in communication.   Christian missionaries and apologists have become increasingly aware that there are various world views within which and by which men think very differently about God, men, and the world. Some pantheists believe, for example, that the material world is evil or an illusion, while a Christian theist holds it is a good creation of God. A complete naturalist believes miracles are impossible, while a supernatural theist accepts them as

actual. When such different thinkers look at the same "fact" or phenomenon they give it radically different meanings.

Chapter 12 of the Gospel of John serves as an example. A certain
phenomenon occurred which three groups witnessed. But each filtered
it through the grid of his own world view. According to verse 28 Jesus
prayed aloud, "Father, glorify thy name." John writes that a voice
came from heaven, saying, "I have glorified it, and I will glorify it
again." The different groups present interpreted the sound in various
ways. The naturalists in the crowd called it thunder. The religionists
claimed it was an angel, and the theists said it was the voice of God.

A world view may be thought of as a pair of glasses through which
one views the world. To someone wearing red glasses, everything will
look red. And to someone with yellow glasses, everything will appear
tinged with yellow. Likewise, to a naturalist every event will have a
natural explanation—even those events that are highly unusual.

Some philosophers say that all facts are "theory-laden"; bare facts
are entirely meaningless. Indeed, the same "fact" can have different
meanings when viewed by different people. If this is so, then the task
of communicating Christianity to someone with a dissimilar world
view is much more difficult than at first appears. Christ's claim, "I and
the Father are one," does not have the same meaning for a pantheist, a
unitarian, or a Christian theist. In line with the pantheist's world view,
this means no more than Christ is a *manifestation* of God, as are all
men. The unitarian takes it to mean Christ is *morally* one with God,
that is, He lived in union with God. The Christian theist, on the other
hand, understands that Christ claimed to be *metaphysically* one with
God, to be of the same essence as God. Indeed, the monotheistic Jews
of Christ's day understood Him to mean exactly that, as is indicated by
their response: "You, a mere man, claim to be God" (John 10:33,
NIV).

One of the tasks of Christian philosophy is to help the communication process between those holding different world views. For it makes
a great difference what kind of "glasses" one has on when he looks at
the world. Some Christians claim that the glasses are "cemented" to
one's face, and can only be removed by supernatural conversion. This
seems unlikely for two reasons. First, from this would follow the
startling conclusion that when one shifts from a theistic to an atheistic
world view (which may happen) it would have to be accomplished by a
supernatural act of God, without any appeal to evidence or argumenta-

tion! Further, how could a naturalist whose glasses are cemented to his face even *understand* the supernatural message he must believe if he sees everything through naturalistic glasses? According to this theory the ability to see supernaturally (the new world view) comes only after conversion; yet one would have to be wearing the new glasses before he could understand the message in order to be converted.

But even if one's world-view "glasses" are not cemented to one's face, it is, nonetheless, a fact that men view things very differently. And different models (or paradigms) are a definite hindrance to the process of communication between people holding them. One task of Christian philosophy, then, is to work on a pre-evangelistic level to get the outsider to look around the edges or through the cracks of his glasses, or to take them off and try a set of "theistic glasses" on for size. Philosophy performs the process indicated by these metaphors through philosophical argumentation. Unless the intellectual ground is cleared and a straight course is cut for the word of truth, it is unlikely that the Christian is truly communicating the gospel of Christ to men of different world views.

Conclusion

The challenge of philosophy for the Christian is twofold. First, there is the general challenge of thinking critically, clearly, correctly, and comprehensively about the world. This is the task of any thinker, Christian or non-Christian. In addition, because of his basic biblical beliefs, the Christian has a special philosophical burden. He uses philosophy in the systemization of these beliefs, and in the philosophical argumentation in defense of Christianity. He needs philosophy to communicate the Christian view to those with other world views. All in all, the Christian depends on philosophy to render the credible intelligible. Philosophy is the tool by which the Christian makes sense out of his faith.

Suggested Readings

Hume, David. *An Enquiry Concerning Human Understanding*
Husserl, Edmund. *Ideas*

James, William. *What Is Pragmatism?*
Plato *The Republic,* books 5–7
Ryle, Gilbert. *Dilemmas*
Sartre, Jean-Paul. *Being and Nothingness*
Spinoza, Benedict. *Ethics*

PART TWO

What Is Knowledge?

⑥ Can We Know?

If you talk to the ordinary man in the street, he will tell you that human beings know many things. We know that one plus one equals two, and that twelve times twelve equals 144. We know that the world has trees and mountains, that people and chairs are a part of our environment. We also know when we are seeing red, and we know that there are other men with minds with whom we talk and live. Thus, it seems a bit strange to be faced with the question of this chapter, Can we know?

Even the skeptic generally does not deny that men are strongly inclined to believe that there is a three-dimensional world of objects which can be bought and sold, used and reused. However, this is not the problem for the philosopher. He is concerned with the rational justification of such belief. The issue is not what we do believe, but what we are justified in believing. It is just at this point that *skepticism* raises its ugly head. As we shall see in this chapter, skepticism takes more than just one form, but all of them take a skeptical attitude toward all or some particular justification of belief.

At first, arguing with a skeptic can be an invigorating experience. But ultimately it becomes frustrating, for a good skeptic is prevented from ever agreeing on any premise, making it impossible for the argument to even get started. Cratylus, a disciple of Heraclitus (Heraclitus taught that a man could never step into the same river twice, because the river was constantly changing), was a pre-Socratic skeptic. Cratylus went even farther than Heraclitus, insisting that no one steps into the same river even once, because both the river and the one stepping into it are constantly changing. This led him to even broader skepticism. Cratylus became convinced that communication was impossible because the speaker, the words spoken, and the one hearing the words were all in constant flux. Thus, whatever meanings the speaker had in mind would be altered by the time they reached the hearer. Therefore, he apparently refused to discuss anything. He felt it was pointless to reply to a question in view of the fact that everything was changing. He would only wiggle his finger to indicate that he had heard the question.

In this chapter we shall examine skepticism. First, we will survey the various kinds of skepticism and their arguments. Second, we will discuss the anti-skeptical arguments which have been developed in response to the skeptics' claims. And finally, we will relate some of the values that skepticism has for philosophy.

Forms of Skepticism and Their Arguments

As noted, there are many forms of skepticism. We have categorized these in five groups: thoroughgoing or complete skepticism; mitigated skepticism; limited skepticism; methodological skepticism; and irrationalism.

Thoroughgoing or Complete Skepticism

There are two kinds of thoroughgoing or complete skeptics. First, there are those skeptics that claim that we have no knowledge whatsoever. We may *believe* this or that, but we are never justified in claiming to *know* anything. Second, there are skeptics of this class who would allow that we do have knowledge of our immediate experiences, but knowledge of anything other than these immediate experiences, perhaps with the exception of logic and mathematics, is impossible.

Sextus Empiricus. Skepticism was known and practiced long before the time and writings of Sextus Empiricus. Most likely, skepticism as a philosophical methodology was developed by the leaders of Plato's Academy in the third century B.C. The Academics, as they were called, rejected Plato's metaphysical and mystical doctrines. Rather, they concentrated on what they thought was paramount in Socrates' remark, "All that I know is that I know nothing." Further, they sought to develop the Socratic method and tactic of questioning.

In the Roman period, the center of skepticism shifted from the Academy to the Pyrrhonian school, probably connected with the school of medicine at Alexandria. This school found its inspiration in the writings of Pyrrho of Elis (c. 360–c. 270 B.C.). He left no writings, but was known as a model of the skeptical way of life, much in the way that Socrates is considered the model of the philosophical way of life. Pyrrhonism, however, is reputed to have been theoretically formulated by Aenesidemus, who taught in Alexandria in the first century B.C.

The fullest and most important formulation of this type of skepticism is that of Sextus Empiricus, who lived and worked in the last half of the second century and the first quarter of the third century, A.D. Little is known of him, except that he was probably Greek, because he seemed to know the subtleties of the language. He also knew details about Rome, Athens, and Alexandria, but we do not know where he was born, where he taught, or where he died. We do know that he practiced medicine.

The *archē*, or motive, for skepticism was the hope of reaching *ataraxia,* the state of "unperturbedness." The history of thought until Sextus Empiricus was one of battles between differing dogmatists. These dogmatists could be characterized by passionate, stubborn belief or disbelief in certain doctrines. These beliefs led to philosophical battles which had disturbed men for centuries. Hence, skepticism was not only an epistemological position, but it also promised a practical consequence—happiness and peace of mind in everyday activities.

Sextus Empiricus' skepticism had three stages: antithesis, *epochē* (suspension of judgment), and *ataraxia*. The first stage involved a presentation of contradictory claims about the same subject. These claims were so constructed that they were in opposition to one another, and appeared equally probable or improbable. To facilitate discussion of these antitheses, *tropes*, or groups of skeptical arguments, were developed. The goal of these tropes was to prove the necessity of suspending judgment about all truth claims. Sextus Empiricus set forth the Pyrrhonian tropes in groups of ten, eight, five, and two. The most famous of these tropes is the group of ten. For example, a tower seen from a distance is square. But the same tower seen up close is round. These two claims, though in opposition, describe the same object. A second example from the group of ten is that the Scythians considered it necessary to sacrifice human beings to Artemis. The Greeks, however, forbade human sacrifice. Again, two opposing claims were made for the same subject.

The second state is *epochē*, or the suspension of judgment. Instead of either asserting or denying any one claim about the subject at hand, one must embrace all mutually inconsistent claims and withhold judgment on each of them.

The final stage is *ataraxia,* a state of unperturbedness, happiness, and peace of mind. When that occurs one is freed from dogmatism. He can live peacefully and undogmatically in the world, following his natural inclinations and the laws or customs of society.

David Hume.   David Hume (1711–1776) was a skeptic in an optimistic age, the eighteenth century. On the one hand, he questioned the knowledge claims of science, mathematics, and even logic. On the other hand, he allowed probabilistic standards for beliefs that go beyond our immediate experience.

At the heart of Hume's skepticism is his attack on the foundations of empirical knowledge. He argues that no generalization about experience is ever rationally justified. No proposition about experience is necessary, or a priori, for one can easily imagine a world where the proposition would be false. For example, "The sun will rise tomorrow morning" is a generalization about experience or reality, but it is not *necessary.* We can conceive of a world quite like ours in which the sun will not rise tomorrow morning.

Suppose that we were to respond to Hume, "The reason we believe that the sun will rise tomorrow morning is that it has risen every morning to this point.'' But Hume would counter that such a statement presupposes that *nature is uniform*. It assumes that nature will not vary its sunrise schedule. This presupposition may be true, but unless we have some reason for believing it, we have no justification for asserting anything supported by it. The uniformity of nature is itself not necessary, since again we can conceive of a world which is random and chaotic. We can imagine a world where oranges tasted like apples one day and pears the next, where water was wet one day and powdery the next. We cannot infer that nature *will* be uniform from the fact that it *has been* uniform; to justify what will happen by what has happened is to beg the question, to give a circular argument, since both depend on the same alleged presupposition. Thus, Hume concludes that induction (arguing from a presupposition) cannot be logically justified at all. For Hume, induction is not a *process of reasoning* at all, but a *habit* of expecting similar events to occur in similar circumstances.

Hume's criticism of induction is actually a strong argument against the claim to know with certainty. We can, however, approach the problem in a different way. We can claim the weaker thesis, namely, that the sun will *probably* rise tomorrow. In this way we show that our conclusion is relative to any body of evidence. Hume has not overlooked this response. His answer is that probability, every bit as much as certainty, depends on the principle of the uniformity of nature. Therefore, if the principle is unjustified in one instance, it will be in the other.

Mitigated Skepticism

Mitigated skepticism is characterized by the rejection of knowledge claims that go beyond immediate experience. However, it does admit some limited kinds of knowledge.

Bishop John Wilkins and Joseph Glanvill. Bishop John Wilkins (1614–1672) and Joseph Glanvill (1636–1680) were early members of the Royal Society, the British scientific organization. They distinguished between infallibly certain and indubitably certain knowledge. Wilkins and Glanvill claimed that infallibly certain knowledge is unattainable by man, because his abilities may be defective or corrupted.

He may be deceived into perceiving connections between the things in the world as necessary, when they may in fact be mere concomitancies.

Indubitably certain knowledge, on the other hand, is possible. According to Wilkins and Glanvill, there are many beliefs we have no reason to doubt. For example, we do assume that the sun will rise tomorrow, and that water will be wet. Indeed, if a man doubted these things, he would be considered disturbed or eccentric by the rest of us. Given the distinction between infallibly certain and indubitably certain knowledge, Wilkins and Glanvill, as well as others of the Royal Society, developed a theory of problem-solving within the limits of "reasonable doubt." This mitigated skepticism remains in the Anglo-American theory of legal evidence.

Immanuel Kant. By his own admission Immanuel Kant (1724–1804) was awakened out of his "dogmatic slumbers" by reading the philosophic debates between David Hume and his opponents. Kant perceived that Hume's arguments questioning the possibility of metaphysical knowledge were strong ones. Kant saw that Hume successfully challenged the optimism of the Enlightenment, and with it Locke's common-sense epistemology, what Locke called "the physiology of the understanding." Kant recognized that the question, Is knowledge possible? was in need of reexamination.

Kant's solution was a radical middle ground. He combined a complete skepticism about metaphysical knowledge with an optimism that universal, necessary (a priori) knowledge about the conditions of possible experience exists. Kant's belief was related to what he called the "Copernican revolution" in philosophy. Just as Copernicus (1473–1543) had changed man's *cosmological* point of view (he showed that the sun, not the earth, is the center of the solar system), so Kant changed man's *epistemological* point of view. Kant posited that the knower does not conform to the object known as previously thought (Locke and his followers believed that the object was "out there," and the viewer merely reacted to its objective qualities.) Rather, said Kant, the known object conforms to the knower. He postulated that for something to be a possible object of knowledge, it had to conform to the mind.

According to Kant, all knowledge *begins* with experience, but there is no knowledge without the contributions of the mind itself. Kant claimed that the mind contributes the "forms of sensibility," space and time, which are necessary for understanding experience. All of our intuitions (perceptions) occur within the limits of time and space, which are the forms by which experience is organized. Kant also catalogued twelve "categories of the understanding," which are necessary in order for us to make judgments about experience. Space and time are necessary conditions for experience to occur at all; the twelve categories (most important of which are *cause* and *substance*) are necessary conditions for evaluation (analysis and synthesis) of experience.

These conditions do not help us gain knowledge of the content (as opposed to the form) of experience, or about what transcends experience. For if an object does not conform to these necessary conditions, it is not a possible object of knowledge. Based on this thesis, Kant identifies three sciences which are not possible. They are: empirical cosmology (a science of a supposed real world); an empirical psychology (a science of a supposed real self lying behind all appearances); and a rational theology (a science of God based on pure reason). Since the object of these sciences is beyond all possible experience, we have no way of knowing if the conditions of experience apply to them. Kant argued that if we construct an argument for God's existence from effect to cause, we illicitly assume that the principle of causality applies beyond the bounds of experience (God is not an object of possible experience).

Thus, in this all too brief summary, we have seen that Kant embraces a *metaphysical* skepticism, while asserting the existence of universal, necessary knowledge about the *conditions* of possible experience.

Limited Skepticism

Limited skepticism is closely related to what we have called mitigated skepticism. In limited skepticism particular types of knowledge claims are questioned by the skeptic. For instance, one may question the knowledge claims made either by the speculative metaphysician or the theologian.

A. J. Ayer.   In his earlier years A. J. Ayer (1910–1970) was an adherent and defender of logical positivism, a movement that dominated the 1930s. His *Language, Truth and Logic* is still the most famous and concise defense of logical positivism in the English language. Along with other logical positivists, Ayer wrote about the elimination of all metaphysics through the analysis of language. This was to be done through the restriction of the term *knowledge* to logically true tautologies and empirically verifiable facts.

On the other hand, it is not nearly so easy to explain how one goes about distinguishing a verifiable fact. The problem is simply this. These statements both appear to be making claims about reality: "It is raining today"; and, "the absolute is lazy." However, Ayer and the positivists argue that the former indeed is about reality but the latter is a pseudo-statement, or nonsense. The question thus for the positivist is how to discern which is a genuine statement about reality and which is not. The tool devised for this task is called the verification principle. The verification principle has an important and varied history, going through numerous formulations and as many refutations. However, the heart of the verification principle is this: Any statement for which we cannot state the conditions that would count for or against its truth, is not a statement about reality, and hence cannot be knowledge.

Given the verification principle, Ayer and others argue that metaphysics can, once and for all, be eliminated. Since metaphysical disputes or claims cannot be evaluated in the light of empirical evidence, they are not *genuine* claims about reality. As a matter of fact, Ayer put it in even stronger language. Metaphysics is not just false; it is *meaningless*.

Antony Flew. What Ayer and the positivists did to metaphysics, Flew did to theology. While Ayer had attacked the meaningfulness of any claim to religious knowledge, it was Flew's attack that brought the issue to the fore. In a discussion recorded in the article "Theology and Falsification" Flew gives a parable of a gardener. He tells of two explorers who find a garden in the middle of the jungle. In this garden there are many flowers and many weeds. One explorer claims that there must be a gardener who tends the plot, while the other explorer denies it. They set a watch, but nothing happens. The believing explorer still affirms his belief in a gardener, but suggests that the gardner is invisible. The two explorers set up an electrified barbed-wire fence and patrol it with bloodhounds. Still nothing happens. The wires never sway, and the bloodhounds never bark. The believer maintains his belief in the gardener. The gardener, so he argues, is invisible, intangible, and insensitive to electric shocks. He has no scent and makes no sound, but he loves and tends the garden. Finally, the skeptic despairs and asks the believer how his gardener differs from no gardener at all.

Flew finds this parable an excellent illustration of the theist's case. The theist begins with what Flew calls "a robust hypothesis which dies the death of a thousand qualifications." Consider the theist who begins by saying that God loves him. On the way to work, his car breaks down. Upon arriving at work, his boss fires him. Yet in spite of all this, he continues to claim that God loves him.

Flew argues that any belief that is compatible with all states of affairs is meaningless, that is, any belief which is not falsifiable is nonsense. Flew declares that the theologian's belief in God is meaningless, since the theist cannot allow anything in experience to count against his position. Flew's clear implication is that if the theologian did allow counter evidence, belief in God would be falsified. Thus, much in the manner of Ayer, Flew will not allow any knowledge claims about God. According to him such claims are not just false; they are, more precisely, meaningless or nonsense.

Methodological or Cartesian Skepticism

In the philosophy of René Descartes (1596–1650), skepticism of the seventeenth century took quite a different turn. For Descartes, skepticism was not the conclusion of some argument, but the method whereby all doubt could be overcome. Descartes claimed that it is possible to arrive at indubitable knowledge through the rigorous and systematic application of doubt to one's beliefs.

In his *Meditations*, Descartes stated his goal:

> Archimedes, in order that he might draw the terrestrial globe out of its place, and transport it elsewhere, demanded only one point should be fixed and immovable; in the same way I shall have the right to conceive high hopes if I am happy enough to discover one thing only which is certain and indubitable.

Descartes was seeking an epistemological Archimedian point which was absolutely certain or indubitable. From there he hoped to derive all knowledge. The tool that Descartes used to arrive at this point was *methodological doubt,* or *skepticism.* He sought to apply this doubt to every belief that he had. If a belief could be doubted, then it did not qualify as his Archimedian point. From his youth Descartes detected that many of his beliefs he once thought were true turned out, in fact, to be false.

Descartes realized that it would be impossible to test individually every belief that he held. All that he needed to do, or so he argued, was to show that the foundation or justification of his beliefs was open to doubt, and the whole edifice would crumble. Descartes recognized that the bases of his beliefs were formed either from his senses or through his senses. But since his senses had deceived him in the past, they failed the test of indubitability. Therefore, the entire foundation of his beliefs collapsed.

However, Descartes was not content to let his doubt rest there. He was determined to press it as far as he could. He suggested that perhaps his senses had deceived him about matters that were both far and small, but were reliable concerning things close up and large. But Descartes concluded that this was not indubitable, because dreams also seem reliable when we are asleep. When we dream, we are often deceived, and think our dreamed experiences are in fact real. We can all remember the dream about the train that was racing toward us while our car was stuck on the tracks. How well do we remember that train! Even now it seems more real than the lengthy freight train that you stopped for this morning. Therefore, there is no *sure* way to separate the dream world from the real.

Or, perhaps it could be argued that there are certain general features of objects that are true of both dreamed and real objects. Is it not true that both a real and a dreamed elephant have at least form, mass, and number? These are certain and indubitable, are they not? No, replied Descartes, for there may be a demon or an evil god who systematically deceives me. These ideas may have no true counterpart in reality.

When Descartes turned to himself, he found that he could doubt that he had a body, arms and legs. However, he could not doubt that *he existed when he was thinking.* Descartes claimed that while he was thinking, even God could not deceive him about his own existence *because there must be an "I" to be deceived.* This truth is called the *cogito*, after Descartes' statement in Latin, *"Cogito, ergo sum,"* which may be translated, "I think, therefore I am." This is the Archimedian point to which doubt led Descartes.

Irrationalism

A final form of skepticism is what we have called irrationalism. It is reflected in the thought of existentialists such as Albert Camus. Camus' thought is built upon the fideistic skepticism of Sören Kierkegaard and Leon Shestov as well as the skepticism of Nietzsche about religion and objective values. While Camus accepts the skeptical arguments of Kierkegaard and Shestov as decisive against rational attempts to explain the world, he rejects their fideistic solution to the crisis. He rejects their "leap into faith," and casts his lot with Nietzsche, who accepts ultimate meaninglessness, since God is dead. The human situation with its constant search for meaning in an essentially unintelligible and absurd world must be recognized and accepted.

Camus' *Myth of Sisyphus* portrays man attempting to measure the nature and meaning of an essentially meaningless and absurd universe. The mythological Sisyphus, eternally pushing a huge rock uphill, only to have it roll to the bottom again, typifies the human condition. Sisyphus "knows the whole extent of his wretched condition." He does not expect to find truth, nor is he anticipating the termination of his struggle. He finds no ultimate value or point in his struggle, yet he will continue on with "silent joy." For Camus, there is no meaning, no knowledge that is objectively true, and no objective value.

Anti-Skeptical Arguments

While an argument with a skeptic may at first be invigorating, we soon recognize that he must be answered. We must show that the skeptical arguments are either false or inconclusive. For this reason, a number of anti-skeptical arguments have been developed, and we will try to survey the most important of these.

Skepticism Is Inconsistent

A good number of philosophers have argued that skepticism is rationally and/or practically inconsistent.

Skepticism is rationally inconsistent. Augustine in *Against the Academics* argued that skepticism is rationally inconsistent. His argument has two stages. Stage one: The skeptic's assertion that we cannot know anything is itself a claim about knowledge. If the skeptic's claim is false, then we need not worry about the skeptic's charge. On the other hand, if it is true, then his position is self-contradictory, because we know at least one thing—that we cannot know anything.

Stage two: But suppose that the skeptic responds by saying that we have misunderstood his claim. He is not claiming that the sentence, "You cannot know anything" is either true or false. He asserts that we cannot know *whether* it is true or false. If this is so, Augustine argues that the skeptic's case is lost just the same. The skeptic's position is shown to be necessarily false, for his is still a claim about knowledge: "For all sentences, we know that we cannot know whether they are true or false." Therefore, total or complete skepticism is rationally inconsistent.

Skepticism is practically inconsistent.   Augustine's argument and those like it may seem valid, but only of interest to those who delight in philosophy. The next criticism of skepticism appeals to the ordinary man or woman. The objection is that while skepticism may be affirmed in the quiet of the philosopher's study, it cannot be lived in the market-place. The skeptic cannot consistently *act* like a skeptic. Can you imagine the skeptic coming to the railroad crossing, seeing the gates down, and yet asking himself if the world is real and if that is a real train thundering down the track? Hardly! He stops and waits just like the rest of us.

Skepticism Is Meaningless

Both objections discussed under this heading relate to the controversy surrounding logical positivism.

The argument from non-vacuous contrast.   To be meaningful, any statement must exclude some states of affairs. In other words, an assertion must not be compatible with *every* state of affairs. Thus, "not-knowing" must distinguish a state of affairs which is different than "knowing." If, however, all states of affairs are "not-knowing," as the skeptic claims, then his whole claim is meaningless. "Not-knowing" would not exclude any states of affairs.

The attack on the verification principle. In its limited forms, the verification principle is often used against a specific type of knowledge, particularly metaphysics and theology (see pp. 50f.). As the verification principle developed, some philosophers argued that the positivist criteria should be applied to the verification principle itself. They asserted that in order for the verification principle to be valid it too must be either purely definitional or empirically verifiable. But how can one verify the principle without begging the question? If the principle is tested against metaphysical and theological statements about the world, the verification principle will prove false. However, if metaphysics and theology are excluded, the principle appears valid. But on what grounds can these be excluded, unless one has already decided what statements are meaningful? Thus, it has been claimed that the verification principle is itself meaningless.

But some have asserted that the verification principle is not subject to the positivist categories, since it is a rule of language. It has a position much like the first principles of logic or the axioms of geometry. If that is granted, the problem for the positivist is that a rule of language can be accepted or rejected. It is a mere proposal. And surely, no defender of metaphysics or theology would accept such a proposal. So what started out as "the turning point in philosophy," as the positivist wanted to call the verification principle, ended as a tempest in a teapot.

Skepticism Is Against Common Sense

As has been indicated earlier in our discussion, the man in the street finds the philosophical skeptic clearly in conflict with common sense. Taking this as their cue, a number of philosophers have developed arguments from common sense.

Thomas Reid and common sense. Thomas Reid (1710–1796), a contemporary of David Hume, was one of the first to appreciate the skeptical import of Hume's arguments. Reid was convinced by both Berkeley and Hume that the principles of modern epistemologists led inevitably to total skepticism.

Reid recognized that given Hume's assumptions, Hume's logic was unassailable. At the same time Reid considered Hume's conclusions clearly false. Thus, Reid set about to challenge Hume's assumptions. Skepticism is inevitable, Reid agreed, only if two of Hume's central presuppositions are true: (1) that the objects of perception are actually ideas or impressions in the mind (this is called variously *the theory of ideas* or *representative perception);* and (2) that our most basic beliefs must be justified by philosophical or rational arguments.

Concerning the first assumption Reid argued that the skepticism and philosophical puzzles which resulted from it constituted a *reductio ad absurdum* argument against it. The theory of ideas led inevitably to a conclusion that was obviously false, namely, that the objective world actually existed in the mind of the perceiver. Reid pointed out that all languages carefully distinguish among the terms that describe the process of perceiving, the mind which perceives, and the object perceived.

Reid also attacked the second presupposition of Hume's epistemology. Reid argued that rational proofs of belief are inappropriate, for they would demand an infinite regress of justifications (each justification would itself need a rational justification, *ad infinitum).* Reid also claimed that these basic beliefs are not rooted in blind prejudice, as Hume supposed. Rather they reflect the very constitution of our rationality, and thus are known through intuition, not demonstration. These beliefs form the basis of all other proofs, but themselves cannot be proved. A number of more modern philosophers have made similar claims. For instance, Wittgenstein argued that the need for justification must end *somewhere.* John Pollock, whom we shall turn to next, claimed that basic beliefs must be viewed as *prima facie* justified. They stand in need of defense only when they are attacked or called into question.

John Pollock and common sense.   More recently John Pollock, in *Knowledge and Justification,* has given a more formalized argument. He argues that we cannot accept the skeptic's argument because "it flies in the face of common sense." He then goes on to present an analysis of skepticism that supports common sense. He says that every knowledge claim consists of evidence and a conclusion. The skeptic asserts, in essence, that the evidence which is contained in the premises of an argument is always true, but the conclusion is always false. We may structure the argument as follows:

Premise 1:	I feel water falling on my head.
Premise 2:	My friends say it is raining out.
Premise 3:	Today's newspaper says that it rained.
Premise 4:	The TV newscaster says that it is raining.
Conclusion:	It is raining today.

The skeptic's claim is that premises one to four are true, but the conclusion is false. Pollock's response is that if the argument is always false, we must decide which one of the propositions in the premises or conclusion is false. In such a case Pollock claims it is always more reasonable to reject one of the premises than to always reject the conclusion. The skeptical argument should, in fact, be considered as a *reductio ad absurdum* of its premises. There must be something wrong with the argument whose conclusion is never in line with common sense.

Skepticism Is in Conflict with Language

A group of philosophers, primarily in the analytic tradition, took their inspiration from G. E. Moore and Ludwig Wittgenstein in formulating what has been called the *paradigm-case argument*. (It is doubtful, however, that either Moore or Wittgenstein ever advanced such an argument.) This approach tries to counter doubt by pointing to paradigm cases, that is, clear and indisputable instances. It is argued that language itself aids this case against skepticism.

The paradigm-case argument has been advanced against a wide variety of skeptical positions. The first step in the argument is to focus attention on a specific case. The critic might begin with a skeptical tenet. For instance, he says, if we cannot perceive material objects, as some skeptics claim, then we cannot see this page. Next, the critic counters by describing a situation clearly antithetical to the skeptical position. The light is sufficient. Our eyesight is not impaired. A book is directly in front of us. We perceive black letters on white paper, and so on. The critic sketches the situation in such basic and obvious terms that we do not hesitate to affirm that we do indeed see the page.

It is important to recognize that the argument leads us to do more than just feel no doubt; it is in fact asserting that we see a page. If it did not make a specific claim, it would simply be a psychological booster, a reassurance that when we have no doubts we are in fact correct. If that were all the argument did it would be philosophically useless. In this case the argument asserts that there are indisputable examples of seeing a page—indisputable because of their relationship to the meaning of the expression "seeing a page." If this circumstance or situation is exactly what we mean when we say "I am seeing a page," how can the situation fail to be a case of seeing a page? The skeptic is refusing to apply the expression to the very circumstances to which the phrase refers.

If the skeptic concedes that the paradigm is a genuine case, then he or she is defeated. If, however, the skeptic persists, the critic points out his dilemma. When the skeptic doubts, surely the words used to express the doubt are to be understood in their natural or usual sense. But if this is so, how can there be a usual sense, since, in denying the paradigm case the skeptic denies the usual sense? If, on the other hand, the skeptic says that his words are being used in a new or different sense, then his claim loses its bite. The critic can then claim that he sees a page in some new or unusual sense.

In recent years, however, the paradigm-case argument has come under serious criticism. Is it legitimate to move from "This is what we call a case of seeing a page" to "This is a genuine case of seeing a page"? The skeptic replies that our language may well be systematically confused so that we call something a genuine case of X but it may in fact be a case of Y.

Skepticism Is Not a Consequence of Induction

As stated earlier, Hume's skepticism is based on our inability to rationally justify induction. Three very clear responses have developed to this Humean critique.

By accepting Kantianism. Some philosophers move to something like Kantianism, and claim some a priori knowledge of a "principle of induction." They argue that certain synthetic propositions about nature (based on the principle of induction) must be true in order for experience to be possible. In other words, our empirical experience presupposes certain synthetic principles. Some philosophers have called this kind of a proof a *transcendental* proof.

By seeking a solution within logic or probability theory.   Discussions of this approach are necessarily very technical, but we will try to explain it as basically as possible. To illustrate: Suppose we know that all ten rocks in a jar are white. Since we know that rocks do not change color by being lifted from a jar, it follows *necessarily* that the first seven rocks we draw out of the jar will be white. On the other hand, if we do not know beforehand the color distribution of the ten rocks, the fact that we have drawn seven white rocks in a row will tell us nothing *necessarily* about our eighth rock. It may be red or black. However, the theory of probability claims it can tell us with a high degree of accuracy what our next draw will be and what the whole set of rocks is like. Suppose we determine the number of possible sets of seven rocks that could be formed out of ten rocks, and suppose further that we have a set of nine white rocks and one nonwhite rock. We will conclude that the possible number of sets containing the nonwhite rock would be greater than the number containing only white rocks. The fact that we have drawn seven white rocks in a row shows the high probability that the entire set is white.

It has been argued that the judgments of probability which are needed to justify our predictions about the future can be established by logic alone. Philosophers with this viewpoint assert that Hume was simply wrong; no inductive inference is necessary to ground assumptions about nature. Theories of probability can be used to prove such predictions.

By denying that induction is a genuine problem.   Still another group of philosophers reject the idea that there is any problem of induction. In their view calling induction a problem is "the scandal of modern philosophy." Two such philosophers are Frederick Will and Antony Flew. They argue, for example, that the fact that oranges have always looked, felt, and tasted like oranges is a good *reason* for assuming they will taste like oranges tomorrow. That is, the *reason* for thinking the orange you eat tomorrow will probably taste like the orange that you ate today is that oranges in the past have always tasted that way. To deny this the skeptic must take the words *reason* and *probably* in ways we do not ordinarily mean them. He must be using the word *reason* to mean "logically conclusive reason." A logically conclusive reason, you will remember, is one where the premises *guarantee* the truth of the conclusion. However, the truth of an inductive argument is not a necessary consequence of its premises. The skeptic then, according to this view, is unhappy simply because induction is not deduction!

The Value of Skepticism

Most epistemologists, both ancient and contemporary, have concluded that skepticism is untenable on both rational and practical grounds. David Hume said, "It [skepticism] admits of no answer, and produces no conviction." However, it would be wrong to think that skepticism is of no value. The strength of skepticism rests in the force of its arguments against dogmatism in areas where one does not have good evidence.

Skepticism raises two very fundamental questions. First, does the epistemologist have *adequate* grounds for his claims to know? There must be sufficient justification for one's beliefs or the skeptic triumphs. And second, are there contradictions or absurdities in one's system? If there are, the system of knowledge *cannot* possibly be true. Thus, the skeptical arguments, regardless of whose they are, point out basic difficulties. If the epistemologist would like to demonstrate the adequacy of his claims to know, the skeptic must be answered.

Thus, from the time of the Greeks onward, skepticism has functioned as a gadfly to challenge the claims of the epistemologist. It is the primer of the epistemological pump.

Conclusion

Having thus examined both the arguments for and against skepticism, we conclude that, while skepticism is not defensible as an epistemological position, it is of value. It acts like a burr in the epistemologist's saddle, demanding that any claim to knowledge is based upon adequate evidence and is free from contradiction or absurdity.

The epistemologist's task has just begun. The problem which now faces him is the need to account for how we do in fact know. It is to this problem that we shall turn in the next chapter.

Suggested Readings

Augustine, St. *Against the Academicians*
Descartes, René. *Meditations on First Philosophy*, meditations 1 and 2
Hume, David. *An Enquiry Concerning Human Understanding*
Sextus Empiricus. *Skepticism, Man and God*
Unger, Peter. *Ignorance*

$\boxed{7}$ How Can We Know?

As we saw in our last chapter there is a small but significant body of philosophers who hold that no knowledge claim whatsoever can be justified. We tried to show why such skeptical claims are themselves unjustified; this is the negative side of the epistemological task. We now turn to the positive side, to show when and how knowledge is possible. Just because some knowledge claim is justified, however, does not guarantee that all claims are genuine. As a matter of fact, we know this from our own experience. Each of us has at times been unjustified by claiming to know things that turned out to be untrue.

In this chapter we want to examine the sources or origin of our beliefs and knowledge. The following sources will be analyzed: the testimony of others, intuition (used here in the sense of instincts, feelings, and desires), reason, and sensory experience. These sources lead to five corresponding logics or criteria for validating beliefs. They are: faith or authoritarianism, subjectivism, rationalism, empiricism, and pragmatism.

Faith or Authoritarianism

Exposition of the Logic of Authoritarianism

By far the most common source of our beliefs is the testimony of others. We begin learning by accepting the beliefs of our family. When we go to school we accept what is said by our teachers and fellow students. Even after graduation we are dependent on the testimony of books, newspapers, radio, and television for an extremely large portion of our knowledge. We accept beliefs as justified when they seem to us to come from good sources.

It is not hard to understand why faith is such an important source of knowledge. First, as individuals we are confined both temporally and spatially. We live in the twentieth century and have no direct access to the myriad of events that occurred in previous centuries. If we are to have any knowledge of these things, we must rely on the testimony of others. We also have no direct access to contemporary events occurring elsewhere, for only God is omnipresent. We are bound by space and cannot know what is happening in Paris right now, unless we have faith in the testimony of others.

Second, we have a *prima facie* disposition to accept the testimony of others. We recognize that it is impossible for us to reason and experience *everything* that can be known. We tend to believe what we are told unless there are clear reasons for suspecting the honesty or competence of our authority. For a moment imagine what life would be like if we refused to accept anything that we were told. If we did not heed warnings, instructions, or advice our lives would be hazardous indeed. We would probably end up in a mental institution. We can conclude that unless there is some certain reason for questioning an authority, generally it is more reasonable to believe than to doubt.

Evaluation of the Logic of Authoritarianism

While authoritarianism is necessary and useful, it cannot serve as the sole criterion of justification for knowledge. There are two decisive reasons for this.

The impossibility of authority as the ultimate criterion. It is always possible to ask why we should believe any authority. In support of the first authority one may appeal to a second authority. However, it is possible to question this second authority and any subsequent authorities that may be invoked. Therefore, we must appeal to something beside authorities. At this point the criterion of validation and source of our belief has ceased to be authority. We may say that some authority knows some piece of knowledge because he saw it, or because he tried it and it worked, or because the information itself is a postulate of reason that should be accepted by all rational beings. But these justifications are pragmatic or empirical rather than authoritarian.

Authorities conflict. Authorities disagree, leaving conflicting and incompatible views. For instance, there are intelligent and honest men and women considered experts on religion who hold that God does not exist. Others, just as intelligent and honest, hold that He does exist. If justification is solely based on testimony, then we have internal inconsistencies on the subject matter. This is a situation the most fundamental law of logic, the law of non-contradiction, will not allow.

It should be noted that the problem of internal consistency is raised for each methodology. In the other logics, however, there is the possibility of external appeal, such as to facts or experience. This is not the case with the authoritarian logic.

When authorities conflict, there are two courses of action that the authoritarian can take. First, he may appeal to reason or experience to settle the dispute. It is simply question-begging to demand that the genuineness of an authority be accepted on its own authority. Most epistemologists would be unwilling to argue in this kind of a circle. Thus, there is often an appeal to reason, experience, or some other criterion. When this is done, however, the source of belief and the method of justification is no longer authoritarianism.

Second, the authoritarian may seek to resolve the dispute by use of the authoritarian criterion itself. There appears to be three ways of measuring authorities: the *prestige* of the original authority; the *number* of those who hold the belief; the *persistence* of the belief.

The prestige of the originating authority in part regulates our faith. If our authority is well-known, honest, and intelligent, then we will be more ready to believe him. But there is a weakness in such an appeal. Prestige must be strictly limited in its validity to the particular subject for which the authority is known. Someone who is an authority on mathematics may be utterly untrustworthy on the subject of botany; the writings of someone who was considered an authority on physics in the eighteenth century would be hopelessly outdated today.

The number of authorities who hold a view is also sometimes used as an index of excellence. For instance, it might be argued that twenty million scientists cannot be wrong about the cause of some disease. But this approach, though often convincing, is unreliable. Twenty million educated persons can be—and have been—wrong. This is possible particularly if they are acting on faith and are unable to check their information against reason or experience.

Finally, the most common use of the authoritarian criterion to resolve conflicts is to appeal to the age of a belief. Those with this view claim that if a belief has persisted over a long period of time, then it must be justified. There is surely some merit to this approach. If some belief has continued for a long time, it is *probable*, since it has not been found to be false, that it has proven useful. However, a belief's long history cannot guarantee that it will not be found false in the future. Moreover, there is at least a sophisticated and subtle appeal here to pragmatism. Those who use this authoritarian approach have given up faith or testimony as the sole criterion of justification and are actually judging truth on the basis of usefulness.

Subjectivism

Subjectivism is a large category which includes diverse methods of epistemology. However, there are important similarities among these methods that justify classifying them together. Usually when we hear of subjectivism, we immediately think of ethical subjectivism or relativism, the lack of absolutes. But this is not the way the term is used here. We mean to emphasize the importance which this approach places on the knower, or *subject*, in the epistemological process.

Exposition of the Logic of Subjectivism

Fundamental to this approach is the contention that the knower has some kind of direct contact with what is known, that is, with the object of belief. Admittedly, this contact is conceived of differently by different philosophers. It may be sensual, as in naive realism, or it may be a kind of intuition, which Henri Bergson (1859–1941) expounded. In either case, our beliefs about reality do not have their source in sense data or the like, but through our immediate contact with the known.

This immediate contact which the knower possesses has important consequences for the problem of justifying one's beliefs. Those who hold this view claim that mere awareness of the contact with objects is the only justification needed. In other words, the experience of awareness is self-authenticating, and the justification for a belief is not to be sought outside of this experience. To demand further justification is both unnecessary and impossible. We might make the same point by saying, "If you experience it, you know it."

According to the subjective position, the awareness from which these beliefs arise is not entirely under the control of the knower. The naive realist, who believes that our beliefs grow out of our direct contact with the known, claims that the experience of reality is not under our control. When we look out the library window, we cannot help but see trees, people, and buildings. The view is the same whether we want it to be so or not. The mystic also claims that the source of belief is not under the control of the knower. But he means something different by this statement than does the naive realist. He means that the mystic experience, that is, the unified vision of reality, or an individual's absorption into the whole, is not something which can be achieved simply as the result of some set procedure. While the mystic can do some things which prepare him for the experience, or make the experience more likely, nothing can be done to guarantee it.

It is helpful, we think, to subclassify the subjective methodology in order to distinguish between rational and suprarational forms of subjectivism.

By far the most common form of rational subjectivism is *direct or common-sense realism,* as it is sometimes called. This approach has been given this name because it has generally been argued that this is the view of the common man prior to philosophical reflection. This is an extreme form of subjectivism, wherein the known is held to be directly perceived "as it is." The source of the knower's beliefs is the result of direct or immediate sense contact with things and people.

A more sophisticated form of rational subjectivism is to be found in the *phenomenology* of Edmund Husserl (1859–1938). For Husserl the common man views the world from the "natural" standpoint. From this view of the world the common man assumes there are indeed material objects such as trees, cars, and buildings, as well as persons. The problem with this natural standpoint is that it cannot serve as the unerring source of our ideas (this will be discussed in detail in the next chapter). We often hold beliefs about reality that we subsequently find to be false.

Husserl, therefore, suggests two reductions, or *epochēs* (suspensions of belief), called the eidetic and phenomenological reductions. These result in access to "pure consciousness," according to Husserl. Consciousness can then be examined or analyzed as the source of our beliefs. There one finds the transcendental ego (the I), transcendental objects which Husserl calls *noēma* (cars, people, buildings as objects of consciousness, not the objects of a "real" world), and ways in which the transcendental ego may be related to these transcendental objects. Thus Husserl considers the source of our beliefs—and their justification—to be consciousness or the mind. Through intuition (a power of the mind or reason), one can come to know the essence of these transcendental objects.

In both common-sense realism and phenomenology, the subject is viewed as being in contact with its objects, and comes to know them through *reason*. We now turn to suprarational forms of subjectivism. It should be noted that we have used the term *suprarational* rather than *irrational*, for these forms do not employ justification *contrary* to reason, but justification *beyond* reason.

Mysticism, a common form of suprarational subjectivism, is often divided into extrovertive and introvertive categories. In extrovertive mysticism the mystic looks out upon a multiplicity of objects and sees them transfigured into a living unity, their distinctiveness somehow obliterated. An example of this type of mystic is the nature mystic, who sees the external world with unusual vividness as the workings of one mind. The introvertive mystic, on the other hand, becomes progressively less aware of his environment and self as separate entities. He speaks of being merged with, identified with, or absorbed into "the one." The subject-object distinction disappears altogether.

A second form of suprarational subjectivism, which has to do particularly with knowledge of God, is *crisis or encounter theology*. In crisis theology the emphasis is not upon identification as in mysticism, but upon confrontation. The similarity beween the two forms is their claim that at least some knowledge is beyond reason.

Martin Buber's (1878–1965) philosophy utilizes this type of theology. He distinguishes between two types of relationships: I-It and I-Thou. In I-It relationships the knower treats that which is known as an object or a thing. He analyzes it, and objectifies the thing which is known. For such relationships, the scientific method is appropriate. I-Thou relationships, on the other hand, are quite different. Here that which is known is itself a subject, and thus not under the knower's control. If the knower is to know the subject, the subject must reveal himself to the knower. In such a revelation situation the Thou stands over against, or confronts, the subject. According to Buber, knowledge is not propositional, but personal. As a matter of fact, this kind of knowledge defies propositionalization. It is ineffable or unspeakable, and beyond reason. At best reason can serve a negative function, demonstrating that it is helpless in this realm. Knowledge about God falls into the I-Thou class.

Evaluation of the Logic of Subjectivism

This methodology seems to point out two things which appear to be correct. First, one feels intuitively that the claim of direct access to the known is intrinsically right. Second, it is indeed correct that the necessity to justify knowledge claims must stop somewhere. Otherwise, one will be caught in an infinite regress of justification. The question, however, is whether experience itself is self-authenticating or whether there must be an appeal to something external.

There are some decisive reasons against considering subjectivism alone an adequate explanation of the origin and justification of belief. First, subjectivism almost always ends in *solipsism*. In every kind of subjectivism except naive realism, one ends up with a world that is simply *his* world. This world is the creation of one's consciousness (as in phenomenology), or is simply not subject to rational criteria (as in mysticism). These claims lead to radically different conceptions of the world. But since experience itself is self-authenticating, there is no hope of judging between these rival worlds. Using the claims of subjectivism alone, the subjectivist cannot consider one kind of subjectivism *better* than another, or better than other viewpoints. Hence subjectivism leads to both solipsism and *relativism*.

Second, subjectivism has difficulty explaining how any of our beliefs can be *wrong*. We know that people have different, incompatible, and even inconsistent beliefs about the world. How can this be, if the knower is in immediate contact with the known through a self-authenticating experience? For naive realism there is a further problem: how is it possible that we thought we saw a lake in the distance, but in fact we did not? Naive realism is at a loss to explain perceptual error.

Third, experience alone is insufficient for belief or knowledge. Knowledge demands not only experience but a conceptual element. Kant put it quite well when he said that sensations without concepts are blind.

Finally, many philosophers would claim that it is simply false to think that personal knowledge cannot be verbalized. Activities, even those which involve confrontation between two subjects, can be reduced to propositional form. It may be true that residual experience may escape what is propositionalized, but that is not because it could not be verbalized, but rather because it has been overlooked.

Rationalism

Throughout the history of philosophy, many philosophers have looked to reason for the origin and justification of beliefs.

Exposition of the Method of Rationalism

At the heart of rationalism is the contention that the source and justification of our beliefs is to be found in reason alone. The rationalist attempts to arrive at apodictic (incontestable) first truths or principles. There are two differing approaches to reach the "starting point" of the system. Descartes began with diverse and unorganized ideas and analyzed them until he reached a single clear and distinct idea, the *cogito*. Others, like Benedict Spinoza (1632–1677), took as their starting point a set of axioms or postulates much like those found in mathematical or logical systems. These principles are known to be true by the light of reason alone, the faculty often called *intuition* by the rationalists.

The starting point for the rationalist must be *certain*. Mere probability will not satisfy him. Therefore most rationalists adopt a methodology that is modeled after mathematics (Descartes even called his methodology "universal mathematics"). From this apodictic or certain starting point rationalists apply deductive techniques, believing that they can deduce the whole of reality. Because the method is deductive, the previous steps guarantee the present conclusion.

It is quite common for a rationalist to employ the ontological argument as a proof of God's existence somewhere in his system. Usually the argument has a functional use, as can be very clearly seen in Descartes' system. Descartes needed some guarantee that the simple ideas which were the immediate objects of his consciousness were indeed representative of objects, that is, things or persons in the real world. He was concerned that he might be systematically deceived by a malevolent demon or an evil deity. This fear, however, was put to rest by the ontological argument. Descartes concluded that God is a perfect being, and thus would not deceive him.

Evaluation of the Method of Rationalism

The rationalist does indeed point out certain things that must characterize an adequate epistemology. Reason is at least a negative test for the justification of any belief. No belief that is contrary to reason can possibly be justified or true. Moreover, the mind plays an important function in the knowing process. That is, there is a conceptual element in knowledge. Without concepts we would be left with undifferentiated experience. The world would seem to be "a buzzing, blooming confusion," as William James described the perspective of very young children.

Several criticisms have been leveled at rationalism. It has been argued by a large body of philosophers that an apodictic starting point can never be the basis for a comprehensive theory of knowledge since it must either be (a) a tautology or (b) incapable of elaboration by deductive techniques. The class of tautological statements would contain propositions such as "1 + 1 = 2," "A is A," and "Bachelors are unmarried males." It has been argued that such statements, while true and absolutely certain, are not informative about the world. If this be so, then such propositions can never be the basis of empirical knowledge.

There is also a problem with a second class of statements, first-person statements about one's private experience. Examples of this kind of proposition are, "I have a pain in my side," or "I have a headache." It should be noted that not all philosophers agree that such statements are either knowledge statements or apodictic. However, even if for the sake of argument we assume that they are, it is very difficult to see how such propositions could be elaborated into a complete account of knowledge using deductive techniques.

There is a question whether a generally agreed-upon starting point can be found at all. For example, the three great classical rationalists, Descartes, Spinoza, and Leibniz, all have quite different starting points. But the problem does not end there. Even if some starting point could be agreed upon and, further, if such a starting point could be elaborated by deductive techniques, it would not necessarily include religious convictions or, for that matter, any religious knowledge.

For instance, let us assume the axioms of Euclidean geometry or some other axiomatic system of logic as our starting point. Let us proceed to elaborate this system using the techniques of deduction until we reach conclusions that are absolutely certain. Would such a system have anything to say about religious epistemology? Probably not. Well, might it not be possible to adopt Descartes' system, and try to extend it so that it would encompass all of knowledge? Most philosophers today would not think so. They generally find his proof for God and the external world unconvincing.

It has been argued that when the rationalist elaborates his system, he inevitably introduces hidden philosophical assumptions or existential premises. Examples of these hidden philosophical ideas can be seen in the philosophy of both Descartes and Anselm. Descartes, in moving from the fact of his existence to an analysis of the kind of existent creature he is, introduces the notion of substance without evaluating it. In the development of the ontological argument Anselm appeals to degrees of perfection and reality, which terms he uses without philosophic examination. In the first formulation of the ontological argument in his *Meditations,* Descartes inserts existential premises into his rationalistic argument. For example, he accepts uncritically that "every cause must have as much reality as its effect." This is never proven or substantiated by Descartes; it is asserted without justification.

Another argument against rationalism is that reason is only capable of demonstrating what is *possible,* not *actual.* Reason can only rule out beliefs or systems that are inherently inconsistent. But one is precluded from appealing to experience. Thus there is no way for a rationalist to determine what in fact is true. Let us illustrate. Either "a yellow Volkswagon is in the parking lot'' or ''a yellow Volkswagon is not in the parking lot'' is true. One of the two is true; both are not. But which one is true? Which one am I justified in claiming to know? Reason alone is helpless in guiding me in this situation.

Empiricism

Some philosophers have attempted to account for beliefs in terms of experience. These philosophers have been called empiricists.

Exposition of the Method of Empiricism

All empiricists hold that experience rather than reason is the source of knowledge. This very general thesis has received very different emphases and refinements, and as such leads to very different kinds of empiricism. Nevertheless empiricists are united in the claim that knowledge ultimately depends on our senses, and what we discover by them.

We must distinguish between the weaker and stronger forms of empiricism. The weaker form is the doctrine that our senses do give us ''knowledge'' in some meaning of the word. Indeed, there are few philosophers in the history of thought who deny this. Those who do deny it, like Plato, so elevate the idea of knowledge that man's experience or senses can never attain it. The stronger form of empiricism, however, claims that *all* knowledge comes from experience. In its most extreme form, it is asserted that no source other than experience provides knowledge at all.

Various reasons have been given for the stronger form of empiricism. Such empiricists claim that every belief is either a direct report of experience or an inference from experience. An example of a direct report of experience would be, ''I now see green.'' An example of something inferred from experience might be, ''There are other minds.'' One exception to this claim that all knowledge comes from experience is mathematical propositions. Such propositions are generally considered to be a priori, not a posteriori. There have, however, been philosophers who have denied this. John Stuart Mill asserted that propositions of mathematics are merely very highly confirmed generalizations from experience. Such a view is not widely held today.

Empiricists also claim that our ideas or concepts are wholly derived from experience. They posit that while it may be true that we can combine ideas or express relations between various concepts without experiencing the resulting ideas, no concepts are themselves a priori. They are a posteriori. If it is true that all our ideas are dependent on experience, then all our knowledge must also be dependent on experience. Empiricists admit that not all knowledge is *immediately* dependent on experience, but it is *ultimately* derived from experience, for the materials from which knowledge is constructed come from experience. John Locke argued that all our ideas are derived either directly from sensation or through reflection on the ideas of sensation. There is literally nothing in the intellect which was not first in the senses. David Hume also reduced all ideas to empirical experience.

Immanuel Kant argued that our ideas are a priori, and that there are a priori truths. However, he cautioned that these ideas and truths only have application when there is experience. For a human being, anyway, reason can only function in conjunction with experience. While Kant did not call himself an empiricist and it would surely be wrong to so classify him, nevertheless he was opposed to what has been called dogmatic rationalism. He denied that there were any forms of knowledge about reality which were derived from pure reason alone.

It is important to note that empiricists do not demand that all knowledge be indubitable. While many would require that certain forms of a priori knowledge indeed be certain, they would allow that a large body of our knowledge is at best only probable.

Evaluation of the Method of Empiricism

Empiricism has a strong appeal to many philosophers for two reasons. First, they believe it gives a more realistic conception of knowledge. Knowledge need not be confined to that which is undoubtable. Second, they argue that empiricism does not prevent one from appealing to experience for knowledge about the world. Empiricism makes it possible to break out of the realm of the theoretical or possible and enter the actual.

In assessing empiricism, however, we find again that it fails as an account of *all* knowledge. Empiricism has more often than not been unsuccessful as an answer to skepticism. As a matter of fact, it has in at least some cases (David Hume) led to skepticism. For, although empiricism has allowed probability as an adequate criterion of justification for knowledge that is *inferred* from experience, it has maintained that the *foundations* to be found in immediate experience are certain.

A good many philosophers are not convinced that *all* concepts can be derived from experience. By far the most problematic are those ideas called *universals* (general terms or characteristics such as "man" or "color," distinguished from individual cases or instances such as "Socrates" or "green"). An empiricist generally argues that the universal is arrived at by abstraction from particular instances. The non-empiricist argues that one would not know which instances to abstract *from* if one had no prior knowledge of the concept. Further, certain ideas such as "equal" or "parallel" are never found in experience; thus the concept cannot be derived from experience.

Closely related to this criticism is the objection that even knowledge of particulars (e.g., a certain man, sound, color, and so forth) is impossible without a conceptual element. The knower must come equipped with concepts, or experience will always remain a buzzing, blooming confusion.

Very recently a number of empiricist philosophers have argued that all experience is a combination of the conceptual and sensual. There is no pure experience. This thesis is by no means agreed upon by all philosophers, and it is not our purpose to either defend or reject such a proposal in an introductory text. Suffice it to note that if this complex view is true, then a more sophisticated brand of empiricism would be needed if one were to adopt empiricism.

Pragmatism

Pragmatism has been advanced as a method for determining genuine from mere verbal disputes, as a theory of meaning, and as a theory of truth. Here, it is our desire to examine it as a possible source and means of justification for our belief about the world.

Exposition of the Method of Pragmatism

At the heart of pragmatism is a radical reinterpretation of the nature of knowledge. Traditionally, knowledge has been defined in static, eternal, and "spectator" terms. Knowledge is, in fact, quite different, according to the pragmatist. It is dynamic. It grows out of the interaction of an organism (in this case, man) with his environment. Because the pragmatist views human beings as constantly interacting with and adapting to their environment, he considers all knowledge to be practical. (This practical approach has led many to call pragmatism anti-intellectual.)

For the pragmatist the proper epistemological method is to be found in the natural sciences. Man applies the scientific method (see chap. 4) to acquire knowledge. (It will be remembered that for the rationalist the proper epistemological method consisted in the adoption of a mathematical model.) The pragmatist considers hypotheses or systems of ideas as *instruments* to help man adjust to his environment. Man's reason is put to its highest and proper use in solving the problems of human existence. Reason seeks to solve these problems by trial and error.

Since our environment is constantly changing, there are no final solutions to any problems man faces. As a matter of fact, man's ability to deal with his environment is in constant flux, so the task is ongoing. Thus, those ideas, beliefs or hypotheses that *work,* that have utility, or are successful are considered to be true. Those which fail may be discarded and considered false.

Two of the most prominent proponents of pragmatism were William James (1842–1910) and John Dewey (1859–1952), both American philosophers.

Evaluation of the Method of Pragmatism

Pragmatism is a practical, in-use account of the origin and justification of our beliefs. It makes no attempt to abstract knowledge from its context. Moreover, like empiricism, it accepts probability as an adequate requirement for knowledge. Furthermore, it does not cut off epistemology from experience. It allows man to seek justification for his beliefs in his experience.

Nevertheless, there are some serious shortcomings of pragmatism. First, pragmatism entails the giving up of *objective* grounds for testing beliefs. Everything is viewed as in constant flux, and as a means rather than an ultimate end. The result is the most radical kind of subjectivism and relativism.

Second, pragmatism has too restrictive a view of the nature of knowledge. To the pragmatist, only practical knowledge is considered true knowledge. This means that much of what has traditionally been considered part of epistemology must be rejected or ruled out. Pragmatism recognizes only the methodology of the natural sciences as valid. One may question absolutizing the scientific method even for the natural sciences, and there is even more reason to question extending the method to *all* areas of human knowledge and inquiry.

Finally, while it is not our primary objective to deal with questions of truth in this chapter, we must note that pragmatism advances a theory of truth that many philosophers consider false. Pragmatism claims that truth is defined as what is useful, what works, or what has good practical results. But it is possible to show that certain statements we know to be false on independent grounds are "true" on pragmatic grounds. For instance, suppose a patient fears he has cancer. He visits a doctor, who runs tests. Sure enough, cancer is present. However, knowing the mental state of the patient, the doctor tells him that there must be surgery but that there is no cancer. The patient comes through the operation with flying colors. The lie has clearly "worked." Therefore, on pragmatic grounds the lie must be true.

It has also been argued that if "true" and "useful" are synonymous, then after one says, "X is useful," it should make sense to say, "X is true." But obviously it does not make sense; the terms are not synonymous.

The reason that such a definition of truth has any plausibility at all is because the phrase "it works," "it is useful," and "it has good practical results" are ambiguous. As has been shown, some falsehood can bring peace of mind, but is this really a *good* practical result? Not all are agreed that it is. Some would argue that it is better to face up to reality rather than attempt to avoid or escape it.

Conclusion

In this chapter we have examined five sources of and methods of justification of our beliefs: faith, subjectivism, rationalism, empiricism, and pragmatism. Each method is best suited for application to a specific kind of knowledge. Faith or the testimony of others is our primary source of our knowledge of the past. Intuition is the ground of our sense of beauty, or taste (our aesthetic sense), as well as ethics and metaphysics for some. Reason functions in both a negative and positive role. It teaches us that beliefs that are contradictory cannot possibly be justified. Reason is also the source of our beliefs about mathematics, logic, and universals. Experience adds to reason the knowledge of the external world, for experience is the source of our factual knowledge. And finally, pragmatism regulates our social and individual conduct where moral norms do not apply.

Suggested Readings

Augustine, St. *The Teacher*
Berkeley, George. *The Principles of Human Knowledge*
Leibniz, Gottfried. *The Monadology*
Locke, John. *An Essay Concerning Human Understanding*
Montague, William Pepperell. *The Ways of Knowing,* ch. 1
Plato *Theaetetus*

⑧ Is Certainty Possible?

The search for certainty has played a large and important part in the history of epistemology. Many philosophers have claimed that certainty or indubitability is a necessary condition of knowing. Plato argued that one can only have an *opinion* about sense experiences because the best that these experiences can attain is probability. Plato contended that true knowledge was always knowledge of the forms or ideas which were both eternal and certain.

In this chapter, then, we will survey some of the more important aspects of this search for certainty. First, we will examine various kinds of certainty which have been advocated by philosophers. And second, we will attempt to enumerate and evaluate the differing types of knowledge that might qualify as certain.

Kinds of Certainty

While certainty has played an important role in epistemology, the nature of that certainty has varied from philosopher to philosopher. We have classified the different kinds of certainty as follows: apodictic certainty, psychological certainty, conventional certainty, pragmatic certainty, and probability.

Apodictic Certainty

By far the highest standard for certainty is apodictic certainty. It requires the *necessary* truth of its object. For this reason, this kind of certainty has also been called indubitability (exclusion of doubt) and incorrigibility (incapable of being corrected or amended). The object of apodictic certainty is impervious to doubt. Sometimes it is claimed that its denial is a contradiction. In recent years, with the increased use of modal logic, one might say that apodictic certainty guarantees truth in every possible world.

Descartes set up an epistemology that was based entirely on this apodictic certainty. In chapter six we saw that he applied methodological doubt to statements that were possible candidates for the starting point of knowledge. He felt that his *cogito* ("I think, therefore I am") filled the role. From this sure starting point, Descartes argued that clear and distinct ideas retained this apodictic or incorrigible certainty. Any claim that did not meet these high standards was excluded from his epistemology.

Psychological Certainty

The standard of apodictic certainty is *so* high that a good many philosophers have sought to lower it, while retaining certainty as a condition for knowledge. This gave rise to the idea of psychological certainty. Here the certainty is not grounded in the object of knowledge or the thing known but in the knower. The knower is certain, or more accurately, *feels* sure. There is no reason to doubt, although one surely *could* doubt, since the object of knowledge is not immune to questioning.

For example, suppose that when you left your home or dorm this morning, you were very careful to shut the door. Once you arrived at school, you were asked by three or four of your friends if you had in fact shut the door. You are *sure* that you did. You distinctly remember pulling it shut, because you dropped one of your books in the process. In this case, it is not that you *cannot* doubt the claim that you shut your door, because with each of the questioners you have a moment of uncertainty and reflection. However, nothing, or almost nothing, would make you give up the claim that the door was closed when you left.

Conventional Certainty

Conventional certainty is quite different from both apodictic and psychological certainty. It is the result of a decision to use our language in a certain way. Usually questions relating to conventional certainty can be solved by consulting a dictionary or some other authority on the subject in question.

To illustrate, it is a convention of our language that we use the word *bachelor* to refer to an unmarried male. A speaker can be certain about this point if he has an understanding of his language. It is not as though there is something inherent in the particular combination of letters in the word *bachelor* that makes it the appropriate term for unmarried male. Clearly, if we wanted to, we could use the invented word *trunt* to express the same concept now conveyed by *bachelor*.

Pragmatic Certainty

Pragmatism is a philosophy of action. If something works or has beneficial consequences, it is true or right. Pragmatic certainty, then, is related to action as well. Our knowledge claims are pragmatically certain if they have been beneficial or have helped us to cope with experience.

C. I. Lewis is one philosopher who advocates this type of certainty. When discussing the correctness of the categories which we apply to experience, he defends their truth or appropriateness on the grounds that through them we are able to deal successfully with experience. In other words, they are true because they work. He does not claim, as Kant does, that these categories are fixed, necessary, or immutable. He allows that it is possible that as science progresses and human needs change, some modification of our conceptual scheme might be desirable. Nevertheless, at present we are sure that they are capable and adequate for now.

Probability

The final kind of certainty would not be considered a certainty at all by some philosophers. A growing number of philosophers have argued that at least for some important kinds of knowledge, sense knowledge in particular, it is both unnecessary and impossible to attain any kind of certainty. Therefore, we should accept what is realistic in these areas: probability.

This appeal can be clearly demonstrated in the philosophy of John Locke. In his important epistemological work, *An Essay Concerning Human Understanding,* Locke says he will "inquire into the original, certainty, and extent of human knowledge, together with the grounds and degrees of belief, opinion, and assent." Probability, for Locke, is to be judged on the strength of the evidence in support of a knowledge claim (this point is discussed at greater length in chap. 10).

Types of Knowledge

In the remainder of this chapter we will discuss various kinds of knowledge which might be candidates for indubitable or incorrigible knowledge. We will examine moral commands, sense experience, self-awareness, logic, and mathematics to see if any or all qualify.

Moral Commands

The argument for the certainty of moral commands.   The argument for the certainty of moral commands is very old, but it has been stated most forcefully by Immanuel Kant. Kant argues that moral imperatives or commands cannot be merely hypothetical. That is, they cannot have the form found in the statement, "If you want to be rich, then you ought to save money." To Kant, such statements rest on desire or inclination and lack *universality*, which is the defining mark of moral knowledge.

Therefore Kant argues that moral commands are categorical imperatives. They have the form found in the statement, "You ought not lie." The "ought" in the categorical imperative differs radically from the "ought" in the hypothetical imperative. The categorical imperative contains the ought of *duty*. Such imperatives are universal and without exception in their demands. On the other hand, hypothetical imperatives are merely expressions of the ought of *prudence*. "If you want to be rich, then you *ought* to save money" could just as easily be stated, "If you want to be rich, then you *would be wise or prudent* to save money." Kant saw that hypothetical imperatives lacked the universality he sought. If one follows the line of argument used by Kant, moral imperatives or commands have two distinguishing characteristics: they are *categorical* and they are *universal*.

Arguments against the certainty of moral commands. It is widely held that ethical choices are arbitrary, or at best they are the product of local conventions or mores. These conventions or mores are not certain, since if we observe the history of civilizations we see changes within the moral code, even in matters of major importance.

Take for example the American standard of morality. At one time in history slavery was thought to be morally acceptable by some, and was even supported by law. Today, most if not all Americans find the idea of slavery morally reprehensible. Or, take the issue of sexual purity. For most of history American society has held that premarital sex and adultery were morally wrong. Today, while there is not universal agreement, a good portion of secular American society would not only deny its immorality but claim that in some cases it might even have healthy consequences! *If* such claims are in fact true, then it cannot also be true that moral commands are categorical and universal in their character.

There is a second, related objection to the certainty of moral knowledge. Some critics point out that people in other cultures have different moral standards than those which we embrace. There is wide divergence of opinion on moral matters in the beliefs and practices of the various cultures of the world. In the midst of such widespread moral relativity, these critics argue, it is impossible to maintain the indubitability of moral commands. Moral relativism, not absolutism, is the only tenable position.

Responses of moral absolutists to moral relativists. While moral relativism is widely held today, it is not without serious problems.

Moral absolutists have responded by advancing objections to moral relativism.

First, they have argued that there is greater unity in matters of morality than the moral relativist allows. There are certain moral standards that all, or almost all, societies embrace. There is widespread agreement on things and actions that have *intrinsic* value. Every society agrees that people are more valuable than things. Disagreement, however, arises over questions of *extrinsic* value. There are differences of opinion and widespread divergence of belief concerning the *means* to bring about the good.

Second, moral absolutists claim that the data which the moral relativist gives us for his conclusions are utterly insufficient. If indeed there is widespread disagreement on moral issues, a point we have seen is questionable, it does not follow that there is no correct moral position; nor does it follow that we cannot discern a morally correct view. The real question for the moralist is whether there are right answers to moral issues and, if so, how we would go about deciding these. Nothing the moral relativist has said even touches on these issues. The moral relativist has merely described the practices and beliefs of people. But if ethics is normative or prescriptive, then the relativist is unjustified in inferring his position from the descriptive data.

Third, moral absolutists point out that if moral relativism is true and every moral choice is arbitrary, then any choice is as good as any other in any ethical context. Hitler's decision to annihilate millions of Jews in World War II was as morally correct as the Underground's choice to try to save and protect the Jews. Or, if we see a child drowning, we will be equally ethically justified in throwing him a rope or throwing stones at him. If all choices are purely arbitrary, then all choices are equally permissible or impermissible. All choices become equally justified or unjustified.

This is indeed a hard pill for the moral relativist to swallow, since even he wants to say that the grossest of crimes is a moral outrage. Yet if the relativist is to be true to the principles of his position, he is prevented from making such condemnations.

Knowledge About the External World

A second candidate for indubitable or incorrigible knowledge is our knowledge about the external world.

Arguments for the certainty of our knowledge about the external world. The arguments for the certainty of our knowledge about the external world are of two quite different kinds. There is the argument of the rationalist Descartes and the empiricist G. E. Moore.

We have already said a good deal about the philosophy of Descartes, but a word of review is in order. It should be remembered that Descartes sought an indubitable or incorrigible foundation on which to build knowledge. It was his contention that our senses could never provide this foundation, since they could be doubted and had in the past been shown to be wrong. Descartes did, however, find this sure starting point in what has been called the *cogito,* "I think, therefore I am." From the *cogito* Descartes argued that indubitable knowledge has two characteristics or properties, clearness and distinctness. Any idea which is both clear and distinct is indubitable.

Now Descartes was ready to tackle knowledge of the external world. He noted that he had an idea of an external, material world. The existence of this idea could be accounted for by any one of three exhaustive possibilities: (1) Descartes might be responsible for the idea. He might have a fertile imagination, and thus manufacture the idea of an external world. (2) God could deceive him, and place in his mind the idea of an external world. God's deception could be systematic, so that whenever Descartes was in a particular state of mind God made it appear that an external world existed. (3) The external world itself existed, and was the cause of the idea in Descartes' mind.

Descartes examined each of these possibilities. He argued that the first possibility is false since his idea of the external world was *impressed* upon his mind. He often perceived the external when his mind was passive. If the idea of an external world was the product of Descartes' imagination, his mind would have had to be *active.* He argued against the second possibility because by definition God is the most perfect being. No greater being than God can be conceived. If this is so, then God could not author a malicious lie.

Descartes concluded that the external world must exist as the cause of his idea of an external world. Such a conclusion is clear and distinct, claimed Descartes, because it is the only alternative that remains of three exhaustive possibilities.

G. E. Moore's argument for the certainty of the external world is quite different from that of Descartes. Moore's proof scandalized many philosophers by its seeming simplicity; they considered it arrogant.

Moore argues for the existence of the external world by proclaiming:
Here is my right hand, and here is my left. Obviously there is an
external world of physical objects!

What was troublesome to some philosophers was Moore's claim that
his method of argumentation was rigorous. He even asserted that possibly no better or more rigorous proof could be given of anything
whatsoever! The premises were true and *known* to be true, and they *did*
entail the conclusion. Why should more be asked? Was not common
sense and the universal assent of the common man on his side?

The objection to the certainty of our knowledge about the external
world.   With the exception of the skeptics, all philosophers believe in
the existence of the external world. But most object to the claim that
this knowledge is certain. They would prefer to call our knowledge of
the external world *probable*. We do have knowledge of the external
world, but that knowledge is not beyond doubt.

This claim is found in the writings of many empiricists, but is
probably best expressed by Hume in his discussions of matters of fact.
According to Hume, matters of fact included knowledge of the external
world, history, and experience in general. He claimed that kind of
knowledge could never be certain because its *contradictory* could conceivably be true. For example, it is possible for you to deny that you
are reading this book. You can doubt such a claim without causing the
kind of formal contradiction that would arise if you denied that $1 + 1$
$= 2$. It is *conceivable* that tomorrow should arrive without the rising of
the sun. Any certainty which we possess on such matters is the result of
custom. We have a habit to expect this to happen. Thus, according to
Hume, any necessity or certainty is psychological. It has its ground in
us, not the world.

If Hume is right, and a good many philosophers have agreed with
him, then there can only be probable knowledge about the world. Our
certainty should be proportional to the evidence in support of that
knowledge. This should not upset us, says Hume, for it only demon-
strates that human knowledge is not like God's knowledge, which is
indubitable.

Self-Awareness

A third candidate for indubitable knowledge is self-awareness, or
knowledge of the self by the self.

Arguments for the certainty of self-awareness. Two quite different arguments for the certainty of self-awareness have been advanced. Descartes is again one of the proponents of such knowledge and the other is John Locke.

Descartes argues that there is an epistemological priority and certainty to one's knowledge of his own existence. Personal knowledge of one's existence is epistemologically privileged. While one may doubt anything he claims to know, one cannot doubt his own existence, because in doubting there is an "I" who doubts. This sort of reflexive proof claims that only existing beings can think and deny that they exist. Descartes held that self-awareness was absolutely indubitable. This was for him the point upon which all other knowledge was to be built.

John Locke also believed in the certainty of man's knowledge of the self, but his approach was quite different than that of Descartes. Locke believed that we perceive simple ideas immediately. These ideas cannot exist in and by themselves. They must inhere in some *substratum,* a "substance" which Locke defines as "some thing, we know not what." It is this substance in which perceivable qualities inhere. Numbered among these substances is the self. Note that self-awareness is only inferred in this argument. However, in a later passage Locke states that our knowledge of ourselves is noninferential. He says that in every mental act (thinking, reasoning) "we are conscious to ourselves of our own being."

The argument against the certainty of self-awareness. Probably the clearest objection to the certainty of self-knowledge has been formulated by Gilbert Ryle. His argument does more than simply deny the indubitability of our knowledge about ourselves; Ryle intended to show that there is no necessity to postulate a mental self or substantial self. Ryle's argument deals with "the systematic elusiveness of the *I*," and proceeds in two stages.

Ryle contended that we can never give a complete description of ourselves, because the present act of describing can always be added to the description, and thus to the knowledge of the self. For instance, we can notice that we are waving our hands, we can notice that we are noticing the waving of our hands, and so on, indefinitely. Whenever we decide to stop an observation, another order of thought will always be possible. Any thought of ours can always be made the object of another thought of ours. Thus it is *logically* impossible to ever give a

complete description of ourselves. This impossibility is in *addition* to
the impossibility due to ignorance. We can never give a complete
description of ourselves or anyone else because we do not know nor
can we remember everything about them.

The second step of Ryle's argument makes an even stronger claim.
According to Ryle, the ''something more'' that philosophers like Descartes and Locke spoke of in experience as the object or thing which
has experience is a phantom. It is the result of being misled by the
word ''I.'' Ryle claimed that the ''something more'' is not an ''I'' or
mental substance which must be inferred from our experiences.
Rather, the ''something more'' is simply the result of the fact that we
(for the logical reasons stated above) can never give a complete description of ourselves.

In response to Ryle's claim two brief points can be made. First, it
may be stated that it is not at all clear that philosophers such as
Descartes and Locke were *misled* in the way in which Ryle claims.
Second, whether or not a description can contain a reference to itself is
a very complex issue. It is a difficult question: Are all self-referring
statements logically objectionable? We can merely note this issue here,
for it is far too complex to settle in an introductory text.

Logical and Mathematical Knowledge

The final possibility for indubtiable knowledge is to be found in the
area of logic and mathematics.

*The argument for the certainty of logical and mathematical knowl-
edge.*   Many, though not all, modern philosophers would argue that
both logical and mathematical knowledge is indubitable or absolutely
certain. They would argue that it is true of every possible world, and
that the denial of these logical or mathematical truths involves a contradiction.

*Objections to the certainty of logical and mathematical knowl-
edge.*   For our discussion here, we will not try to settle whether logic
and mathematics are purely formal disciplines. We will, however,
examine objections to the certainty of logical and mathematical knowledge.

The reason, so critics claim, for the absolute truth of logical propositions is that they say nothing about the world. They may indeed apply to reality (at least to acknowledge that reality is not contradictory), but they tell us nothing positive about what is occurring in reality. It is argued that their truth depends upon their form *alone*. Logic tells us what is possible and what is impossible, but not what is actual.

John Stuart Mill made it quite clear that he was not sure of the truth of the laws of logic. He wrote that the laws of logic are empirical generalizations, and, as such, are open to correction. He argued that just because we cannot conceive of another set of logical laws, it does not follow that another set of logical laws is impossible.

W.V.O. Quine, a contemporary philosopher, views knowledge in terms of a "web of belief." He argues that at the center of the web are those beliefs that we hold with greatest certainty, but he claims that even these *could* be given up. Among the beliefs at the center of the web are beliefs about logic. Quine denies that there are any purely formal or analytic beliefs or statements which are incapable of surrender or modification. He says that we tend to retain our belief in the matters at the center of our web because any change in this area would demand radical revision of our picture of the world, and we tend to resist this as much as possible.

Conclusion

It should be noted that while philosophers do disagree about the possibility and nature of certainty for any particular kind of knowledge, this in no way undercuts our claim to know—unless one makes apodictic certainty a necessary condition of all knowledge. Human knowledge is, at least in some respects, fallible or probable. Only God can know everything necessarily and incorrigibly. This does not mean that we, as humans, have no indubitable knowledge, although good philosophers will disagree concerning its nature and extent.

We should relate our present discussion to several issues at the heart of Christianity: God's knowledge, its communication to us (particularly as revealed in the Bible), and our knowledge of God's revelation and great acts in history. Is God's knowledge as communicated to us in the Bible certain, indubitable, or true? Or is it a mixture of truth and error, knowledge and opinion, with varying degrees of probability?

It is our firm conviction that God's knowledge as communicated in the Scriptures is infallible (certain, indubitable, and wholly true). But how is this possible, given the considerations that have been raised in this chapter? The answer is to be found in certain attributes which the Bible teaches are a part of the divine nature. Among God's attributes are omniscience, truth, perfect goodness, and omnipotence. Each of these attributes is crucial to the point we are making. Human knowledge is probable and fallible in part because our knowledge is partial. Sometimes we are wrong simply because we are ignorant of some relevant fact or facts. Such cannot be the case with God because God knows *everything*, both the actual and the possible (Ps. 139:1–6). Moreover, God's knowledge is true. That is, it *corresponds* to reality (Exod. 34:6; Num. 23:19; Deut. 32:4). Thus, neither ignorance nor error characterize God's knowledge.

But, is it not possible, as Descartes suggests, that God is a deceiver? Perhaps He knows the truth but withholds it intentionally from us! Perhaps we come to think that there is an external world, other minds, and moral virtue when in fact there are no such things. It is here that the biblical teaching concerning the perfect goodness of God is important (Ps. 34:8; 119:68; 145:9; Matt. 19:17; Luke 18:19). This attribute of the divine being guarantees that God would not *intentionally* mislead or deceive us.

We must, however, raise one final issue with respect to our discussion of the Bible. Is it not possible that all we have said is true, but that God might be unable to communicate His knowledge without error, making it less than certain or indubitable? Such might be the case were it not for the fact that Scripture teaches that God is also omnipotent or all-powerful (Matt. 28:18; Luke 1:37; 18:27). Therefore, if God does possess the truth, and if He has the will or motivation to communicate it (both points we have demonstrated above), then He cannot lack the power to communicate it to men. Hence, it seems clear that any conceivable reason for denying the indubitability or infallibility of God's revelation in the Bible is answered.

While the Bible is infallible, our understanding and hence knowledge of it is only fallible. (For example, most of us can remember coming to a clearer or changed understanding of a biblical text.) Even though the evidence for such a central event of the Christian faith as the resurrection of Jesus is overwhelming, it is nevertheless possible (though highly improbable) from a purely *empirical* point of view that the resurrection did not occur or that it was a hoax. This is simply because the resurrection is an empirical event or a matter of fact, and its contradictory is possible. This could just as well be said about our experience of salvation—perhaps it was a hoax!

A number of apologists and theologians have noted two important problems with this attack on our knowledge of God and His actions. First, while certainty cannot be attained, nevertheless we are commanded by God to make a total and unconditional commitment of our lives and fortunes to God. The depth of our commitment clearly exceeds the evidence that we possess. Second, when believers discuss matters of religion, it is obvious that they would rather surrender their belief in the fact that $1 + 1 = 2$ or in the law of non-contradiction than their belief in God's existence and love. Again, the believers' faith is not proportional to the evidence.

Apologists and theologians have argued that we must distinguish between certainty and certitude. Certainty has been the subject of this chapter, and is in principle impossible when we are dealing with matters of experience, a part of which is the resurrection and our experience of saving grace. However, the reason that God demands total and unconditional commitment and that the believer holds so tenaciously to his belief in God and His love is that the believer has *certitude* concerning these beliefs. Certitude is that added assurance given to the believer by the *internal witness* or *testimony* of the Holy Spirit. God's Spirit bears witness with our spirit to the truth of spiritual matters (I John 3:20; 5:8–10).

Suggested Readings

Ayer, A. J. *Language, Truth and Logic*
Descartes, René. *Rules for the Direction of the Mind*
Hume, David. *An Enquiry Concerning Human Understanding*
Husserl, Edmund. *Cartesian Meditations*
Kant, Immanuel. *The Critique of Pure Reason,* preface

$\textcircled{9}$ How Do We Perceive the External World?

In this chapter we will deal with a central problem of perceptual knowledge. The question that is raised is whether or not what we perceive retains its existence and character independent of us as perceivers. Or to put it another way, what do we perceive when we perceive? There are three fairly distinct positions that are held on this subject. They are realism, dualism, and idealism. In this chapter we will discuss these three methods of interpreting the relationship of objects to their knower.

Realism

There are at least two distinct and significant forms of realism which warrant individual attention, primitive realism and common-sense realism.

Extreme or Primitive Realism

Exposition.   The most natural and simple way of interpreting the relationship between subject and object is to understand every experienced object as existing independently of any observer. The realist would say that just as your feet can be under the desk without depending on that relationship for their existence, so too any object can be known to you (the subject) without being affected by you. This position is the unreflective view of the ordinary man in the street. It is generally only after an introduction to some philosophical problems that one begins to question this position.

Evaluation.   There are at least three reasons that most philosophers find fault with this view. First, it is virtually a universal experience to at some time be wrong in a judgment about a perception. Perhaps you saw a brown rope on the ground but mistook it for a snake. You were sure that you saw a snake, but you were incorrect. This sort of error is hard to account for if it is true that we are in immediate contact with objects, and our relationship to them does not affect them. Second, extreme or primitive objectivism has no way to account for illusory or hallucinated objects. For instance, suppose you seem to see a pink elephant tap-dancing on the ceiling. Obviously, you are mistaken, but how can primitive realism explain the pink elephant's existence in your perceptual field? As a matter of fact, the hallucinated pink elephant may seem more "real" to you than a genuine elephant, which you have never seen. Third, it is clear that all perception of objects is dependent on factors in the visual context. Extreme realism does not take this into consideration. However, it is an important point and will be discussed in detail below.

Common-Sense Realism.

Exposition.   Common-sense realism, at least initially, seems to moderate the problems of extreme realism and yet avoid the artificiality which one immediately feels with dualism and idealism. Common-sense realism agrees with extreme or primitive realism that physical objects are independent of or external to the mind, although they are directly and immediately observable to it. What distinguishes the two views is common-sense realism's understanding of the unreal, the illusory, or hallucinated object. Such perceptions are subjective, and their objects occur exclusively within the mind. Thomas Reid and G. E. Moore are just two examples of prominent philosophers who have held positions of this general type.

Evaluation. Common-sense realism has the advantage of resolving the second criticism brought against extreme or primitive realism. According to common-sense realism, illusory objects are *not* independent and external to the mind, but are in some sense the product of it.

However, the other criticisms must still be answered, even if they have less force against common-sense realism. Since physical objects are both external to the mind and in direct contact with it, how can we be mistaken about an object which is real? Moreover, once the epistemologist has admitted that illusions and hallucinations are internal to and relative to the observer, how can he deny that *all* perception bears some relativity to the observer?

Because such criticisms have been leveled against this moderate form of realism, dualism has arisen.

Dualism

We will distinguish between two kinds of dualism, the representative perception or "copy theory" of knowledge, and phenomenalism.

Representative Perception

By far the most common form of dualism is "the copy theory" of knowledge. It has had such prominent defenders as Descartes, Locke, and Hume. More modern empiricists have developed a theory of dualism called "the sense data theory."

Exposition. This form of dualism recognizes two distinct and independent orders of existence. First of all there are ideas, that is, impressions or sense data which are the immediate objects of perception; these are directly and immediately present to our consciousness. Second, there is an independent and external world which we *infer* as the cause of the sense data perceived by our consciousness.

Epistemological dualists have viewed the nature of the ideas and their causes differently. Some have held that both the ideas and their causes are material, while others have contended that both are mental or immaterial. Most common has been the view that the ideas are mental or psychological, and their causes are material. Some philosophers, however, have thought that the ideas are material and the causes immaterial. Representative perception claims that the "thing" we perceive is numerically distinct from the cause of our perceiving it.

Let us guard against a possible confusion here. We are discussing *epistemological* dualism, not *metaphysical* dualism. Metaphysical dualism postulates a psycho-physical, or mind-body dualism (see chap. 12). Epistemological dualism is *not* concerned with the relation of the mind to the body or ideas to brain processes, but merely with the relationship that the data of our experience has to the supposed causes of it.

There are three fundamental arguments for this form of dualism. First, this position is able to deal with illusion and error. Second, dualism conveniently handles perceptual relativity. And third, dualism can distinguish and explain the difference between what are called primary and secondary qualities.

Unquestionably, the strongest reason philosophers have embraced epistemological dualism is because of a philosophical argument against realism called "the argument from illusion." We all can remember riding down a road in a car on a warm day, looking ahead some distance, and seeing what appeared to be a puddle of water or a small pond on the highway. However, as we drove closer we found that there was no water at all. Someone who holds that we are in direct contact with the objects of perception is not able to give an explanation for the illusion or perceptual error. Another example of perceptual error occurs when we partially submerge a stick in the water. We perceive the stick as *bent,* but upon removing the stick we find that it is straight. Our perceptions have misled us. If it were true that we perceive objects directly, this phenomenon would not occur.

A second line of argument has to do with perceptual relativity. If you look at a quarter on a table directly from above, the coin looks round. But if you take the coin in your hand and elevate one end about forty degrees, a funny thing happens. The coin no longer looks round but eliptical. It is the same coin as the one which appeared to be round; how can we account for the change in appearance if we are perceiving the object directly?

A third argument advanced in favor of dualism would not be accepted by all philosophers. It is an argument from the distinction between primary and secondary qualities. A group of philosophers have argued that physical objects have two differing kinds of qualities or properties—those that are quantitative and those that are not. The quantitative properties, or primary qualities, are number, position, size, shape, duration, mobility, and mass (inertia). Another way of distinguishing between primary and secondary qualities is to realize that spatial and temporal qualities are primary qualities. On the other hand, non-quantitative properties, or secondary qualities, are color, sound, smell, taste, and most tactual sensations.

Three important differences are said to exist between the two kinds of qualities. The primary or quantitative properties form a continuous or homogeneous series. Each quantity can be precisely determined by comparison with other qualities of the same kind. This is not so for the non-qualitative properties: they are discontinuous, heterogeneous, and incommensurable. For instance, how can one compare green and blue? Moreover, if one knew only the colors of blue and yellow, it would be impossible to make him understand the nature of green.

A second difference between primary and secondary qualities is that the quantitative properties of an object are known through a number of senses, although generally these qualities are best apprehended through sight and touch. On the other hand, the non-quantitative are known through a single sense. For example, number is revealed by all five senses, while color is known only through sight.

Finally, a third difference between the two kinds of qualities is that the quantitative qualities can be shown to exist by both *direct* observation and also *indirectly* through their effect upon other objects. It is contended that non-quantitative properties, however, lack ascertainable effects and cannot be known without direct observation. For example, the shape of an object is discernible both by looking at the thing and by observing the imprint which it makes in clay. On the other hand, the taste of a fruit is discernible only in the perceiver's mouth. It cannot be recorded or objectively defined.

Evaluation.   The chief objection to this view, even if one accepts the arguments for dualism, is that the arguments presented thus far support only the conclusion that sometimes we do not perceive objects directly (i.e., when we are deluded or when perceptual relativity is involved). Thus, there is a need to give arguments that will extend epistemological dualism to all instances of perception. Here we have three auxiliary arguments.

First, it has been pointed out that there is no *intrinsic* difference between perceptions we have that are true and those that are erroneous or illusory. For example, the eliptical quarter and the round quarter both seem to be equally real. If we are perceiving something different when we perceive an illusion, so it is argued, then we should expect our experiences to be different in each case. From the nature of our experience we should be able to tell whether it is true or illusory. However, this is not possible. Any ability that we possess to distinguish between veridical (true) and illusory perceptions depends on context or past experience.

Second, it is argued that we are justified in extending dualism to all cases. For example, suppose that we see a silo from about half a mile away. From this distance the silo appears to be *round*. As we get closer, however, we realize that the silo has *eight sides*. It only *appeared* round from our original distance. The original perceptions, now *considered false,* and the later perceptions, now *considered true,* form a perfect series. It is not as though the earlier perceptions were dark and the later perceptions were light with the glow of truth, for there was no break between those perceptions that made the silo appear round and those that showed it to be octagonal. There was no change in any condition except that of distance. Because true and delusive perceptions may form a continuous series, with respect to both their qualities and the conditions in which they are received, we can extend dualism to all perception.

Third, it has been noted that all our perceptions, both those that are veridical and those that are delusive, are in some degree dependent upon eternal conditions such as light, and also upon the perceiver's physiological and psychological state. In cases that are habitually delusive or veridical we are not apt to notice the importance of external conditions. But these conditions do influence perception. For instance, when we look at the page of a book, we assume we are seeing the book as it "really" is. Nevertheless, we must admit that our experience of the page of our book requires more than that the page simply exist. Many other factors enter into our perception of the page, such as the amount of light, the distance at which we view the paper, the background or surface against which the book is placed, and the state of our nervous system and eyes. If we vary these conditions we will find that our perception varies also. For instance, if we squint our eyes, the page will look fuzzy and we will not be able to read it. Many philosophers have concluded that, although our perceptions are not wholly dependent on external conditions, these conditions do affect our perceptions. Thus, we are justified in claiming that all cases of perception demand the introduction of some form of epistemological dualism.

Even with these three auxiliary arguments, a number of objections have been made against dualism. If it is claimed that we always perceive an idea, impression or sense datum, how can we falsify—or verify for that matter—such a claim? It would seem that we would need a perspective outside of the process (the kind of perspective that none of us can have) to determine the truth or falsity of the dualist position. Indeed, no *empirical* fact will count either for or against the position. Thus, dualism is not an empirical theory, capable of proof or disproof from experience, but at best a philosophical theory.

More serious, however, is the claim that dualism or representative perception seems to lead to skepticism. If it is true that there are two realms, one of the mind with ideas and sense data and one of an external world with objects and persons, then our ideas will be true when they copy reality and false when they do not (or when they are distorted copies). But how can we discover when this agreement exists and when it does not? We can judge whether a photograph is a good one or a bad one by comparing it with the original object. But is this possible with perception? It would seem to require a perspective that no human being can have, a perception outside the perceptual circle. Therefore, it is argued that at best we must be agnostic about the exact nature of the "real" world.

Philosophers have sought various ways to defend dualism against this charge. Descartes claimed that ideas must resemble their causes or objects because God is a most perfect being, and thus not a liar. Other philosophers have argued that at least the primary qualities of external objects are known through more than one sense; one sense can and does correct the other. Take the partially submerged stick as an example. To our sight it appears bent in water. But, still submerged, it will *feel* straight to touch. In this way our sense of touch corrects our sense of sight. Still other philosophers argue that any perception occurs in a context, and it is this context and our past experience that keep us from taking delusive or illusive perceptions as veridical. Once we take the stick out of water, we are no longer deluded. We come to know that sticks which are submerged in water appear bent. Furthermore, when we learn about light and the laws of refraction through a medium, we realize why a stick will appear bent in water, although it is in fact straight.

There is another objection which is directed particularly against the dualism which distinguishes between primary and secondary qualities. As we noted, primary qualities are quantitative, while secondary qualities are non-quantitative. But if all the physical causes of perception are primary properties, then it follows that secondary qualities—and with them the immediate objects of perception (ideas, sense data, and impression)—must belong to a realm different from that of the physical properties. Thus, what began as a numerical duality between sense data and the objects which we infer from them has in fact become a theory about *qualitative* duality or difference.

Since the objection only has consequences for a small group of contemporary philosophers, we shall not dwell on the problem. Suffice it to say that the difficulties can be overcome by simply putting the so-called secondary qualities back into the physical world. For instance, color itself and the varying shades of color might be explained as various intensities of light waves reflected from objects. Thus, our perception of color would also have a physical cause.

Still another objection applies to all forms of dualism. At the heart of this criticism is the fact that the physical causes which supposedly *cause* sense data can only be located in the space and time of the sense data themselves. This is an important point. Suppose that we are perceiving a table. We immediately perceive, it is argued, not the table, but a sense impression or data. Thus, *sense impression exists only as a state of our experience*. Furthermore, it could not exist independently from us. However, from the way in which we receive sense data, we realize that they are the effects of external causes. In this case we would call the cause the "real table," to distinguish it from the internal or perceived table. According to the theory, this "real table," as simply the product of inference, is incapable of being experienced since we are limited to our own states of experiences.

Here is the problem. This inferred table must exist in a space other than the space of the perceived table, since numerical difference requires difference of spatio-temporal position. Where, however, can this "real" space be? The only space which we can *conceive* is the space which we *perceive*. But this is the space in which the perceived table and all sense impressions inhabit! This perceptual space is too internal and subjective to be the home of real tables, chairs, and horses. Thus, one must look beyond for a suitable resting place for the "real table." The difficulty is that it is impossible to think or conceive of any space that is external to the space that is perceived. The space that is experienced is the space in which one finds his body, the earth, and the space in which the farthest stars revealed by telescope exist. However, the dualist has claimed that this perceived space is the domain of sense data, and therefore not good for the inferred, "real" world to exist.

The same difficulty can be argued for the dualists' view of time. It is impossible for there to be a time other than that which is experienced.

Phenomenalism

"Phenomenalism" is the name of a special form of dualism which originated in the philosophy of A. J. Ayer.

Exposition.   Ayer begins by presenting and evaluating the argument from illusion. He clearly recognizes the importance of the argument for the introduction of sense data into one's epistemology. His evaluation of the argument is most interesting. Ayer states that when the argument is understood as an empirical claim or as a matter of fact, it is inconclusive. For example, when one examines the subsidiary arguments given to extend the necessity of sense data to *all* instances of perception, one sees that each of the arguments rests on a premise which is open to question. The first argument depends on the assumption that since true and delusive perceptions are perceptions of objects of different types, the perceptions should be qualitatively distinguishable. The second argument rests on the premise that if perceptions differed with respect to their qualities and conditions of occurrence, they could not be arranged in a continuous series. The third argument asserts that material things can exist and have properties without being causally dependent on some observer.

Ayer holds that each of these crucial premises is open to question. Moreover, the first two of these premises are not open to any empirical proof or disproof. Ayer offers a surprising suggestion. He admits that the introduction of sense data *as a matter of fact* cannot be justified.

However, he advances the introduction of sense data *as a matter of language*. Ayer points out that it is epistemologically more convenient to talk about the external world in a *sense data* language than in a *material object* language. Notice that the ground of justification for the introduction of sense data has shifted from an empirical to a pragmatic base.

What are some of the advantages that Ayer thinks make such a language superior? (This is important since many philosophers might find such talk not only inconvenient but also incredible.) First, since statements about sense data are statements about the way things *appear* or *seem* to an observer, such statements are incorrigible or indubitable. Suppose you say that a black and white page *seems* to be before you. According to Ayer, you cannot be wrong about what appears to be the case unless you are lying, ignorant, or misusing the language. It is true that there may *in fact* be no page before you, but you cannot be mistaken about what *appears* to be so. As we shall see, this ability to deal with perceptual error will be argued as an advantage of Ayer's epistemology. Thus, if phenomenalism is acceptable, it offers certain foundations for knowledge. They are sense data statements.

Second, the introduction of sense data language leaves open the question whether an external world exists and if so, of what kind. Some philosophers have argued that the world is wholly material, while others have held that reality is entirely immaterial. Still others have claimed that the world is *both* material and immaterial. The advantage of talking in a sense data language is that the whole question of the nature and existence of an independent, external world is left open. No questions are begged, as when for instance we appeal to language in support of material objects since our language is a *material object language*. Sense data language only tells us about the way objects appear.

Third, any sentence of the sense data language will always be *true* when a sentence in the material object language is *true*. In other words, the sentence "There appears to me to be a new car" will always be true when the statement, "There is a new car" is true. Thus, the sense data language will always *save the truth* of the material object language.

Ayer's account of knowledge can also explain error. Statements in sense data language may be true even when the corresponding propo-

sitions in the material object language turn out to be false. For example, we may *appear* to see a lake a mile down the road, but there may
in fact be no lake. According to Ayer's thesis we have no problem with
perceptual error. We did *seem* to see a lake, and this was correctly
conveyed by the sense data statement. On the other hand, as we have
said, there is no lake in reality. This too is handled without difficulty
by denying the truth of the material object language sentence.

Evaluation.   Almost every criticism, and a few more, that can be
made of the view we called dualism has been made with equal force
against phenomenalism. Dualism was criticized because it was in principle beyond proof or disproof, and thus was not an empirical theory.
Ayer grants this for his position. But instead of abandoning the position, he attempts to turn the criticism into an advantage rather than a
disadvantage.

This move may be both applauded and criticized. At least before,
dualism had been justified as *empirically necessary.* Now something
intervenes in our perception of the world which is merely a linguistic
convenience. Why remove ourselves in such a way from reality? For
these and other reasons, Ayer does not now, nor did he ever, have a
large following for his form of epistemology.

Before leaving this discussion, it is worth pointing out that *in practice* Ayer presents us with an ontology that makes sense data the
ultimate entities or constituents of reality. Since Ayer admits that his
epistemology leaves the questions of the existence and nature of reality
open, in practical terms we are left with sense data, or more precisely
sense data *statements,* as the ultimately real. At best this consequence
is novel, but false in light of the history of philosophy.

Idealism

Having examined realism and dualism and having raised some of the
problems with each of these positions, we turn now to our third alternative, *idealism.*

In general, idealism may be defined as the view that objects, particularly material objects, cannot exist independently of some consciousness of them. Thus all reality may be reduced exclusively to conscious
beings and their states. This position may be divided into a weaker
form and a stronger form.

The Weaker Form

The name most commonly associated with idealism is that of Bishop George Berkeley (1685–1753). Berkeley (pronounced *Bark*-lee) was roughly a contemporary of John Locke and David Hume.

Exposition.   Berkeley's views were really the logical outgrowth of a number of epistemological claims which were widely held during his time. A good number of epistemologists had conceded that the object perceived in illusion and perceptual error is wholly internal to the perceiver. Moreover, the belief that the immediate objects of perception are ideas, impressions, or sense data was widely accepted. John Locke had argued that *only* the primary qualities exist or inhere in the objects themselves. The secondary qualities, such as color, smell, and so forth, are merely *powers* objects posses to produce certain effects in perceivers. Thus, the actual existence of these secondary properties becomes internal to the perceiver.

Berkeley was sufficiently astute to see that if an argument could be given for the subjective character of secondary qualities, a similar and parallel argument could be made for the internal and subjective nature of primary properties. What had begun as a world of sense data or ideas, on the one hand, and their physical and objective causes on the other, has now been left behind. In its place is a world in which *all* the facts of existence are reduced to those characterized wholly by conscious beings and their states or ideas. There is no independent world or reality outside of experience. This is summarized in Berkeley's famous dictum, "To be is to be perceived."

What the epistemological dualist calls an inferred, independent, and external world of material objects is reduced to a subjective, dependent, and internal system, with generally fixed and regular relations between specific states of consciousness. You may wonder how the experience of physical states is now distinguishable from subjective experiences. The answer is that the so-called "physical" states or experiences can apparently be shared by a number of minds. What distinguishes one's experience of seeing a giant redwood from seeing a pink elephant is that only one perceiver sees the pink elephant. Anyone who meets certain conditions will *share* the experience of the redwood. It is important, however, to note that Berkeley claimed that the redwood as well as the pink elephant has *no* existence outside conscious experience.

If existence and perception are so intimately related, the natural question that comes to mind is, What happens when an object is not perceived? Does it cease to exist? According to Berkeley's account it certainly would seem to go out of existence. Berkeley, however, had an answer for this problem. He claimed that God, who never slumbers nor sleeps and who is omniscient and omnipresent, continuously perceives all objects everywhere. While objects may at times lack *human* perceivers, they never lack a *divine* perceiver and thus continuous existence is guaranteed.

The principal reason Berkeley argued for such an improbable view was the same reason which led to the substitution of dualism for realism. Epistemologists became increasing aware of the dependence of experienced objects on the perceiver. You will remember that epistemological dualists noted that certain properties were "influenced" by the states of the perceiver and the context in which the object was perceived. Berkeley simply applied this relativity to the primary or quantitative properties as well. He found that man's experience of the shapes, sizes, hardness, softness, and weight of objects was every bit as dependent on conditions in the self as were secondary qualities. The argument can be put something like this:

> All properties which are relative are subjective.
> Primary properties are relative properties.
> ∴ Primary properties are subjective.

The logic of Berkeley's argument is unavoidable—given the truth of the premises. The major or first premise must be accepted by those who hold to the subjectivity of secondary qualities because of their relative character. Berkeley showed that primary qualities were also relative. Therefore, the conclusion that both primary and secondary qualities are subjective seems inescapable.

Evaluation.   The first and immediate objection (or reaction) to such a view is that it reduces trees, mountains, and thundering locomotives to the same immaterial stuff that dreams, pink elephants, and ghosts are made of. Surely, this cannot be true. Berkeley had a ready answer, however, to this objection. He claimed that mental states may be divided into two classes, the first consisting of perceptions caused by something beyond us and the second containing perceptions that both exist in and are caused by our minds. The first class is "physical" and constitutes the order of nature, while the second class is what Berkeley calls the *psychical* and includes the private and exclusive possession of each self. Psychical experiences lack the *regularity* and *community* of "physical" ideas. However, the only causal agency for ideas that we know is *conscious will* (our psychical ideas are the product of our conscious will). "Physical" ideas, therefore, must also be the product of a will somewhat like ours, only infinitely wiser and more powerful. Therefore, Berkeley claims that God is the source of our ideas of a material world, to which we ignorantly attribute existence independent of our consciousness.

For most of us such an answer is entirely inadequate. It goes contrary to common sense and the universal intuition of the human race. Even Hume (whose views on rationally justifying the existence of the material world left something to be desired) saw that what he called Nature had not left it to us to decide whether the external world was real or not. We immediately and intuitively grasp the necessity of the reality of the material world.

Berkeley's answer gives rise to another problem for the theist. Berkeley's claim that the "physical" world's source is in the will of God but has no independent external existence, would seem to cast doubt on the integrity of God. It would appear, at least on the surface, that God is misleading us so that we believe that there is an independent world when there is not. Berkeley might reply that God is not responsible for our erroneous conclusion—we are. We decide that the "physical" world exists independently. But this is not sufficient. Our intuitions and the evidence seem to point so strongly in the direction of an independent, external, and material world that it is hard to see how a perfect, honest, and loving God could refrain from telling us of our error.

If we do grant that the immediate objects of perception are ideas (this is by no means universally accepted), then we may ask about their causes or origin. There are at least two possibilities, independent material objects or an infinite spirit. Which of these possibilities seems more probable? Certainly, the former is the more simple and more likely. Furthermore, as a rule, causes are found to resemble their effects.

Another objection to idealism is its impracticality. While one may hold this kind of an epistemological theory, it is indeed difficult to *live* as an idealist. Think of what would happen if you began to treat your wife, husband, mother or father as merely minds with ideas caused by infinite spirit! It would not be long before you found yourself in deep trouble, and not just philosophical trouble.

The Stronger Form

Surprisingly, Berkeley's views are not the most extreme position that one might take with regard to the existence of the material world.

Exposition.   Berkeley and his followers were careful to insist that their doctrine applied only to the individual facts of experience. The laws and relations that unite these facts or terms were to be excluded. However, Immanuel Kant moved the process of subjectifying existence another step further. Kant claimed, at least according to some interpretations, that the form and relationship of the so-called facts of our experience is the product of the mind. He argued that our intuitions or sensations of the physical world come to us *in space,* and our experience of reflection or memory occurs *in time.* Moreover, our representations (somewhat similar to ideas) are related by certain rules or categories such as causality, necessity, or unity. Space and time are called *forms of intuition,* and causality, necessity, unity, and others are called *categories of the understanding* (see pp. 88–89). These forms and categories are a part of what Kant calls a *transcendental* psychology. While not all philosophers have interpreted Kant as saying that these forms and categories are exclusively mental, he does claim that they are principles by which the mind operates, and we do not know if they apply to things-in-themselves (things as they really are, apart from our perception of them). Indeed, there are philosophers who would argue the stronger view that these forms and categories *cannot* apply to things as they are.

One final stage yet remains. Kant's followers, particularly Johann Fichte (1762–1814), Georg Hegel (1770–1831), Friedrich von Schelling (1775–1854), and Arthur Schopenhauer (1788–1860), though they differed on details, reduced even the self to subjectivity. Not only were the forms and the relations of experience subjective, but the *ground* of these forms and relations, the individual self, was subjectivized.

The argument for such a position is that the *various* experiences of finite selves constitute the experience of an "absolute self." This absolute self is itself subjective in character. Here the relentless movement toward subjectivity and hyper-solipsism is complete. Nothing has escaped the idealists' sword.

Evaluation. The same criticisms used against the weaker form of idealism apply here also; the range of applicability to the stronger form is simply greater. Such claims call into question the integrity of God, who, according to the idealistic perspective at least, seems to be deceiving us. Such philosophical views are incapable of being put into practice in real life, as we saw on p. 147. Furthermore, the total solipsism of this final form of epistemology would seem to destroy any hope of humans communicating with one another, or transmitting knowledge.

Conclusion

In this chapter we have examined three views on the nature and independence of the material world and the knower. *Realism* postulates that we are in direct contact with an independent, material, external world. *Dualism* asserts the existence of two realms, one of ideas, impressions, or sense data and another of material objects. The existence of the material world is inferred as the cause of our ideas or sense data. *Idealism* reduces all "the world" to the realm of the subject or subjectivity. In its most extreme form even the self is assigned to this domain.

We have shown that each of these positions is open to some objections. Idealism, because of its strongly counter-intuitive nature, has never had a wide following. Dualism, on the other hand, has been widely advocated in the twentieth century, although it is presently experiencing less favor than it did in the first half of the century. Some philosophers have come to believe that dualism is actually not an empirical theory capable of proof or disproof. Also, such a view seems to lead to either skepticism or idealism. Skepticism would follow if we *cannot* guarantee the relationship between the realm of the ideas and what is inferred, namely a material world. It seems logically inescapable that idealism will follow if dualism is introduced on the grounds that we *can* distinguish between primary and secondary properties of objects. The argument that infers the subjectivity of secondary qualities from their relativity works equally well for the subjectivity of primary qualities, and ultimately the subjectivity of all things.

Therefore, though we are aware of the problems of realism, we remain unconvinced that some sophisticated form of realism is incorrect. It best accords with our common sense. While atheists and theists who do not accept the claim that God is perfectly good may be skeptical about the argument that God is not a deceiver, those who hold to the biblical view of God find this view significant. Descartes was correct—God cannot and will not deceive us into believing that there is an independent, material world if such is not the case.

The objections against realism do not seem insurmountable, given what we know about the physiology, the psychology of perception, and the functioning of the material world through the natural sciences—particularly physics.

Suggested Readings

Ayer, A. J. *The Empirical Foundations of Knowledge*
Berkeley, George. *The Principles of Human Knowledge*
Descartes, René. *Meditations on First Philosophy,* meditation 6
Kant, Immanuel. *The Critique of Pure Reason*
Merleau-Ponty, M. *The Phenomenology of Perception*
Moore, G. E. "Proof of an External World," in *Philosophical Papers*

10   How Are Beliefs Justified?

As we come to the close of the section on epistemology, we will turn our attention to *epistemic justification,* the way we justify our claims to know. Traditionally (from Plato onward) for something to be known it at least had to be believed by someone and that belief had to be true. However, philosophers realized that belief and truth alone were not sufficient for knowledge. Something more had to be added. At a minimum there had to be evidence, that is, support or justification for holding that belief. Modern epistemologists speak of this as the *logic* or *structure* of epistemic justification.

Before turning to a discussion of the structure of justification, it is essential to note that in contemporary discussions of epistemology there is a certain independence among the concepts of truth, knowledge, and justification. Truth and justification can be seen to be different concepts in that someone may be justified in believing some

151

proposition *p* but *p* may in fact be false. Similarly, one could be justified in believing *p*, and yet we could deny that he *knew p*, since *p* is false. In other words, justification is a necessary condition of a belief being true and counting as knowledge, but it is not alone a sufficient condition.

In general terms there are two alternative logics or structures of epistemic justification, *foundationalism* and *coherentism,* or *contextualism.*

Foundationalism

Most philosophers until quite recently held some form of foundationalism, whether they spoke of their procedure of epistemic justification in those terms or not.

Definition and Exposition

Foundationalism is the view that there is a structure of knowledge whose foundations, though they support all the rest, are themselves in need of no support. Epistemic justification, then, is pyramidal. The beliefs or propositions in the lowest tier are justifiably believed without appeal to any other reason, and hence constitute a foundation for knowledge. Each belief or proposition in the higher tiers is justified on the basis of propositions or beliefs lower in the pyramid.

Foundationalism, then, usually consists of two claims. First, there are directly justified beliefs. And second, any person has sufficient number of these beliefs to build justificatory pyramids that are topped with *indirectly* justified beliefs.

Epistemologically basic beliefs. It may be helpful to look more closely at each of these levels. Epistemologically basic beliefs or propositions constitute the lowest tier of the justification pyramid. The most important characteristic of these beliefs it that their justification is *not* inferred (some philosophers have even argued that they *cannot* be inferred) from any other beliefs or propositions. For this reason, their justification is said to be direct, and they constitute direct or immediate knowledge. They have been called "intrinsically acceptable," "*prima facie* justified," or "intrinsically credible" beliefs by other philosophers. At any rate, they make up the foundation upon which all knowledge is built. Some would take this as analogous to the axioms of a geometric system. They are absolutely primitive.

Mediate or indirect justification. All beliefs that are supported by epistemologically basic beliefs are said to be justified *mediately,* or indirectly. The resultant knowledge is called *mediate*, or indirect, knowledge. We can now explain more clearly how mediate justification is thought to be related to immediately justified belief(s). The idea is that, while some beliefs may be supported by other mediately justified beliefs, if we progress sufficiently far down the pyramid of justification, sooner or later we will arrive at directly justified beliefs (epistemologically basic beliefs or propositions). The line of descent in general will not be direct; usually the belief we start with in the higher tier will rest on several beliefs, each of which in turn will be supported by several beliefs. Thus, the typical picture is that of multiple branching from the original belief, much like a tree. If we turn the "foundation" metaphor on its head, we can say that each mediately or indirectly justified belief stands at the origin of a more or less multiple branching tree structure which ultimately terminates in an immediately or directly justified belief or proposition.

The relationship between higher and lower beliefs in the pyramidal structure. Let us now explain what we mean when we say that the foundational beliefs *support* the mediate beliefs. These epistemologically basic beliefs function in two ways. Some basic beliefs serve as logically conclusive reasons for certain non-basic beliefs. The connection is analytic and known a priori. (Some philosophers have argued that the relationship could also be a posteriori.) Without claiming that either of the following statements is a basic belief, the relationship is analogous to the relationship between the statement, "Tom is a bachelor" and the statement, "Tom is an unmarried male."

Second, certain epistemologically basic beliefs (beliefs lower in the pyramid) may function as reasons in a much looser, less conclusive way. Such reasons are called contingent, logically good, or *prima facie* reasons. These are *good* reasons for some mediate knowledge, but they do not logically *guarantee* that knowledge. For some philosophers, beliefs about appearance or sensation are epistemologically basic. If we accept that, then we can understand the contempo-

rary philosopher Wilfred Sellars' description of perceiving red as epistemologically basic. Sellars would say, "I am being appeared to,
redly." To Sellars, this is a good reason for thinking that there is
something red in front of him. Further sensations convince him that he
is looking at a ripe, red apple. Notice, however that "being appeared
to, redly" is not a *logically conclusive* reason for a man to think he is
seeing an apple. He may conceivably have the same sensation if he is
undergoing brain surgery and a certain portion of his brain is stimu-
lated.

Support for Foundationalism

Foundationalists typically cite the *regress argument* in favor of their
structure of epistemic justification. The regress argument attempts to
show that the only alternatives to foundationalism are circular justification or the equally unacceptable infinite regress of justification. To
return to the tree idea of justification, there are only four conceivable
terminations for any branch:

(a) It ends in an immediate, directly justified belief (an epistemologically basic belief).

(b) It ends in an unjustified belief.

(c) The original belief reoccurs within the justification chain so that
the branch forms a loop.

(d) The branch continues infinitely.

It is possible that in any tree one branch might assume one form,
while another branch a still different form. The regress argument,
however, assumes that justification and hence knowledge is only possible if each branch assumes form (a) above.

Let us examine a tree where each branch has form (a). Since each
branch ends in an immediately or directly justified belief, which itself
needs no justification, the regress is terminated along each branch.
Hence, justification is transferred along each branch to that original
belief.

Next let us assume there is a branch of the form (b). It is argued that
with form (b) *no* element will be justified. Our original belief will only
be justified if the belief supporting it is justified. However, in form (b)
when we come to the termination of the branch, the belief upon which
all other beliefs depend for their justification is itself unjustified. Thus,
since it is unjustified, the beliefs it supports are unjustified.

With form (c) we have a justification chain which forms a closed loop. Here the problem is circularity. To make our example more understandable, let us call our original belief *p*. *P* will only be justified if *q* is justified. *Q* will be justified if *x* is justified. But we find that *x* will only be justified if *p* is justified. So ultimately, belief *p* is only justified if *p* is justified. This is a viciously circular argument, and begs the question.

Finally, form (d) above deals with a branch with no terminus. No matter how far we extend our branch from its point of origin, we find that the last element is itself a belief that is mediately or indirectly justified. Therefore, no matter where we examine this structure, we find that the necessary condition for mediate justification (i.e., a directly or immediately justified belief) is lacking. Failing this necessary condition of justification, each belief back to the original is itself unjustified.

The conclusion of this regress argument is something like this. Higher-level beliefs are justified if and only if every belief that supports them is justified. Since justification must come to an end, the structure for each belief must terminate in an immediately justified belief. If the foundation fails to be immediately or directly justified, then the pyramidal structure of justification collapses. This argument has had a firm grip on epistemologists throughout the history of philosophy.

Criticisms and Objections

The recent strategy for attacking foundationalism is to claim either that it is an ideal incapable of attainment *or* that it is in some sense incoherent.

1. *There are no incorrigible statements that can serve as epistemologically basic propositions for perceptual knowledge.* To understand this criticism we need to review a bit of the history of epistemology. As we said in our discussion on indubitability, some epistemologists held that for any claim to count as knowledge, it must be indubitable or incorrigible. As time passed, it was considered necessary that at least the basic propositions (foundations) be incorrigible. This would insure infallible foundations for our knowledge. Hume argued that any knowledge of the external world (what he called

matters of fact) was, in principle, fallible. That is, it would always be conceivable that the contradictory could be true. But even after Hume some epistemologists sought infallible foundations. Ayer, for example, sought them in sense data and Husserl in an analysis of the structure of consciousness. Most epistemologists were unconvinced, however, by Ayer's and Husserl's attempts, for they argued that the candidates for infallible basic propositions about the external world were either not knowledge at all or not incorrigible.

Response to this criticism has been of two kinds. First, one can continue to maintain that there are sufficient basic propositions to build a comprehensive epistemology. In this case one would be rejecting Hume's criticism. Second, one might accept Hume's analysis and assume that it is not necessary for all epistemologically basic propositions to be incorrigible. Philosophers characteristically hold that some basic beliefs are incorrigible (e.g., mathematics and logic) and some are not (e.g., the external world). Thus, the contemporary foundationalist John Pollock divides epistemologically basic propositions into those that are incorrigible and those that are *prima facie* justified (these are not incorrigible). Other philosophers call this latter class intrinsically acceptable or credible.

For example, we begin with the presumption of the truth of a belief. In the absence of any reason for rejecting this *prima facie* justified belief, we are justified in believing it. This does not mean that such a belief could not be wrong or that it will not be revised. The acceptance of *prima facie* justified beliefs is simply a recognition that (1) justification must in fact stop somewhere and (2) not all knowledge is capable of incorrigible foundations. Pollock calls any belief that functions as a reason for rejecting a *prima facie* justified belief a *defeater,* because it shows the belief to be wrong. Both responses by foundationalists affirm that at least some knowledge rests upon indubitable foundations.

2. *There are no directly justified beliefs which can serve as epistemologically basic propositions or beliefs.* The second objection bears a similarity to the first, but it is a more serious attack on foundationalism. In answer to the first criticism it was possible to grant the objection and still maintain the view (although that was not the only way to defend foundationalism). On the other hand, this second criticism is aimed directly at one of the central claims, that there are immediately or directly justified propositions.

The objection goes like this. Any spontaneous claim, observational or introspective (e.g., "I am being appeared to, redly"), brings with it almost no presumption of truth when we consider the claim by itself. We usually accept claims as true because of our confidence in a whole body of background assumptions. Included in these assumptions are the reliability of the observer, the conditions under which the observations were made, and the kind of objects about which the claims are made. In sum, so the argument goes, the acceptance of any claim is (even if not consciously) dependent upon and hence determined by inference from these conditions. Therefore there are no directly justified beliefs or propositions.

This objection seems to be incorrect on a number of grounds. Even if it were true, it attacks only knowledge of the external world. Although this is admittedly an important part of our knowledge, there are other kinds of foundationalists. More pointedly, William Alston has argued that this objection contains a confusion. Alston says it appears to substantiate the claim that there are no directly justified beliefs but in fact it does not. Upon close scrutiny we see that the criticism is not directed against the observer who makes an introspective or observational claim, but against us for accepting his claim. That is, there is a subtle shift from the first-person to the third-person perspective. All that our second objection shows is that we would have different grounds for accepting the claims of the observer than we would for making those claims ourselves. An observer could very well be directly justified in accepting a belief, while we at best would be mediately justified in believing that claim.

3. *Foundationalism in the end leads either to an infinite regress or dogmatism.* Further, opponents argue that foundationalism will be guilty of an infinite regress of justifications if we say we must know the grounds on which our basic propositions are justified. For it will always be possible to demand that we have grounds for knowing the grounds, and so forth. On the other hand, if it is not necessary to know the grounds on which our basic propositions are justified, then we end up with dogmatism. A dogmatist simply asserts—without the possibility of justifying reasons—that the foundations (i.e., the epistemologically basic propositions) are justified.

There are, however, two replies to this objection. The first is to claim that there are self-warranting or self-justifying beliefs or propositions which constitute the foundations of knowledge.

A second response is suggested by William Alston and hinted at by

John Pollock. Alston distinguishes between two types of foundationalism, *iterative* foundationalism and *simple* foundationalism. Alston rejects iterative (repetitious) foundationalism on the ground that it does lead to an infinite regress as charged. On the other hand, he argues that simple foundationalism escapes the charge of an infinite regress *without* falling into the trap of dogmatism. It avoids the infinite regress by grounding knowledge in immediately justified basic propositions without demanding that we know these foundational beliefs are justified. The rationale for such a move is that justification must stop somewhere. Alston asserts that the charge of dogmatism too can be escaped. In most cases our basic beliefs are not challenged, either by some other belief or by some other person's objection. Thus, usually the question of dogmatism or arbitrariness is not an issue. Pollock would seem to agree when he calls some epistemologically basic propositions *prima facie* justified. A belief is justified until proven unjustified.

But what if there *is* some challenge to a basic belief? How can we avoid dogmatism here? Alston answers that while it is true that simple foundationalists require that some beliefs are immediately justified, the view recognizes that all beliefs require some mediate justification. For foundational beliefs, this mediate justification will be some valid epistemic principle which gives the conditions for a belief's justification but does not include holding other justified beliefs. The believer will be immediately justified in holding that belief because he thinks that principle is valid and the belief in question falls under that principle.

For example, suppose we believe that it is a valid epistemic principle that appearances under normal lighting, perceived by a reliable observer, are generally correctly reported. Then we will be immediately justified in believing that we see red if the lighting is good and we are reliable observers. Alston's point is this—the reasons we have for accepting immediately justified beliefs are necessarily different from those we have for accepting mediately justified beliefs. Alston calls the reasons given for immediately justified beliefs "meta-reasons"; they have to do with the reasons for regarding a belief as justified. Thus the charge of dogmatism is avoided.

Another possible way to respond to the charge of dogmatism, which takes us very close to the first reply, is simply to point out that the basic premise(s) is *justified;* it is *self*-justifying because it is self-evidently true. And it is self-evidently true because when one examines the meaning of the predicate he finds that it is the same as the meaning of the subject. Others claim that some premises are self-justifying because they cannot be denied without contradiction or inconsistency.

4. *The foundational or epistemologically basic beliefs do not constitute logically necessary reasons for believing higher-level propositions.* This objection is much like our first criticism, which claimed there are no incorrigible or indubitable epistemologically basic beliefs. Here the argument is that the epistemologically basic beliefs, or beliefs lower in the structure, do not constitute logically conclusive reasons for holding beliefs higher in the pyramid. In other words, they do not guarantee the truth of the higher-level beliefs.

The answer to this criticism may take one of two approaches. First, we may attack the criticism directly by claiming that the objection is false. In general the problem centers on our knowledge about the external world. For example, it is argued that the belief that we appear to see a house is not a logically conclusive reason for claiming that there is a house. We can be wrong about what we think we are sensing. One can reply, however, that there are logically conclusive reasons lower in the structure.

A second response is to accept the claim that not all reasons that constitute mediate justification are logically conclusive, but at the same time assert that logically conclusive reasons are not necessary in all cases. One could claim that all that is necessary is that reasons be *good* reasons. To demand that all justification be logically conclusive is to require that all our knowledge be indubitable. As we have seen, a good many modern philosophers think such a view is unnecessary and impossible for certain kinds of knowledge, particularly empirical knowledge (see our discussion in chap. 8).

5. *There are insufficient epistemologically basic or immediately justified beliefs or propositions for a comprehensive epistemology.* The criticisms discussed to this point can be answered in favor of the foundationalist, particularly if one is willing to take the more moderate stance. These final two objections, however, are less decisive in favor of either foundationalism or its opponents. The way one judges the correctness and severity of these criticisms will determine whether one is an epistemological foundationalist or a coherentist.

The position may be summarized as follows. The structure advocated by the foundationalist may be defensible. Simple foundationalism may avoid both infinite regress and dogmatism. There may be immediately justified beliefs and beliefs lower in the epistemic structure which might serve as reasons for beliefs higher in the structure. *But* it is argued that there are not sufficient epistemologically basic or immediately justified beliefs to serve as a foundation for all kinds of knowledge. Thus, it is claimed, foundationalism fails as a comprehensive structure for epistemic justification.

To judge this criticism one would have to formulate an epistemology for each area of knowledge (e.g., mathematics, logic, natural science, history, etc.) along a foundationalist model and evaluate its effectiveness. Such a task exceeds the space limitations of this chapter. However, John Pollock has attempted this in his book *Knowledge and Justification*. It is his contention that sufficient foundations can be found.

6. *Theory-ladenness makes basic propositions impossible.* This criticism grows in large measure out of the ideas of philosophers of science such as Thomas Kuhn and Paul Feyerabend. They have argued that there is nothing like pure experience or fact against which we may test our beliefs to see if they are justified or true. Rather it is *theory* (a picture of the world) which operates at all levels of experience. These philosophers have argued that theory determines what will be considered a fact; alternative theories about the world will produce differing facts.

The application of this thesis to foundationalism is as follows. Foundationalism *requires* that there be basic propositions which are directly justified. However, if theory-ladenness is true, then it would seem that *all* our beliefs are affected by theory. Hence the distinction between the lower and higher levels of the pyramid collapses.

Not all philosophers agree with Kuhn and Feyerabend. There are at least two ways to reply to the criticism. First, one may essentially reject the claim, arguing that there are bare facts. These bare facts do not change, but they are capable of *different interpretations*. Second, one can deny the more radical form of the argument, while accepting a more moderate form. One can argue that theory is at work at all levels, but it does not lead to differing facts. One can indeed deny what is sometimes called conceptual relativism. On the contrary, there is a world, and, while there may be theory involved, the closer a belief is to this world the less theory-laden it is. These less theory-laden beliefs or propositions are both epistemologically prior and immediately justified.

Coherentism or Contextualism

The major alternative to foundationalism is *coherentism* or *contextualism*. Sometimes this view is also called "the nebula theory of justification." We must note that there is both a coherence theory of *justification* and a coherence theory of *truth*. They are *not* the same. Here we are discussing the coherence theory of justification.

Definition and Exposition

Coherentism is the belief that there are no epistemologically prior or basic beliefs, and that "justification just meanders in and out through our network of beliefs, stopping nowhere." There is, if you will, no bedrock in justification. Whereas foundationalism is often conceived as pyramidal in structure, coherentism is pictured as a "web of belief." There is a mutual relationship between various beliefs, so that one supports a second while the second and a third may support the first.

Generally, philosophers such as Willard Quine have argued that the beliefs closer to the center of the web are given up with greater reluctance. Surrender of beliefs close to the center of the web leads to radical changes in our picture of the world. Suppose that our belief in material objects is near the center of the web, as it most certainly is. Then, consider what kind of a revision of our understanding of the external world would be necessary if we rejected physical or material objects. Because there are no epistemologically basic propositions, beliefs are simply justified by other beliefs without terminating anywhere. This web effect has led some philosophers to call this system of epistemic justification the *nebula theory*.

Support

Much of the material used in support of coherentism has already been discussed in the objections to foundationalism. The support for coherentism is in one sense negative in nature. Foundationalism, so it is argued, is a fine *ideal* but *not attainable* in practice. The heart of the criticism is the claim that there are no basic propositions. Coherentists believe that there are no, or at least not sufficient, immediately justified beliefs. Also, theory-ladenness prevents the possibility that such beliefs should exist.

A contextualist will contend that none of the objections against his view is so serious as to be decisive and, since he believes that foundationalism is a failure, this is the best that one can do. He believes that one must be realistic.

Criticisms and Objections

There are at least two objections to coherentism. Whether one will become a coherentist generally depends on his evaluation of the viability of foundationalism and the acceptability of the contextualist's response.

1. *The coherentist theory of justification leads to an infinite regress.* If there are no foundations or basic propositions which are immediately justified, so it is argued, we have an infinite regress of justification—and ultimately the failure of any belief to be justified. When there are two alternatives, one of which involves an infinite regress, generally philosophers accept the other solution. In this case, the nebula theory threatens to become an infinite regress.

In response to this criticism coherentists have argued that the problem is not nearly as serious as it appears. It is not necessary that to hold any belief one must explicitly have gone through the whole process of justification. All that is necessary, so the coherentist argues, is that if one is asked a reason for his belief, he can justify or give a reason for it. Hence, one need never in practice be driven more than three or four steps down the chain of justification. If this is so, then the fear of an infinite regress is more theoretical than actual.

In response the foundationalist argues that this misses the point. One must go back more than two or three links on a long chain to explain what is holding up the bottom link. Otherwise one never gets to the "peg" holding up the whole chain. The coherentist's response is that he finds an explanation that does not end in an immediately justified belief every bit as acceptable as one that does. Moreover, he questions the contention that an infinite regress is a threat, and even denies the impossibility of such a regress.

2. *A coherence theory of justification is cut off from the world.*   It has been argued that the nebula theory of justification cuts us off from the world, for one can be "justified" in believing anything whatsoever. All that is required is a sufficiently coherent group of beliefs, no matter how outlandish. For instance, suppose a person rejects all the evidence from his senses. Whatever looks fat he says is really skinny; whatever looks green is actually red, and so on. Just so long as the resultant set of beliefs are coherent, there would be nothing wrong! All that is necessary to make this work is the one claim that our senses mislead us *systematically*.

If this criticism is correct, and some philosophers who defend coherentism talk as if it surely is (e.g., Quine talks of conceptual relativism or radically differing views of the world), this is a difficult consequence for most to accept. However, it should be noted that some defenders of this theory of justification believe it does not lead to a lack of contact with the world. Donald Davidson and Hilary Putnam have argued that if we accept the theory-ladenness of our beliefs, and most defenders of coherentism do, then theory and world are intermingled; they interpenetrate. We grasp the world through our picture or theory about it. The relativism that would result from being cut off from the world is not even possible, since theory and experience interpenetrate. If this is true, then conceptual relativism cannot be made coherent. As a matter of fact, Davidson and Putnam have both argued that conceptual relativism is only possible where theory and world are thought to be distinct and divorceable elements, making possible alternative mappings of the theory to the world.

Conclusion

There are Christian epistemologists on both sides of the issue of epistemic justification. At some point both foundationalism and coherentism approach one another. If a foundationalist will allow basic beliefs that are not incorrigible and reasons that are not logically conclusive, and if a coherentist will accept the view that beliefs at the outer edges of the web are farther from experience, then the two views have some important similarities.

In conclusion it is appropriate to mention that there are two consequences of any view which a Christian epistemologist cannot accept.
They are relativism or agnosticism about the real world. Views that
clearly entail either of these must be rejected.

Suggested Readings

Alston, William P. "Has Foundationalism Been Refuted?"
Philosophical Studies 29 (May 1976): 287–305
_____. "Two Types of Foundationalism," *The Journal of Philoso-*
phy 85 (April 8, 1976): 165–85
Aristotle *Prior Analytics*
Pollock, John. *Knowledge and Justification*
Quine, Willard. "Epistemology Naturalized," in *Ontological Rela-*
tivity and Other Essays
Williams, Michael. *Groundless Belief: An Essay on the Possibilities of*
Epistemology

PART THREE

What Is Reality?

11   Is Reality One or Many?

One of the most persistent problems in philosophy is that of the one and the many. Is reality one or many or both? If reality is one, then how do we explain its apparent multiplicity? If reality is really many, then how do we explain the seeming oneness or unity of reality? Finally, if reality is both one *and* many, is the one in the many, or is the many in the one? In other words, which is most basic—the one or the many?

Monism:
Reality Is One But Not Many

The classic representative of monism in the Western world is the early Greek philosopher, Parmenides. An analysis of his argument for the oneness of all reality illustrates the position of monism and outlines the basic alternatives open to those who disagree.

The Parmenidean Argument for Monism

The basic argument for monism from Parmenides is summarized as follows:
(1) Reality is either one or many.
(2) If reality is many, then the many things must differ from each other.
(3) But there are only two ways things can differ: either by being (something) or by non-being (nothing).
(4) However, two (or more) things cannot differ by nothing, for to differ by nothing means not to differ at all.
(5) Neither can things differ by something or being, because being is the only thing that everything has in common, and things cannot differ in the very respect in which they are the same.
(6) Therefore, things cannot differ at all; everything is one.

Now let us examine the premises. Number 1 seems true by the principle of the excluded middle, that is, either one or the other opposite is true, with no middle ground. Number 2 seems true by definition; if things differ, then there must be a difference. Number 3 seems true by the principle of the excluded middle. Number 4 appears to be true by definition, for "no difference" seems to be just another way of saying "differ by nothing." Finally, number 5 seems solid, for how can things *differ* in the very respect in which they are the *same* (i.e., not-different)? The conclusion number 6 follows logically from these premises.

Anyone who wishes to avoid the conclusion of monism—that all reality is one—must object to some premise 1 through 5. More precisely, the dilemma for non-monists (pluralists), is to show how things can differ either by being (that which is) or by non-being (that which is not). Indeed, the positions taken by the pluralists after Parmenides follow along these two lines. But before we examine these pluralistic views, we must first examine the view of Zeno, the famous disciple of Parmenides. Zeno tried to prove his master's monism by paradoxes.

Zeno's Paradoxical Proofs

Zeno's basic argument goes something like this:
(1) If we assume reality is many, then absurd or impossible consequences follow.

(2) Absurdity is a sign of falsity.

(3) Therefore, it is false that reality is many.

(4) Hence, reality must be one.

This kind of argument is known as a *reductio ad absurdum*. Let us take a couple of Zeno's illustrations of this kind of argument for monism.

First, if reality is many then it can be divided. But if a space between A and B can be divided in half, then so can the half space be divided in half, and then *that* half space be divided in half, and so on infinitely. But there is not an infinite space between A and B, but only a finite space. Hence, we end with the absurd conclusion that the space is both infinite *and* finite at the same time.

Further, Zeno argued that for the same reason, Achilles could never catch a tortoise. For in order to catch up to the tortoise, Achilles must first catch up halfway. And before he can catch up halfway, Achilles must catch up half of half, and so on, infinitely. However, an infinite amount of space cannot be traversed (at least, not in a finite amount of time). Hence, Achilles will never catch the tortoise.

The same kind of argument can be applied to anything that is many, since whatever is divisible is subject to such a reduction. Since the only non-absurd conclusion left is that all reality is one, all rational persons should become monists. So goes Zeno's argument.

A Reply to Monism

Zeno's paradoxes have been rejected by philosophers for several reasons. First, one need not assume as Zeno does, that (all) reality is *mathematically* divisible. Perhaps only some reality is mathematically divisible, or perhaps reality is not *infinitely* divisible. Maybe there is a point at which a line or space can no longer be split. This final, tiny, unsplittable item of reality is what the atomists called an *atom* (literally, "indivisible").

There are counter-examples to Zeno's view. In modern math a point is dimensionless. Yet an infinite number of dimensionless points make up a line, which has dimension. If Zeno were correct, this could not be so, for according to his view each little part of a line would have to have dimension (and further divisibility).

Parmenides' argument has been attacked in two ways. First, some claim that things can differ by "non-being," which is, nonetheless, a real difference. Second, others insist that things can differ in "being" and still be genuinely different. Thirdly, perhaps the easiest way to criticize Parmenides is to point out that his premise number 5 begs the question. It says "things cannot differ in the very respect in which they are the *same*." But this assumes that they are the "same" (or one) in order to prove that they are one, which argues in a circle.

Let us turn our attention to the four basic pluralistic alternatives to monism.

Pluralism:
Reality Is Many

In response to Parmenides' argument, philosophers after him took one of four basic positions. Two groups said reality differs by "non-being" (atomists and Platonists) and two insisted that reality differs in "being" (Aristotelians and Thomists).

Atomism: Things Differ by Absolute Non-Being

The atomists, such as Democritus and Leucippus, argued that reality is constituted of innumerable and indivisible atoms, which together fill the void of space. Besides differing in size and shape, the atoms differ in *space*. That is, each atom occupies a different space in the Void. The Void is any empty container; it is literally nothing. Hence, the basic way one thing (atom) differs from another is by nothing or non-being.

The Void in itself is absolutely nothing—pure emptiness. And yet by occupying different places in this empty space each thing (atom) in the universe is really different from each other thing. So the atomist's solution to Parmenides' dilemma was to affirm that things do indeed differ by nothing or non-being—by absolute non-being.

Philosophers have noted a number of criticisms of atomism. First, atomists do not really answer Parmenides' challenge that differing by *absolutely nothing* is not differing at all. Second, most modern thinkers reject the atomistic concept of space as a *container*. Rather, space is thought of as a relationship. Finally, atoms, once thought to be hard and unsplittable pellets of reality, have been both split and "softened" into energy by modern science.

Some modern pluralistic philosophers think of the ultimate units of reality as "monads" (as did Leibniz), which are a kind of qualitative "atom." Others speak of "eternal objects" (as did Whitehead), which are unchangeable and potential qualities that may "ingress" into the real, changing world. These revisions of ancient atomism indicate a rejection of the atomistic solution to the problem of the one and many. However, modern pluralists do not escape the logic of Parmenides' dilemma: how can these units of reality (actual or potential) really differ in being or in non-being? Unless there is a real difference in being, then Parmenides wins—all is one.

Platonism: Things Differ by Relative Non-Being

Plato provides a somewhat different answer to Parmenides. He spoke of a "receptacle" in which the mixture of all things is contained (this is the analogue of the atomist's Void). Later, however, he also used the principle of "otherness" to distinguish one thing from another. This has been called differentiation by relative non-being, because it affirms that all determination is by negation. For example, we define or identify the pencil by showing that it is *not* the table, not the floor, and not everything else. This does not mean that there is not anything else, but simply that the pencil is not everything else. Hence, this is called the principle of *relative* non-being, since relative to everything else the pencil is not everything else. All differentiation is by negation. A sculptor "differentiates" the statue from the stone by chiseling away (negating) all that is not the statue. In this same way, suggested Plato, everything in the real world (i.e., the world of Ideas or Forms) can be differentiated from everything else.

There are a number of ways this solution can be criticized. First, Parmenides would ask how differing by non-being (relative or not) can be a *real* difference. If being is what is real, then non-being would be what is not-real. Hence, if things differed only by non-being, there would be no real difference between them. Second, other philosophers would ask how *all* determination can be by negation. How would the sculptor know when to stop chiseling the stone unless he first had some positive idea of what the statue was to be? Finally, if all determination (and differentiation) were by negation, then it would take an infinite number of negations (of everything else in the universe) in order to know the identity of anything. But this is impossible for a finite mind.

Aristotle: Things Differ in Their Being (Which Is Simple)

After Plato the next most significant answer to Parmenides was that of Plato's most famous student, Aristotle. The ultimate items of reality in the universe for Aristotle were not atoms (as for Democritus) or ideal Forms (as for Plato), but were Unmoved Movers (gods). There were forty-seven or fifty-five of these Simple Beings, depending on which astronomer was right (each Mover moved a different sphere of the heavens). These beings were simple (uncomposed of form and matter) or pure forms of Being. Each was a simple being in itself and yet differed from the others, which were also beings. They literally differed in *being,* since they were beyond space and moved everything in space. All forms in the material world differed in their matter (and space), but pure Forms (gods) had no matter, so they differed in their very being. Each was an uncomposed being and as such it differed from the rest.

A number of criticisms can be mentioned. First, Aristotle himself (or a later editor of his *Metaphysics,* book 12) noted a serious problem: in a universe with multiple gods there would be no unity. Indeed, it would not be a *uni-*verse, since each Being (Unmoved Mover) operates in his own separate sphere, uncoordinated with the others and unsupervised by a superior Being. Second, Aristotle does not really answer Parmenides' problem of how things can differ in their very being if there is no real difference in their being, since each is a *simple* being. If each Being is the same in its being with the others, then there would be no difference between them.

Aquinas: Things Differ in Their Being (Which Is Composed)

Aquinas made a unique contribution to the problem of the one and the many. He argued for *both* unity and diversity within being itself. Aristotle thought of being as simple; Aquinas thought of finite being as compound or complex. Finite being for Aquinas was composed of actuality and potentiality. There can be different kinds of beings, depending on their potentiality. Some beings (like men) have the potential for being rational; others (like tomatoes) do not. These different potentials are *real.* For example, there are real differences among the potentials of an acorn, a monkey, and an Albert Einstein. Potentials make a difference, argued Aquinas, in the kind of thing a being is.

Aquinas's answer to Parmenides, then, was twofold. First, according to Aquinas, Parmenides begs the question by *assuming* a univocal view of being. If being is understood as meaning *entirely the same thing,* does not one necessarily end in monism? Second, if one understands being as analogous (similar), then there can be many different beings all sharing in being. The doctrine of the analogy of being, as used by Aquinas, shows how things can be many in their being (there can be many different beings) since they have different potentials.

There is unity in being since, for Aquinas, only one thing *is* Being (God); everything else *has* being with differing potentials. God is pure actuality; every other being has potentiality in its being. Hence, the actuality of every finite being is analogous to God's actuality, since it has actuality and He is actuality. However, finite beings have potentiality in their being and God does not.

Aquinas apparently gave an adequate Christian answer on the level the problem was posed, that is, on the level of being. In short, one must either (1) accept some kind of analogy of being, (2) accept monism, or (3) take the problem out of the category of being and place it in other terms. This latter alternative was taken by Plotinus.

Plotinus:
Unity Goes Beyond Being

For the pantheist Plotinus, there is something more ultimate than being; it is *unity*. God is the One who goes beyond all being, knowledge, and consciousness. From the One flows (emanates) all multiplicity, the way many radii flow from the single center of a circle. Hence, the many are in the One, in contrast to pluralism which holds that the One is in the many.

All multiplicity *and all being* flows from ultimate unity. In fact, there are *degrees* of being, depending on the degree of unity a being has. The most unified of all beings Plotinus called Mind (*Nous*), and beneath Mind on the great chain of being is Soul (or World Soul). The last link at the very bottom in the chain of being is matter. Plotinus considered matter the most evil, because it is the most multiple. Evil, then, is a necessary outflowing (emanation) of the One (God) who is beyond all good and evil.

Plotinus's response to Parmenides is twofold. First, unity, not being, is the ultimate category in the universe. Therefore, there is no difference in either being or non-being on the highest level; the One is absolutely simple. Second, on the level of being, things differ by their *degree of unity;* some things have more unity in being than others.

Philosophers have several objections to Plotinus's ideas. First, Plotinus does not really answer the problem. He does not show how there can be both oneness and manyness *in* being simply by taking the problem *beyond* being to the One (or Unity). Second, critics assert that Plotinus's One must have reality status. And if being is that which is real, then the One is not actually beyond being. Third, many philosophers object to talking about "amounts" or "degrees" of being, as though being were quantifiable. Objects may have different degrees of properties or perfections, but *being* is not a property, and therefore does not come in amounts. Being is a representation of a given set of properties. Finally, how can the One go beyond all thought (and the law of non-contradiction) when every thought the monist has about the One is subject to the law of non-contradiction?

The Christian Trinity:
A Model for the One and the Many

Some Christians have suggested that the solution to the age-old problem of the one and the many is the orthodox Christian belief that there are three persons in one God. Here there is both plurality (of persons) and unity of essence.

Elaborating the Trinitarian Model

Since at least the time of Augustine, Christians have seen great explanatory value in the trinitarian model. A number of plaguing questions are immediately answered by the Christian concept of a tri-unity of persons in one Godhead. The questions, "Was God lonely before He created the world?" and "What did He do before He created?" are immediately answered by the concept of the Trinity. For the trinitarian, God was in perfect, eternal, and unbroken fellowship within Himself prior to creation. He did not *need* anyone external to Himself with whom to commune. Why, then, did God create men, if not for fellowship? The trinitarian can respond: because God *wanted* to share His love (and be loved); not because He *needed* to do so.

These answers do indeed flow naturally from the doctrine of the Trinity, but do they help in solving the ontological problem of the one and the many? Some evangelicals seem to think so. They insist that the tri-unity of God shows that on the most ultimate level of reality in the universe (that is, God's level), unity and diversity are equally fundamental realities. Unity in God is no more fundamental than plurality, and plurality is no more basic than unity. God is equally a unity in plurality and a plurality in unity.

In this sense, for the trinitarian both pluralism and even modified monism (as Plotinus) are wrong. Pluralists hold that reality is primarily many and only secondarily one. Monists, on the other hand, insist that reality is fundamentally one and only many in a secondary sense. Often monists will say that ultimate reality is one actually and many potentially. In this respect, for a monist the many is rooted in the one, whereas for the pluralist the one is grounded in the many. In short, monists and pluralists differ on what is more fundamental—the one or the many. However, some trinitarians argue that in the Godhead unity and multiplicity are *equally* fundamental.

Evaluation of the Trinitarian Solution

First of all, it seems right to insist that unity and plurality are equally fundamental to the orthodox Christian understanding of the Trinity. Two extremes must be avoided. God is not *basically* three persons connected only by an interpersonal link of fellowship. This would mean that the one nature or essence of God is weakened to a mere relational connection among the three individual persons. This extreme leads to tri-theism, a form of polytheism. The other extreme is to consider God fundamentally one in essence and that humans are at best only different manifestations or modes of that one essence. This extreme leads to modalism or unitarianism. It is essential to the orthodox Christian teaching on the Trinity to view God as fundamentally and eternally both three and one, as well as three in one, and one in three.

Granting the above explanation of the fundamental nature of both unity and plurality in God, the question still remains whether this solves the ancient problem of Parmenides about how things can differ in their very *being*. The answer seems to be that the Christian doctrine of the Trinity does *not* solve this problem of how there can be many beings, since there are not many beings in the Trinity. God has only one being; the belief that there are many beings in God is tri-theism, which is not the orthodox doctrine of the Trinity.

The Bible teaches that God is one in being or essence, but three in person. Attributing personhood to God's essence or attributing essence to God's personhood is to confuse the two categories. The two are distinct but not separated (or separable) in God. If this is so, then the fact that there are three *persons* in God will be of no help in explaining how there can be many *beings* in the universe. For a solution to the problem of the one and the many *on the level of being* we are thrust right back to the alternatives set up by the Parmenidean dilemma.

Conclusion

Monism in the strict sense argues for only one being in the universe. Everything is one in its very being. There is no diversity *in being;* there is only identity. Pluralism in the strict sense insists that being is essentially multiple; there are many beings. Whatever unity these beings may have is based on their own individual and multiple existences and is secondary to it. Theists, or at least Christian theists, by contrast argue that there is a real unity and a real diversity of being in the universe. Christian theists do not view being as univocally identical wherever it is found. Beings are similar (analogous), but not identical to one another. Yet there is a unity of being, since God is the one being from whom all other beings derive their very being. God *is* being; everything else *has* being because He gives it being (John 1:2, Rev. 4:11). "In him we live, and move, and have our being" (Acts 17:28). God is an infinite being; and all creatures are finite beings.

Since creatures are in some sense like their Creator, then there is a similarity *in being* between Creator and creatures. However, God is infinite and creatures are finite, so there is also a genuine difference. This difference is a part of the essence of the creatures, and it makes it possible for there to be two or more beings that are genuinely different. Apart from this similarity of being, all would be one monistic whole. All apparent diversity and multiplicity would, in the final analysis, be illusory. But the theist insists that such is not the case, because there are *many* different finite beings, all of whom derive their essence from the *one* infinite being.

Herein the theist sees an answer to the ontological problem of the one and the many posed by Parmenides. Things do not differ by nothing, but by something. That is, creatures are *really* different from God. He is the infinite cause of their being, and they are the finite being that He causes. God is a necessary being, and creatures are contingent.

Suggested Readings

Aquinas, Thomas. *De Ente*
Aristotle *Metaphysics,* book 12
Lucretius *The Nature of Things*
Plotinus *Enneads*
Plato *Parmenides*
Plato *The Republic*

12 The Relationship Between Mind and Body

Often the most simple and obvious ideas, upon critical examination and reflection, show themselves to be complicated and profound. The commonplace in our experience can expose the depths of our ignorance. What are we closer to than ourselves, and yet the simplest question that we can ask about ourselves—What am I?—produces the most profound perplexity. The question of our nature is one of the hardest to answer and one of the most important.

The question of man's nature, while simple and fundamental, has the greatest philosophical consequences. Morality, religion, metaphysics, and law all depend on our answer to this question. Both morality and law presuppose that men are moral agents who have responsibilities, and who can incur guilt and be worthy of praise. Machines or robots have no responsibilities and thus are worthy of neither praise nor blame. If men are robots, then law and morality as traditionally conceived are misguided at best and pure nonsense at worst. Most religions, and Christianity in particular, assume that humans are spiritual beings, capable of communion with God, who is the supreme spiritual being, and of surviving the dissolution of their bodies in death. Again, if man's nature is material, then religious practices and hopes are in fact ill-conceived. This issue is highly significant, and some answer must be found.

Monistic Theories of Man

One large class of answers to the question, What am I?, may be generally called *monistic* theories of human nature. We shall discuss the following general approaches: materialism (including extreme materialism and the identity theory), idealism, and the double-aspect theory.

Extreme Materialism

The oldest philosophical mind-body theory is materialism.

Exposition.   In its most extreme form, materialism is the view that *we are our bodies*. It is clear that we have bodies, and that they are material. "We" are identical with "our bodies"; we are nothing more than our bodies. Whenever we use personal pronouns, we refer only to bodies, ours and others.

Extreme materialism's advantage is its simplicity. Some bodies belong to animals, while others belong to men or women. So viewed, a person's identity is nothing obscure or metaphysical, at least with respect to the *kind* of thing he or she is.

A second advantage of extreme materialism's view of man is that it eliminates the debate about the relationship between body and mind. According to this perspective, there is no longer a problem concerning the connection of the two; there is no more question about how one can act upon the other. Extreme materialism makes these questions unnecessary.

A third benefit, so some might argue, is that it solves the questions concerning human death. The death of a man is simply the cessation of those functions which constitute life. Human death exactly parallels animal death. The end of person is identical to the end of his body, which will ultimately return to dust.

A fourth reason some accept extreme materialism is that it has an explanation for everyone's concern with his own body. Because we *are* our bodies, the health or well-being of our bodies is the health and well-being of ourselves. Any threat to our body is a threat to us. Such concern is universal, regardless of one's religious or philosophical beliefs. Some would claim this is strong evidence for extreme materialism.

Criticisms.   In spite of the antiquity of this position, it has been beset by enormous difficulties. Most philosophers throughout the history of thought have maintained that any theory, even the most absurd, is superior to that of extreme materialism.

The strongest objection to materialism is the criticism of the central thesis that we are identical to our bodies. We are nothing more and nothing less than physical matter. But if this is true, it follows that anything that can be said about our bodies can be said about us, and anything that can be ascribed to us can with equal justification be asserted of our bodies. If there is something that can be said about us but not about our bodies, then we have shown that our bodies and ourselves are different entities.

Given this claim of identity, we may now ask, Is there *anything* that is true of our body which is not true of ourselves, or vice versa? We can say, for example, that we and our body have the same weight. To give our correct weight is to give the correct weight of our body.

But not all assertions work this way. We can ascribe praise or blame to ourselves. However, it is absurd to ask (except in a very metaphorical way) which part of our body is guilty. The whole man is guilty and the whole man seems to be more than just a body. Suppose a shoplifter is caught by a policeman, who says that he is going to arrest him. What shoplifter would respond that *he* should not be arrested, only his *hand* should be booked at the police station? The policeman will take the whole person to the station. Or, assume that you do well in a philosophy class. It makes no sense to praise your brain for its success. The point is that we cannot without great incongruity ascribe *moral predicates* to physical objects like our bodies.

The problem with what has been called *mental predicates* is even greater. Let us examine the concepts of anger and love. Suppose we are angry with a roommate. What sense can we make of the question, *Where* are we angry? Is our head or chest angry? We are angry all over; it makes no sense to try to localize our anger. It will not do to reduce anger to certain physiological changes in our body, such as increased adrenalin in the bloodstream. This is not what we mean by anger. The same can be said of love. It makes no sense to speak of our brain or heart being religious. If we are religious, it is not our body that is religious. It is the *whole* man, and this is more than just his body. If we love God, it is not only our body that loves him. We love him with our whole heart, soul, mind, and strength.

The problems become even more pronounced when we discuss *epistemological predicates,* those propositions about belief and knowledge. Truth or falsehood is impossible to determine solely on a material or physical basis. Assume that at the present someone believes that it is 1872. This belief is false, but what physical state or part of the body can be identified with the false belief? A physiologist might give us a complete description of all the physical states that one might be in at any particular moment, but it would be impossible to distinguish some of these states as true and others as false.

The Identity Theory

The identity theory is a recent version of materialism, presented and defended by J. J. C. Smart and H. Feigl, among others.

Exposition.   The identity theorists use the philosophical distinction between meaning and reference, or connotation and denotation. For example, the "morning star" and "evening star" have different meanings or connotations. However, both expressions have the same denotation or referent—the planet Venus.

Armed with this distinction, the identity theorists claim that mentalistic and physicalistic terms have different meanings or connotations, but that they do as a matter of fact have the same denotations or referents, namely physical phenomena. Not only is the "morning star" and "evening star" an example of this identity but also "water" and "H_2O," as well as lightning and a specific type of electrical discharge. In each of our examples above the discovery of the identity was more than a philosophical discovery; it was, at least in part, an empirical or factual discovery. Sometimes this identity is called *de facto* identity.

With regard to mental predicates, they will be shown to be *de facto* identical with brain states, so the identity theorists predict, once science learns more about the function of the brain.

Criticisms.   It should be clear that materialism formulated in terms of the identity theory, with its *de facto* rather than logical identity between physical and mental states, does indeed avoid many of the traditional criticisms of older materialism. A thought, for instance, can be identical with a brain event even if a person knows his thought without knowing about the brain, because there is no logical identity between the two, only *de facto* identity. The identity between the thought and the brain state would be an empirical discovery.

The identity thesis, then, is in part an empirical theory which claims that for each particular mental event to occur some particular brain state must exist. However, the evidence which could decide whether there is a correlation between mental events and brain states is inadequate. We cannot determine whether the theory is true or even probable, although many scientists take it seriously and use it to guide their research. Even if the theory were shown to be true or highly probable, this would not be enough to establish the identity thesis. The identity thesis does not just hold that mental and physical events are related in some systematic, possibly even law-like way, but that they are one and the same event, namely the physical event.

Often the claim that the mental and physical event is the same is supported by appeals to conceptual considerations, ''Ockham's Razor'' (the simplest explanation is preferred), analogies with other scientific methodologies, and the goal of a unified science. All of these considerations are noble and praiseworthy, but they do not decide our question.

Another objection to the identity theory is the location problem. While it makes sense to ask the location of a physical event, it is absurd to ask the location of a mental event. Since two connotatively different things are the same event only if they occupy the same space, it cannot be the case that thoughts and brain events are identical.

Still another criticism to the identity theory is that it cannot account for a distinguishing feature of mental events, namely their privileged access by the subject who has them. An essential characteristic of a thought that is ours, so it is argued, is that we have privileged access to it. If mental events were really reducible to, or even basically, physical events, then they would be public. *Any* person would be in as advantageous a position as the subject to report the mental occurrence. The fact that this is not so suggests that mental events are not physical events.

The central problem for materialists of whatever form is that they attempt to reduce man to nothing but his body, or matter. Philosophically and theologically this does not seem to be justifiable.

Idealism

The opposite extreme of materialism is idealism.

Exposition. Idealism, as we discussed earlier (p. 144), is most prominently associated with Bishop George Berkeley. He maintained that the mind and its perceptions are the only things that exist: to be is to be perceived. Thus, man is not reducible to matter, but is reducible to mind (see chap. 7).

Criticisms. Despite the brilliance and skill of Berkeley's arguments, his idealism has never seemed very plausible. Few have agreed that a simple statement about putting one's hand on his forehead is ultimately equivalent in meaning to a highly complex and sophisticated statement about the sense perceptions of God. While there may be some value to viewing the world as Berkeley did, in the end it yields an incoherent and impractical picture of reality. It too is guilty of the reductive error.

The Double-Aspect Theory

A final form of monism is the double-aspect theory.

Exposition. The double-aspect theory holds that the physical and the mental are simply different aspects of something that is itself neither physical nor mental (although some philosophers claim that it is both). The most notable thinker who took this approach to the mind-body problem is Benedict Spinoza (1632–1677). Spinoza claimed that man could be considered an extended, bodily being as well as a thinking being. Neither of these characterizations alone or in combination exhaustively describe the underlying substance of man. According to Spinoza these different aspects of man are full descriptions of man under differing categories. Man can be described from a psychological and from a physical aspect. Other philosophers have preferred to talk of these as differing *levels* rather than aspects.

While some philosophers have limited the double-aspect theory to man alone, others have called themselves *panpsychists,* ascribing to all physical objects a corresponding mental aspect. Spinoza claimed this was true, although he believed that in some entities the mental aspect was so crude or primitive it did not deserve the name "mind."

Criticisms.   While the double-aspect theory does attempt to transcend traditional mind-body problems, there are two reasons given for rejecting it.

First, it is argued that there is a need to explain the nature of the underlying unity. Spinoza called it "God or Nature." But this is confusing and contradictory, since God is infinite and nature is not. Herbert Spencer in the nineteenth century called this underlying unity "the Unknowable." To P. F. Strawson, a contemporary philosopher, the unity is the *person,* an entity capable of both physical and mental predicates. We can ascribe to it both states of consciousness and corporeal characteristics. But such a description is no help, it is argued, and we are back to the starting point. In response to this criticism some philosophers have claimed that it is not necessary to know *what* something is, but only to know *that* it is. While we cannot define the what, we still know that it does exist.

A second problem for the double-aspect theory is that we need a clearer definition of the word *aspect.* The advantage of talking about differing aspects or viewpoints is that the differences are not inherent in the thing under discussion, but exist in the *way* the thing is approached; in relation to purposes, outlooks, or conceptual schemes, and so on.

Some philosophers have distinguished between the aspects by approaching man "from the inside," as subject, or "from the outside," as object. To view man from the inside is to view him mentally, and to view him from the outside is to view him physically. But some would argue this is of no help, since talk of insides and outsides already presupposes a physical body "surrounding" a central self or mind, which begs the question if the underlying unity is neutral. Other philosophers have said "inside" and "outside" are only metaphors. If so, then they must be defined before any progress can be made.

Some philosophers have found the double-aspect theory unacceptable because it does not advance our understanding of the mind-body problem; it merely gives us more verbal baggage. Others claim that it is indeed helpful; the fact that it cannot fully explain the view does not prove it to be false.

Dualistic Theories of Man

Dualistic theories of man distinguish not only between the meanings (connotations) of mental and physical expressions but also between their referents (denotations). As we shall see, there are radically different theories of nonidentity. Some hold the expressions refer to differing *substances*, others to differing *events*, others to differing *properties* or *relations*, and still others to differing *states*. We shall discuss five forms of dualistic theories: interactionism, parallelism, preestablished harmony, occasionalism, and epiphenomenalism.

Interactionism

The simplest and most common dualistic way of expressing the relationship between our bodies and our minds is interactionism.

Exposition.   According to interactionism, minds and bodies together constitute the human person in this present state. Mind and body causally act upon one another in that mental events may cause bodily events, and vice versa.

This position finds support in the way in which we often describe our experience. Pain, a mental event, can cause us to wince or withdraw a hand, which are bodily events. Our thoughts can either slow or hasten the rate of our heartbeat. Fear can cause us to perform physical acts such as lifting a heavy object that normally would be beyond our powers. Finally, our emotions can cause us to shake or tremble.

We also describe bodily events as having mental effects. A decaying tooth can cause a dull ache, a bright light can produce an afterimage, and a fine piece of music can bring us a sense of well-being.

Descartes presented interactionism in its classic form. He held that there are two kinds of substances, mental substance and corporeal ("extended") substance. According to Descartes, the defining property of the mental substance is that it thinks, and the essential characteristic of a corporeal substance is that it is extended (has spatial magnitude). Man alone possesses both of these substances, and in the human person the one can effect events in the other. They form a single system of interacting parts. (While Descartes formulated his view in terms of *substances,* the position might just as easily be formulated in terms of mental events or states. Commitment to interactionism does not entail a commitment to mental substance.)

Criticisms. In spite of its popularity, two major objections have repeatedly been brought against interactionism. The first objection is empirical in character. Some have charged that interactionism contradicts the physical principle of the conservation of matter and energy: if interactionism is true it means that physical energy is lost when physical events cause mental events, and gained when mental events produce physical events.

The second criticism grows out of the radical distinction which Descartes makes between the mental and the physical. If indeed they are as diverse as Descartes claims, then how can they ever be causally connected? It would appear that one could not effect the other.

Both of these objections, however, can be answered. With respect to the first objection one can respond that the principle of the conservation of matter and energy does not apply to the complicated area of brain phenomena. Or one might deny that energy is lost or gained at all, and thus the conservation principle is intact. It could be argued that it is not necessary to postulate the loss of physical energy in performing the non-physical.

The second objection, that the mental and physical are too diverse to be causally connected, rests on the assumption that a cause contains all the same properties as the effect. This assumption is not widely held today. For instance, electrical activity may result in a magnetic field, which in turn may affect the position of a piece of iron. In this example there is no apparent similarity between cause (electrical activity) and effect (the movement of a piece of iron). Would we, however, be justified in denying a causal relationsip among the effects above? One might answer that we are not justified in deciding a priori what can and cannot be causally connected. Moreover, we are not required to ex-

plain *how* a causal relationship exists before we are justified in asserting *that* one does exist. Further, the Christian would assert that though
God and man are diverse in their natures, they have a causal relationship.

There is, however, a third objection to interactionism that is more
troublesome. The criticism is that mental events are not causes but
rather are the *outcome* of physical events, which are the actual causes.
Notice that the claim is different from materialism or the identity
theory. This objection does not *reduce* mental events to the physical; it
claims that the causality goes in one direction, from the physical to the
mental (see *epiphenomenalism*, p. 191). As physiology continues to
advance, so it is argued, we will see the priority of the physical. Then
the causal power of the mental will be seen to be an illusion. Given the
present state of scientific knowledge, it is impossible to determine
whether this objection to interactionism is justified.

Parallelism

Parallelism is one of the views about the relationship of mind and
body that emerged as a response to the objection that the mental and
physical are too diverse to be causally connected.

Exposition.   Parallelism holds that the mind and the body are correlated in a systematic manner but that there is no interaction, direct or
indirect, between either. The mind and the body are like two trains
running side by side, parallel but unconnected. The motivation for this
view is clearly to avoid the problems of interactionism. Having concluded that causal interaction is impossible, the parallelist simply
claims that every mental event is systematically correlated with some
physical event or events. Whenever the mental events occur, so do the
physical, but neither can be said to be the cause of the other.

Criticisms.   Parallelism seems to be unacceptable on at least two
grounds. First, there are cases when mental activity ceases but bodily
functions do not, as in a comatose individual. Even more generally this
occurs (to a lesser degree) during normal sleep. If there is a one-to-one
correspondence between mind and body, how can these two
phenomena be explained?

There is, secondly, a more serious reason for rejecting parallelism.

This position is at odds with our usual empirical procedures. The parallelist is forced to admit that the systematic connection between mental events and their corresponding physical events is *purely accidental*. This runs counter to a whole trend in modern scientific method and statistical technique which would deny that such a high degree of correlation could be purely accidental. If we are ready to accept the supposed systematic relationship as the product of chance, then we must be equally ready to accept that some of the most solid findings of science might be the result of chance. If this is so, then the whole structure of modern science and its methodology is undermined.

Preestablished Harmony

Preestablished harmony is a slight, but important variation on parallelism. Leibniz argued that God made mind and body perfect mechanisms, and at their origin synchronized them. By this preestablished harmony they would be forever in phase without subsequent intervention. This theory gives the philosopher a way to relate mental and physical substances or events.

In this view God replaces the chance of parallelism to avoid the troublesome second objection. But the seeming relationship between mind and body is still quite weak, for there is no causal relationship. They merely have parallel, preestablished histories.

Occasionalism

Occasionalism, a view held as early as Augustine, is another response to interactionism, and as such is related to the previous dualistic theories.

Exposition.   Many philosophers after Descartes accepted his radical distinction between mind and body, and did not accept causal interaction between mind and body. At the same time most thinkers admitted that there did seem to be some kind of systematic relationship between the two substances. There was a need to explain how this could be.

A group of philosophers, the most notable of which were Arnold Geulincx (1625–1669) and Nicholas Malebranche (1638–1715), developed a theory which claimed that God is the connecting link between mind and body. When we will (mental) to move our foot, then on that occasion God moves our foot (physical). Or if there is a car in our field of vision (physical), God causes a visual image of a car (mental) to be seen. Occasionalists commonly used the analogy of two clocks that are synchronized not because of some direct causal connection but because they had the same maker. Mental and physical events do not ever affect one another, but they are rather the result of God's activity.

The occasionalists were so thoroughgoing that they denied any causal relationship between any natural events. God's causal intervention was necessary for even the simplest of actions, such as one billiard ball striking another billiard ball. As it turns out, God is the single true cause in the universe. Without His providential intervention none of the regularities in nature would occur.

Criticisms. Occasionalism only gained popularity for a short period of time, but it is important to study as a transition to more sophisticated views of mind and body.

There are two reasons for rejecting occasionalism. The first is that occasionalists see no relationship between mind and body. Any supposed connection is mere illusion, caused by God to appear as a connection. What is more problematic is that occasionalists deny any genuine causal connection even in natural events (our billiard ball example).

The second objection is that the theory pictures God in a way entirely out of keeping with the biblical record. God is continually intervening within the causal chain. God is making our arm move, a visual image appear, and two billiard balls strike one another. The Bible teaches that, while God *can* intervene directly into His creation, He often uses what have been called *secondary means* to accomplish His purposes. For example, in creation God made vegetation, trees, animals, and man, but He then commanded them to produce "after their kind" (Gen. 1:11, 12, 21, 24, 25, 28). This is not to deny that He is ultimately in control of secondary means of providence, but it does deny that God is the single, proximate cause of everything that happens.

Epiphenomenalism

Epiphenomenalism is an old theory, but it is still attractive to some philosophers today.

Exposition.   If we reject parallelism, preestablished harmony, and occasionalism because we feel that there is overwhelming evidence for some kind of causal connection between the mind and the body, then epiphenomenalism is an attractive alternative. Epiphenomenalism holds that the causal relationship or interaction goes only in one direction, from body to mind. Thus, physical events have mental effects, but not vice versa. Epiphenomenalism, properly understood, is not merely a sophisticated materialism. There are genuinely two entities or substances, mind and body. There are genuine mental events, but their occurrences are *entirely* dependent upon the physical. The physical is primary, the mental is by-product.

The chief support for epiphenomenalism is to be found in the contention of modern science that the physical world is an autonomous system. It is claimed that someday our knowledge will advance to the point where it will be possible to explain all events in the physical world—even human behavior—in terms of physical events and physical laws. While verification of this prediction is not yet possible, those who hold the theory live in hope of such a prospect.

Criticisms.   The primary objection to the epiphenomenal theory is that in spite of the epiphenomenal claim to the contrary, mental events apparently are able to cause physical events. Epiphenomenalists argue that the supposed mental causal efficacy is an illusion. The brain event that causes a wince *also* causes the sensation of pain. Because the sensation of pain occurs slightly prior to our wince, we incorrectly assume that the pain causes the wince. In fact, we know nothing of what is taking place in the brain. Epiphenomenalists assert that some brain event can and will in fact be shown to precede our experience of pain.

Conclusion

The problem of the mind and the body remains a source of philosophical dispute. Some philosophers have attempted without success to show that it is not a real problem. As we have seen, there have been many proposed solutions to the problem, but there is at present no solution that is decidedly superior on purely philosophical grounds. Most contemporary philosophers of mind hold to some form of the identity theory, interactionism, or epiphenomenalism, at the same time recognizing that there are problems with each view.

As Christians, however, we can go a little further, even if we cannot settle all the philosophical issues. First, although many contemporary philosophers have adopted the identity theory, which is a highly sophisticated form of materialism and monism, such a position is clearly contrary to the teaching of Scripture. The Bible unmistakably teaches that man is more than the purely material. Man's body was taken from the dust of the ground, but God breathed His breath into man (Gen. 2:7). Man, then, is *something more* than simply a body. Christian theologians have disagreed whether that something more is merely immaterial or whether it is soul and spirit. The point of agreement, however, is that man is not reducible to matter. Therefore, unqualified monistic theories must be rejected.

But that is not all. For Christian theologians are agreed that an important part of the something more which characterizes man is that in Scripture, he is said to have been created in the image and likeness of God (Gen. 1:26, 27). Male and female are the bearers of God's image. While we may disagree as to the exact nature and content of that image, we are agreed that it is this aspect of our constitution that gives us our immense worth. Although people are sinners and worthy of eternal punishment, they are of infinite value because they bear the image of God. Man is so precious to God that He sent His son, Jesus Christ, to die for us.

Suggested Readings

Aristotle *De Anima*
Descartes, René. *Meditations on First Philosophy,* meditation 2
Evans, C. Stephen. *Preserving the Person*
Hobbes, Thomas. *Leviathan*
MacKay, David. *Clockwork Image*

13 Is Man Free?

One of the most important and yet controversial philosophical questions that we must face is the issue of free will. Again, it should be emphasized that morality, law, religion, as well as metaphysics all have a stake in our answer.

Imagine an experience many of you may have had. Suppose you were invited to go out for a pizza with a group of your fellow students. At the same time you knew that this chapter had been assigned in your philosophy class. What would you do? You weighed the alternatives. Would there be another time before the next class to read this chapter? What would the consequences be of coming to class without reading the chapter? On the other hand, who else was going to go out for pizza? Someone you wanted to meet or get to know better? When would there be another opportunity like this for a break from your studies? You had a choice. You deliberated, and you decided to study. As you now read this chapter, it is with the distinct feeling that your decision was free and you were responsible for the actions which you are now performing. This is an example of one of the arguments advanced by some in favor of *free will.*

Physical determinism, on the other hand, in its most extreme form rejects free will. It has been around throughout the history of thought, but the issue as currently discussed has been generated by developments in the natural sciences since the sixteenth century. A central presupposition of emerging science was universal causation, the belief that every event has a cause and that there are no uncaused events. Furthermore, it was assumed that events occur in orderly patterns, which make possible the formulation of causal or natural laws. On the basis of these laws and a knowledge of the actual causes at work in a situation, it is possible to predict with great accuracy what will occur.

For example, on the basis of what we know about the action of water on soil, and because we know that such action is in fact taking place in a certain river valley, we can with great precision predict the course of erosion in that valley. Concerning events about which we cannot now make such predictions, there is *in principle* no reason why we could not. Our lack of knowledge about both the laws and the present cause are our only hindrances. As we learn more of the causes of earthquakes and develop methods to detect when these causes are at work, then we will be able to predict both the time and severity of earthquakes. These theories about universal causation and total predictability have been traditionally called *determinism.*

What makes these assumptions troublesome with regard to man's behavior is that man is also an object in the natural world. Thus, if universal causation and total predictability reign throughout the natural order, then it would follow that man's behavior is also causally determined and predictable. This seems, at least at first blush, to be in conflict with free will.

There are at least two ways that we can divide this subject. The simplest and most common is to discuss the question in terms of the various positions that are taken with regard to it: hard determinism, soft determinism, indeterminism, and libertarianism. A less usual but very helpful way of examining the issue is in terms of the apparent conflicting claims of freedom and determinism. Some philosophers have taken the positions to be *incompatible,* and affirmed one while rejecting the other. Some philosophers have argued that upon closer examination it is clear that freedom and determinism are *compatible*. Still others have claimed that they are neither incompatible nor compatible in the senses above, since they are answers to quite different questions and are not comparable at all. In this chapter we will use the more common method of dividing the topic, although we will refer to the issues of compatibility and incompatibility as we think that they help to make the positions clearer.

Before turning to our discussion of the various views, we must attempt to define *freedom*. As will become apparent in the debate, incompatibilists and compatibilists disagree on what constitutes freedom. Antony Flew defines these views nicely. According to Flew, incompatibilist freedom may be defined as the view that there are no contingently sufficient non-subsequent conditions for a person choosing to act in a particular way. Roughly this means that there are no conditions prior to an action that determine that action. On the other hand, compatibilistic freedom is the position that there *are* contingently sufficient non-subsequent conditions for a person's decision to act in one way and not another. More simply, compatibilist freedom maintains that there can be conditions prior to an action sufficient to determine that action, and yet that action can be free.

Determinism

As mentioned above, determinism is the belief that *all* events are governed by laws. Admittedly, these laws are not like those passed by a legislature. Rather they are statements of conditions under which certain effects or events inevitably occur. Likewise there are conditions that determine the conditions of that effect, conditions that determine those conditions, and so on backwards *ad infinitum*.

Determinism may be divided further into "hard" determinism and "soft" determinism.

Hard Determinism

Exposition. Hard determinism accepts an incompatibilist view, that freedom and determinism cannot be reconciled. Everything that exists has antecedent conditions, known or unknown, which determine that that thing could not be other than it is. Everything, even every

cause, is the effect of some cause or group of causes. This is equally
true for every past event as well as every future effect. While it is
unlikely that such a thesis is held by the man in the street, determinists
claim that it is assumed at every point in the common man's daily life.

Since we as human beings are a part of the world, the principle of
determinism applies to us as well. It applies to what we may call the
physiological states and changes in our body such as height, weight,
growth, pulse rate, and so forth, as well to our purposive and delibera-
tive behavior.

Hard determinism, in particular, is often mistaken for fatalism.
Fatalism is the view that what happens is inevitable, regardless of what
we do or do not do. Whether we struggle or fail to move a finger, the
same things will happen. Hard determinism, on the other hand, holds
that things happen because of antecedent causes, our own behavior
being one of these causes.

Criticisms.   This form of determinism has been widely criticized,
for it seems to run directly counter to a universal and strongly-held
human belief that at least some human actions are free. Some have
objected that hard determinism as an a priori principle of our reasoning
cannot be proven, since we do not know all the laws that govern the
physical universe, let alone human behavior. Defenders of hard determinism respond by saying that while we do not now know all the laws
that produce effects, science has made great progress in this area and
determinism is in line with our growing knowledge. Moreover, so it is
claimed, there are no reasons for thinking that we could not someday,
through the steady advance of science, come to know all, or almost all,
of these laws.

There are, however, much more serious consequences to this view.
Hard determinism seems to radically undercut the ground for morality.
If it is a fact that effects are totally determined and could not have been
otherwise, what can we make of the traditional moral concepts of
"merit," "praise," and "blame"? It would seem, if determinism is
true, that we would never be justified in punishing any criminal, no
matter how terrible the crime. Nor would it ever be appropriate to
praise a person for an action, no matter how heroic.

Hard determinists have two general lines of response to this criticism. First, they claim that the general conceptions of morality are

consistent with hard determinism. They argue that all the view claims is that actions are determined by antecedent causes. Therefore, punishment or praise will count as an antecedent cause for some future behavior. That is, punishment or praise may determine, in part at least, some future behavior of the person receiving it or those observing it.

Those who object to determinism, however, point out that such a conception of morality opens a Pandora's box, and misses the key notion in morality. The danger is that we could consider ourselves justified in punishing or praising people regardless of their actions, simply to produce certain effects that we deemed to be good. This is the heart of the problem. Traditional conceptions of morality have almost universally ascribed praise and blame on the basis of human responsibility. If the hard determinist account of action is true, it is difficult to see how anyone can be *responsible* for his actions. The only basis of either praise or blame is to be found in its consequences. This is a hard pill for most to swallow.

Second, the hard determinist may respond that the objection merely shows that our moral conceptions as traditionally conceived are in need of revision in light of our present knowledge about the world and human behavior. The idea of human responsibility must be rejected, so the hard determinist's line goes. As a matter of fact, the rejection of moral responsibility will produce a healthier rather than a weaker society. It will bring good rather than evil. The fact that we know that we are not responsible for our behavior will provide the basis for a more satisfying personal life (for example, we will not be introspective or critical of ourselves), as well as giving us the ground for a more rational and humane system of interpersonal relationships (we will not try to punish people for their crimes). Moreover, so the hard determinist tells us, this position frees us from worries about the future. While it is true that our actions may make some difference, the possibility of change is limited. We can now have the fortitude to accept what comes. Chance is excluded. All human action is ruled by heredity and environment.

The critic claims that not only is hard determinism unproven and contrary to our conception of moral responsibility, but that this form of determinism is inconsistent with the human activity of deliberation and our sense of freedom. Often, before we act, we deliberate. Deliberation is difficult to define or describe without using metaphors. It is weighing of evidence, considering this alternative and that, and attempting to anticipate consequences of possible courses of action. Whether we are conscious of them or not, whenever we deliberate we assume a number of presuppositions. The most crucial presupposition is that certain things are up to us. It is up to us what we are going to do. If we are in the power of another person or at the mercy of circumstances beyond our control, it makes no sense to deliberate. One can only wait and see what will happen.

If some things in our experience do genuinely depend on us, then we must have freedom to perform them. But just what we mean by *freedom* here is not clear. Do we mean merely that an alternative action is logically possible? That is, although you came to college, it was logically possible for you to take a job. If that is all we mean, then the claim to be free appears, at least to some philosophers, to be quite trivial. Or, does freedom require that alternative actions are causally or actually possible? Or conversely, that no action is causally determined or necessary? The hard determinist denies that any alternative action is causally possible. Every action is causally necessary. Thus, freedom in the former sense, which most people assume, is not a reality according to the hard determinist. It is an illusion, as Spinoza puts it.

The hard determinist says, so much the worse for the ideas of human freedom and deliberation. One imagines that he deliberates, but that is exactly what it is, an imagination. It is conceit that leads us to think that we are the masters of our behavior. Spinoza uses an interesting example. He asks us to suppose that a stone has been thrown into the air, and suddenly becomes conscious. The stone, Spinoza argues, would believe that it was the source of its own motion, because it was conscious of its behavior at that point but unaware of the real cause of its action. It is a fact that we are *sometimes* mistaken in our belief that an action is the result of deliberation. Therefore, it is at least possible that we are always wrong in believing that our actions are the consequence of our deliberation.

From our discussion it should be clear that hard determinism can be maintained, but only at the cost of revising some of our most cherished beliefs. We must change our views on moral responsibility, and we must be willing to grant that the ideas of deliberation, choice, and freedom are illusions. For many philosophers this is too high a price to pay, and thus they seek alternative positions, one of which is soft determinism.

Soft Determinism

Many philosophers desire to retain both determinism and responsibility, and therefore turn to soft determinism.

Exposition. There are many versions of soft determinism, but they all have three claims in common: (1) determinism is true, and therefore events including human behavior, voluntary or otherwise, arise from antecedent conditions, making alternative kinds of behavior impossible; (2) voluntary behavior, however, is free to the degree that it is not performed under *external compulsion;* and (3) in the absence of external constraint the causes of voluntary actions may be traced to certain states, events, or conditions within the agent, namely his will or volitions, choices, decisions, and/or desires.

It is important to this view that two things be true. The first is that freedom be definable in terms of compatibilist freedom. That is, there may be antecedent conditions which determine an action, and yet that action is free. The second may be illustrated by the following three examples. In the initial case, suppose you are told to get out of the room. Someone comes in and picks you up and carries you out against your will. In such a case the action of leaving the room is not free, and you cannot even be called an agent of the action. In our next case someone comes in and tells you to get out of the room, and holds a gun to your head. You get out of the room. This is a case of external compulsion; you act and are thus the agent of the action. In the final case you are told to get out of the room. However, there is no external constraint used in this instance. You are told of all the advantages you will receive by leaving the room. Because of the character and desires you have developed, you leave the room. Your character and desires made it causally necessary that you should act as you did, but there is no external constraint, so you are said to be free.

Soft determinism is the view, then, that we are free and therefore sometimes responsible for our actions, provided there is no external constraint. We are merely acting in accord with our own choices, desires, and volition.

Criticisms. There are at least two objections to soft determinism. The first criticism is that soft determinism does not escape the problems of hard determinism if our desires, character, and volition are themselves determined. As a matter of fact, we can imagine a case where we clearly would not be responsible. Suppose that we acted in accord with our desires and inner state, but that these states were in fact induced by hooking us up to some machine.

The soft determinist would be little concerned with this objection, however. He does not deny that even our desires, character, and volition have causes. But it must be remembered that the requirement for a free act is that it be produced without external constraint. In the example above the soft determinist would respond that there was external coercion and that the action above was not free, and therefore not an argument against the soft determinist position. The desires and will can be constrained.

The second objection is not so easily dismissed, for it takes us to the heart of the debate between a soft determinist and a libertarian view of action. It has to do with what is meant by "could have done otherwise." Having decided and acted upon that decision, could we have done otherwise? Some soft determinists deny that the question should even be asked, for it is without meaning. According to this view, to say that we could have performed another action means simply that we *would* have done otherwise *if* those inner states which determine our actions were different. To say we could have decided otherwise is only to say that had we concluded to decide differently, we would have decided differently. This is of course trivially true, but really does not get to the heart of the matter.

Philosophers opposed to this form of determinism have responded in at least three ways, all similar in thrust, but highlighting different aspects of the issue. First, the usual response is that an agent is not free unless he possesses contra-causal power. That is, an agent must be able to do otherwise. Second, philosophers such as C. D. Broad and Keith Lehrer have argued that the soft determinist understands "could we have done otherwise" as a hypothetical "could we have done otherwise" *if*. This may be a possible meaning for the phrase, but it is not the sense needed to justify our usual moral conceptions of blame and praise. For these concepts we must have the categorical sense "could we have done otherwise," period. Third, Richard Taylor in his book, *Metaphysics,* says that alternative courses of action may be viewed in two ways. They may be taken as a disjunctive sentence, I can *either* study philosophy *or* go to sleep. Or, alternative courses of action may be stated as a conjunctive sentence, I can *both* study philosophy *and* go to sleep. The first sentence is true if only one of the two options is true (one alternative might not be a live option). In the second sentence both alternatives must be true. Contra-causal power must be possible. On this point we reach the deepest point of disagreement with soft determinists, who simply deny that claim. Soft determinists assert that all that is necessary is that we have reasons, we decide, and we carry out decisions without external compulsion.

Simple Indeterminism and Libertarianism

Two views that are directly opposed to determinism are simple indeterminism and libertarianism.

Simple Indeterminism

Simple indeterminism has few supporters, because of all the views to be presented it seems least likely to be true.

Exposition. Indeterminists deny a compatibilist interpretation of freedom. Determinism and freedom are incompatible, as in hard determinism, but there is also a denial of determinism. According to the indeterminist, the only meaningful (correct) understanding of freedom is the incompatibilist view. Further, he will argue that at least one and possibly many events are not caused, that is, they are independent of antecedent events. The simple indeterminist contends that the most likely candidates for these uncaused events are our own free actions. There is no scientific law, or law of any kind for that matter, under which our actions can be categorized. There is here a very clear sense in which a free act could have been otherwise. If it was in fact uncaused, then, even taking preceding and accompanying conditions into consideration, some other action was possible; one did not have to do what was done.

Some defenders of indeterminism would even extend this idea of an uncaused event beyond human actions to the physical or natural order. To support this contention these thinkers invoke Heisenberg's principle of uncertainty or indeterminancy, which was the basis for the quantum theory in physics.

Criticisms.   Most philosophers find that upon reflection, this simple form of indeterminism has little plausibility. First, it is reasonable to conclude that an event in the natural order has a cause—even when we do not know what that cause is. Only very small children speak about the toy that simply broke without any reason. Most thinkers generally concede that we do not know *all* causal relationships, and an apparently uncaused event only seems so because of our ignorance.

Second, the position has little plausibility with regard to human actions. Suppose we assume that some actions, in particular those that are free, are not caused at all. The resultant picture of man will not be the determinist's puppet, to be sure, but what is substituted is less than satisfactory. The understanding of man that now emerges is that of an erratic, jerking phantom, making moves and actions without rhyme or reason. He moves at one time this way and at another time that way, but in both instances without any cause!

Human actions in such a state are manifestly free and uncaused, but it is questionable at best if we have anything to do with them. What makes this account so unacceptable is that, while it retains freedom, it does so at the cost of responsibility. It is difficult to see how such behavior could be *our* behavior. How can actions that are out of our control justifiably be called our behavior? The end of this view of action would seem to be the rejection of all responsibility for actions of this kind. How could such action be our *responsible* behavior?

Libertarianism

Libertarianism seeks to overcome the difficulties of both determinism and indeterminism.

Exposition.   Like some of the other positions which we have discussed, libertarianism holds that determinism and freedom are incompatible. That is, libertarianism holds an incompatibilist view of freedom. Libertarians believe that our free actions are neither caused by another (as in determinism) nor are they uncaused (as in indeterminism). Rather, they are self-caused. Hence, the view is sometimes called *self*-determinism because of the theory of personal agency.

A human being (person or self) is sometimes, although admittedly not always, a self-determining being. We are, in other words, sometimes the cause of our own behavior. The libertarian holds that for an action to be free it must be caused by the agent who performs it, and it must be done in such a way that no antecedent conditions are sufficient for the performance of that act. If an action is both free and rational, the action must be done for a reason, although the reason is not the action's cause. This means that we could always have done otherwise. At least two possibilities were live options.

This account of freedom is the only one which does justice to the deeply-ingrained intuition that we do have contra-causal power. Second, this view alone makes any sense of the activity of deliberation. All the positions examined to this point, so it is argued, really do not properly account for human deliberation. Third, libertarians find both determinism and indeterminism objectionable, so they conclude that the only remaining alternative, libertarianism, is true.

Criticisms. First, empiricists object to the metaphysical notion of a *self* or *person* in this view. Since the time of Hume, it has been popular to criticize the idea of the self as a substance which endures through time. For a thoroughgoing empiricist, the person or the self is a mere collection or bundle of things or events. The libertarian view runs directly counter to this popular conception of man. But, says the critic, outside of the claims of the libertarian theory of action (and the claims of certain religious beliefs), it is impossible to empirically prove that man is anything more than an assemblage of physical things and processes. For those of us with religious beliefs rooted in the Bible, such proof is not necessary. However, some philosophers would find this view unacceptable. A materialist would argue that death ends all, and that man is wholly reducible to matter. Libertarians respond by noting that even Hume presupposes the real existence of an ''I'' or entity behind his impressions which gives unity to them.

Second, some question the libertarian conception of causality. Libertarianism holds that an agent, who is not an event but a substance, is nevertheless capable of causing another event. That is, a free agent can cause events to occur, namely, his own actions, without anything else causing him to so act.

Richard Taylor, who advocates a libertarian view, admits that the

libertarian concept of causation is so different from the usual concept
that we should not even give it the name "cause." Taylor argues that
we should not speak of agents *causing* their actions, but rather as
originating, initiating, or simply *performing* them.

Thus, it would seem that the acceptability of the libertarian view of
freedom is going to rest on three considerations. Do selves or persons
of the type described exist? Is the libertarian conception of causality
plausible? And, finally, does it make sense to speak of persons causing
their actions but not causing their existence?

The Two-Level Theory

We now come to the last of our possible positions on freedom and
determinism. This view maintains that beliefs in determinism and free
will are in some sense independent.

Exposition. The two-level theorist contends that the compatibilist's concern with laws that might govern human behavior is
ill-founded. There are no laws that govern what we call free human
behavior (deliberating, choosing, and action). However, unlike the
libertarian, the two-level theorist does not consider the categorizing of
decisions and actions of persons even a *conceptual possibility.* He
claims that the scope of determinism is restricted by an analysis of the
nature of action and choice.

A key contention of this position is that we are sadly confused if we
seek *causes* of human actions and decisions. Events have causes. Even
physical movements of our body have causes. Human actions, on the
other hand, are not explained by an appeal to causes, but by giving
reasons, or purposes. For example, the raising of an arm is a physical
event. We can ask, "Why did the arm go up?" It will be adequate to
respond that the muscles in the arm tensed, causing the arm to be
raised. Quite a different question is, "Why did *you* raise your arm?"
Here the request is for reasons, not causes. An adequate answer here
might be, "To hail a cab." What is important to see about these two
cases is that the latter does not seek the specification of antecedent
conditions. Reasons are essentially different from causes.

The upshot of this account is that two-level theorists claim that all
traditional discussions of the free-will problem are misconceived, for
they grant the determinist the possibility of causal explanation for

human action. Once this is refuted, says the two-level theorist, we will no longer be bothered by the traditional problem of the relationship between determinism and free will.

Criticisms. The criticisms of the two-level theory are much like those of libertarianism. The two-level theory again involves the conception of a self or person as a substance enduring through time (see p. 203).

The two-level theory does raise another problem, however. What is the relationship of *reasons* to *causes?* It seems intuitively clear that the two are related. While it is true that the tensing of the muscles in your arm is part of the cause of your arm raising, it may be only the instrumental cause, not the efficient cause. It seems obvious that your desire to get a cab had some relationship to the tensing of the muscles in your arm (see chap. 12 and the discussion of how mental events can cause physical action).

Conclusion

It should be clear from the discussion and evaluation of hard determinism, soft determinism, simple indeterminism, libertarianism, and the two-level theory that several answers have been given to the question of human freedom. Our discussion leads us to think that simple indeterminism has the least plausibility. Also, we find hard determinism difficult to accept, although there are some Christians, albeit small in number, who find it acceptable. Most Christians would take their stand among the remaining three views.

Some Christians are greatly influenced on this subject by the idea of theological determinism. Theological determinism is the view that God ordains every event and situation; man does not have the capacity to choose or influence his own ultimate destiny. This issue, hotly debated in Christian circles, has been purposely omitted in this chapter. It is based on varying interpretations of Scripture and is, therefore, a theological question more than a purely philosophical one. Nevertheless, one's views on such theological matters as the nature of God's omniscience and predestination will certainly affect what philosophical options one finds acceptable.

Suggested Readings

Edwards, Jonathan. *Freedom of the Will*

Holbach, Baron. *System of Nature*, chs. 11, 12

James, William. "The Dilemma of Determinism" in *Essays in Pragmatism*

Luther, Martin. *The Bondage of the Will*

Taylor, Richard. *Metaphysics*

14 Does Man Survive Death?

One of the most interesting questions that a philosopher is called on to examine is that of immortality. Do we survive our funeral? This question might be found in at least two places in a philosophy textbook. Because of the close connection of the afterlife with religious belief, it might be discussed in the Philosophy of Religion section. (However, we should note that there is a certain independence between belief in God and belief in immortality. Such openly atheistic philosophers as J. M. E. McTaggart and C. J. Ducasse both believe in immortality.) Or, because the whole question of immortality reduces quickly to a problem of the nature or constitution of man, it might be discussed in the section on Metaphysics. Is man the same person after death as before? What survives?

We will be focusing our attention almost exclusively on the metaphysical arguments for and against man's survival after death. We will first examine the most prominent arguments against immortality; then we will evaluate the arguments for immortality.

Arguments Against Immortality

In general, opponents of immortality have made an effort to show that the arguments for immortality are inadequate. Th.: mortalists, as we may call them, have claimed that in the debate over immortality the burden of proof rests with the immortalists. Survival after death is not simply an "open question." There is, so they claim, an overwhelming presumption in favor of mortality, and this is operative in the first argument against immortality.

The Universality of Human Mortality

Exposition.   The argument against immortality is an empirical one. Mortalists point out that it is a universal and indisputable fact that all men and women die. All our friends die; everyone we know will die, given sufficient passage of time. So certain is death that "all men are mortal" has become a truistic example in logic. Most people would find it contradictory indeed if, upon reading of an air crash, they were informed that a passenger had died and yet survived. Such a consequence seems logically impossible.

Criticisms.   The argument from the universality of human mortality at best establishes only that the burden of proof rests with the defender of immortality. However, beyond that point the argument seems to miss the central claims of the immortalists. First, note that both mortalist and immortalist agree that if the normal course of events is followed, all humans will eventually die. The real issue is over the question of what follows death. The claim that there is universal human mortality really does not speak to this issue. The fact that "all men are mortal" is a truism does not in and of itself prove that humans do not survive their death. Or, put more strongly, the fact that all human lives terminate in this world has no logical connection to whether they continue in another world.

Perhaps one of the reasons philosophers use universal mortality as an argument against immortality is the ambiguity of the word *mortal*.

"Mortal" may simply mean capable of death, as when we say, "I am a mere mortal, and cannot live forever." On the other hand, the word can mean "final," as in a "mortal blow" to an idea. But it begs the question to assume that the latter meaning is to be applied to death.

Second, even as an empirical or factual argument, the universality of human mortality is not a valid proof against immortality. Not all humans have died. Both Enoch (Gen. 5:24) and Elijah (II Kings 2:11) did not die. If death followed by annihilation were true, it would seem that no explanation could be given for these two clear counterexamples. Furthermore, the death and resurrection of Jesus Christ is the central counterexample to the mortalist position. Christ survived death and returned to tell us about it. Jesus Christ's death and resurrection is the guarantee or pledge that human beings like us will survive death (John 11:25, 26; I Cor. 15:12-22). Biblical Christianity not only teaches that the dead survive but also that the living shall be translated into incorruptible bodies at Christ's return (I Cor. 15:51-58).

The Analogy of Nature

Exposition. There are a number of arguments which have been used by mortalists against belief in immortality. These arguments are physical in nature and have come to be called arguments from the analogy of nature. A forceful statement of these arguments is to be found in Hume's *On the Immortality of the Soul.* In this treatise Hume gives a number of forms of this argument.

First, explains Hume, when two objects are so closely connected that some change in one brings a proportionate change in the other, we ought to conclude that when the change is so great in the former that it is totally dissolved, there will be the total dissolution of the latter. The application should be clear. Our bodies and minds are related in this way. Changes in our bodies produce proportionate changes in our minds—small pains lead to minimal mental confusion while great pain leads to total mental collapse. The total dissolution of the body at death is accompanied by the total dissolution of the mind.

A second analogy from nature which Hume gives is drawn from the fact that no form in nature can survive if it is transferred from its original environment to a different environment. Trees cannot exist in water any more than fish can live in the air. As a matter of fact, a relatively slight change in our atmosphere would make life as we know it on this planet impossible. If the earth were a relatively small distance closer to the sun, all life would be burned from our planet. Since this is so, what reason is there to suppose that our soul or mind can survive such a radical change as the dissolution of our body?

The similarity in anatomy between animals and men constitutes a third analogy for Hume. From comparative anatomy we learn that animals resemble men. Is it not natural to assume that there is also a resemblance between the souls of animals and of humans? If so, then it would follow that either animals are immortal as well, a position generally unacceptable to immortalists, or both animals and human beings are not immortal.

The fourth and final analogy is found in the constant change in this world. Though the world may indeed appear to be stable, it is in constant flux. As a matter of fact, the world gives evidence of frailty and dissolution. Since this is so, Hume concludes that it is wrong to assume that one form of life, the single most fragile form at that, is immortal and indestructible.

Criticisms.　　The first analogy is grounded in the interrelatedness of body and soul, and the claim that a change in the one will bring about proportionate change in the other. This analogy assumes an interactionist view of the relationship of mind or soul to body, and an unusual form of the position at that. As we have seen (chap. 12), a good many philosophers would reject this solution to the mind-body problem. Moreover, this analogy presupposes that a change in either element or substance will bring about a *proportionate* change in the other. Modern physics has called into question such uniform relationships between cause and effect. Certain effects are greater than their cause, and vice versa.

Furthermore, and most importantly, Hume assumes that the proportionate response in the mind or soul to the dissolution of the body would be the corresponding dissolution of the soul. But why should this be? Is this a logical necessity? Is there empirical evidence in support of Hume's contention? To gain that kind of evidence one would have to experience death. Some would point to the findings of people like Raymond Moody and Elisabeth Kübler-Ross[1] as

1. See Raymond A. Moody, Jr., *Life After Life* (New York: Bantam, 1976); and Elisabeth Kübler-Ross, *Questions & Answers on Death & Dying* (New York: Macmillan, 1974).

counterevidence. Moreover, the testimony and resurrection of Jesus Christ is the decisive answer to the claim of Hume.

The second analogy, that man's soul cannot survive an environmental change as trees cannot live in water and fishes cannot exist in the air, begs the question. Hume simply assumes what he must prove, that the soul of man is incapable of existence when the body is dissolved. Hume has no *empirical* evidence of what happens to a human being's soul after he dies, although such evidence is readily available for a submerged tree or a fish in air. Suppose that we only saw a frog when it was in the water. Observing that most animals are fit either for land or for water, we might conclude that frogs cannot exist both in the water and on the land. This, however, would in fact be false, and the only way we could know the life conditions of a frog would be through observation.

The third analogy, taken from comparative anatomy (what is true of animals will be true of human beings because they resemble one another in certain ways), is surely fallacious. Resemblance or similarity is *not* identity, and analogies are weak where there are great differences. As a matter of fact, the differences between human beings and animals cast grave doubt on Hume's analogy.

The fourth analogy is unconvincing as well. Because *some* or even *most* of what we observe about the world is in flux or change, that in no way proves the change or dissolution of *all*. One might maintain that the argument is not intended as a proof, but only shows what is more probable or what the rational person will believe. This claim might seem plausible at first, but in the end must be rejected. The concept of change has undergone radical revision since Hume's day. Change was once viewed as decay and dissolution, but this is not the case in modern science. Matter itself is now thought to be indestructible; at best one can transform matter into energy. Thus, this last of Hume's analogies is false in light of the modern understanding of matter and change.

The Body-Mind Dependence Argument

Exposition. The most popular and impressive of the arguments against immortality is the "body-mind dependence argument." Those who advance this view claim that it has received powerful confirmation from modern brain research. Simply put the argument is as follows.

The activity of the mind is dependent upon the body. We know that the brain is not immortal, ceasing to function at death. Further, all evidence points to the fact that our mental life is bound up with our brain structure and bodily energy. It is rational to conclude, then, that mental activity ceases with the cessation of bodily life, in particular the life of the brain. Bertrand Russell admitted that the argument is only one of probability, but it is as certain as most scientific conclusions.

Criticisms.   Two things need to be said of this argument. First, it is true that in our present existence the functioning of our minds is somehow dependent on our bodies. We can all recall instances where we were unable to think well because of the state of our physical bodies. When we have the flu, we find ourselves below par not only physically, but also mentally. Second, the body-mind dependence of our present existence proves nothing about the conditions of a future existence. To conclude anything we would have to observe that future life. It could be that the conditions of that existence are quite different from those of this present life.

Immortality

We are now ready to examine the evidence that is given in support of immortality. We shall first discuss the kinds of immortality doctrines, and then examine the arguments for immortality.

Kinds of Immortality Doctrines

Immortality, or survival after death, has been viewed in at least three ways: the immortal-soul doctrine; the reconstruction doctrine; and the shadow-man or minimal-person doctrine. Each of these is an attempt to describe how a man might survive his funeral.

The immortal-soul doctrine.   The immortal-soul doctrine is at least as old as Plato, and is clearly set forth by him. He believed that human beings are essentially *composite beings.* We are more than simply bodies. We are something else, something which is different in kind—an incorporeal soul. Plato held that for the duration of a life the soul was imprisoned in the body. The soul was nevertheless a substance, and as such was capable of survival independent of anything else.

Another crucial point of Plato's doctrine is that the soul is the real, true, or essential person. One's body is changing and decaying. The soul, on the other hand, is the real person. Thus, since it is the soul that survives death, the real person is immortal. *We* can be said to survive our funeral.

The reconstruction doctrine. In its purest form the reconstruction doctrine is simple and clear. It is the view that after death our body will be resurrected and our person reconstructed. There are some important differences between the immortal-soul doctrine and the reconstruction doctrine. The immortal-soul doctrine holds that the real person escapes intact at death. But, the reconstruction doctrine maintains that to have a genuinely human and personal existence we must have a body. We must have human corporeal form to be a genuine person. This body is resurrected or reconstituted after death by an act of omnipotence. God calls us back into existence, and we become an immortal person.

The shadow-man or minimal-person doctrine. The shadow-man or minimal-person doctrine is an attempt to capture the best elements of the two former positions. It is interesting that this view closely approximates the understanding of orthodox Christianity. Tertullian, one of the church fathers, defends a position similar to this in *De Anima*. The theologian and philosopher Thomas Aquinas (1224–1274) defends a version of this position at length in the "Treatise of the Resurrection" in his *Summa Theologica*. And most recently a version of this doctrine has been forcefully defended by Paul Helm.

This position claims that the real person is a shadow-man or minimal-person which is sufficiently human and corporeal that the perennial problems of identification (Do *we* really survive?) and individuation (Can we distinguish ourselves from others after death?) can be overcome. At the same time the shadow-man or minimal-person is also sufficiently incorporeal and immaterial that it has no difficulty in escaping unharmed from the ordinary earthly body when it is buried.

Evaluation. Before turning to an examination of the arguments which immortalists have given in defense of their position, it may be well to limit the field of doctrines to which the arguments will have application. We shall defend the shadow-man or minimal-person doctrine, but discuss arguments offered in support of the immortal-soul doctrine since it has played such a central role historically in philosophical discussions of immortality. Thus, we will critique the reconstruction doctrine here.

The reconstruction doctrine seems problematic on two grounds. First, there is the problem of identification. How can we know that the resurrected or reconstituted persons are identical with the original persons? How is it possible to guarantee that the reconstituted person is not a mere replica or a brilliant forgery? Two responses have generally been offered. It might be argued that God will infallibly ensure that the torments of hell and pleasures of heaven are granted to the right people. It might also be claimed the person himself cannot fail to know whether he is the original or a brilliant forgery. Opponents of the reconstruction doctrine reply that appeals to the cognitive and executive abilities of omnipotence or the supposed privileged status of the person in question are inadequate. The crux issue is the *possibility* of honest error. In spite of all our efforts we cannot be absolutely sure that the reconstructed person is the person he claims to be. But could God be involved in a case of mistaken identity? Granted, sheer omnipotence will not prevent the possibility of error, but God is more than mere omnipotence. He is also omniscient and truth, and so these problems could not arise.

Second, a resurrection or reconstitution doctrine demands one of two possibilities at the death of the person. The person may cease to exist (be annihilated) until the last day, being reconstituted at that time to enjoy either the blessings of heaven or the torments of hell. Such a position seems to be precluded by what the Bible says about the present state of those who have died (Luke 16:19-31; II Cor. 5:8; Phil. 1:23). They are *now* either with the blessed or separated from God. Or, one might avoid these difficulties by claiming that immediately after death the individual receives a resurrection or reconstituted body. One thus avoids the problem of temporary non-existence or annihilation, but in the process creates another difficulty. The passages in the New Testament that speak of resurrection do so in terms of groups, and eschatologically (i.e., "on the last day") rather than individually and periodically (Dan. 12:1, 2: I Thess. 4:13-18; Rev. 20:1-10). For these reasons, Christians reject the pure reconstruction doctrine.

Arguments for Immortality

The philosophical arguments for immortality go back at least to the time of Plato and Aristotle.

The argument from the simplicity of the soul. In one of Plato's Dialogues, the *Phaedo,* Cebes, one of the leading characters, is concerned that at one's death the soul disperses or decomposes. Socrates argues that this is not the case.

Socrates begins by declaring that only certain *sorts* of things can decompose or come apart. Here he distinguishes between things that are composite and things that are simple, or uncomposed. The composite things are always changing; they are never constant. On the other hand, things that are simple or uncomposed are, most probably, constant and unchanging. If, then, the soul is of this latter group, then it is probable that the soul does not change or come apart. This argument rests on two important assumptions. First, things which are simple are unchanging. And, second, the soul is simple.

The argument from the analogy with forms or ideas. This second argument is Platonic in origin, and closely related to the previous argument. This argument presupposes Plato's general theory of Forms or Ideas. Plato taught that for every significant word, such as "justice," "goodness," "triangle," or "man," there is a corresponding, abstract Idea or Form. These Forms are eternal, unchanging entities, intelligible to the intellect in the same way that material objects are sensible to our senses. These Ideas stand for general classes of things, and the particular instances of these Ideas (one just action, one good deed, one triangle, or one man) "participate in their appropriate Form."

Plato uses this general theory in two ways to show that the soul is immortal. First, the soul is the faculty of the body that *knows.* The Forms are the real objects of knowledge. Moreover, all genuine knowledge is certain, and certainty is a property only of that which is unchanging. Since the Ideas (the things known) are eternal and unchanging, then the soul (the knower) must resemble the Ideas, and be eternal and unchanging.

Second, the soul is the principle of life, and is therefore equated with the Form of life. Life is incompatible with death, as is equality with inequality or justice with injustice. No principle admits of its opposite. Life cannot be overcome by death. Hence, Plato concludes that since the soul, as the Idea of life, is deathless and eternal, so our immortal part is not destroyed by death and will exist somewhere in another world.

The argument from reminiscence. This argument too is from Plato, who presented two quite different forms of the argument, though the conclusion is the same. In the first form of the argument Plato begins from the premise that we have some knowledge of a priori truths which we have not acquired in this life. An example of this kind of knowledge is the conclusion of the Pythagorean theorem (Meno 81–86B). The other form of the argument begins with the premise that we all possess certain ideal concepts such as perfect equality or perfect justice. These concepts cannot have been gotten from our present experience, since neither of them is fully instantiated or embodied in this life (Phaedo 73A–77A). Plato concludes that we must have been acquainted with these truths at some time in the past, prior to the embodiment of the soul. The soul inhabited the realm of the Forms. Thus Plato argues that the soul not only outlives this body, but pre-existed it.

Christians reject this argument because it entails the belief in the pre-existence of the soul, a belief which finds no support in Scripture and is contrary to the Christian doctrine of the origin of the soul.

The argument from rationality. This argument is not found explicitly in the writings of Plato, but the central ideas of the argument are there. In the *Phaedo* Socrates distinguishes between the physiological explanations for human activity and the motives which an agent has for behaving in the way he does. There is, so it is argued, no necessary connection between the concepts of physiology and a man's motives for his behavior (see p. 204).

This thesis is developed into a formal argument by the contemporary apologist C. S. Lewis. Lewis argues that rationality is more than nature (i.e., it is supernatural). Rationality cannot have arisen from purely material causes. Because of the supernatural nature of rationality, the bodily occurrences associated with rational behavior cannot be wholly explained by the natural sciences.

Objections to Arguments for Immortality

Within the Platonic dialogues themselves are criticisms of the arguments for immortality. For instance, after the argument for immortality from the simplicity of the soul is given, Cebes challenges the thesis that simplicity implies eternality. He asks why we should not view the relationship of the soul to body like that of a weaver to his coats. The weaver may make many coats and outlast them. But why is it not possible that the weaver is outlived by the *last coat?* The soul is long lasting but not eternal, according to this analogy.

Strato, another figure in the *Phaedo,* attacks the argument from simplicity more directly. He asks why the soul may not simply cease to exist. It is true that the soul cannot undergo change in its parts (it has none), but that does not preclude the possibility that someday it will wear itself out and perish.

It is not our purpose to give an exhaustive exposition of the criticism in Plato's writings. It should be clear that some of the arguments depend heavily upon Plato's theory of Forms (abstract or general terms). Others demand acceptance of views that are contrary to biblical teaching (such as the preexistence of the soul). Still another rests heavily on the thesis that the knower must resemble the thing known. Rather, we want to examine objections of a much more serious kind. The criticisms which follow claim for the most part that there is an *in principle* or *inherent* impossibility in the contention that we can survive our own death.

The problem of identification. We have discussed a version of this criticism earlier, in connection with the reconstitution doctrine. The objection, simply put, is that even if we were able to survive death, we could never be sure that what survived was *us.* Even if we grant that the soul is the "real" us and that the soul survived death, we could never preclude the possibility that what survived was a person uncannily similar to us.

We might answer the anti-immortalist that memory might serve to verify that we were the same person as the pre-mortem individual. If we remembered experiences about ourselves which happened prior to death, then there might be justification for claiming that we are the same person. This would be particularly true if the experiences that we had after death could in some way be related to those before death.

In response to this, opponents of immortality argue that memory is fallible, and we could be deceived. There are three appropriate replies. First, just because our memory is fallible does not mean that all instances of remembering are false. The fallibility of our memories only shows that we *could* be wrong, not that we *are* wrong. As mentioned above, if the experiences before and after death are related, there would be the strong probability that our memory was reliable. For example, suppose that the experiences are stages in some thought process such as telling a story or participating in a discussion. In such a case there would be strong *prima facie* evidence that these stages were the product of a single intelligence.

Second, the fallibility of memory is only a decisive argument against immortality if personal identity is defined in terms of memory. But to do so is to confuse a metaphysical and an epistemological question. Memory is necessary for us to *know* ourselves after death; this is an epistemological question. But even if memory fails and we do not *know* that we have survived death, it does not follow that we do not *in fact* survive death; this is a metaphysical issue.

Third, in the last analysis we can indeed depend upon God's memory to guarantee the correctness of the re-identification of each person. Since He is omniscient and totally truthful, we need not be concerned about the fallibilities of memories.

The problem of individuation.   One of the central contentions of the immortalist is that survival is *personal*. It would not be enough if at death we were absorbed into some world soul, and lived on endlessly in a non-personal existence. We must live on *personally*. This idea of personal existence demands the ability to individuate or distinguish persons. The mortalists claim that our present principle of individuation is a body. If we are told to find out how many people are in the philosophy class, then we count bodies. If, however, we are told by a number of people that they will be at an event in spirit, we have no way of counting the spirits present!

This problem seems to have a direct and simple reply. It is true that our present principle of individuating persons is by way of bodies. But this fact does not prove that it is the *only* way of distinguishing persons. All the argument establishes is that in the post-mortem state prior to the resurrection there would have to be a different principle of individuation.

Moreover, it is helpful to note that the problem is not peculiar to human survival after death. For in Christian theology there is the belief in a whole host of spirit beings other than God: angels, demons, and Satan. Thus, if they can exist as individual spirits, then there is no reason that men cannot also do so.

The problem of rationality. This objection is directed specifically at the argument from rationality (there is such a radical difference between the physical conditions of human behavior and the motives men ascribe to their behavior that we must be dealing with different things—a physical body and an incorporeal or immaterial soul). Opponents of immortality offer two criticisms of this argument. First, they argue that even if the physiological conditions of human behavior are so diverse from the motives for that behavior, we do not have any grounds for saying that they are *not* logically related. Possibly, as we come to know more about each area, we will also find that there is a definite relationship between the two, and that one might even be reduced to the other. Second, even if we grant the argument from rationality, that does not prove that the difference between the physical and the rational is something immaterial or incorporeal and could therefore survive the dissolution of the body.

We should not, however, allow the mortalist off the hook too easily. While we do have a great deal to learn about physical behavior and the mind, there have been numerous attempts to reduce the mental to the physical, and *all* have failed. While it is always *logically possible* that a reduction could be carried out, there are good reasons for thinking that it is *empirically impossible* and in fact will never be accomplished (see our discussion of the mind-body problem in chap. 12). Furthermore, while it is true that the "something more" than the physical does not have to be mental or incorporeal, there are good reasons for thinking it is (again, see chap. 12).

The problem of the intelligibility of "surviving one's death." One of the common contemporary criticisms of immortality by mortalists is that the phrase "surviving one's death" has no meaning at all. We are familiar with the words and thus think we know what is being said, but upon analysis that phrase is shown to be without any meaning.

The reasons behind this claim are twofold. First, a condition of surviving one's death is the ability to have experiences that are at least successive if not continuous before and after death. That is, we must have some pre- and post-mortem experiences that are related to one another in such a way that they will constitute some evidence that we are dealing with the *same* person. But, so it is argued, this is impossible, because a logically necessary condition of experience is that we have sense organs. And sense organs are just the things that are possessed by someone with a body. It is argued that if we lack a body we are without sense experience. Therefore, the claim to have survived our death is unintelligible.

Second, it is said that our language about persons is language about an object that can be *met,* that we can encounter in experience. Person language then is body language. Some defenders of immortality deny corporeal existence, and thus the use of person language about post-mortem experience is incoherent or unintelligible.

A number of philosophers, a prominent one being H. H. Price, have disagreed. We can conceive of non-corporeal experience. Except for materialist views of man, philosophers grant that even in his embodied, present state man has non-corporeal experience—thinking, willing, imagining. Because of the present interrelationship of the mind and the body, the body has a part in these activities, but there is reason to believe from the nature of the experience that thinking, understanding, and other mental activities could be carried on in a disembodied state. For instance, Plato would have argued that thinking could be better pursued without the encumbrance of a body. There is no reason to claim that all experience in a disembodied state is impossible, which is the claim of the mortalist.

It is also pure assumption on the part of the mortalist that we will not be able to meet the person after death. (The Christian holds that once the resurrection takes place we will have bodies, and can be met.) But even in the disembodied state there is reason to think that individuals can be met. Throughout Scripture spirit beings confronted and were met by men. On some occasions heavenly beings appeared to human beings and were recognized as angels (Matt. 1; Luke 1, 2). Thus it is false to deny that spirit beings can be met.

The problem of the intelligibility of "the next world."   The final criticism of mortalists has to do with what we mean by "the next world." Defenders of immortality speak of "here" and "the hereafter." What is meant by this? *Where* is the next world, strictly speaking? The critic says that if we cannot answer that question, then our claim that men arrive in the next world after death is nonsense.

The *exact* answer to this question cannot be given, however. *That* there is an afterlife and *that* it bears some resemblance to this life is abundantly clear from Scripture. The exact nature of that existence is not totally spelled out for us. For instance, even though we are given glimpses of what that life is like (Rev. 21, 22), Bible-believing Christians do not all agree how those glimpses should be understood. Is the description literal or is it figurative language about a real place? Is heaven a material place "up there"? One cannot answer these questions with certainty, but let us again emphasize what is clear and certain for the Christian: an afterlife *really* does exist. It is not the figment of anyone's imagination.

Moreover, from a purely philosophical perspective there is reason to think that there is space other than physical space. For instance, think now of a tiger in a cage. The tiger and the cage are spatially related, but how far is the tiger from your desk? You cannot answer that question, for the tiger is in perceptual space, not physical space. There is no *logical* reason for denying that the afterlife is in a non-physical space, although it could well be in physical space.

Conclusion

It is our judgment that there is, on purely philosophical grounds, no decisive reason for rejecting immortality. There is, in fact, positive evidence that we do survive our own death.

For the Christian the question of an afterlife is decisively answered by Jesus Christ. As God's Son, He knows whether there is life after death. As one who has passed through death to life, He is uniquely qualified to answer the question of immortality. He clearly affirms that there is life after death (Luke 16; John 11).

At death there remains what Paul Helm calls a minimal person and what Peter Geach calls a surviving mental remnant of a full person. This minimal person no longer has a body but remembers things about his past, including the embodied state. The minimal person has thoughts about his rememberings, and is able to reason (see Luke 16). Nothing requiring a body is possible at this time, however. At the resurrection the minimal person is reunited with his resurrection body, and then lives on eternally in a re-embodied existence.

Suggested Readings

Geach, P. *God and the Soul*

Helm, P. "A Theory of Disembodied Survival and Re-embodied Existence," *Religious Studies* 14 (March 1978): 15–26.

Hume, David. "Of the Immortality of the Soul"

Penellum, T. *Survival and Disembodied Existence*

Plato *Phaedo*

15   Are There Other Minds?

Not only is the philosopher interested in the nature of reality and of man but also in how each of us knows that there are other minds, beings with thoughts and feelings just like ours. This question has been discussed widely in contemporary philosophy by English-speaking philosophers primarily within the analytic tradition, and continental philosophers predominantly within the phenomenological and existential traditions.

In this chapter we will first discuss the traditional argument offered in support of the belief in other minds, the argument from analogy. Then, since it has been widely criticized, we shall look at the major alternative solutions that have been suggested to this question.

The Argument from Analogy

Exposition

To argue by analogy usually means that we assume that if a given phenomenon A is consistently associated with another phenomenon B, then when we come to a phenomenon *similar* to A we can justifiably conclude that it is related to a phenomenon *similar* to B.

With respect to other minds we begin with our own minds. We observe that there is a correlation between our mental states, on the one hand, and our physical states and/or behavior, on the other. Further, we observe that there are other bodies similar to ours and that they exhibit behavior like ours. Therefore, by way of analogy, we are justified in assuming that mental states like those we experience are associated with other bodies in the same way that our mental states are associated with our bodies. For example, we know that a glass of iced tea on a hot day will refresh us and quench our thirst. Therefore, when we see someone else drink a glass of iced tea on a hot summer day, we are justified in thinking that he will be refreshed and that his thirst will be quenched.

Criticisms

The argument from analogy seems obvious, and for many years was taken to justify our belief that there are other minds. However, this argument has come under serious attack in contemporary philosophy. The objections may be stated as follows.

Arguments from analogy are weak. The first criticism is about analogical arguments in general, and is the least radical objection. It is argued that analogical arguments are weak, and that the analogical argument for other minds is particularly weak. Such critics point out that the argument from analogy would be relatively strong if we were first able to observe the correlation of mental and physical states in a large number of cases. For instance, suppose that we had observed the correlation between fire and smoke in thousands of cases and under various conditions. Then, if we were driving down the street and saw smoke pouring out of a house, we would be justified to conclude that there was a fire.

With the argument from analogy for other minds, however, we are prevented from appealing to *any other case* but our own. If we could appeal to the experience of others then the argument from analogy would be unnecessary. We would already know that other minds exist on independent grounds. Furthermore, the responses and behavior of other bodies are often quite different from ours. For example, when we drink iced tea and are refreshed, we may say, "Ahhh." Others, after drinking a glass of iced tea on a hot summer day, may smile and sing the Lipton tea jingle. How can we be sure that the differences in behavior are not indications of differences in mental events?

As we said earlier, this criticism is the least radical since a defender of the argument can reply that the argument from analogy attempts only to show a degree of probability.

There is no way to check the correctness of the argument. The second objection is more specific, for it attacks a special feature of the analogical argument for other minds. In most analogical arguments we can check directly the conclusion of the argument. Let us return to the fire-smoke analogical argument. If challenged about our inference that there is a fire, we can check directly on our conclusion by driving to the scene of the smoke. In other words, we can always in principle do without the analogical argument. However, with regard to the existence of other minds, it has been traditionally denied that this is possible. We cannot dispense with our argument, as it is the *only* means of proof.

One may ask why this inability to check the correctness of the argument renders it ineffective. The answer that some contemporary philosophers have given is that no conceivable observation could count against the argument. We have, so it is argued, no criterion for its truth or falsity other than the claim itself, and therefore the argument must be considered nonsense, since it cannot be verified.

The validity of the argument depends on our ability to learn from our own case. A major objection to the analogical argument for other minds is that it depends for its validity on our ability to learn from our own circumstances what a mental attitude is.

The first criticism was formulated by Wittgenstein. The analogical argument, he claimed, demands that we pick some mental state (pain or anger, for instance), and then re-identify that state whenever it recurs. The problem with this demand is that it does not allow for the possibility of incorrect identification. Behavioral and other external, objective checks are precluded, so there is no conceivable way to determine if we have made a mistake. Wittgenstein argued that the distinction between a correct identification and a mistake is essential, and without it we end up with a notion of identification that is meaningless.

The second argument against learning from our own case is that of the contemporary philosopher P. F. Strawson. His argument is more difficult to understand. He says that the idea of a mental attitude necessarily involves the idea of objects, things, or persons to which it can be significantly applied. By definition, a mental attitude may be applied to oneself and to others. Applicability to oneself and others is an *essential* characteristic of a mental event. Thus, before we can know what is meant by a mental event we must know what is meant by *both* oneself and the other. Thus the argument from analogy is used to show that there is another with a mind, but, so it is argued, the proof will not work unless we assume the conclusion of the argument.

Defenses of the Argument

In spite of the attacks on the argument from analogy, some philosophers have consistently defended it. Chief among its defenders has been A. J. Ayer. The primary defenses of the argument follow.

Verbal behavior counts for the argument.   In response to the claim that the argument is weak, Ayer has emphasized a special feature of this argument, namely, that people can speak. Since people can speak and since their accounts of their mental states sound much like our mental states, then we have something more substantial to go on in our argument than mere behavior.

Those who find the analogical argument unconvincing reply that speech can be understood only if it is accompanied by correct non-verbal behavior. If this is so, then again we have come to the place where we must depend on non-verbal behavior, and this differs from person to person.

The argument can be checked more directly.   One cannot ask any more of a method, so it is argued, than that when we examine its conclusions directly, they turn out to be correct more often than not.

The argument from analogy meets this requirement. We assume that there are other people besides ourselves, and that these other people make analogical inferences about feelings and thoughts that we have. When we check their conclusions about us, we find out that they are generally true. For instance, when we scream and pull our hand off of a hot stove, they conclude, correctly, that we are in pain. When other people see us sitting around with a frown on our face, they rightly surmise that we are depressed. Generally, they are correct about our mental attitudes.

Whether they actually make inferences from analogical arguments is beside the point, for they most certainly *could*. That is enough. Further, there is no need to be concerned because the only cases that can be more directly checked are our own. All or most arguments involving inferences utilize a restricted class of instances. What is important is that the class of instances be relevant. The analogical argument, so it is asserted, meets this test.

Opponents of the argument from analogy have argued that it is in principle impossible for more than one person to check directly on the conclusion. They claim that general publicity is an essential requirement of any argument. Of course, one may with equal justice question why this is necessary.

A criterion of correctness is not needed in all cases of identification. The analogical argument for other minds was criticized on the grounds that we cannot learn from our own case. Two replies have been made to this objection. First, it has been claimed that a criterion of correctness is not essential to *every* case of identification. Second, Ayer has contended that the required identification of a mental state can be accomplished without resorting to some public phenomena. One can with equal justification satisfy the requirements of identification by appeal to other private sensations.

An Alternative Form

Some philosophers have argued that the difficulty with the form of the argument from analogy which we have presented is that it is an argument from *extrinsic* rather than *intrinsic* analogy (see chap. 20, on religious language). It is claimed that the intrinsic analogy argument overcomes the criticisms of the extrinsic analogy.

The revised argument goes as follows. A being's activity is dependent upon its nature. Others have rational activity. Therefore, there must be other rational minds. The argument is even more convincing if one accepts the premise that an effect resembles its cause.

Alternative Arguments for the Existence of Other Minds

Because a good many philosophers, particularly within the English-speaking analytic tradition, have become dissatisfied with the argument from analogy, a whole host of alternative solutions have arisen in the current debate. We will examine the most significant alternatives.

Behaviorism

If one rejects the argument from analogy, the most obvious recourse is to advance some form of behaviorism.

Exposition. Behaviorism, as applied to the question of other minds, is the view that all mental attitudes or psychological expressions are fully reducible to behavior or physical states. Some philosophers would say that these expressions are completely understood in the light of behavior. If this is so, then the argument from analogy is unnecessary, since the behavior *is* the meaning of the expression, not merely a ground for inference in an analogical argument.

One of the advantages claimed for this position is that it is in principle open to public check. For instance, when we say that we are in love, we are asserting something about behavior in specific circumstances. We are talking about showing kindness, getting married, and having children. Anyone who says he loves a member of the opposite sex, and yet is consistently cruel or indifferent, does not want to marry, and refuses to have children is on shaky ground in claiming to be in love.

Criticisms. An extensive criticism of behaviorism is not our goal here, since it is far more than just a theory about other minds. However, any criticism of behaviorism in general weakens its use as a solution to the problem of other minds (see also the criticism of materialism in chap. 12).

There is, however, an objection to behaviorism that does relate directly to the problem at hand. It has been argued that a behavioristic account of certain first-person psychological statements is invalid. When we are in intense pain, we do not claim to be in pain on the basis of certain behavior which we observe in ourselves, but because of the circumstances causing that behavior.

This objection has gained considerable importance with a group of philosophers who consider it a decisive reason for rejecting *both* behaviorism *and* the argument from analogy. The reason is that both arguments claim a contingent (non-necessary) relationship between mental states and behavior. This objection shows that this is not so. The connection between mental attitudes and behavior is *logical,* or *conceptual.* There is no need to observe and correlate mental states with behavior because it is not a contingent matter. The relationship is necessary.

Wittgenstein

A number of philosophers have found that the views of Ludwig Wittgenstein, the father of *logical behaviorism,* support this last objection. The distinguishing feature between behaviorism and logical behaviorism is that behaviorism sees the relationship between mental states and behavior as contingent while logical behaviorism considers it conceptual or logical.

Exposition. Wittgenstein asked, "How do words refer to sensations?" His answer is that there is only one possibility; "Words are connected with the primitive, the natural expression of sensation and used in their place." That is, words are conceptually related to and used as symbols for perceptions. Although Wittgenstein does not elaborate, certain followers of Wittgenstein (Norman Malcolm, for instance) claim that this is Wittgenstein's answer to the question of reference between mental states (sensations) and behavior (expressions).

Further, these philosophers argue that this understanding of sensation expressions has a number of advantages. First, we can explain why our first-person sensation statements have importance for us. Such sensation statements as "ouch" have the significance of natural expressions of sensation and emotion. Second, Wittgenstein's understanding of expressions of sensation is said to explain the logical features of psychological statements. This is why it would be absurd to conclude that one is in pain only by observing one's own behavior. It also explains the impossibility of error about being in pain. If a person burns himself on a hot stove, he does not wonder whether or not he is in pain.

Criticisms.   In spite of the advantages of Wittgenstein's analysis of expressions of pain, there is a problem. Yet a cry of pain seems to contradict the statement, "He is not in pain." Since most logicians hold that only statements can be contradictories, there is a problem with the denial that a cry of pain is a statement.

Wittgenstein, however, held that pain statements ("I have a headache," for example) are never *exactly* like cries of pain. Sometimes the utterance is more like a natural expression and other times less, dependent on the context. Wittgenstein, then, provided three criteria for present-tense utterances of sensations and emotions: (1) These expressions cannot be mistakenly spoken; (2) they can be pretended or feigned; and (3) they can be made without self-observation.

These further considerations give rise to a host of problems. First, how can they all be true at once? How can it be possible that they cannot be uttered *mistakenly* but they can be *pretended?* The most hopeful approach is to claim that sensation expressions, like natural expressions, can be feigned. One can make an insincere groan. Such a groan is like a lie, and a lie is a statement. The next problem is with the incorrigibility of the expression. At best it appears that some revision is necessary in the incorrigibility claim. One must say that present-tense, first-person pain statements are corrigible (correctable), but not in all the ways other statements are. They are simply corrigible in the sense that they can be pretended or feigned.

In addition to the objections to Wittgenstein's analysis of psychological statements there is a criticism which Wittgenstein himself foresaw. It was that one might reach the conclusion that the sensation itself was *nothing.* But Wittgenstein denied that this was the impression he wished to give. Rather, he argued that he wanted to turn his face from the picture of the inner process. He was anxious to get away from the mysterious and concentrate on the public. Despite Wittgenstein's protestations, however, he was not totally successful in dispelling the suspicion that the sensation is nothing. It was difficult to turn his face from the inner process without leaving the distinct impression that the sensation did not exist.

P. F. Strawson

Strawson's position arose out of the problems with Wittgenstein's argument for the existence of other minds.

Exposition. On many points Strawson is in agreement with Wittgenstein. He agrees that skepticism about the existence of other minds is senseless and pointless. He also accepts the view that the relationship between mental states and behavior is not contingent but logical or conceptual.

At the same time, Strawson rejects some of Wittgenstein's central contentions. Strawson holds that the association of first-person, present-tense statements with natural expressions is both confusing and unnecessary. Moreover, he differs with Wittgenstein on the possibility of a private language, for he sees no problems with the invention of a private language. We might invent a personal language in which we have names for sensations, even if those sensations do not have external or public expression.

From what has been said so far it might be concluded that Strawson holds that the relationship between sensations and behavior is contingent, but he does not. How does Strawson avoid this conclusion? He argues that general agreement is necessary before there can be a common language. The fact that we agree about the appearance of blue, green, red, and so on makes it possible for us to have a common *impersonal* color language. This is not true for language about pain, however, since we cannot talk about the appearance or shape of pain. This precludes the possibility of a common impersonal pain language. There is, however, something that we are in agreement on—pain behavior—and on this basis we may have a common *personal* or *private* language. Strawson's idea is that there is a *logical adequacy* for ascribing psychological statements to other persons.

Nevertheless, it is important to emphasize that before one can have a concept of pain, he must be willing to ascribe it to others, for by definition pain is something that *belongs to someone*. It is for this reason, it should be remembered, that Strawson considers the argu-

ment from analogy inadequate. We need other minds before we can
have a concept of pain.

Criticisms.   At some points Strawson's views are identical with the
defenders of the argument from analogy, and at other points he agrees
with Wittgenstein. Where this is so, his views are open to the same
kinds of criticisms.

A. J. Ayer, however, has brought some criticisms which apply
particularly to Strawson's views. Ayer's first objection is that Strawson's notion of logical adequacy for ascribing psychological predicates
to persons is obscure and unjustifiable. Ayer is surely right that we
could wish for more clarity in Strawson's notion of logical adequacy,
but he does not make it clear why he thinks that it cannot be salvaged.

Ayer's second major criticism is Strawson's reason for holding that
the argument from analogy and the resultant philosophical skepticism
about other minds cannot be stated coherently. Ayer thinks that Strawson's objection to the argument from analogy is that it is circular. It
attempts to justify belief that there are other persons by relying on the
premise that one knows oneself to be a person. Such an argument
assumes exactly what is to be proved.

Most philosophers have concluded that Ayer has simply misunderstood Strawson. Strawson in fact argues that the trouble with the
argument from analogy is that it uses the concept of a person and *at the
same time* rejects the rule that a necessary part of the concept of a
person is the idea of mental attitudes based on behavior.

John Wisdom

Although John Wisdom's views on the problem of other minds in no
way constitute a *theory* about other minds, his ideas have been exceed-
ingly important. He was greatly influenced by the thought of Wittgenstein, and like Wittgenstein believed that a philosophical problem bore
resemblances to an illness. According to Wisdom, a philosophical
problem is an indication of a deep-seated intellectual disorder related to
our insistence on thinking in terms of language of misleading models.
The philosophical difficulty is "cured" when we no longer think in
terms of such inappropriate models. In this sense, philosophical problems are not *solved,* but rather are *dissolved.*

The cure for philosophical illness is insight. Unfortunately, inappropriate models are followed in large part unconsciously. By bringing the offending model to consciousness and showing the way our thought has incorrectly depended upon it, insight and freedom to think correctly are gained.

Wisdom also applies this method to demonstrate the nature of our knowledge about other minds. The first step is to induce philosophical perplexity by focusing on the problems raised by the most attractive answer to us. The task of the philosopher, then, is not to present us with an alternative model that is correct or true, but to point out the multitudes of statements that express our knowledge about other minds. In doing this the philosopher shows each such statement has its own logic, and that logic is similar to the logic of any other statement. Wisdom claims that by comparing these similarities and differences as well as the variety of ways in which we might or do know about other minds, we come to have a true grasp of the nature of our knowledge about other minds.

The problem with Wisdom's views is that they point up helpful ways in which to clarify the problem, but few solutions are offered. Unless one subscribes entirely to the thesis that the problem is dissolved when properly understood, then Wisdom is of limited help.

Conclusion

In this chapter we have examined the most common argument for the existence of other minds, the argument from analogy. While the argument from analogy has been widely criticized in contemporary thought, it seems to be as defensible as any of the alternatives. Clearly, it is not without its detractors, but none of the objections offered against it seem to be decisive.

Suggested Readings

Husserl, Edmund. *Cartesian Meditations,* meditation 5
Plantinga, Alvin. *God and Other Minds*
Strawson, P. F. *The Concept of Persons*
Wittgenstein, Ludwig. *Philosophical Investigations*

16   What Is Truth?

As we come to the close of this section on reality or metaphysics, we want to examine the question of truth. What is truth? If philosophy is ultimately tied up with truth, it is important that we try to define truth, and explain how it can be determined.

In this chapter we shall discuss the four major theories of truth: the coherence theory, the pragmatic theory, the performative theory, and the correspondence theory. Though the coherence and correspondence theories appear first in the history of thought, we will discuss the correspondence theory last and defend it as the correct account of truth.

The Coherence Theory of Truth

The coherence theory of truth is one of the two traditional theories of truth. It was held by the great rationalist metaphysicians such as

Spinoza, Leibniz, Hegel, and F. H. Bradley. For a short time it en-
joyed some support among logical positivists such as Neurath and
Hempel.

Exposition

Definition.   According to the coherence theory of truth, a statement
(some philosophers like the word *judgment* better) is true if and only if
it *coheres* or is consistent with the other statements of the system. Each
statement of the system is related to every other statement by implication. There is an analogy to this theory of truth in pure mathematical
systems. To test any statement for truth one simply observes if it
coheres with the other statements of the system. The system of coherent statements is different for the rationalist metaphysicians and the
logical positivists. For the rationalists the system is a comprehensive
account of the universe or reality. The logical positivists, on the other
hand, see the system of statements as the scientific picture of the world
as described by the contemporary sciences.

Given this view of truth, there are at least two interesting consequences. First, it is characteristic of the system that each part depends
on its relationship to the other parts. From these relationships meaning
and truth are derived. This is called "the doctrine of internal relations." Because of this thorough interrelatedness of knowledge, all
knowledge becomes necessary within the system.

A corollary to the doctrine of internal relations (and a distinction of a
coherence theory of truth in general) is that there are *degrees of truth*.
The truth of any particular statement is intimately connected with, and
can only be exhibited by, the truth of the statements of the entire
system. It thus follows that any particular statement or group of statements will only be *partially* true, and conversely, partly false. It is the
system of statements that is wholly true.

Support.   Various arguments are given in support of this theory of
truth. First, it is a common means we all use to evaluate the truth
content of statements or ideas we are confronted with. We reject various claims because they are inconsistent with our experience. For
instance, if someone told us that he had met a ghost or the great
pumpkin, we would reject the story because it does not cohere with the
rest of our experience. This is not only true with regard to ghost

stories, so it is argued, but is also the case in scientific investigation. Suppose someone told us that he had "dropped" an egg, but it did not fall to the ground. It remained suspended in midair. We would not believe him, because it is inconsistent with what we know of science, and with our own experience of what is possible.

Second, we find a similar understanding of truth in systems of pure mathematics. The test for the truth of any new proposition is its coherence with the other propositions of the system, and ultimately with the axioms of the system. In pure mathematics the test is more than a merely practical one; it is a logical one. A statement is coherent with the other propositions of the system when it is logically deducible from them.

Third, knowledge of the past is judged to be true or false in terms of its coherence (or lack of coherence) with what we know of the past. Coherence, not correspondence, is the test of historical knowledge, for there are no observable, corresponding states of affairs or facts to compare belief with (see pp. 247ff.). One can only compare the statement "George Washington was the first president of the United States" with other statements in documents or history books, and information in works of art.

Fourth, according to defenders of the coherence theory, it is incorrect to think that we can verify even statements in the present by pointing to corresponding facts. Such an approach assumes "that there is a solid chunk of fact" with which we have direct contact and to which all thought must adjust itself. Such thinkers observe that what some philosophers consider a brute fact is actually just a judgment or set of judgments. They claim that verification consists rather in the *coherence between* the initial judgment and the set or system of judgments.

Criticisms

While coherence is a *necessary* condition of truth, we shall see that it is inadequate as a theory of truth; it is not a *sufficient* condition as well.

A statement may be consistent (coherent) with one system but inconsistent with another. From our discussion, it should be clear that defenders of the coherence theory of truth depend heavily on pure mathematical systems as models. However, this reduction of truth to a mathematical model produces a number of difficulties. For one thing, in pure mathematics there are often alternative systems. In modal logic there are various axioms, allowing us to make a deduction in one system that is denied by another system. The upshot of this is that an axiom or statement may be coherent with one system of judgment but incoherent with another. This may be acceptable in mathematics or logic where we are only trying to deduce certain statements from a given system, but concerning science or empirical knowledge such a consequence creates serious difficulties.

A statement may be coherent with a system of judgments, but not applicable to the real world.   In pure mathematics we are interested only in the relationships between various statements. We want to show that certain conclusions can be derived from a set of statements, following various rules for operating on them. For instance, we can show that we can deduce the statement, "2 plus 2 is equal to half of 8" from a given set of statements and rules. It will not, of course, count against a mathematical statement that it has no application to the world. But empirical statements of science and everyday experience purport to tell us about the world, and thus need some stronger meaning to be true. In other words, coherence only guarantees that a statement may *possibly* have application to the world. It does not demonstrate that any statement *actually* has application to the world.

It is logically possible to have two coherent systems.   It is at least logically possible to have two internally coherent systems of statements which are, however, mutually incompatible so that both cannot be true without sacrificing the law of non-contradiction. A defender of the coherence theory could reply that we should then accept the more comprehensive system as true. However, this does not alleviate the problem, because it is equally possible that these internally coherent but mutually incompatible systems could also be *equally* comprehensive.

If the coherence theory is true, then, there is no way to decide between the systems in question. The rejection of an empirical statement in the end is quite different from the rejection of a mathematical statement. We may reject a mathematical proposition because of its failure to cohere, but we reject empirical statements because they are inconsistent with a body of beliefs that we believe to be true on independent grounds. That is, we believe the system of our everyday beliefs to be true about the world on grounds *other than* coherence. Thus the coherence (or lack of it) of a new judgment is simply a practical test, not a determination of truth.

Even in mathematics coherence is only a criterion of truth, and does not determine the meaning of truth.   A number of philosophers have argued that even in mathematics a coherence theory of truth is simply one *criterion* (that is, it assigns the conditions for using a statement) of truth, not its *meaning;* the actual criterion for the truth of empirical statements is correspondence with the nature of the world. In both cases, however, a true statement states some fact about the world. Regardless of whether "A is B" is a mathematical or an empirical statement, if it is true, then "A is B" *corresponds* to some fact, A is B.

The doctrine of degrees of truth is untenable.   Even if we restrict the doctrine of degrees of truth to mathematical statements, it appears to be false. The reason that this doctrine seems plausible at first is that it is ambiguous. There are at least three ways to interpret the idea of "partial truth." The first is that some statement is both true and false. It contains some truth *and* some falsity. If so, however, the truth that it contains is wholly true and that which is false is wholly false. To deny that is to give up the most fundamental law of logic, the law of non-contradiction. A second way to understand this doctrine is that some statement is both true and false in the same way at the same time. This is clearly false, if the law of non-contradiction holds. Finally, it may mean, and this seems to be what a coherence theorist has in mind, that any statement is only a *part* of the truth. The *whole* truth contains many more propositions. This is certainly correct, but it does not keep that which is only a part of the truth from being entirely true in the part to which it corresponds.

The Pragmatic Theory of Truth

Pragmatism was a dominant force in American philosophy during the first half of the twentieth century. While there are few philosophers today who call themselves pure pragmatists, the movement has left an indelible mark on American philosophy. We will examine a distinctive theory of truth which grew up with pragmatism. It will be helpful in dealing with this theory of truth if we build our discussion around the three central figures in pragmatism—Charles Sanders Peirce (1839–1914), William James (1842–1910), and John Dewey (1859–1952).

Charles Sanders Peirce

Peirce's view of truth.   Peirce (pronounced *Purse*) sought to relate truth to observable practices; his understanding of truth was in contradistinction to that of Descartes. Descartes thought that a proposition was true when we had a clear and distinct idea of it. Peirce reacted to this subjectivism, and rejected Descartes's view. He felt that a proposition could *seem* to be clear and distinct without really being clear. Peirce's theory of meaning, sometimes called the *pragmatic maxim,* bases the meaning of a proposition on the bearing it has on the conduct of our lives.

Peirce called his approach *pragmaticism,* and argued for a public understanding of truth. Truth could not be conceived apart from its *practical* relationship to doubts and beliefs within the framework of human inquiry. Metaphysical visions of truth such as those set forth by Spinoza and Leibniz were, for Peirce, in violation of Ockham's Razor (p. 183). Men and women search for belief; the search for truth is, in practice, the search for belief. Truth is the consequence of the experimental method, and will ultimately be agreed upon by the scientific community.

Evaluation of Peirce.   We shall say more about the identification of truth with practice in our discussion of William James. Suffice it to say here that a number of key notions in Peirce's view of truth lack practical consequences; thus they too would presumably fall when examined under the principle of Ockham's Razor. What is the experimental or practical difference between Descartes's "absolute fixity of truth" and Peirce's "opinion which is fated to be ultimately agreed to"?

These, however, are minor objections when viewed in light of the criticisms to be made of pragmatism's central thesis that truth is related to practical consequences.

William James

Both William James and John Dewey sought to apply the pragmatic notion of meaning to truth. There was, however, a decided difference in the application and results achieved by each man, and in James's hand Peirce's method undergoes crucial transformation.

James's view of truth.   When Peirce talked about practice bearing on truth, he was talking about the results of the scientist or the experimenter. He claimed that only this sort of experience is important for our understanding of truth. Furthermore, said Peirce, experience is very general in nature, not particular. Given the scientific flavor and the public nature of his views, Peirce was interested in experience stated according to general rules or regularities for a *group* of observers.

Both of these views of Peirce were modified by James. First, James was interested in the particular and the concrete, as opposed to the general and abstract. Second, James's understanding of what constituted experience was quite different from Peirce's. Rather than the results of the scientist, James was concerned with the effects of a *belief* in the private and personal life of the individual.

James defined the role of thinking in light of these concerns. The function of thought is not to imagine reality, but to produce ideas that will satisfy an individual's needs and desires. Thought functions primarily as a problem-solver. In the area of science, truth is determined by verification, for such ideas are necessary to predict and to cope with experience. Thus, scientific truth meets the criterion of practical interest.

However, James said that scientific truth gives us no criteria for metaphysical and theological beliefs. Since meaning and truth are related to consequences, James argued that an individual could regard metaphysical and religious beliefs as true if they provided him with what James called "vital benefits." Vital benefits are consequences that help an organism survive in its environment. Thus, according to pragmatic principle, if belief in God "works" satisfactorily for us, then we will be justified in believing it, and it will be true. James's famous statement is that the true is "the expedient in the way of our thinking," just as the right is "the expedient in the way of our behaving." In other words, truth is determined by consequences.

Objections to James's view of truth. Bertrand Russell (1872–1970) and Arthur O. Lovejoy (1873–1962) were two of the most severe critics of James's pragmatic theory of truth. First, both Russell and Lovejoy argued that the notion that something is true if it "works," which is central to James's view of truth, is ambiguous. Lovejoy pointed out that a belief may "work" in two very different ways. We may say it works if predictions we make on its basis are in fact fulfilled. On the other hand, we may say that a belief works if it contributes to our motivation and effort.

But a belief may work in one of these ways and not in the other. Let us consider a particular belief, that an extremely rich uncle loves us. On the basis of this belief we predict that we will receive great wealth upon his death. This belief may motivate us to do things for this uncle that we would not do otherwise, such as mowing his lawn. Likewise, it may help us in times of great poverty to endure the lack of earthly goods. But when this uncle dies, he may leave us out of his will, and we may not receive a penny. Thus our belief "worked" to motivate and encourage us, but it did not "work" to benefit us financially. Russell makes a similar point. When a scientist claims that a hypothesis works, he means that he can deduce a number of predictions that are confirmed in experience. However, these predictions or their results may not necessarily be *good,* and so may not "work" to benefit mankind.

Second, Russell claimed that James's view of truth ignores the way we usually understand truth. Consider the following two sentences: "It is true that it is sunny out"; and "It is useful to believe that it is sunny out." If James is correct, then these two sentences are identical in meaning. When we believe one, we believe the other. There should be no transition in our mind from one to the other—but there obviously is. Therefore, the two sentences cannot be identical in meaning.

Moreover, on pragmatic grounds we will be bound to declare certain sentences true that we know on independent grounds to be false. Consider the case of a patient who comes to a doctor. The patient suspects cancer and is emotionally unstable because of this fear. The doctor examines the patient and finds overwhelming evidence that there is cancer. However, because the doctor feels that the patient either will refuse the needed surgery or will not do well in surgery, he tells the fearful patient that nothing serious is wrong. Reassured by the words of the doctor, the patient goes through the surgery and recovers. Telling the patient that nothing serious was wrong "worked." But was it true? On pragmatic grounds we must say yes, but on independent grounds we know that it is *not* true.

Third, Russell argued that James's notion of truth was, in practice, useless. To say that belief is true in light of the consequences, is to say that the results of holding it are better than the results of rejecting it. But how can we be sure of the results of holding any belief? We may underestimate or overestimate their effect.

John Dewey

Dewey developed a theory of truth which was in keeping with his pragmatic method, and may be identified with the phrase, "warranted assertibility."

Dewey's view of truth. Dewey began by pointing out that it is easy to subscribe to the belief that truth is a correspondence between an idea or statement and a fact. However, this can also be understood outside the context of inquiry, reflective thinking, and problem solving. What does "correspondence" mean in practice? What is the relationship between ideas and facts in practice, that is, in the context of investigation?

According to Dewey, an investigation is always instigated by an initial state of doubt. The doubt is real, not theoretical. One is uncertain about the surroundings. It is impossible to understand the use of ideas and facts unless we first understand the purpose in undertaking the inquiry, that is, to answer doubt and uncertainty.

Serious inquiry begins with the formulating of one's doubt into a problem. Within this context an idea is a possible solution to the problem. An idea is more than simply that which is directly perceived. It extends beyond what is perceived to what is (as yet) unperceived.

Facts, said Dewey, are used in inquiry to mark off or set what is secure and unquestioned. Facts guide inferences by prompting new ideas, and new ideas promise new facts, which in turn verify the ideas. Facts are not abstract, and they always occur in the context of inquiry. Thus, the correspondence between ideas and facts comes from their working relationship in the context of inquiry.

Ideas, then, *become* true when their "draft upon experience" is verified by the promised facts. According to Dewey, truth is not antecedent to a context of inquiry. Furthermore, truth is a mutable idea. It "happens to an idea" when it is verified, or "warranted."

Objections to Dewey's view of truth.   There are a number of problems concerning Dewey's view of truth. First, it is argued that truth is certainly antecedent to its verification. Truth is not something that "happens" to an idea. It is not a time-dependent, acquired property. Suppose, for example, that a crime is committed on Tuesday. On Friday we have enough evidence to place the guilt on Jones. The statement "Jones committed a crime" cannot be true on pragmatic grounds until Friday, but we know good and well that it was true on Tuesday. As a matter of fact, on Dewey's interpretation we should not be able to convict Jones. "Jones committed a crime" is not true until Friday, and the crime was committed on Tuesday.

Both Rudolf Carnap and G. E. Moore attacked Dewey's view of mutable truth. Carnap pointed out that there is a distinction between *truth* and *confirmation*. It does make sense to say that a statement is confirmed today, but not that it may be true today and not yesterday or tomorrow. Dewey has merely confused truth with confirmation. To accept his view will ultimately lead to the surrender of the law of non-contradiction.

G. E. Moore, on the other hand, stated that there is only one way we can make a belief true. We will make the belief, "It will rain tomorrow" true only if tomorrow *we have a part in making the rain fall.*

The Performative Theory of Truth

The performative theory of truth is most prominently associated with P. F. Strawson.

Exposition

Until Strawson's analysis, it was assumed by all philosophers, irrespective of differences on other matters, that terms like "true" and "false" were descriptive expressions. It is this assumption that Strawson challenged. He argued that "true" is a *performative* expression. In using a performative definition one is not making a statement but

performing an action. According to Strawson, to prefix a statement by
"It is true that . . . " we are not making a comment on the statement,
but agreeing with, accepting, or endorsing the statement. To say "It is
true that the sky is blue" is not to say anything more than "I agree that
the sky is blue."

Strawson not only recognizes the performative use of "true," but he
recognizes also another use of "true," which he calls expressive. The
expressive use is often signaled by such phrases as, "So, it's true
that . . . "; "Is it true that . . . ?"; or "If it is true that . . . ." In each of
these utterances, the word "true" expresses surprise, doubt, astonish-
ment, or disbelief. In this case, too, "true" does not contribute to what
Strawson calls the *assertive meaning* of what is said. It has no
statement-making role.

Criticisms

The most serious objections against Strawson's position are as
follows.

*Strawson does not distinguish among performative expres-
sions.* Philosophers have distinguished a number of kinds of performatives. Even if we grant that "true" is sometimes used as a
performative, it differs from such other performatives as "I grant . . .,"
"I accept . . . ," "I concede . . . ," "I admit . . . ," and "I insist . . . ."
At least some of the expressions, such as "I concede . . . ," "I accept . . . ," or "I insist . . . ," suggest an adversary background, or context of argument. "That's true" does not function in this way. Moreover, a performative such as "yes" needs distinction from "it is true
that . . . ." The former indicates what philosophers call *bare assent,*
while the latter indicates a considered opinion, as in, "I have studied
the evidence and conclude that . . . ."

*The hypothetical syllogism contradicts the performative analysis
of "true."* P. T. Geach has made the following criticism of Strawson's position. He presents this hypothetical argument:

> If x is true, then p.
> X is true.
> _____
> Therefore, p.

Strawson would claim that the second premise is a performative. "*X* is true" should be interpreted as an agreeing performance. But it cannot be argued that the "*x* is true" of the first hypothetical premise is an agreeing performance. That is, if we say "If *x* is true, then *p*," we are *not* agreeing with or accepting *x*. If this is the case, then the explanation of "true" offered by Strawson is not the same in both premises. We no longer have a valid argument form, and one of the most fundamental argument forms (*modus ponens*, that is, the affirmative form) now becomes invalid. This argument, so Geach contends, shows that Strawson's analysis is faulty.

It has been argued that Geach's criticism rests on a misunderstanding of the way in which performatives function in logical arguments. Here is an example of a clear case of a performative argument:

> If I promise to help, I will do it.
> I promise to help.
> _____
> Therefore, I will do it.

There is an occurrence of a performative use of "I promise" in the second premise but not in the first. Still the argument is valid. This argument shows that the fallacy of equivocation is *not* committed simply because an expression has a performative use in one premise of an argument and a non-performative use in another. Difference in meaning, not function, constitutes equivocation.

While it is true that Strawson does discuss "true" as a performative, he does not claim that this is the whole story. We should remember that he talks about an expressive use. Presumably, the first premise above would fall under this analysis.

Performatives cannot account for "blind" uses of the word "true." A blind" use of the word *true* occurs when a person describes a statement or group of statements as "true" without knowing what that statement or statements are. For instance, suppose someone says, "Every statement our philosophy teacher makes is true." It is reasonable to assume that the speaker does not know everything that the philosophy teacher has said. Therefore, he cannot be agreeing with or accepting these statements. Moreover, if we were to substitute the actual statements themselves for the phrase "every statement," we would change the meaning of the sentence. Hence, "Every statement our philosophy teacher makes is true" does not, as Strawson claims, have the same performative meaning.

In response to this criticism Strawson has modified his position. He admits that when a person asserts that a statement is true, he at least in part makes a statement about a statement.

The Correspondence Theory of Truth

While the correspondence theory of truth has a long history, and was known in its essential features in antiquity, the term *correspondence theory* has gained popularity primarily through the writings of Bertrand Russell. The correspondence theory of truth holds that truth consists in some form of correspondence between a belief or a sentence and a fact or a state of affairs.

There are many examples of the correspondence theory of truth, but we will examine three formulations which demonstrate the salient features of the theory. We will discuss the positions of Aristotle, G. E. Moore, and Alfred Tarski.

Aristotle

Exposition.   Aristotle gives a definition of truth that is, on examination, clear and simple: "To say of what is, that it is not, or of what is not, that it is, is false; while to say of what is, that it is, and of what is not, that it is not, is true."

According to Aristotle, substances are characterized by the fact that they can at differing times have opposite qualities. But do statements or opinions fall under this criterion? The statement, "It is raining out" may appear to be true today and false tomorrow. But Aristotle rejects this suggestion, for he thinks this conclusion rests on a misunderstanding. In this example there is no genuine alteration in the *statement itself,* but in the *fact* outside (it is raining), by which the statement's truth or falsity is measured. "For it is by the facts of the case, by their being or not being so, that a statement is called true or false."

Aristotle speaks of the facts as a kind of causation. The facts *cause* the truth of the statement by asserting that fact. It has been noted that what Aristotle calls a *cause,* many contemporary philosophers would be more likely to call a *criterion.*

Criticisms.   What we might call the Platonic-Aristotelian correspondence theory of truth had not long been formulated when a problem or criticism was brought against the view. It was suggested by
Eubulides, a member of the school of Megara. (This school seems to
have been in conflict with a good many of the basic Platonic-
Aristotelian positions.) Eubulides's objection to the correspondence
theory has been called the "liar paradox." Eubulides asks his hearers
to consider a man who says, "I am lying" or "I am now uttering a
falsehood."

The problem with this statement should be obvious. The utterance is
true if it is false, and false if it is true. Thus, in at least one case, the
correspondence theory of truth seems to result in an utterance meaning
its opposite. Furthermore, because of the Aristotelian dependence on
fact for the truth or falsehood of a proposition, we have at least an
apparent problem. The related matter of fact *is* the truth or falsity of
the statement. This "paradox of the liar" has been much debated both
in ancient and contemporary philosophy, and it has been assumed that
any adequate theory of truth must give a satisfactory answer to this
problem.

One possible answer to the paradox is to insist that the claim "I am
lying" is self-destructive or self-defeating and, therefore, is not a truth
claim at all. To use mathematical language, sentences like this constitute the null set. (Another answer to this problem will be suggested by
the work of Tarski, below.)

G. E. Moore

One may choose either Bertrand Russell (1872–1970) or G. E.
Moore (1873–1958) as a representative of the modern formulators and
defenders of the correspondence theory. We have chosen Moore because his position is easier for the beginning student to understand.

Moore's early views.   Moore and Russell were lifelong friends
and colleagues at Cambridge, forging their philosophical positions
against their earlier training in idealism. Moore's early views on truth
are contained in a series of lectures which he gave in 1910–11.

According to Moore, truth and falsity are properties of what he
called propositions. A proposition is identified with the *meaning* of an
indicative sentence. In hearing and understanding a spoken sentence

and in seeing and understanding a written sentence, something is apprehended by us which is more than the mere sentence. While the *act* of apprehension is the same in all cases, *what* is apprehended is different in various sentences. Acts of belief and sentences can only be called true or false in a secondary sense, but it is a proposition that is in fact the bearer of truth or falsity.

Moore's later position. Moore returned to the questions of truth and falsity in his later writings, although he modified his views somewhat. In his later work he talked about beliefs rather than propositions. He defined the difference between a true and a false belief as follows: When a belief is true, that which is believed is a fact; when a belief is false, that which is believed is not a fact.

Moore also asserted that there are no such things as propositions. Moore expressly said that truth does *not* consist of three parts: a believer, a belief, and some other thing called a proposition. In his most developed treatment, Moore argued that the truth of a belief consists in a relationship between a person and a *fact*. Thus in Moore's more mature thinking facts replaced propositions. He explicitly said that the relationship between the belief and the fact is one of correspondence. Facts exist in the same sense that chairs and tables exist.

There is one problem that Moore does not address. It has to do with false beliefs and the existence of false facts. Russell and others were much concerned with this issue, and clearly denied that false facts exist. If they did exist, false facts would clutter up the ontology of the world. Rather, false beliefs fail to correspond to *anything*. For instance, when we falsely believe that the moon is made of green cheese, our belief corresponds to nothing.

Alfred Tarski

The twentieth-century Polish logician, Alfred Tarski, has picked up and amplified the medieval idea of "true" as a straightforward adjective of a straightforward object in a sentence. His treatment of the topic is considered by most philosophers as one of the classics of modern logic. While his concern is primarily with the idealized language of logic, some argue that what Tarski says is applicable (with some minor revisions) to ordinary language.

According to Tarski, truth is a property of sentences. A sentence is true or false only as it is a part of a particular language. (The medieval scholastic theologians and philosophers were sensitive to this point as well.) Take for example the sentence, "Man is a car." This sentence is only true or false in relation to some concrete language, and would be true in a language where the word *car* meant what we now mean by *mammal*.

Moreover, Tarski denies that a sentence which asserts that sentence *S* is a true sentence of *L* (a particular language), can itself be a sentence of *L*. Such a sentence would belong to what Tarski call a *meta-language*, a second-order language in which talk about the first-order language is possible. By so doing Tarski has offered another possible resolution of the liar paradox, since any sentences asserting either the truth or falsity of sentences of *L* would not belong to *L* but to a meta-language.

Finally, Tarski defines truth in terms of correspondence. The sentence, "Snow is white" is true if and only if snow is indeed white. Truth then is a property of sentences, and involves a relationship between a sentence and reality.

Conclusion

In this chapter we have examined four principal theories of truth: the coherence theory of truth; the pragmatic theory of truth; the performative theory of truth; and the correspondence theory of truth. We have argued that the first three theories of truth are inadequate, that the correspondence theory alone is sufficient. As Christians, we cannot accept any theory of truth which results in either relativism or agnosticism. The Bible clearly declares that man can know the truth, and will be held responsible for such knowledge.

Suggested Readings

Ayer, A. J. "The Criterion of Truth" in *Philosophy and Analysis,* ed. M. Macdonald
Bradley, F. H. *Essays on Truth and Reality,* chs. 7, 11
James, William. *The Meaning of Truth*

Moore, G. E. *Some Main Problems in Philosophy,* chs. 6, 13–16

Strawson, P. F. "Truth" in *Philosophy and Analysis,* ed. M. Macdonald

Tarski, A. "The Concept of Truth in Formalized Languages" in *Logic, Semantics, Metamathematics*

PART FOUR

What Is the Ultimate?

The Relationship Between Faith and Reason

17

One of the most basic issues facing the Christian in philosophy is how to relate faith and reason. What role, if any, does revelation have in determining philosophical truth? Conversely, what role, if any, does reason have in determining divine truth? These are not easy questions, and Christians have answered them in different ways.

Before these views can be understood, the terms *revelation* and *reason* must be defined. "Revelation" is a supernatural disclosure by God of truth which could not be discovered by the unaided powers of human reason. "Reason" is the natural ability of the human mind to discover truth.

The solutions to the issue of which method is a reliable source of truth are divisible into five basic categories: (1) revelation only; (2) reason only; (3) revelation over reason; (4) reason over revelation; and (5) revelation and reason.

Revelation Only

Some philosophers have claimed that revelation alone can be considered a legitimate source of man's knowledge. Such thinkers exhibit a mistrust of human reason as an avenue to truth.

Sören Kierkegaard

According to Sören Kierkegaard (1813–1855), the father of modern existentialism, the human mind is wholly incapable of discovering any divine truth. There are several reasons for the impotence of human reason.

Man's fallen state.   Man is alienated by sin from a holy God. Indeed, God is an "offense" to men who are in a perpetual state of rebellion against Him. Man is suffering from what Kierkegaard called a "sickness unto death" (the title of one of his works). The very nature of man's sin makes it impossible for him to know the truth about a personal God, since it is this very God whom he is passionately ignoring or rejecting.

God's transcendence.   Man cannot know any truth about God because God is "Wholly Other." God is not only an offense to man's will, but He is a "paradox" to man's reason. Although Kierkegaard does not claim that God Himself is absurd or irrational, nonetheless, God is suprarational; the truth of God is paradoxical or seemingly contradictory to us. Because this God utterly transcends or is "beyond" reason, there is no way for reason to reach beyond itself to God.

No positive role of reason.   The very best that reason can do is to reject the absurd or irrational, but it cannot be of any positive help in attaining divine truth. Christian truth can be known only by what Kierkegaard called a "leap of faith." By this he means a sheer act of the will in face of blinding rational odds. Thus a believer may go beyond reason in a personal commitment to God by faith alone. Kierkegaard's illustration of this point is Abraham's response to God's command that he sacrifice his beloved son, Isaac. By faith alone and

without any ethical or rational justification, Abraham willingly as-
cended Mount Moriah to offer his son Isaac in obedience to God.

Proofs are an insult to God.   According to Kierkegaard, any rational attempt to prove God's existence is an insult to God. It is like a
lover insisting on proving the existence of his loved one to others while
the loved one is present. Indeed, no one even begins to prove God
unless he has already rejected God's presence in his life, says Kierkegaard. Proofs are unnecessary for those who believe in God and
unconvincing to those who do not believe. The only "proof" of Christianity is suffering, according to Kierkegaard, for Jesus said, "Come,
take up the cross, and follow me" (Mark 10:21b).

Historical evidence is unhelpful.   Kierkegaard asked, Can eternal
happiness be based on historical events? His answer was an emphatic
and resounding "no!" The eternal can never be based on the temporal.
The very best the historical can provide is probability—but the believer
needs *certainty* before he will make what Paul Tillich called "an
ultimate commitment to the ultimate." Only by faith in the Transcendent can one transcend human and historical probability and encounter God.

As a Christian, Kierkegaard believed that God entered time in
Christ. He also believed the events of Christ's life to be historical,
including His virgin birth, crucifixion, and bodily resurrection. However, Kierkegaard believed that there was no way to be absolutely
certain these events actually occurred. What is more, Kierkegaard
believed that the historicity of these events was not even important.
The significant fact is not the *historicity* of Christ (in times past) but
the *contemporaneity* of Christ (in the present) by faith in the believer.
He wrote:

> If the contemporary generation had left nothing behind them but these
> words: "We have believed that in such and such a year that God ap-
> peared among us in the humble figure of a servant, that he lived and
> taught in our community, and finally died," it would be more than
> enough.[1]

---

1. Sören Kierkegaard, *Philosophical Fragments* (Princeton, N. J.: Princeton University Press, 1936), p. 130.

Karl Barth

One of the most famous theologians of the contemporary Christian church is Karl Barth. Like Kierkegaard, Barth argued that God is "Wholly Other" and can be known only by divine revelation.

Need for supernatural revelation.   Barth, too, believed that fallen man is incapable of knowing a transcendently holy God. Barth held that all attempts to reason one's way to God were futile. This is why Barth felt comfortable writing an introduction to a book by the atheist Ludwig Feuerbach (1804–1872), who argued that God is nothing but a projection of human imagination. However, Barth held that what man cannot do "from the bottom up" by reason, God has done "from the top down" by supernatural revelation. For Barth the Bible is the locus of God's revelation. It is the instrument through which God speaks. In itself the Bible is only a propositional record of the personal revelation of God to His people, but the Bible *becomes* the Word of God to us as God speaks through its human words.

Barth's "no" to natural revelation.   God does not speak to us through nature, for man is fallen and, hence, has completely obscured and distorted God's revelation in nature. Even the "image of God" in man is not a "point of contact" but a point of conflict between God and man. Barth was emphatic that the human mind has no ability to know God. In fact, Barth answered the question whether man even has a capacity to receive God's supernatural revelation with a book entitled *Nein [No!]*. Human reason has neither the active nor passive capacity for divine revelation. God must supernaturally give the ability to understand His revelation as He gives the revelation itself.

Reason Only

On the opposite end of the faith-and-reason spectrum are the rationalists, who claim that all truth is discoverable by human reason. Indeed, some go so far as to claim that nothing is truly known by revelation at all. Others give some status to revelation, but make reason the sufficient and final test of what is and what is not true in the allegedly supernatural revelation.

Immanuel Kant

Kant was himself of devout and pious Lutheran heritage. In his famous *Critique of Pure Reason,* which laid the basis for much of modern agnosticism, Kant claimed to critique speculative (theoretical) reason in order to "make room for faith."

Reason demands we live "as if there is a God."   Despite the fact that we cannot know (by speculative reason) if God exists, we must live as if there is a God because our practical (moral) reason demands this. That is, reason demands that we *postulate* God's existence in order to make sense out of our moral duty in this life. For unless we live as if God exists, there is no way to fulfill the command to achieve the greatest good.

Reason demands we live "as if miracles do not occur."   The essence of what Kant accomplished, however, is depicted in the title of his book, *Religion Within the Limits of Reason Alone.* By use of what Kant called "practical reason," Kant laid down the basis for the trend to de-supernaturalize religious belief. Kant did not say nor did he believe that there was no supernatural revelation from God in the Bible. He did insist, however, that we must judge all the alleged supernatural revelation by means of "practical reason alone." He held, for instance, that reason demands that we give up belief in the resurrection of Christ and, in fact, in any biblical teaching contrary to this "reason." Concerning this rational approach, Kant admitted that "frequently this interpretation may, in the light of the text [of the revelation], appear forced—it may often really be forced." As to any biblical miracle, Kant insisted that if it "flatly contradicts morality, it cannot, despite all appearances, be of God (for example, when a father is ordered to kill his son [as Abraham was in Genesis 22])".

Benedict Spinoza

An even more radical example of the "reason only" view is the Jewish philosopher, Spinoza. He believed that all truth is known only by means of self-evident axioms. Anything contrary to these axioms or not reducible to them is to be rejected as irrational—whether it is in the Bible or not.

Geometric rationalism. Beginning with what Spinoza considered the irreducible axioms of human thought, he "deduced" all the necessary truths about God, man, and the world. First, according to Spinoza, it is rationally necessary to conclude that there is only one "substance" in the universe of which all things, including all men, are but modes or moments (this is clearly a sort of pantheism). Likewise, "evil" is but an illusion of the moment or particular. The universe as a whole is good, just as a mosaic as a whole is beautiful, despite the seeming ugliness of an individual piece.

Spinoza did not trust sense perceptions; they are not, he said, the source of truth. Truth resides only in ideas—more precisely, in the perfect Idea. Truth is known only by a rational intuition.

Anti-supernatural rationalism. Few writers in the modern world were more militantly anti-supernatural than Spinoza. Applying his rationalism to the Bible, Spinoza concluded that Moses did not write the first five books of the Old Testament nor receive them in revelations from God. He considered it "irrational" to believe in the miracles recorded in the Bible, or in any miracles. He said, "We may, then, be absolutely certain that every event which is truly described in Scripture necessarily happened, like everything else, according to natural laws."

Spinoza was certain that "nature's course is fixed and unchangeable." He was uncompromising in his insistence that "a miracle, whether a contravention to, or beyond nature, is a mere absurdity." This means, of course, that Spinoza would insist that the resurrection accounts in the Gospels must be rejected. In short, any part of biblical revelation which did not accord with Spinoza's naturalistic rationalism had to be considered inauthentic. This is about as clear an example of "reason only" as can be found in the history of philosophy.

Reason Over Revelation

There are others whose emphasis on reason is not nearly as radical as Spinoza's. Their view of reason and revelation could more properly be defined as reason *over* revelation. This view is ascribed to some of the early Christian Fathers, such as Justin Martyr and Clement of Alexandria.

Alexandrian Fathers

Justin Martyr believed in divine revelation, but in addition to the Bible he held that "reason is implanted in every race of man." In view of this he held that those among the ancient Greeks who "lived reasonably are Christians, even though they have been thought atheist." This included men such as Heraclitus and Socrates.

Clement of Alexandria was even more eulogistic of human reason. In a famous passage in his *Stromata* he wrote, "Before the advent of the Lord, philosophy was necessary to the Greeks for righteousness." For philosophy "was a schoolmaster to bring 'the Hellenic mind' as the law, the Hebrews, 'to Christ.'" Not only did Clement exalt human reason but at times even identified it with divine revelation. He believed that Plato spoke "through the inspiration of God." He did not hesitate to reinterpret divine revelation in view of his own platonic kind of reasoning. In this way these early philosphical Christians set the stage for later, even modern, Christian rationalists who exalted reason over divine revelation.

Modern Higher Criticism

Perhaps the best example of those who hold the "reason over revelation" view are known as "liberals" or "higher critics." Roughly speaking, this refers to a theological movement which sprung from seventeenth- and eighteenth-century European thought. It was influenced by Spinoza, Kant, and Hegel, who concluded by human reason that parts or all of the Bible are not a revelation from God. Higher critics have included men such as Jean Astruc (1684–1766) and Julius Wellhausen (1844–1918). In contrast to the historic, orthodox view that the Bible *is* the Word of God, liberals believe that the Bible merely *contains* the Word of God. When they apply the canons of human reason or modern scholarship to the Bible they feel that some parts of it are "contradictory," and others are simply myths or fables. Some Old Testament stories are rejected by these critics because the events seemed to be "immoral."

Another group of men who exalted reason above revelation were the Deists of the seventeenth and eighteenth centuries. Men such as Herbert of Cherbury (1583–1648), Charles Blount (1654–1693), and John Toland (1670–1722) minimized or negated the supernatural elements of the Bible. On the more popular level was the American, Thomas Paine (1737–1809), who in his famous book *The Age of Reason* leveled a bitter attack on the numerous passages of Scripture that seemed to him to contradict human reason. And Thomas Jefferson literally cut the miracles from the four Gospels and pasted the de-supernaturalized remains in a scrap book. It was later published as *The Jefferson Bible*. It ends thus: "There laid they Jesus, and rolled a great stone to the door of the sepulchre, and departed." The rest of the story—the resurrection of Christ—is a miracle that cannot, thought Jefferson, be accepted by good reason.

Both the higher critic and the Deist, then, hold reason over revelation. These thinkers themselves determine what parts of an alleged revelation are *really* not revelations at all. This attitude is still held by theologians today, especially those who deny that the Bible is wholly true in everything it affirms. Anything in the Bible—whether it be God's command to the Israelites to kill the Canaanites or Paul's teaching on the role of women—that does not accord with the "acceptable canons of human reason" is rejected by them.

Revelation Over Reason

Opposite those semi-rationalists who exalt reason over revelation are those strong revelationalists who exalt revelation over reason. In the latter category are men like the early church father Tertullian and, in later times, men like Cornelius Van Til.

Tertullian

Tertullian is sometimes stereotyped as a "revelation only" proponent. This is based on the single statement, "I believe because it is absurd." Actually Tertullian never used the Latin word *absurdum*. Instead, he used the word *ineptum*, which does not imply contradiction but simply "foolishness." He was probably claiming no more than Paul did in I Corinthians 1, that the gospel seems "foolish" to the unbeliever. On other occasions Tertullian spoke of the need of using "the rule of reason." He also spoke against those who were "content with having simply believed, without full examination of the grounds of the traditions" they believed.

It is true, nonetheless, that Tertullian exalted revelation above human reason. In one famous passage he cried out: "What indeed has Athens to do with Jerusalem? What concord is there between the academy and the church?" Obviously, philosophers were not exalted by Tertullian. He declared:

> Unhappy Aristotle! who invented for these men dialectics, the art of building up and pulling down; an art so evasive in its propositions, so farfetched in its conjectures, so harsh in its arguments, so productive of contentions . . . retracting everything and really treating of nothing!

As far as Tertullian was concerned, philosophers were "those patriarchs of all heresy."

Tertullian not only considered philosophy unhelpful, but held that it is not at all essential to the believer. Revelation is all that really counts. In fact, he said, "it is the more to be believed if the wonderfulness be the reason why it is *not* believed." The believer reasons *about* revelation but never *against* it. Revelation stands over reason; reason does not stand over revelation. Tertullian, unlike Kant, did not believe in "revelation within the limits of reason" but rather "reason within the limits of revelation."

Cornelius Van Til

Perhaps the best example among contemporary evangelical thinkers of one who exalts revelation over reason is the Reformed theologian and apologist, Cornelius Van Til (b. 1895). His view is often called *presuppositionalism* because it strongly stresses the need to "presuppose" the truth of revelation in order for reason to function. For if there were no God—the Christian God—who created and sustains the very laws and processes of reason, then thinking itself would be impossible. Reason, for Van Til, is radically and actually dependent on revelation.

The problem with Christian rationalism.   According to Van Til, the difficulty with other Christian views of faith and reason is that they exalt reason over God. They ground God in reason, rather than recognizing the truth that reason is based on God. The existence of the sovereign God of Christianity is the most basic assumption in a Christian system of philosophy. God is the creator of human reason. Hence, all reason must be His humble servant, not His master. Reason stands under God's judgment but never sits in judgment of God. God's revelation, then, will always be over man's reason, never the reverse.

God is not subject to laws of logic.   The view held by many Christians that God is subject to the law of non-contradiction is rejected by Van Til. Logic applies only to the created, not to the Creator. God is sovereign over all—even over the laws of thought. According to Van Til, the Christian must never capitulate the transcendence of God to anything, even to the most fundamental rules of human reason.

The proper use of human reason.   If one must presuppose the truth of revelation and hold that the law of non-contradiction does not apply to God, how does Van Til escape the "revelation only" position? What rule is there for reason as it relates to divine revelation? Van Til claims that God's revelation is not God. Since God transcends His revelation, it is not inconsistent to hold that logic applies to the revelation but not to God Himself. Further, Van Til uses reason as a servant of the revelation and even, to borrow the title of one of his books, "In Defense of the Faith."

In a succinct summary of his position, called "My Credo," Van Til argued that other Christian thinkers were not sufficiently rational. That is, they did not carry reason far enough. He declared, "The traditional method . . . compromises God himself by maintaining that existence is only 'possible' albeit 'highly probable,' rather than ontologically and 'rationally' necessary."

In view of this, many followers of Van Til see his system as a kind of transcendental argument which contends that it is absolutely necessary to presuppose the divine revelation in the Bible before one can consistently think, communicate, do science, or make any sense out of life or his world. It does seem most fair to understand Van Til as one who does not negate reason but simply exalts revelation above it. What Van Til is vigorously opposed to is the opposite, that is, exalting reason above revelation. Human reason must never stand in judgment of God or His revelation in Scripture.

Revelation and Reason

The last category comprises those Christians who believe there is an interrelationship between revelation and reason. Two great thinkers stand in this tradition: Augustine and Aquinas. The difference between them is largely a matter of emphasis.

Saint Augustine

Augustine (354–430) came to Christianity from a background of Platonic philosophy, while Aquinas wrote in an Aristotelian tradition. Both men, however, believed the scriptural injunction (from the Septuagint, Isaiah 7:9), "Unless you believe, you will not understand." The basic relation of reason and revelation is that the thinking Christian attempts to render the credible intelligible. He tries to reason about and within his revelation. There is even a sense in which one can reason for revelation, though never against it.

Faith is understanding's step.   In Augustine's words, "faith is understanding's step." Without faith first one would never come to a full understanding of God's truth. Faith initiates one into knowledge. In this sense Augustine fully believed that faith in God's revelation is prior to human reason. On the other hand, Augustine also held that no one ever believes something before he has some understanding of what it is he is to believe. In fact, Augustine asserted that no one should believe a revelation which he has not first judged by good reason to be worthy of belief. He said, "Authority demands belief and prepares man for reason. . . . But reason is not entirely absent from authority, for we have got to consider whom we have to believe, and the highest authority belongs to truth when it is clearly known." But since Augustine believed that faith is prior to reason, it seems best to entitle his view "revelation *and* reason."

Understanding is faith's reward. While Augustine believed that "faith is understanding's step" he also held that "understanding is faith's reward." The reward for accepting God's revelation by faith is that one has a fuller and more complete understanding of truth than he could have otherwise. Indeed, taking from revelation insight into the nature of the unchangeable God and man's mutable mind, one can devise a valid proof for God's existence which borrows no premise from God's revelation. The proof "stands on its own two feet" philosophically, although one would perhaps never understand this proof apart from the revelation of God in Scripture. The "proof" goes something like this:

(1) My mind understands some immutable truths (such as 7 + 3 =
    10).
(2) But my mind is not immutable.
(3) A mutable mind cannot be the ground of immutable truths.
(4) Hence, there must be an Immutable Mind (that is, God).
The philosophical "understanding" of God that comes via this proof is
by no means the only kind of understanding into which one is inaugu-
rated by faith, but it is one kind.

According to Augustine, faith is a prerequisite for the full understanding of God's revelation. A partial understanding of the basic
content of the gospel is, of course, necessary before one can believe it,
but the full understanding of Christian truth is subsequent to saving
faith. Fallen man's sinfulness obscures his ability to see the truth
before saving faith is exercised.

Thomas Aquinas

Aquinas (1224–1274) considered himself to be a faithful follower of
Augustine. Many philosophers hold that the basic difference between
them is that Aquinas took the Christian *truth* of Augustine and put it in
the *terminology* of Aristotle (rather than the terminology of Plato
which Augustine used). In addition to this there does appear to be a
shift in emphasis, for Aquinas does stress the role of reason more than
Augustine; at least he speaks more about it.

God's existence can be proven. Aquinas recognized that not all
men can prove the existence of God. This is so for many reasons. First
of all the mind is finite, and second it is fallible. In addition most men
do not have the time or inclination to engage in the arduous task of
elaborating a philosophical proof. For these reasons, said Aquinas, it is
necessary for men to first believe in God's existence—otherwise few
men would possess the knowledge of God. According to Aquinas,
belief that God exists is necessary because "the investigation of the
human intellect for the most part has falsity present with it. . . . That is
why it was necessary that the unshakeable certitude and pure truth
concerning divine things should be presented to men by way of faith."
In short, Aquinas held that man is subject to the *noetic* effects of sin,
that is, the influence of sin on his mind. "We are bound to many things
that are not within our power without healing grace—for example to

love God or neighbor. The same is true of believing in the articles of faith." But, continues Thomas, "with the help of grace we do have this power."[2]

Despite the influences of sin, by faith in God's revelation man receives the God-given ability to overcome this deficiency. For "sin cannot destroy man's rationality altogether, for then he would no longer be capable of sin." Aquinas held that with the aid of revelation man can come to understand certain truths about God and even "prove" them philosophically.

Thomas listed "Five Ways" God's existence can be proven, most important of which is the following "Cosmological Argument."
(1) Finite, changing things exist.
(2) Every finite, changing thing must be caused by another.
(3) There cannot be an infinite regress of these causes.
(4) Therefore, there must be a first *uncaused cause* of every finite, changing thing that exists.

Aquinas believed this argument stood validly on philosophically justifiable premises which were not borrowed from revelation. The fact is, however, that no philosophy has ever devised such a proof for the Christian God without first being influenced by the revelation of God in the Bible.

Supernatural truths are known only by faith. Not only is faith *prior* to reason or understanding God's nature, but some truths of God, such as the Trinity and other mysteries of the faith, are knowable *only* by faith. We may know that God exists by reason, but we know that there are *three persons* in one God only by faith.

Revelation alone is basis for belief in God. Aquinas is emphatic that the only true basis for believing *in* God is divine authority or revelation. According to Thomas, "It is necessary for man to receive by faith not only things which are above reason, but also those which can be known by reason. . . . " The best that reason can do is to show *that* God exists; divine authority is the only ground for believing *in* God. Reason and evidence bear on "belief *that*," but not on "belief *in*." Aquinas held that one "would not believe [that] unless he saw

---

2. Thomas Aquinas, *Summa Contra Gentiles*, I. 4. 3–5; *Summa Theologica*, II–II. 2. 6, ad 1.

that [the revelation is] worthy of belief on the basis of evident signs or something of the sort." On the other hand, neither unbelievers nor demons believe *in* God, even though they believe *that* God exists.

Reasonable evidence is support for belief.   Faith in God is not based on evidence but on the authority of God Himself through His revelation. Nevertheless, the believer does find reasonable *support* for his faith in experiential and historical evidences and miracles. As we have noted (chap. 5), faith is more *meritorious* (Heb. 11:6) but reason is more *noble* for a believer (Acts 17:11). Even though one cannot reason *to* belief in God, he can find reasons *for* it. In fact faith may be defined as "the ability to reason with assent." In this way, Aquinas was apparently in accord with Augustine concerning the interrelatedness of reason and revelation.

Faith is prior to reason philosophically; no non-Christian ever offered proofs for the *Christian* God. Yet reason is prior to faith *personally;* one does not believe *in* a God or His alleged Word if he has no evidence *that* it is true.

Conclusion

In the final analysis there is an essential agreement among Christians on the relationship between faith and reason. Most believers attempt to render the credible intelligible. Most reason *about* or for their faith, even if they do not claim to reason *to* it.

The Impossibility of Total Separation

Any attempt to totally disjoin reason and revelation seems unfruitful if not impossible. Even those who hold strongly to a "revelation only" view provide arguments or reasons of some kind to support it. By the same token, any attempt at pure rationalism is frustrated by the fact that *everything* cannot be proved; something is always presupposed or simply believed.

The pure revelationist must recognize that there must be some way of distinguishing a false revelation from a true one. Even the Bible commands the believer to "test the spirits" and "beware of false prophets." But how can one "test" for truth without some truth test?

There is, however, an important distinction to make between the use of reason to discover *whether* something is a revelation of God or not (which is legitimate) and the use of rationalism to determine *what* in the Bible is revelation and what is not (which is not legitimate). Belief is unworthy and blind unless it tests *whether,* but it is unjustifiably dogmatic if it attempts to determine *what* in the revelation is or is not true. For it is foolhardy to believe everything without reason, and it is arrogant to assume everything must be acceptable to our reason before we can accept it as God's Word.

The Basic Confusion: Belief In and Belief That

It seems that much of the debate among Christians concerning which view of faith and reason is correct depends on which view of "faith" one takes. Those stressing "faith *in*" seem to be correct that one needs no reason for it. If God Himself is not a sufficient ground for believing *in* Him, then no amount of rational proof will help. The only "reason" anyone should believe *in* God, say these Christians, is that He is God. On the other hand, if one is speaking about "faith *that*" God exists, it would seem that evidence or reason does bear on this question. For how does one know *that* it is God speaking (rather than one's own imagination) unless he has some way to distinguish truth from falsity?

"Belief that" seems to be logically prior to "belief in." Surely no thinking person should "believe in" something if he has no *reason* to "believe that" it is. Who would march down a church aisle and say "I do" (belief in) before a congregation if he has no evidential or rational grounds for "believing that" someone he loved stood next to him at the altar?

Epistemology and Ontology

There is a difference between *the way* we know reality (epistemology) and *what* we know about reality (ontology). The "revelation only" proponents appear to be ontologically correct that God is the ground of all truth. If God exists and is the source of all truth, then of course all truths come from "the top down." However, epistemologically we must start from "the bottom up" and discover whether or not God does indeed exist. In the epistemological sense, then, reason is prior to revelation, since reason must be used to evaluate whether or not the Bible is indeed a revelation. Once this question is settled, then reason cannot be legitimately used to reject any of that revelation. Reason must take its place *under* revelation and not stand in judgment over it.

There is some truth in all of the basic views on reason and revelation:

(1) "Reason is over revelation" is correct in that reason is epistemologically prior to revelation. The alleged revelation must be tested by reason.

(2) "Revelation is over reason" is right in the ontological sense. God created reason and it must be His servant, not His master.

(3) "Revelation only" is correct in the sense that ultimately and ontologically all truth comes from God.

(4) "Reason only" has some truth, since reason must judge epistemologically whether the alleged revelation is from God.

(5) "Revelation and reason" is correct because it properly assigns a role to each and shows their interrelationship. One should reason about and for revelation, otherwise he has an unreasonable faith. Likewise, reason has no guide without a revelation and flounders in error.

Suggested Readings

Aquinas, Thomas. *Summa contra Gentiles,* 1
Augustine, St. *On True Religion*
Geisler, N. L. *Christian Apologetics,* part one
Holmes, Arthur. *Faith Seeking Understanding*
Van Til, Cornelius. *Defense of the Faith*

18   What Is Meant by "God"?

While most people have a belief in God, their concepts of God vary greatly. Basically, there are five different ways to view God: (1) *Theism* holds to a God who is both beyond and in the world (God is transcendent and immanent); (2) *Deism* believes God is beyond but not in the world (God is transcendent but not immanent, at least not in any supernatural way); (3) *Pantheism* believes God is in the world but not beyond it; in fact, God *is* the world (God is immanent in the universe but not transcendent over it); (4) *Panentheism* contends that God is in the universe the way a soul is in a body. That is, the universe is God's "body" and God is the "soul" of the universe; (5) *Finite godism* believes that God is beyond the universe but is not in supreme control of it (as opposed to theism); the universe is not God's "body" (as opposed to panentheism).

There are, of course, many variations within these five basic

categories of belief. For example, some finite godists believe there is
only one finite god (*finite monotheism*); others believe there are many
finite gods with one who is supreme among them (*henotheism*); and
still others believe there are many finite gods, each with his own sphere
of activity (*polytheism*). But for purposes of classification we may
think primarily about five different concepts of ''God.''

Theistic Concept of God

The theistic concept of God is common to the Judeo-Christian tradition. It is the description of the God of the Bible. Three of the greatest
classical thinkers who articulated this view were Augustine, Anselm,
and Aquinas. Some important modern proponents include Leibniz and,
more recently, C. S. Lewis.

Basic Elements of a Theistic View

There are at least three basic elements of a theistic view of God,
dealing with the nature of God Himself, the nature of creation, and the
nature of God's activity.

God is both beyond and in the world.   According to theism, God
is not the world (or the universe), but is ''beyond'' it or ''more than''
it. That is, God is transcendent. The universe is finite or limited and
God is infinite or unlimited. Further, God is ''in'' the universe. That is
to say, God is immanently present as the sustaining cause of the universe. In short, God's relation to the world is analogous with a painter's relation to his painting. The painter is *beyond* the painting, but he
is also reflected *in* the painting and is the cause of it. However, the
theist would protest that this analogy does not go far enough, for God
is continually, personally, and intimately involved with sustaining the
universe, whereas the painter can walk away from his painting once it
is painted.

Creation is ex nihilo.   Theism holds that the world is dependent on
God for its very existence. Without God's creative sustenance, the
world would not exist. Traditionally this doctrine has been called creation *ex nihilo* (''out of nothing''). By ''out of nothing'' theists mean

that there would have been *nothing* else unless He had made *something*. Theists hold that God did not make the world out of anything else.

The doctrine of *ex nihilo* creation stresses the radical contingency of everything other than God. God alone is a Necessary Being. That is to say, He is a Being that cannot *not* be. Everything else in the universe is contingent (something that *can* not be). But what *can* not be must be *created* in order for it to exist; it must pass from non-being to being. The theist belief means that God did not create the world out of Himself (*ex Deo*), as in pantheism, or out of some preexisting stuff (*ex hulēs*), but out of nothing else (*ex nihilo*).

God can act supernaturally in the world. Supernaturalism is a third implication of theism. The naturalist who does not believe in God considers the universe to be "the whole show." The theist, by contrast, believes that there is more—namely a supernatural realm. The theist believes that the world is radically dependent on an all-powerful God who created and who continually sustains the world. If this is true, it follows logically that such a God can also *intervene* in the world. This kind of special intervention in the world is called a *miracle*.

Theists do not believe that natural laws are fixed and immutable and, hence, inviolable. They believe that natural laws are descriptions of the regular way God works in His creation, not prescriptions of how He must work. Miracles, then, are events manifesting the irregular or special way God works in the world. It is essential to theism to maintain the possibility of miracles. In short, if there is a God who can act in the world, then it follows that there can be special acts of God (miracles) in the world.

Evaluation of Theism

There are several arguments leveled against theism. We will mention here only those which come from "atheologians" or atheists, since the alternate views of God will be discussed below.

God is impossible. There are two kinds of arguments given to show that the theistic conception of God contains contradictions. One form of the argument goes like this: If God were really all-powerful, then He could make a stone so heavy that He could not lift it. But if He could not lift it, then He would not be all-powerful. Hence, no such God can exist.

In response, some theists have noted that God cannot do something which is impossible by definition. As it is impossible to make a circle square or to create another uncreated God, theists hold that it is impossible for God to make a stone that He cannot lift. Other theists explain that the problem begins with the use of a *double negative:* "If God can*not* make a stone that He can*not* lift, then He is not omnipotnent." If we were to put this into logical notation, however, the statement would read: "Any stone which God can make, He can lift." Worded this way, the statement does not present any limitation to God's power.

A second atheistic objection is that God by nature must be self-caused, which is impossible. But according to theism, everything must be caused except God, who is not caused by anything else. The critics counter that if God is the cause of everything, then He must be self-caused. But this is impossible, for one cannot cause his own existence. A cause is ontologically prior to its effect; but a being cannot be ontologically prior to himself. God cannot simultaneously be causing His own existence and being caused.

The theist's response is that this involves a mistaken notion of God. God is not a *self*-caused Being; He is an *un*caused Being. And there is no contradiction in affirming that God is not caused by another or by Himself but is a Necessary Being who always and necessarily existed. Theists also note that not *every* thing needs a cause, only *some* things need causes, namely, contingent or created things. The Creator is not a creature, and so does not need a cause either beyond or in Himself. He

Evil is incompatible with God.   The other major objection to theism is based on the problem of evil. It has often been stated in this form:

(1) If God is all-powerful, He could destroy evil.
(2) If God is all-good, He would destroy evil.
(3) But evil exists.
(4) Therefore, there is no such God.

The theist responds by first pointing out that premise three places an unjustified time limit on God. It says, in effect, that since God has not yet done anything to defeat evil we are absolutely sure He never will. But this cannot be known for certain by any finite mind. It is possible that God will yet defeat evil in the future. This is indeed what Christians believe, for it is predicted in the Bible (Revelation 20–22).

Second, it may be that God cannot destroy evil without destroying freedom—which is acknowledged even by most atheists as good. It may be that the only way God could eliminate evil, strictly speaking, would be to make robots out of men. But if men were reduced to machines, there no longer would be a *moral* world. For a moral world is possible only where there are moral (personal) beings. Without a moral world there would be no *moral* problem of evil.

The theist points out that if we grant the existence of the theistic God we automatically have an answer to the problem of evil. The argument may be stated as follows:

(1) Since God is all-good, He has the *will* to defeat evil.

(2) Since God is all powerful, He has the *power* to defeat evil.

(3) Evil is not *yet* defeated.

(4) Therefore, evil *will* one day be defeated.

That is, the very nature of the theistic God demands that He will do whatever good is possible to be done about the situation. If it does not now *seem* to men as finite beings that this is so, it is because we cannot see the "whole picture" or the "final end."

Deistic Concept of God

Deism is a desupernaturalized form of theism; its view of God is the biblical view of God minus miracles. One famous American deist, Thomas Jefferson, literally cut all the miraculous passages out of the Gospels and pasted the desupernatural remains in a scrapbook. It has since been published as the "Jefferson Bible."

The two major elements of deism are its perspectives on the nature of God and the nature of the world.

God Is Beyond the World

The deist believes in the transcendence of God. God is more than the universe; He is the Creator of the world. In this regard, deism sides with theism in its opposition to dualism (especially the dualism of Greek philosophy) which considers the world and God as two coeternal realities. For the deist, the existence of the world is dependent on God and not independent of Him.

The World Operates Naturally

All deists believe that the world operates by natural law, but they differ on the reason for their naturalism. Some deists hold that God *cannot* intervene supernaturally in the world, while others say that He *will not*. Let us call these, respectively, the "hard" and "soft" forms of deism. We must note that few deists believe that God is disinterested in man, since any God interested enough to make man would surely be interested enough to help him.

The "hard" deist generally adopts a belief in the immutability of natural laws. He believes in effect that God's "hands are tied" by what He has created. This idea has its roots in the deism of the eighteenth century. The phrase from the Declaration of Independence referring to man's "inalienable rights" reflects the strong deistic belief in natural law.

The "soft" deist believes that God's lack of intervention is due to the fact that He does not desire to interfere with our lives. Some believe that it would reflect poorly on God's character as a perfect Creator if He had to constantly "repair" His creation by miraculous intervention. Others simply stress the desire of God that man as a free and autonomous creature "live on his own." But whatever the reason, deists deny the fact of miracles or at least their necessity in God's relation to the world.

It is important to note that deism encourages a natural piety and worship of God (including prayer) as well as a strong emphasis on moral law. Indeed, one of the justifications of the American Revolution was the deistic belief that the moral laws of God are higher than the laws of man. The deists of the eighteenth century believed that it was therefore sometimes necessary to break the tyrannical hold of human government in order not to violate the inalienable rights of "life, liberty and the pursuit of happiness" given by the Creator.

Evaluation of Deism

Aside from the external criticisms of deism that can be seen in contrast to other views of God, there are several internal problems.

Miracles. A central embarrassment to deism is the fact that it denies miracles while it affirms creation, for in a very real sense creation is the greatest miracle of all. Why claim that the God who created the world from nothing does not have the ability to make something out of something (such as wine from water)? This central inconsistency is not easily answered without special pleading.

Natural law.   The deist's strong view of scientific natural law is now discarded by modern science. Scientists no longer speak of unbreakable prescriptive "laws" but of descriptive "maps" or "models." The universe is no longer "closed" but is open to the unusual and the irregular. Therefore, from the scientific point of view there is no reason that miraculous events cannot be a subclass of the "unusual" in nature. To be sure miracles will be more than merely unusual; they will have moral and theological characteristics as well. But a miracle will be *at least* a scientifically unusual event. And in this sense miracles are not unscientific.

Relation of God to world.   Deism is built on a mechanistic model, claiming that God is a machine-maker and the world a machine. However, the theist rejects the mechanical model for a *personal* one. God is related to us more like a father is to his children. And what father would not "intervene" to rescue his children who were in need?

In this regard some theists have pointed out that nothing is really *caused* by natural law. Natural law simply *describes* what is caused by God. For example, a mathematical law tells us that if one has five pennies in his pocket and puts three more pennies in his pocket, he must then have eight pennies there. But that mathematical law can never put any pennies in a pocket. In the same way, a natural law is only a way of describing how God causes things to happen regularly, and is not itself a cause of anything.

Pantheistic Concept of God

Pantheism is often thought of as an "Eastern" concept of God and theism a "Western" concept. This is not strictly true, however, since there are Western pantheistic systems (such as Spinoza and Plotinus) as well as Eastern non-pantheistic ones (such as Sikism).

Types of Pantheism

All pantheisms are actually forms of monism, not pluralism. They hold that reality is ultimately one, not many. More precisely, the many exist in the one rather than the one in the many. In other words, pantheists believe that God encompasses all there is. Within this framework five types of pantheism may be distinguished.

Absolute pantheism.   This form of pantheism teaches that there is only one single reality. The Greek philosopher Parmenides is an example of this view (see pp. 167–68). He argued that there can be only one reality; the rest is illusion. Parmenides reasoned that if two (or more) beings existed, they would have to differ. But there are only two ways to differ: by being (something) or by non-being (nothing). However, said Parmenides, two things cannot differ by being because that is the very respect in which they are identical. And they cannot differ by non-being because to differ by nothing is not to differ at all. Therefore, concluded Parmenides, there can be only one Being. The fact that things seem to be many is nothing but an illusion. Logic demands that all things are one.

Emanational pantheism.   In his neo-Platonic form of pantheism, Plotinus (see pp. 173–74) admitted that there is a multiplicity in the universe, but insisted that all multiplicity unfolds from the absolute simplicity of the One (God). The universe is created *ex Deo* (out of God); the world is an emanation of God. All that exists unfolds eternally and necessarily, as a bud unfolds into a flower. Multiplicity flows from simplicity as radii flow from the center of a circle. God (the One) is beyond all being, knowing, and consciousness. The One is the Absolute Unity which by emanating outward to mind (*Nous*) becomes knowing by reflecting back on its absolutely simple Source (the One). The simple duality of knower and known gives rise to World Soul, which contains all other souls as part of its genera. These souls inform or animate matter, which is the farthest emanation from the center of Absolute Unity. Matter is the most multiple of all, and the closest to absolute Nothing or non-being.

Multilevel pantheism.   In Hinduism, Sankara's pantheism is multilevel. The highest level of reality, *Brahman,* is beyond all materiality and multiplicity. Brahman is revealed or manifest, however, on other levels. The next level down from the highest and absolute level is the Creative Spirit, *Isvara,* who in contrast to Brahman is a personality, a "He." The third level is World Spirit (*Hiranya-garbha*). Unlike Plotinus's emanational pantheism, these three levels are not a cascading emanation, one deriving from the other, but are three descending levels, each of the same ultimate reality (Brahman). The world (*virāj*) is not total illusion, but is simply the lowest degree of reality, grounded in Brahman.

Modal pantheism. The rationalist Benedict Spinoza developed a *modal* form of pantheism. He postulated one absolute Substance in the universe of which all else is but a *mode* or moment. That is, reality is essentially or substantially one, but modally many. Looking at reality "from the top down," as it were, there is only one infinite and necessary Being (God). But viewing reality "from the bottom up," there are multiple aspects or dimensions. These aspects or modes, however, are not separate beings. There is nothing *beyond* infinite Being; all reality is *within* the infinite ocean of Being. The appearance of separateness and multiplicity is due to the deception of sense perception. By the use of self-evident axioms the mind can and does deduce the truth that all reality is one.

Developmental pantheism. Both Plotinus and Sankara held to "vertical" pantheisms, in which the movement from One to many is from "the top down." Hegel, on the other hand, developed a kind of "horizontal" pantheism, wherein Absolute Spirit unfolded itself *developmentally* in history. Hegel believed that history is "going somewhere," headed toward a goal or end. The phenomena or happenings of history are a manifestation of Absolute Spirit.

Hegel's dialectical development of the Absolute goes something like this: When one posits Being, the most that can be said, he has thereby also asserted non-being, the least that can be said. But from the tension of opposites (Being and non-being) emerges *becoming*. World reality, then, is a state of becoming. God's manifestation in history is developmental.

With the exception of Parmenides's absolute pantheism, all other pantheistic views grant that some kind of distinction (though no division or separation) exists in reality. Whether, however, the distinction is emanational, modal, or developmental, each view holds that reality is ultimately One and that the many exist only in the One.

Basic Elements of a Pantheistic View

There are several distinctinve elements involved in pantheism. Each may be seen in contrast to theism.

The nature of God.   God is non-personal. Personality, consciousness, knowledge, and so forth, are lower levels of manifestation. The highest level of reality is beyond personality. It consists of absolute simplicity.

The nature of creation.   Creation is not *ex nihilo,* as in theism; it is *ex Deo* (out of God). There is only one "substance" in the universe and everything is an emanation of it.

Relation of God and the world.   In contrast to theism which holds that God is beyond the universe and separate from it, the pantheist believes that God and the universe are one. God is the All and the All is God. Some pantheists speak of the world as an illusion. In this sense the world is not God; it is nothing. But whatever reality exists in the universe is the reality of God.

Evil is not real.   In the stricter forms of pantheism, evil is a mere illusion, an error of mortal mind. Evil *seems* to be real, but it is not. It is due to the deception of our senses; it is a result of thinking partially rather than wholistically about reality. The Whole is *actually* good; it only *seems* evil if one is looking at a part separate from the Whole.

Evaluation of Pantheism

A number of criticisms have been leveled at pantheism. Some attempt to show it is false; others simply argue that it is not *necessarily* true.

Sense perception.   Absolute pantheism assumes that our senses deceive us. Many philosophers reject this in favor of a more common-sense approach to reality. Why assume that the obvious is totally incorrect? Even the pantheist trusts his senses when he reads a book containing pantheistic truths—otherwise he would not be able to receive the truth through the ink spots on the paper. Furthermore, in everyday existence, pantheists must trust their senses like everybody else. They must step out of the way when they see or hear a train, or else they will be killed.

Parmenides.   Parmenides's rigid pantheism is based on the question-begging assumption that Being must be understood univocally (in entirely the same sense) rather than analogically (similarly). It is, of course, true that there can be one and only one Being *if* Being means entirely the same thing wherever it is found. But the pluralist insists that Being does not mean that all entities are entirely the same, but only *similar*. A finite being is a different *kind* of being (a dependent kind). If, then, Being is understood analogically, there can be more than one being in the universe.

Evil as an illusion. Non-pantheists are bothered by the denial of the reality of suffering, pain, and evil. If evil is not real, they ask, then where does the illusion come from? Why is it so universal and why does it *seem* so real? Why does the illusion of the pain hurt as much as real pain?

Ex Deo creation. If God is a Necessary Being, that is, one that cannot *not* be, and if creation is contingent, then how can creation be "out of" or "part of" God (the Necessary)? Is this not a contradiction in terms?

Panentheistic Concept of God

Panentheism means all-in-God. It is perhaps better understood, however, as God-in-all or God-in-the-world. The panentheist believes that God is in the world much like a soul is in a body.

Basic Characteristics of Panentheism

The most fundamental difference between theism and panentheism is that the former is a monopolar and the latter a bipolar view of God.

Bipolar theism. In one sense the panentheist is a bipolar, or dipolar, theist. He believes that God and the world are two poles of one overall reality. In this regard panentheism is a kind of "halfway house" between theism and pantheism. The theist believes God is *beyond* the world (and in it); the pantheist believes God *is* the world; but the panentheist holds that God is *in* the world.

Alfred North Whitehead and Charles Hartshorne are contemporary proponents of the bipolar view. According to these philosophers, God has a potential pole that is not the world, and an actual pole which is the world. The potential pole is eternal and infinite; the actual pole is temporal and finite. The actual pole of God (His "body") is constantly changing. Hence, the view is sometimes called "*process* theology." Because this changing pole is finite, panentheism can be classified as a form of finite godism (see p. 284).

The panentheist reacts strongly against the classical theist's monopolar God, arguing that such a God could not relate meaningfully (or interdependently) with the world. This is why panentheism is sometimes called neo-classical theism.

God's relation to the world. Theism claims that the world is dependent on God but God is independent of the world. Panentheists, however, insist that God is as dependent on the world as the world is dependent on Him. That is, God and the world are interdependent. The world, they say, is the actualization of God's pure potential pole. These pure potentials (called God's "primordial nature") enter the dimension of space and time and are actualized in the organistic whole of the world (called God's "consequent nature").

Value and evil. All happenings of the world, including all acts of good and beauty, are preserved or "stored" in God's consequent nature. This consequent nature as enriched by the achieved value in the world is sometimes called God's "superject" nature by panentheists. Every event in the world is at any given instant either positively absorbed into ("prehended") or negatively rejected by the organistic whole of the world. That which at a certain moment is incompatible with the unity of the positive whole is called "evil." The same kind of event, however, at a later moment in the ongoing world process may fit into the whole, and thereby be called "good."

Creation is ex hulēs. Panentheism has much in common with ancient Greek dualisms. As in dualism, panentheists hold that both poles are eternal. The physical pole (God's "body") is not created out of nothing. It was always *there;* creation is a continual process of forming it *ex hulēs,* that is, out of matter or stuff already there. In fact, properly speaking, God is not a sovereign Creator of the world (as in theism) but a Director of world process.

Evaluation of Panentheism

There are several aspects of panentheism that have been criticized by other philosophers. The first of these centers on the nature of God.

Bipolar incoherence. The bipolar theist objects to the theistic God's alleged unrelatedness to the world. He claims that an infinite eternal being cannot meaningfully interact with a finite temporal being. The theist responds by pointing out that the problem is not resolved but only intensified by putting these opposites *within* the nature of God. It is one thing to say with the theist that an infinite can *relate* to a finite (made in His image and likeness), but it is quite another to say that God *is* an infinite finite. How can there be a contingent *and* a necessary pole in one God? How can God be at once both eternal and temporal? At this point incoherence, if not contradiction, seems to destroy the panentheistic view of God.

Sacrificing God's supremacy. In panentheism God has been "demoted" from world Creator to cosmic Controller, from a being transcendent over the world to one dependent on it. But how can *both* the world and God be depending on each other for their existence? Is this not as incoherent as suggesting that the bottom brick is holding up the top brick at the same time the top brick is holding up the bottom brick?

Can God actualize His own potential? Aristotle argued that no potential (mere capacity) can actualize itself. Clay does not mold itself into a statue. Some outside force, or actuality, must work on it in order to make a form out of the formless clay. This idea is an argument against the concept of the bipolar God, who seemingly actualizes His own eternal potential in the world.

Whitehead posited "creativity" as the "ultimate principle" in order to avoid the above difficulty, but this only creates another problem. If creativity is the ultimate principle, then there is some reality apart from "God" on which He is dependent. But if there is some reality beyond the panentheistic "God," then this God turns out not to be God at all.

Evil and panentheism. Numerous objections have been leveled against panentheism's view of evil. Philosophers have asked the following questions: (1) Where is all this value panentheists claim is "stored" in God's consequent nature? The world does not *appear* to be getting better. (2) Why is God engaging in the costly "experiment" of creation at our expense if He cannot, because He is finite, even guarantee the outcome? Does He not have even the power to call off the experiment? (3) Who can worship a God who is not infinitely good nor in sovereign control of the situation? (4) How can a purely finite God ever assure us that evil will be overcome?

Finite Conception of God

Actually, finite godism is the broad category of which there are two subcategories: the view that there is a one-pole finite god, and the view that there is a two-pole finite god (panentheism). Since there is a good deal of overlap, we will discuss the monopolar finite godism.

There are numerous examples of the finite god view in the history of philosophy. Plato's Demiurge fits the category, as do Aristotle's 47 or 55 Unmoved Movers or gods who move "the spheres." In modern times David Hume gave impetus to the idea of a finite god by citing the problem of evil. Hume claimed that the best an imperfect world such as we have can prove is a finite and imperfect god. This is the case for two reasons. First, a cause need only be *adequate* to its finite effect. Second, on the principle that cause must resemble its effect, it is necessary to conclude the cause, like its effect, is imperfect. John Stuart Mill, after Hume, also concluded this, arguing that evil's existence makes it highly unlikely that an all-powerful, all-good God exists. William James came to the same conclusion. Perhaps the strongest representation of finite godism in America, however, was Edgar Brightman (1884–1953). Brightman considered God a sort of "struggling hero," who desired good for the world but was unable to guarantee it.

Exposition of Finite Godism

Rather than examine any particular finite godist we will simply summarize some central tenets of the belief. Perhaps the best way to understand finite godism is by way of contrast to theism.

The nature of God is limited.   Theism proclaims God is unlimited in power and goodness. Finitism finds this unbelievable in view of persistent and pervasive evil in the world. If God were all powerful, He could destroy evil, and if He were all good, He would destroy it. But since evil is not destroyed, God must be limited in power and/or goodness. The belief in an absolutely powerful and perfect God does not account for the surd (irrational) evils—the waste, cruelty, and injustice in the natural world, to say nothing of God's lack of intervention in "man's inhumanity to man."

The struggle with evil. According to finite godism, there is a salutary effect of understanding God as finite; it gives us more motivation to fight evil. For if God is all-powerful and the outcome is guaranteed in advance, then why should I struggle against evil? An absolute God can and will take care of it on His own. If, on the other hand, the outcome depends on me and what I do actually counts for eternity, then the limitations of God provide the highest motivations for service.

Evalation of Finite Godism

Numerous objections have been offered to the finite conception of God. We will mention briefly three of them.

A finite God needs a cause. Some have pointed out that a finite god cannot be God at all. The principle of causality states that *every* finite, changing being has a cause. The finite god, then, is only a gigantic creature who himself is in need of an infinite Creator. As Aristotle would say, every finite changing thing passes from a state of potentiality to a state of actuality. But no potentiality can actualize itself—wood cannot build itself into a house. Hence, there must ultimately be an Actualizer of all finite beings who has no potentiality or limitations of His own.

A finite God cannot solve the problem of evil. William James, who was himself a believer in a finite god, focused the problem for finite godism when he wrote, "The world is all the richer for having a devil in it, *so long as we keep our foot upon his neck*" (italics added). But therein is precisely the problem: a finite god cannot guarantee victory over evil. Only an all-good and all-powerful God can assure us that our labor for good is not in vain. And without this assurance, proper motivation for good will sag.

Evil does not prove God finite. Evil and imperfection in the world does not prove God is finite. God may have some good purpose for evil, either (a) known to us, or (b) not known to us but known only to Himself. The only way one can refute this possibility is either (a) know the mind of God, or (b) prove there is no God. Since the anti-theist has no access to the former and no success at the latter, one need not give up the belief in an infinite God. The theist may agree that this is not the best of all possible worlds, but he does insist that it is the best possible *way* to attain the best possible world. That is, it is possible that permitting evil may be the precondition for achieving the greatest good (as immediate pain is often the best way to permanent pleasure).

Conclusion

There are many ways to conceive God. From the Christian point of view God is seen as an infinitely powerful and good Creator and sustainer of the world. He created man with free choice and has allowed evil for a good purpose, that is, to ultimately defeat it and to achieve the greater good. The theistic God is both transcendent over the world and immanent in it. Pantheism, by contrast, sacrifices God's transcendence, while deism denies His supernatural immanence. Finite godism, whether monopolar or bipolar, reduces God to a creature and offers no sure hope of victory over evil. Hence, what the Christian knows by faith in God's revelation, the Bible, is confirmed by human reason.

Suggested Readings

Aquinas, Thomas. *Summa Theologica,* 1
Augustine, St. *The City of God*
Brightman, E. *A Philosophy of Religion*
Hartshorne, Charles. *Philosophers Speak of God*
Ogden, Shubert. *The Reality of God*
Spinoza, Benedict. *Ethics*
Whitehead, A. N. *Adventures of Ideas*

19 Does God Exist?

Before we can answer the question, Does God exist? we must determine which concept of God is in view. In this chapter we will be speaking of the God of Christian theism (see chap. 18). The focus will be on the question whether or not an all-powerful, all-good, infinite Creator and sustainer of the whole universe exists.

There are various postures taken on this question. Some offer what they call conclusive arguments for God's existence. Others offer what they insist are proofs that God does not exist. Still others hold that we cannot know whether or not God exists. Another group of thinkers prefers to suspend judgment on the whole matter. Finally, there are those who say they have good reason to believe that God exists but there is no rationally inescapable proof of His existence.

We Know for Certain God Exists

There are two basic kinds of arguments claiming rational certainty about God's existence. The first is a posteriori, arguing from effect to cause, and the other is a priori, arguing from the idea of God.

The Arguments from Effect to Cause

There are two main forms of this argument: the one begins with ideas and argues to God and the other begins with contingent facts. This first form of the argument is represented by Augustine (354–430) and Descartes (1596–1650).

Augustine's argument from truth.   St. Augustine's form of this argument may be summarized as follows:
(1) There are some necessary and unchangeable truths (ideas) such as 7 + 3 = 10.
(2) But a finite mind, such as mine, is not unchangeable.
(3) An unchangeable truth cannot be based in a changeable, finite mind.
(4) Therefore, there must be an infinite, unchangeable Mind (that is, God) which is the basis for all unchangeable truths.

There are two basic criticisms of this argument. First, some question whether or not any necessary truths about reality exist. Mathematic "truths," they say, are merely definitional and stipulative—they are not informative about reality. The second criticism asks why an immutable idea cannot arise in a finite mind. Why cannot one *think* about an immutable or necessary truth unless one is an immutable or necessary being?

Descartes's argument from the perfect idea.   A later correlative to Augustine's a posteriori argument from "immutable truth" is Descartes's argument from the "perfect idea." His reasoning proceeds this way:
(1) I have imperfect ideas (for example, I doubt).
(2) But one cannot know the imperfect unless he knows the perfect.
(3) However, an imperfect mind cannot be the source of a perfect idea.

(4) Therefore, there must be a perfect Mind which is the source of my idea of perfection.

Objections to Descartes's argument follow similar lines as those of Augustine's. First, some ask why an imperfect mind cannot imagine the idea of perfection. Second, why must doubt be called "imperfect"? Perhaps doubt is an accurate (or, perfect) representation of the actual state of affairs. The third criticism is that both Augustine and Descartes assume, without proof, that ideas need *causes*. This invokes the principle of causality without logical justification.

Aquinas's argument from contingents to God. Another major form of the a posteriori proof for God was presented by Thomas Aquinas (1224–1274). The heart of his reasoning is as follows:
(1) Every effect, by its very nature, needs a cause.
(2) Every contingent being is an effect.
(3) Hence, every contingent being is caused.
(4) Therefore, it follows that the cause of every contingent being is not contingent, but Necessary (that is, God).
The opponents of this proof for God cannot object to the first premise because it is true by definition, that is, an effect by its very nature is something which is caused. It is saying no more than every person with a navel had a mother. The problem comes with proving that the world has a "navel" (i.e., that it is an effect). There are two main objections. First, some ask, must every contingent thing be caused? Why cannot a contingent being simply exist uncaused? Second, even if every individual, contingent being is caused, why must the whole composition of contingent beings be caused? Perhaps the parts are caused but the whole universe is uncaused. Such critics claim that to say otherwise is to be guilty of the fallacy of composition.[1] It is like arguing that a whole mosaic must be the same shape as each piece of tile or glass. Third, some ask why the cause of a contingent being cannot be another contingent being. Why must it be a Necessary Being?

---

1. A fallacy of composition mistakenly views the properties of the whole as having the same characteristics as the parts. ("Each member of the football team is the best in the league; therefore the whole football team is the best in the league." This is not necessarily true.)

Arguments from the Idea of God

The second major attempt to prove God's existence comes from St. Anselm (1033–1109). Since Kant's day this argument has been known as the *Ontological Argument*. There are at least two forms of the argument.

Argument from the idea of the most perfect Being conceivable.   In meditating upon God, Anselm concluded that God by definition must be the most perfect Being possible or conceivable. For if one could conceive of anything more perfect, then that would be God. His argument unfolds this way:
(1) God is by definition the most perfect Being conceivable.
(2) The most perfect Being conceivable cannot lack anything.
(3) But if God did not exist, He would lack existence.
(4) Therefore, God must exist.

This argument has come under two basic criticisms. First, Gaunilo, a monk in Anselm's day, contended that the fact that he could conceive of a perfect island did not mean such an island actually existed. Anselm insisted in response that an island by definition need not be absolutely perfect in the same sense that God by definition must be absolutely perfect. Therefore a "perfect" island might exist in the mind but not in reality, but God, to be perfect, must exist in reality.

The second criticism is held more widely to be decisive. Immanuel Kant insisted that Anselm wrongly assumed that existence is a property of perfection. On the contrary, said Kant, existence is not a predicate or attribute of a concept. Anselm assumed that the concept must be instantiated, that is, that an example of it had to be found in experience or reality. But since existence is not a property of perfection, then positing God's non-existence takes nothing away from the absolute perfection of the idea in one's mind. In short, it is *possible* that God does not exist. And if this is so, then it is not rationally necessary that God exists. No one, therefore, can use this argument to claim that God exists for certain.

Argument from the idea of a Necessary Being.   The second form of Anselm's argument is more difficult to criticize. It has also been held by philosophers such as Descartes, Spinoza, and Charles Hartshorne. We may summarize Hartshorne's argument as follows:

(1) The existence of a Necessary Being must be either (a) an impossible existence, (b) a possible but not necessary existence, or (c) a necessary existence.
(2) It cannot be impossible, since it is not a contradication in terms to affirm "a Necessary Being necessarily exists."
(3) It is a contradiction to affirm that a Necessary Being (one that cannot *not* exist) is a possible Being (i.e., one that *can* not exist).
(4) Therefore, a Necessary Being necessarily does exist.

This argument seems to avoid all the criticisms of the first, since: (1) only a Necessary Being (not a perfect island, or the like) *necessarily* exists, and (2) existence is not being used as a property. In fact, the argument is not based on the concept of God as an absolutely perfect Being but as a *Necessary* Being.

Two other criticisms have been leveled at this form of the ontological argument. The first insists that necessary existence is "smuggled" into the argument under the *concept* of God. Just because a triangle must be *conceived* as having three sides does not mean that a triangle actually exists. Likewise, it is argued, simply because God must be *conceived* as necessarily existing does not mean that He actually exists. Some feel this objection misses the target, because triangles and all other things—*except God*—need not be conceived as actually existing. But if God is necessarily existent, they insist, then He must necessarily *exist*. A Necessary Being by His very nature cannot *not* exist.

A second criticism has been offered by some, namely, that it is *logically* possible that God does not exist. One can argue that granted, *if* a Necessary Being does indeed exist, then it cannot have a possible (i.e., contingent) kind of existence. But it is always *logically possible* that no Necessary Being exists.

Third, some have insisted either that the very concept of a Necessary Being is inconsistent or contradictory. Some even say it is impossible (this will be discussed below under attempted disproofs for God). But such critics claim that one need not claim that the concept is impossible to invalidate the ontological argument. They say that even if it is *possible* that the concept of a Necessary Being is contradictory, then it is possible that such a being does not exist. If it is possible that the concept is contradictory, then it is not necessary that it is non-contradictory. And since no theist has offered a widely held and convincing argument to prove that the concept of a Necessary Being is *necessarily* non-contradictory, then no absolutely certain conclusion follows from the ontological argument; it is always *possible* that the very concept of God is contradictory. In short, if it is rationally possible that the very idea of a Necessary Being is contradictory, then the existence of such a God is not rationally necessary.

We Can Know for Certain God Does Not Exist

Most arguments against the existence of God have not claimed absolute certainty. Here we will consider only those which do make that claim.

Argument from Evil

There are numerous ways to state this argument. We will use two of the more lucid ones.

Argument from the fact of evil.   The most famous form of this argument is as follows:
(1) If God is all-good He will destroy evil.
(2) If God is all-powerful He can destroy evil.
(3) But evil is not destroyed; it still exists.
(4) Hence, there is no such God.

The theist cannot plead that (1) God is finite and therefore cannot overcome evil, nor that (2) God is imperfect and does not care to destroy evil, nor that (3) God was ignorant of what evil might occur when He created the world. For each of these denies some tenet of theism.

The theist does object to this attempted proof on two grounds. First, he suggests that perhaps there is no way (at least for the present) to destroy evil without destroying the greater good of free will. If this is true, then allowing evil to continue may be a necessary concomitant of the fact that God wills the greatest good. Second, the theist objects that the atheist places a time limit on the defeat of evil. The atheist argues in effect that since God has not *yet* defeated evil, He *never* will. But the theist points out that the atheist could not know this unless he were omniscient.

Argument from the opposition of good and evil. Some atheists have attempted to disprove God by insisting that the following propositions, (1) God exists, and (2) Evil exists, are mutually exclusive propositions. God is absolutely good, and evil is opposed to good. Therefore, they cannot coexist.

The problem with this argument is that it assumes a premise which the atheist has not supplied. The missing premise must read, (3) God has no good reason for allowing evil. But the theist can simply point out that (a) God may have a good reason for allowing evil which is known only to Himself, or (b) God may have a good reason known to some but not fully recognized by all, especially by atheists. In view of this, unless the atheist is omniscient, he is not in a position to say there could be no good reason known to God. In fact, if there is an all-good God, then whatever reason He has for evil is automatically a *good* one, since it flows from His good will in accordance with His infinitely good nature. Thus the atheist cannot logically disprove the existence of God on the basis of the existence of evil.

Arguments from the Nature of God

Some atheists have argued that the very nature of God as defined by theists proves that God is impossible. There are several forms of this argument.

A self-caused Being is impossible. Jean-Paul Sartre argues that if God is not caused by another, and if everything is caused, then God must be causing His own existence. But a self-caused Being is impossible. A cause is always ontologically prior to its effect, and one cannot be prior to himself. Put another way, an effect is what is being actualized, and a cause is what is actualizing. But one and the same being cannot be in both of these contrary positions simultaneously. To cause, one must be in the process of actualizing, and to be caused one must be in the state of potentiality. But one cannot be both at the same time.

The theistic response to Sartre is brief. First, God is not a self-caused Being; He is an *un*caused Being. A self-caused Being is impossible, but an uncaused Being is not. Second, theists do not hold that *every* thing is caused, but only that *contingent* things are caused. A

Necessary Being does not need a cause, since He exists by His very
nature.

Necessary existence is impossible.   Another kind of ontological
disproof of God can be summarized as follows:
(1) God by nature must be defined as a Necessary Existent.
(2) But necessity cannot apply to existence; necessity is a characteristic of propositions, not of reality.
(3) Therefore, there cannot be a Necessary Existent.

First, the theist asks how one can know that "necessity" cannot
apply to existence. Perhaps it applies to both propositions and existence. We should not legislate how words can be used; we should
instead listen to how they are being used. As Wittgenstein would say,
language is a game we play, and the game has rules (see p. 51). It is our
task to find out what *is* meant by a word, rather than whether or not it
has meaning.

Second, other theists insist that if the second premise is true, that is,
if necessity cannot apply to existence, then the premise itself must be
false. In short, it is self-destructive, because it claims to be *necessarily*
true about existence. To put this another way, (a) either the statement
in proposition 2, above, is necessarily true, or (b) it is not necessarily
true. If (a), it is self-defeating, and if (b), then a Necessary Being may
indeed exist. In either case, this argument does not disprove God.

Third, some claim that this attempt to disprove God's existence
misunderstands what theists mean by necessity. The necessity a theist
claims is *ontological,* but not logical. It begs the question to say that
the theist cannot use the term "necessity" in this way but must use the
term only in a logical sense.

God has impossible attributes.   Some have insisted that God cannot be all-powerful. If He were all-powerful, then He could do
anything—even make a stone so heavy that He could not lift it. But if
He could not lift it, then He would not be all-powerful. This objection,
of course, is easily answered by noting that God cannot do what is
impossible by definition (see p. 274).

Other forms of this argument have been offered in an attempt to
show that *two* or more of God's attributes are incompatible. How can
God be *free,* for example, and still be a *Necessary* Being? But clearly

God is necessary with regard to what He *is,* and free in respect to what He *does.* Still others would claim that God cannot be all-loving *and* all-just. How can He really love all men and yet justly punish them forever in hell? But the theist responds that a truly loving father will not force his children to obey his commands and desires when they come of age. It is truly just *and* loving to allow free creatures to choose their own destiny.

There have been other attempts to show that two or more of God's attributes are incompatible (for example, that God is a spirit and yet acts in the physical world). But these do not amount to disproofs of God—they simply lead to a modification of the theist's *concepts* of God. Sometimes such arguments are simply category mistakes (see p. 19) that incorrectly assume what is true of finite creatures must also be true of an infinite Creator.

Argument from the Nature of Freedom

Some have contended that God cannot exist because man is free. Jean-Paul Sartre argued this way:
(1) If God exists, then all is determined by Him.
(2) But if all is determined, then nothing is free.
(3) However, I am free.
(4) Hence, God does not exist.
Theists respond in several ways to the loopholes in this argument. First, strong determinists, such as Jonathan Edwards (1703–1758), have denied that man is free in the sense Sartre contends. Men are "free," says Edwards, only in that they may do what they *desire,* but it is God who gives them their desires (see chap. 13). Other less deterministic thinkers (soft determinists) insist that *both* are true: God causes or determines what happens, *and* men freely choose how to act. God is the primary cause, and men are the secondary causes of what they freely choose. Another response is that God causes all things by His wisdom operating through human freedom, but not by His power coercing it. Some theists view God as the Creator and men as "sub-creators." They insist that God sovereignly wills to give men freedom, knowing how they will exercise it. Thus He remains in control by His omniscience. In any event, it is clear that there are a number of ways to avoid the conclusion that God does not exist if men are free.

We Cannot Know If God Exists

The view that we know God exists is called *theism*. The position that we know God does not exist is called *atheism*. The belief that we cannot know whether God does or does not exist is labeled *agnosticism*.

Two Kinds of Agnosticism

One form of agnosticism claims that we *do not* know if God exists; the other insists that we *cannot* know. The first we will call "soft" and the second "hard" agnosticism. We are not here concerned about "soft" agnosticism, since it does not eliminate in principle the possibility of knowing whether God exists. It says in effect, "I do not know whether God exists but it is not impossible to know. I simply do not have enough evidence to make a rational decision on the question." We turn, then, to the "hard" form which claims that it is impossible to know whether God exists.

Impossibility of Knowing God Exists

Most modern forms of agnosticism have their roots in the thought of Immanuel Kant. While Kant himself *believed* in God, he felt, nonetheless, that no one could *know* God existed. There are, he felt, two basic reasons for this rational agnosticism.

Appearance/reality disjunction.   Everything we know comes to us through our senses a posteriori, but it is formed and categorized a priori by the categories of the understanding (see p. 89). The mind without the senses is empty, and the senses without the mind are blind. That is, the content or "stuff" of knowledge is provided through sensation but the final form or structure of knowledge is given by the mind.

This being the case, there is no way for the mind to *know* reality (the *noumena*). We know things only *after* they are formed by the mind, not before. Only the thing-as-it-appears-to-me is known, not the thing-in-itself. In Kant's terms, one can know only the *phenomena,* but not the *noumena*. And since God is a noumenal reality, then it follows that God cannot be known by pure reason.

Kant argued that all attempts to know God by pure reason fail because they illicitly assume an ontological argument. They may begin from experience of the phenomena (as in the cosmological argument), but sooner or later they go beyond experience by assuming (illegitimately) an ontological concept of a Necessary Being. But this is precisely what cannot be done, because there is "a great gulf fixed" between noumena and phenomena. We cannot get beyond appearance to reality. Hence, any such argument, cosmological or otherwise, is doomed to failure.

Antinomies of reason. There is a second reason Kant gives for the impossibility of rationally knowing or proving God. He points out that contradictions result whenever one assumes that the categories of the mind apply to reality. These paradoxes of pure reason prove that reason has wandered "out of bounds." The proper role of reason is within the phenomena of experience. Reason cannot penetrate the noumenal thing-in-itself. One can know only *that* the world-in-itself is, but not *what* it is.

Kant gives a number of examples of these antinomies of reason. Each thesis is opposed by an antithesis, both of which must be posited but neither of which is compatible with the other when applied to the real world. For instance, *thesis:* there must be a first cause of the world, since everything must have a cause; but, *antithesis:* there cannot be a first cause, for if everything needs a cause then so does the first cause, and so on infinitely. Hence, we are left with the impossibility that opposites are true. Since this is impossible we must give up the hope that reason applies to noumenal reality. We are left, then, with complete agnosticism. Reality cannot be *known.* And what applies to reality as a whole includes God in particular.

We must live as if there is a God. Giving up the knowledge of God is not the same as giving up God. In fact, Kant was a devout believer in God. He insisted that men could not—or at least should not—live without God. All men, Kant argued, seek happiness in harmony with duty. But such is not attainable without positing the existence of God. Hence, what we cannot prove by pure reason we must posit by practical reason. That is, we must *live as if* there is a God. However, we must never by theoretical reason try to prove the existence of God. We must remain agnostic because of the very nature of the knowing process.

Evaluation of Agnosticism

There are three basic criticisms of the "hard" form of agnosticism.

Not all reasoning leads to antinomies.   It may very well be that antinomies prove that some reasoning is not valid about reality. Zeno's paradoxes, for example, may prove that some reality (for example, the world of space and time) is not infinitely divisible. However, not all reasoning need end in antinomies. Indeed, some of the very examples Kant uses are not genuine antinomies. In these cases either the thesis or antithesis is not true, or else an underlying premise is false. For instance, Kant assumes that the principle of causality implies that *everything* must have a cause. But if one assumes that only *contingent things* need a cause, then contradiction does not follow.

Basic categories of the mind must apply to reality.   Implicit in Kant's argument from antinomies to agnosticism is the premise, "No contradictory premise can be true about reality." This is precisely why Kant says that pure reason cannot apply to reality—because it ends in contradiction. But if the rational law of non-contradiction applies to reality, then there is at least one principle of the understanding that applies to reality. In fact, since the principles of identity and excluded middle (see p. 168) are inseparably related to the principle of non-contradiction, Kant allows that at least these principles of reason apply to reality. Further, Kant admits we know *that* reality is there (though we do not know *what* it is) and that it is the cause of the phenomena we do know. But if he claims that the *noumena* is causing the *phenomena,* then he has himself applied the principle of causality to the noumenal realm.

Inconsistent nature of total agnosticism.   Another way to state this objection to Kant's agnosticism is to point out that it is inconsistent to affirm that one *knows* that he cannot know anything about reality. How can one know this without some knowledge of reality? If the agnostic insists that he is not making any positive statement about reality but only a negation (that he *cannot* know it), then this too is impossible. Every negation is actually a definite statement which implies some positive knowledge. How can one know for certain what reality is not unless he knows something of what it is by contrast?

Some agnostics may claim that they cannot know infinite reality (that is, God) but only finite reality. But even here there are several problems. First, the very denial of knowledge of an infinite implies some knowledge of the infinite. One must know what cannot be denied of God if he knows what can be denied of God. Further, when one says, "I cannot know the Infinite," another may justly ask, "You cannot know *what*?" If the agnostic does not have some knowledge of the infinite, then the very denial is meaningless, since he cannot know even the meaning of the term *infinite* in his denial.

If the denial means only that one cannot know the infinite infinitely, then most theists would readily agree. Man is finite and hence cannot know in an infinite way. But this limited agnosticism, which humbly admits it does not have an infinite understanding of the infinite, is a long way from denying *all* knowledge of the infinite.

We Must Suspend Judgment

The skeptic neither affirms nor denies God's existence. And in contrast to the agnostic, the skeptic does not say it is impossible to know. For agnosticism too is a form of dogmatism—negative dogmatism. The skeptic claims to take a much more tentative attitude toward knowledge. He is not sure that God is or is not, nor is he sure whether man can or cannot know God. In fact, the complete skeptic is not sure of anything (see pp. 84–87).

Justification of Skepticism

In the ancient world skepticism grew out of Platonism. Platonic dialogue was reduced to debate and debate degenerated into doubt. It was believed that the two sides of any topic could be so debated that a stalemate would inevitably result. This being the case, the wise man would suspend judgment on all truth questions.

Skeptics developed a number of *tropes* (ways of arguing, see p. 86) which were used as justifications of their doubt. A brief restatement of these will shed light on the position.

Relativity of perceptions. A standard source of doubt through the ages has been the fact that there are numerous perspectives one can have on any given subject. Depending on the angle of perception, a square plane may look like a rhombus or even a straight line (if viewed from the edge). Who, then, is to say that his particular perspective is the true or correct one?

Deception of sense perception.   Our senses often deceive us. An oar looks crooked when it is partially submerged in water. But the skeptic carries this observation a step further, claiming that if we are sometimes deceived then we may always be deceived. In view of this the wise man does not trust his senses. But since the senses are the source of all our knowledge about the world, it follows that we must be skeptical about everything.

Equipollence of all arguments.   Any given issue has at least two sides; each side can be argued with equal sophistication. In the final analysis, then, one cannot be sure of either side. Every thesis has an antithesis. The paradox of human reason demands that we doubt the truth of either.

Impossibility of knowing reality.   At best we know only appearances, not reality. But with only surface knowledge one cannot attain any underlying essential truth. The skeptic holds that doubt about the true essence of things is necessary.

We cannot know caused connections.   Many skeptics have attacked the principle of causality, which non-skeptics use to discuss ideas beyond the world of their experience. The modern skeptic, David Hume, insisted that causal connections were based on "constant conjunction." We see things joined in experience, but we can never rationally justify that they are connected in reality. Simply because the sun always rises *after* the rooster crows does not mean it rises *because* the rooster crows. This is called the *post hoc* fallacy. If this is so, says the skeptic, then we must ever remain skeptical about reality.

Limitation of knowledge.   All finite knowledge is fragmentary. But fragmentary knowledge can never be the basis of any certain conclusions. We all recognize that an innocent party can appear guilty based on partial evidence. One must have all the facts to be sure.

Response to Skepticism

The skeptic is surely partially correct, for *some* knowledge is relative and tentative. But it does not follow from this that *all* knowledge is inadequate. There are several reasons for rejecting skepticism.

Skepticism does not suspend judgment on all things. In the final analysis, skepticism is as dogmatic as any other view. The skeptic is *certain* that skepticism is true. Or, put another way, he will suspend judgment on everything *except his skepticism*. He doubts everything but the need to doubt everything.

Why doubt, if there is no reason to doubt? There are some legitimate reasons to doubt some things. When one has no evidence, very slim evidence, or equal opposing evidence, then doubt may very well be called for. But when one has overwhelming evidence or even good evidence, then there is no reason to doubt. Why should one doubt that other people exist or that the world exists? Why should one doubt his own existence?

Absolute doubt is impossible. Both Augustine, who at one time was a skeptic, and Descartes, who engaged in methodological skepticism, concluded that absolute skepticism is self-defeating. Augustine said that one must exist before he can doubt. Descartes saw that the more one doubts, the more certain he is that he is doubting. So the greater the doubt, the greater the certainty.

No one lives total skepticism. One of the practical arguments against skepticism is that not even the most ardent skeptic can actually *live* his skepticism. He does not suspend judgment on whether his food is safe to eat, or else he would soon poison himself. Nor does he suspend judgment on whether he should walk on a freeway, or else he would soon be hit by a car. But some ask, what good is a philosophy that cannot be lived? Even the Scottish skeptic David Hume admitted that he would sometimes have to take release from his skeptical thoughts by playing a game of backgammon.

If skepticism is not a necessary or even proper attitude toward truth, then the door is open for anyone who wishes to look for good evidence for the existence of God. This leads us to our last position.

We Have Sufficient Reason to Believe in God

Even if there were no rationally airtight arguments for God's existence, there may be some very good reasons for believing in it. Very
few, if any, scientific theories are beyond falsification, but many of
them (such as the theory of gravitation) have very good evidence to
support them. Many Christians hold that belief in God functions like a
scientific model—it is internally consistent and adequately explains all
the facts of experience. If so, then there are grounds to claim there is
good reason to believe in God.

Other theists point out that the objections to theistic arguments are
indecisive. Even if the theistic arguments are not logically necessary,
they may be sound. If, for example, we grant that a contingent being
exists, then how can we avoid concluding that there is a Necessary
Being? Is it reasonable to believe that something comes from nothing?
If not, then, since something exists, it follows that Something has
always existed. And if there is a contingent being, then Something
must necessarily be a ground for its contingency. For by definition a
contingent being cannot be uncaused or self-caused; it must be caused
by another. But *all* beings cannot be caused; one Being must be the
Causer. And this Being cannot be contingent, or it too would be
caused. It seems reasonable, then, to conclude that a Necessary Being
exists.

Those who object that the universe as a whole could be this Necessary Being are using the word *universe* differently than the scientist
does. Such critics cannot mean the *observed* universe, or the universe
which is subject to *change* or subject to the Second Law of Ther-
modynamics (that the amount of available energy is decreasing). In all
of these cases the scientist speaks of a changing, limited and, therefore, contingent universe. But the critics must mean *universe* in the
sense of an eternal, unchanging "whole" which is necessary and uncaused, and is *more than all the finite parts* of the universe. But in this
sense they have simply replaced what the theist means by "God" or a
Necessary Being with the word "Universe."

One does not defeat the reasonableness of the theist's argument for a
Necessary Being by renaming it "the Universe." Either the atheist
claims that something comes from nothing or else that something always was. The atheist has a choice. He may assert that all the contin-

gent parts of the universe are *equal* to the whole and therefore the whole is also contingent (since adding up contingents only yields a contingent). Or, he may claim that the whole universe is *more* than all the parts; the parts are caused or dependent but the whole is not caused—it is simply there (as Bertrand Russell said). But once the atheist admits there is an eternal, uncaused something which is more than all the finite parts of the universe and is the cause upon which they are dependent, then he has acknowledged what the theist has argued for all along, namely, God.

Once the atheist has acknowledged this much, all that remains is to see whether this Necessary Being is personal, good, and so on. The theist appeals to the principle that "nothing comes from nothing." Since there are personal beings in the universe, and since the personal cannot arise from the non-personal, nor the good from non-good, then the necessary ground of all personhood must itself be personal and good. And since this Necessary Being is infinite, then He must be infinitely good. Despite the fact that this argument may not *convince* all unbelievers, there is no reason to say that the believer does not thereby have good reason to believe in God.

Conclusion

There are five major positions regarding the existence of God. Those who attempt to prove that God's existence is a logical necessity beg the question by assuming the existence of God, or at least the existence of *something* from which they infer God's existence. Further, both agnosticism and skepticism are self-defeating positions. The theist, therefore, is open to offer good reasons for his belief in the existence of God. Such good reasons are supplied by the arguments for an infinite, necessary, and personal Being which theists call "God."

Suggested Readings

Anselm, St. *Proslogion*
Geisler, N. L. *Christian Apologetics,* chs. 12, 13
Hick, John. *The Existence of God*

Hume, David. *Dialogues Concerning Natural Religion*
Kant, Immanuel. *The Critique of Pure Reason*
Lewis, C. S. *Mere Christianity*, part one
Plantinga, Alvin. *The Ontological Argument*
Tennant, F. R. *Philosophical Theology*, vol. 1

20 How Can We Talk About God?

If God is infinite and our language is finite, then how is it possible to engage in meaningful talk about God? For if language is empirically grounded and God is a trans-empirical Being, then it would seem that no talk about God can be truly descriptive. There are three basic answers to the problem of the nature of religious language. Some say it is *equivocal,* that is, the meaning of words as we understand them is applied to God in an entirely different way; others claim meaning must be *univocal,* applied in entirely the same way; and still others contend it is *analogical,* applied in a similar way. (Some prefer a twofold classification of *literal* and *symbolic.* In this case, univocal and analogical would be subdivisions of "literal.")

God-Talk Is Equivocal

All those who insist God-talk is equivocal claim that an infinite God always transcends the ability of finite language to express Him. God-talk is not descriptive of the way God *is*. Some of these thinkers say God-talk informs us of what God *does*. Others insist it can only reveal what God *is not*. And still others claim God-talk is only about the way God desires us to *live,* or merely to *think* about Him.

Negative God-Talk

Plotinus (see chap. 11) believed that God-talk is basically negative. This perspective is called the *via negativa* (the way of negation). Plotinus argued that God is absolutely and simply One; He is beyond all duality. But all our statements about God have a duality (subject and predicate). Further, God is simple but our ideas about Him are multiple; we give many attributes to God but He is One in essence. Plotinus claimed that since all our ideas are finite forms, and since God is infinite and beyond all form, then there is no way we can talk positively about God. Even the word *One* as applied to God means "not many," a negation.

Many other philosophers, especially mystics, agree with Plotinus. They insist that God can be "known" only intuitively by mystical union. But such an intuition is dependent on prior negation. We must negate all finite conceptions of God until we evoke a pure intuition of His majesty. Such an intuition necessarily defies any positive description.

The problem with this position is that all negations imply some positive knowledge. One cannot say God is "not-that" unless he has some knowledge of the "that." Further, how would one know what does not apply to God unless he knows what does apply? In short, negations imply prior affirmations.

Extrinsic Analogy

There is another approach to God-talk in Plotinus that has been adopted even by some Christian thinkers. Plotinus argued that we call God "good" only because He causes goodness in things. We call God "good" in the same way that we call food "healthy"—food itself does not possess health, but food *causes* health in an organism. Likewise, we call God "good," "true," and so forth, not because He really *is* these things but because He *causes* them in others. As a matter of fact, argued Plotinus, the Cause of Being cannot have being, for "He had no need of Being, who brought Being to be.'' Creation, then, is not *like* the Creator. There is only an extrinsic, causal relationship between God (the Cause) and creation (His effects).

Christian thinkers have pointed out several problems with this equivocal view of God-talk. First, it conflicts with the biblical claim that creatures are "like" God, or made "in his image" (Gen. 1:26; 9:6; James 3:9). Second, it leads to complete agnosticism about the nature of God, and we have already noted that total agnosticism is inadequate (see chap. 19). Finally, some ask how God can give perfections He does not have to give. How can He produce what He does not possess? Can something come from nothing?

Symbolic Language

Perhaps the most common form of the argument for equivocal God-talk is the insistence that religious language is purely symbolic, mythical, parabolic, metaphoric, or the like. Some say that religious language contains qualified "models" which are evocative but not descriptive. Others consider such language a collection of "ciphers." These thinkers agree that God-talk cannot be literal.

At the core of this position are two main arguments. First, literal God-talk would be idolatrous. The existentialist Martin Buber (1878–1965) contended that idols are idols whether they are metal or mental. Ideas or concepts can cause "the eclipse of God." Sören Kierkegaard insisted that since God is "wholly Other"; our attempts at language about Him are like arrows shot in His direction—they are always far short of their target.

Second, only symbolic or mythological language is religiously *evocative*. The neo-orthodox theologian Emil Brunner (1889–1966) argued that a belief in the Bible as a propositionally descriptive revelation of God is "Bibliolatry." It is worshiping a "paper Pope." According to Brunner, the Bible is only a personal revelation geared to evoke a personal response from us. Paul Tillich (1886–1965) insisted on the symbolic nature of God-talk, since nothing from our empirical experience is literally true of the "Ground of Being" (God). Karl Jaspers (1883–1969) spoke of preserving myths and ciphers of God because they are "openings to Transcendence," whereas objective language has no religious value. Common, then, to all these positions is the belief that religious language is not *descriptive* of God but is merely *evocative* of an experience with God. Only subjective, metaphorical, or mythical language can call one "beyond" the empirical to the transcendent.

There is some validity to this position. First of all, surely straightforward, unqualified literal talk from the finite world does not have a one-to-one correspondence with the infinite, transcendent God. No finite concept can capture the infinite. Second, symbolic language, that is, metaphors and the like, play a very important function in religious language. Even though they are not *literally* descriptive of God, they nevertheless evoke a response in the reader/hearer to the object of religious language (God). And since gaining a response from the reader/hearer is an important purpose of God-talk, it is essential that the metaphorical aspect be preserved.

However, there is a serious problem in claiming that *all* God-language is *purely* metaphorical or symbolic. Tillich himself recognized this, and was later forced to acknowledge that there must be at least one non-symbolic truth about God (namely, He is "Being" or "Ground of Being"). For unless one knew that something was literally true, how could one know that everything else was *not* literally true (that is, symbolic)? As others have noted, even a metaphor, such as "God is a rock," must have some literal truth behind it. For while God is not finite or limited in extension as a rock is, He is nonetheless enduring or unmovable.

Equivocal God-talk is described in several other ways. Some speak of religious language as "pointers," "parables," or "myths." What all of these have in common is the belief that human language does not inform us about what God *is* but only about how He desires us to live.

Activity Language

The medieval Jewish philosopher Moses Maimonides (1135–1204) claimed that religious language, although largely negative, does possess a "positive" element. It is a positive description not of God's attributes but of His *activity*. It does not inform us about God's essence (which is unknowable) but about His *actions*. What God *is* remains unknowable; only what God *does* can be known. By activity language we can know that God *does* good, and *speaks* truth. We may not conclude, however, that God *is* goodness and truth.

But here again we are left with total agnosticism. How do we know we cannot know anything about God? How can we negate things about Him without prior knowledge of His positive attributes? If what God does is no indication of what He is, then He could *be* evil even though He *does* good.

From the Christian perspective, however, we do know many positive things about God. The Bible says God *is* love (I John 4:16); He *is* holy (Lev. 19:2); He *is* truth, and so on. Even though we cannot comprehend Him completely (I Cor. 13:12), we nevertheless do apprehend Him clearly (Rom. 1:23). What obscures God is not so much man's finiteness but his sinfulness. Men are blinded by sin (II Cor. 4:4) and "suppress the truth" (Rom. 1:18, RSV).

Univocal God-Talk

In view of the agnosticism that is essential to equivocal God-talk, many Christian thinkers have insisted on the *univocal* nature of religious language. The essential arguments for this view were laid down in the thirteenth century by the Franciscan thinker Duns Scotus (1265?–1308).

Arguments for Univocal God-Talk

In its basic form, this is an "either/or" argument. Either we have a univocal understanding of the terms we use of God, or agnosticism results. If the term "good," for example, does not have the *same* (univocal) meaning when applied to both God and man, then we cannot know what it means when applied to God. And if *all* God-talk is nothing but terms with equivocal meanings, then we know nothing about God.

If our concepts are not equivocal, and if one rejects univocal concepts, then there remains only one alternative: analogical concepts. However, argued Scotus, if there is even an element of "sameness" in an analogy, between meanings of terms applied to men and applied to God, then this element is really univocal. If, on the other hand, the analogy has no identifiable element of sameness, then it is neither univocal nor truly analogical, and we must conclude that the two meanings are really equivocal.

In other words, we must either have a univocal concept whose meaning can be clearly defined and applied to God as well as creatures, or else we are launched into an infinite regress of non-univocal concepts. Thus we must conclude that sooner or later one must have a clear univocal concept of terms which may be used of both God and creatures without changing their meaning. Without this basic tenet, we must conclude that theological language, or language applied to God, is uninformative.

Platonic Univocal Language

For Platonists, religious language is a kind of *logos* (discourse) about the *theos* (God). Plato had described reality as consisting in a set of Forms which are a subset of the ultimate Form (the *agathos,* or Good). When one speaks correctly about the Good (which Christians later identified as God), then the form of his language gives the very essence of the ultimate Good (or God). That is, the very ideas expressed in our language correspond with the Ideas (Forms) in the spiritual world (or, as Christians would have it, in the mind of God). There is, then, a kind of one-to-one correspondence between the true ideas in our mind (as expressed in language) and the Ideas in God's mind. The great Christian Platonist, Augustine, used the following illustration. We have certainty, he argued, because the idea God has produced in our minds by divine illumination is the exact replica of the original idea in His mind, just as the impression of a ring on a wax tablet is the exact replica of the ring.

Evaluation of Univocal God-talk

The Platonic implications of the univocal view of religious language have occasioned both ancient and modern criticisms. Thomas Aquinas summarized the ancient criticisms of univocal predications of God in the following arguments.

Criticisms.   First, no effect of God is equal to its cause. All effects (creatures) exist in a multiple way, whereas God is absolutely simple. Hence, there is no way a quality of a creature existing in a multiple way can be applied univocally (in entirely the same way) to the simple Creator.

Second, no creature has the same mode of being as God. Each

creature is contingent, while God is necessary in His existence. It follows, then, that "being," or any characteristic of being cannot describe God and creatures in entirely the same way.

Third, to describe two or more entities one must speak of what they have in common, or in what way they differ specifically, such as by some property or accident (that is, by what qualities they *possess* but not what they *are* essentially). But since God does not share any essence with another (He is the only infinite, necessary Being), and since He has no accidents (whatever a Necessary Being "has," He *is* essentially), then it follows that nothing can be said univocally of God and creatures.

Fourth, whatever describes two entities univocally is simpler than both, at least in theory. For the characteristic common to both is simpler than both things which have it in common. But nothing is simpler than God, either in reality or in theory. Hence, nothing can be said univocally of God and creatures.

Fifth, whatever describes two entities belongs to them both by way of participation. That is, they both participate in the common attribute describing them. But God does not participate in any common nature; He transcends all else. Therefore, nothing can be said univocally of God and creatures.

Sixth, God is prior to all else and all else is subsequent to Him. That is, God *is* Being, essentially, but all other things *have* being by dependence on Him. But if "being" describes God essentially (by priority), and describes all other things only by subsequence, it is certainly not used univocally.

At the basis of these arguments is another reason Aquinas rejected univocal God-talk: the fact that God is infinite and creatures are finite. No finite characteristic can be applied univocally to an infinite Being. Univocal God-talk would mean that either God is finite or our concepts are infinite, which are both impossible. And finite concepts cannot have a one-to-one correspondence to an infinite God.

In addition to the criticisms of Aquinas, univocal God-talk has had some hard times in the wake of Wittgenstein's rejection of the Platonic, essentialistic view of language. According to Wittgenstein, there are no universal forms of meaning. The same word or concept can have different meanings in different contexts. Meaning is determined by usage, and usage is based in different "forms of life" (see p. 51). If this is so, then there are no eternal and essential forms of meaning represented by language which can be univocally applied to God. The contemporary view of language is that speech functions more like a *mythos* than a *logos*. That is, language, particularly God-language, has more disclosure power than descriptive power.

Even though this criticism may in its extreme forms imply a kind of agnosticism about God, it seems safe to say that there is at least an element of truth in it. A word may indeed have differing meanings in different contexts. Sometimes the same *sentence* differs in meaning in different contexts. The Platonic idea of a univocal concept whose Form remains constant does not fit our experience with language. Further, whatever form our finite expressions may have, it does seem to be a gross form of verbal idolatry to suppose that such forms can convey to us the very essence of an infinite and transcendent God. The only form that corresponds univocally to an infinite Being would be the very infinite essence of God Himself. And this essence no finite mind, ideas, or words can capture.

Contributions of the position.   Despite the fact that univocal one-to-one descriptions of God seem impossible, there are two important contributions made by this position.

First, as we concluded in the above discussion about negative God-talk, there must be some positive element in our knowledge of God. Every negative presupposes a positive. But if there is a positive element, then it must be understood univocally or else it has no positive content.

Second, if God-talk is to avoid complete agnosticism, then there must be a univocal element in it. Scotus clearly showed that analogous concepts will not suffice. They reduce either to agnosticism (by way of an infinite regress) or to a univocal concept as the basis of the analogy which provides the "sameness."

In brief, if the concepts applied to God are not univocally *defined*, then they are indeed equivocal. They must be *understood* univocally, or else they are actually different concepts represented by one word (as the word *bark* represents two different concepts). The *understanding* of the basic meaning of every term appropriately applied to God must be the same understanding of the meaning when used in reference to creatures. If, for example, the term "being" is defined as "that which is" when it is used of a man, then it must be understood to have that same meaning when applied to God. Without this common meaning there can be no positive description of God. But this univocal definition or meaning cannot be ascribed to God in a univocal way, that is, without qualification. For God does not exist *in the same way* that creatures do.

Analogous God-Talk

If both equivocal and univocal descriptions are not viable forms of God-talk, as has been claimed by many critics, there remains only one alternative—analogy. But, as has already been indicated, analogous concepts reduce to agnosticism or else to univocal concepts. Where, then, does this leave us? In skepticism? As we will observe, skepticism is not the inevitable answer.

The Meaning of Analogous God-Talk

The answer seems to be a combination of univocal concepts and analogical *judgments* (or *predication*). That is, terms used of God must be *defined* the same (univocal) way but cannot be *applied* the same (univocal) way. In fact, before the terms can be appropriately applied to God, all finitude must be negated or purged from them. In short, the characteristic signified by the term is univocally understood, but the *mode* of signification (that is, the finite context in which we know the term) cannot be applied to an infinite God. For example, goodness as we know it is in a finite form (mode). Only when we purge from our concept of goodness the finite form or context in which we know it can we apply goodness as such to God. In short, what goodness is by its very nature can be appropriately applied to God, but how goodness is known by us cannot be applied to Him. Since we know goodness only in a finite mode, we must negate the finite "package" and apply the pure perfection to God in an infinite way.

Criticisms of Analogy

The contemporary philosopher Frederick Ferré has laid down the basic criticisms of the use of analogy in religious language. He gives five arguments against it.

First, says Ferré, why do analogists select some qualities from creation and reject others? Why not assume God is responsible for all characteristics found in creation? That is, why apply only goodness and truth to God? Evil and ugliness are also found in the world He made.

Second, Ferré points out that any word torn from its finite context becomes entirely empty of meaning. Meaning is inseparably linked to the limited circumstances from which it arises. Therefore, no term can be applied to an infinite God without losing all of its significance.

Third, Ferré argues that analogy rests on the unjustified philosophical assumption that an effect must resemble its cause. However, effects often do not resemble their causes. Broken glass, for example, does not resemble the hammer that breaks it. Those who argue for a similarity between cause (God) and effect (world) overlook the fact that "cause" as understood in this world is finite and as applied to God means infinite. This is an equivocation.

Fourth, Ferré contends that analogy is based on an alleged similarity of beings. But since the similarity cannot be expressed univocally (for this would depart from analogy), and it cannot be expressed analogically (for this would launch an infinite regress, as Scotus showed), there is no basis for the alleged similarity of beings.

Others have stressed similar points against analogy. The most common objection is refutation by counter-example. It is argued that many effects obviously do not resemble their causes. Why, then, should we assume God is like the world He made? Mosquitoes cause malaria but do not resemble malaria. Hot water causes eggs to harden, but water itself is not hard.

Qualifications of Analogy

Before addressing the specific objections to analogy it may be helpful to note the limitations placed on analogy by some theists.

First, they insist that there is only a basis for analogy when there is an *intrinsic causal relation,* not simply an extrinsic one. Hot water has only an extrinsic relation to the hardness in the boiled egg, but it has an intrinsic relation to the heat in the egg. Heat causes some things (such as eggs) to harden, but causes other things (such as wax) to become soft. Since these are opposite effects, it is obvious that the relationship is only extrinsic, since a cause cannot possess opposite characteristics essentially. But since heat does communicate heat there is an intrinsic relation between the heat in the water and the heat in the egg.

Second, there is a basis for similarity between God and creatures only when the characteristic caused is essential and not merely accidental to the effect. For instance, musicians give birth to non-musicians (*per accidens,* that is, accidentally), but humans generate humans (*per se,* that is, essentially). It is accidental to one's humanness whether he is tall or short but it is essential to humanness that one is a rational being. Therefore, there is no reason to attribute to the cause what is accidental to the nature of the effect, but it is necessary to attribute to the cause what is essential to the nature of the effect.

Third, according to some theists, an effect need not resemble an *instrumental* cause (that *through* which the effect comes to be). It does resemble, however, the *principal efficient* cause (that *by* which the effect is produced). For instance, the student's exam does not resemble his pen (instrumental cause), but it does resemble his mind (the principal cause).

Finally, an effect need not resemble the material cause (that out of which something is made) but only the *efficient* cause (that by which something is made). The sun causes clay to harden into bricks, but the sun is not a brick. Electrical energy produces light in a bulb, but the same energy produces motion in a motor. The result in each case depends on the material on which the cause operates.

Theistic Response

In view of these qualifications, the theist answers the objections as follows.

First, only *some,* not all, characteristics found in the world can be appropriately applied to God, because only some characteristics flow from the *principal, efficient* cause in an *essential* way. Other characteristics derive from instrumental or material causes, or else are merely accidental.

Similarly, God is spirit, but He creates matter. Matter is not *like* God (although it derives its reality from God), for it is limited in form and extension. Its physical limitations are essential to the very *conditions* of its creation.

Second, contrary to Ferré's claim, words do not lose *all* their meaning when abstracted from their finite conditions. Goodness *as we know it* is finite, but goodness *as such* is not. It is possible to define goodness (univocally) as "that which is desirable for its own sake," without any implications of finite limitations. That is, the quality signified can be unlimited, even though the *mode* of signification, or context, is limited.

It may be true, however, that some words do lose their meaning when all finite limitations are negated. An infinite rock, for example, seems impossible; the term *rock* appears to be empty and vacuous when all limitation is removed. The key to discerning which characteristics may be appropriately applied to God and which may not is this: those positive qualities in the world that are not by their very nature limited can be applied without limitation to God. Since evil, ugliness, and the like are not positive qualities but the absence of good, beauty, and so on, these cannot be applied to God. Also, since material extension, limitation, and change are not by their very nature unlimited, neither can they be applied to God. However, truth, beauty, goodness, oneness, and so on, are not necessarily limited. Hence, these may be applied to God.

Third, many theists argue that the effect (creation) does resemble the cause (God). The psalmist said, "The heavens declare the glory of God" (Ps. 19:1). Man was made in God's "image" and His "likeness" (Gen. 1:26). "Does He who implanted the ear not hear? Does He who formed the eye not see?" (Psalm 94:9, NIV). How can God give what He does not have to give? Can something come from nothing? Quite the contrary. If God has created intelligent beings then He must be intelligent. A transcendent Cause is more perfect than His effects; He cannot be less perfect. God is beyond human goodness, intelligence, and so on.

In short, if God is an actuality and if He actualizes (creates) the existence of other things, then there must be some similarity between the actuality of God and His effects. For act communicates act; the cause stamps its "form" (that is, determinative perfection) on the effect. Everything in creation bears one or more of the perfections of God. The higher forms of creation (such as men) are more like God, and have more godlike perfections, than the lower forms (plants).

In all these alleged counter-examples, there is a confusion between some accidental characteristics of the effect (or the material condition, or the instrumental cause) and the essential nature of the effect. Mosquitos, for example, are not the cause of malaria, but only the instrument through which the parasite is passed. There is an *essential* similarity, however, between the malaria parasite in the mosquito and the one in the malaria victim. Malaria parasites do produce malaria parasites that resemble their progenitors. Likewise, the moving hammer communicates motion to the glass, which breaks. Motion creates motion. There is an essential similarity here, too, even though the broken glass does not look like the hammer. All causes stamp their "form" on their effects in some way. Therefore, theists look around in the world to behold its perfections. Whenever one is found, it is stripped of its limiting connotations and applied to the infinitely perfect Creator of all good things (James 1:17).

Fourth, theists contend that they do not use the word *cause* in an equivocal way, as critics claim. *Cause* may indeed mean either infinite cause or finite cause. "Cause" as such, simply is "that which can produce or actualize something." If the cause is itself in some way actualized, then it is obviously not an Uncaused Cause (or God). The Uncaused Cause, the theist claims, is infinite. All other causes are limited in some way. Only God is pure actuality; He has no potentiality in His essence to become anything that is not already. All other things have the potentiality to not exist. For they are created and, hence, they can be annihilated.

In short, there is no equivocation on the term *cause*. There are simply different orders or kinds of causes. God is an *unlimited* cause; all other causes are limited. The word *cause* has the same meaning (univocal) in all cases, but is simply qualified as "unlimited" when used of God in contrast to man, who has only limited causal power.

Fifth, theists claim that the similarity of beings can be expressed or defined univocally. All beings exist. The term *existence* is always defined the same way, namely, "that which is," or "that which is actual." Beings are not held to be identical by theists (that would be pantheistic), for they believe that there are many beings, and these differ from each other. Finite beings are similar to but different from the infinite Being, God. However, the term *being* (or more properly, "existence") is univocally *defined*. The difference comes in the way the term is *applied* to God and creatures. God *is* Being in an infinite way, and creatures *have* being only finitely.

Other objections to meaningful God-talk have been expounded in contemporary philosophical analysis. Two of them are worthy of note here. First, some object to applying action predicates to God, such as, "God caused Lazarus to rise" on the grounds that one cannot act without a body. This objection, however, is built on the unproven assumption that all causal action is exactly like physical causal action. On the contrary, there is mentally caused action. Psychosomatic studies, as well as our own experience, would seem to indicate that our minds do cause action in physical objects.

A second objection from contemporary philosophy comes from the tradition of logical positivism. Some thinkers claim that the principle of empirical verifiability eliminates all meaningful God-talk (see chap. 2). The principle of empirical verifiability would limit all meaningful statements to empirical matters of fact. But since God is by definition a trans-empirical Being, this would imply that all God-talk is literally nonsense. There are many objections to this principle. Some have pointed out that it is too restrictive: it eliminates statements that are obviously meaningful even to empiricists (such as empirical generalizations of science, like "all swans are white." This is not empirically verifiable unless one observes *all* swans, a practical impossibility). Others have objected that the principle attempts to *legislate* meaning and not listen to it.

Conclusion

There are three basic views of the meaning of religious language. Some hold that terms applied to God have a totally different meaning (equivocal) than those applied to creatures. Many within this group stress the *negative* nature of religious language. Others emphasize the symbolic and evocative role of religious language, as opposed to a purely descriptive function. The second major position claims God-talk is univocal. Here the *positive* aspect of understanding God is stressed. Analogy, on the other hand, insists that no term can be predicated in a one-to-one, univocal way of an infinite God.

It appears that there is an element of truth in all these views. First, it seems clear that if we are to avoid total agnosticism about God, then all knowledge of God cannot be purely negative. There must be a positive element which is univocally defined. On the other hand, those stressing analogy are correct when they contend that no term can be taken from the finite context and conditions of human experience and applied to an infinite being in entirely the same way. This is where the truth of the *via negativa* comes in. Unless we negate all finite limitations of these terms and apply only the univocally understood context to God in an analogous way, we engage in verbal idolatry.

Finally, there is more to religious language than the purely descriptive; God-talk must be evocative. It must be not only talk *about* God, but talk *from* God that calls us to respond *to* God. The language of revelation must involve propositional descriptions of God, or else we would not know to whom we are responding. But it must involve more than the mere propositional; it must evoke a response to a Person (God). In short, adequate God-talk is both talk *about* God (positive and descriptive) and talk which elicits from us a response *to* the transcendent God. In order to perform all these functions it must have both positive and negative elements as well as both descriptive and evocative functions.

Suggested Readings

Aquinas, Thomas. *Summa contra Gentiles,* book 1
Ferré, Frederick. *Language, Logic and God*
Flew, Antony. *The Logic of God*
Geisler, N. L. *Philosophy of Religion,* part 3
Mondin, Battista. *The Principle of Analogy in Protestant and Catholic Theology*
Ramsey, Ian. *Religious Language*

21 The Problem of Evil

Perhaps more controversy has been generated over the problem of evil than any other issue surrounding the question of God's existence. Some claim evil disproves God's existence; others insist it proves His absolute perfection. We will proceed in our discussion with a survey of the various answers to the question of evil.

God and Evil

There are three basic ways of relating God and evil. First, one may affirm the reality of evil and deny God (atheism). Second, one may affirm God and deny the reality of evil (pantheism). Finally, one may attempt to show the compatibility of God and evil. Since this last view breaks down into a number of variations of theism and dualism, we will discuss each separately.

Illusionism: Denying the Reality of Evil

Monistic views affirm God and deny the reality of evil. This is true of both Western and Eastern forms of pantheism. The Hindu pantheist, Sankara, argued that only *Brahman* is reality. The external world (māyā) is *illusion*. The only basis for the world is *psychological,* not ontological. It *appears* to be something, the way a rope appears to be a snake until one gets closer to it. Brahman (God) causes the world and evil in the same way that the rope causes the "serpent" to appear.

In the West, Spinoza argued that all evil and imperfections in the world are a necessary part of a total picture of infinite good. It is an error to believe that one tile in a mosaic is ugly when the whole picture is beautiful. As Christian Science boldly proclaims, "Evil is but an illusion, and has no real basis." It is simply "an error of mortal man."

The Christian theist rejects illusionism for several reasons. First, illusionism is a complete denial of the reality of sense perception. Why should one assume that his senses are totally untrustworthy? If this were true, even the pantheist would have no means of acquiring truth about reality. Second, if evil is an illusion, why does it *seem* so real? The illusion of pain hurts as much as real pain. Finally, why is this "illusion" so universal and persistent? Where did it come from? Could it be that the statement, "Evil is an illusion" is itself an illusion? Perhaps (as Freud would say) this is precisely what we would *wish,* but for that very reason the idea is suspect.

Atheism: Denying the Reality of God

The atheistic position is at the opposite end of the spectrum from the pantheistic one. Pantheists affirm God and deny evil; atheists affirm evil and deny God.

If God exists, He is not essentially good. One atheistic argument is presented in the form of a dilemma.
(1) Either (a) morality is right because God willed it or else (b) He willed it because it is right.
(2) But if (a), then God is arbitrary about what is right, and He is not essentially good.
(3) And if (b), then God is not ultimate, since He is subject to some standard beyond Himself.

(4) But in either case—if God is not essentially good or not ultimate—God is not what theists claim Him to be.

(5) Therefore, no theistic God exists.

The theist may answer this dilemma by taking either "horn." Voluntarists claim that good is based on God's will but insist that God is sovereign but not arbitrary. Essentialists contend that God's nature is the ultimate norm in accordance with which His will cooperates. If the latter is so, then God wills what is essentially good without there being some ultimate standard beyond Himself. The ultimate norm for all good flows from the will of God but only in accordance with the nature of God. Thus God is neither arbitrary nor less than ultimate.

God should destroy all evil.   The classic way of stating this objection based on evil is as follows:

(1) If God is all-good, He will destroy evil.

(2) If God is all-powerful, He can destroy evil.

(3) But evil is not destroyed.

(4) Therefore, there is no all-good, all-powerful God.

But, as was stated in chapter 19 (p. 292), there is an implied time limit on God in premise 3. And second, it is *possible* that there is no way to destroy evil without also destroying the good of permitting free creatures. Indeed, the argument may be restated to prove just the opposite of what the atheists intend. For if there is an all-powerful God, then we have the assurance that evil will be defeated without destroying freedom. It may be argued this way:

(1) If God is all-good, He will defeat evil.

(2) If He is all-powerful, He can defeat evil.

(3) Evil is not *yet* defeated.

(4) Therefore evil will one day be defeated.

In short, grant that the theistic God exists and there is automatically a solution to the problem of evil. Thus if the grounds for believing God exists are good (see chap. 19), then evil is explained.

God and evil are logically incompatible.   Other atheists have insisted that God and evil are mutually exclusive.

(1) God and evil are opposites.

(2) Opposites cannot exist simultaneously.

(3) But evil exists.

(4) Hence, God cannot exist.

The problem with this argument is that the atheist fails to prove that God and evil are actually contradictory. They may be only contrary but not contradictory. The problem may be focused by restating the argument with the missing premise supplied.

(1) God exists.

(2) Evil exists.

[(3) There is no good purpose for evil.]

(4) Therefore, both (1) and (2) cannot be true.

(5) But we know (2) is true.

(6) Therefore, God cannot exist.

The difficulty here, of course, is in proving premise 3 to be true. The only way one can be sure God could not possibly have any good purpose for evil is either (1) to already know God is not all good, which begs the question, or (2) to know the mind of God, which is presumptuous for any finite being. Again, if there is an all-good God, it follows automatically that He does have some good purpose for allowing evil, even if no human being knows what that good purpose is. The only way left open to the atheist is to show God does not exist on some grounds other than the existence of evil.

An important point sometimes overlooked by the non-theist is that since the point disputed here is logical or conceptual, all the theist needs to do is show some *possible* explanation for evil to defeat the non-theist's claim. Theists are not obligated to show *in fact* that this is the case.

God and evil are practically incompatible.   Some atheists grant that evil and God are not necessarily *logically* incompatible but insist, nevertheless, that there is a *practical* incompatibility. In other words, it is logically possible that God has a good reason for allowing evil, but there is actually no reason to believe He does. They argue that no one would exonerate Eichmann of his blame in the Nazi holocaust on the mere grounds that it is logically possible he had some very good reason to kill all those Jews. Likewise, why should God be excused simply because it is possible He has some good reason for allowing evil?

The reply from a theistic standpoint points out that Eichmann (a finite sinful human being) and God (an infinitely good Being) are obviously in different categories. Even though it is *conceivable* that Eichmann had a good reason, there is *no evidence* that he did, and there is much evidence that he did not. There is *good evidence,* on the other hand, for believing that God has a good reason for allowing evil— His own infinitely good nature is all the reason one could ever need.

Theists use a double standard.   Atheists object to the above and similar arguments on the grounds that God is being excused from evil on the basis of a kind of double standard. John Stuart Mill objected that God regularly does what people are sent to jail or severely punished for doing. For example, God through nature inflicts sickness, pain, and even torment on humans. And eventually, God takes everyone's life—a crime called "murder" in any other case. Why should God be excused and men condemned for these heinous crimes?

What this objection fails to recognize is that God is a set of one. God is sovereign over life—He created it—and hence He has the right to take it (Deut. 32:39; Job 1:21). There is a rule that governs the activity of life-taking and it does apply to all in that class. It just so happens that there is only *one* Being in the class. The rule is this: only the Being who creates life has the right to take it.

In a lesser sense there is an analogy of this in our experience. There are shrubs in your neighbor's yard as well as in yours. You are sovereign over the shrubs in your yard and can cut them down if you wish. You are not sovereign over your neighbor's shrubs, however, because the neighbor owns them. Therefore, it is right for you to destroy your own shrubs for kindling wood, but wrong for you to destroy your neighbor's. In like manner, since God is sovereign over all life, it is not wrong for Him to take life for some good purpose known to Himself, especially if death is (as the Christian claims) the way God brings us to a better place.

Why did God create a world that would sin?   Perhaps the most plaguing contemporary criticism of theism from evil is the insistence that God could have avoided creating a world that would sin. According to theism, God could have made:
(1) No world at all.
(2) A world with no free creatures.
(3) A world where free creatures would not sin.
(4) A world where free creatures would sin.[1]

---

1. A fifth alternative, namely, that God could have created a world where creatures were free but must sin, is an impossibility (since freedom necessarily entails the possibility of not sinning).

But of the four choices open to God, choices 1 through 3 would seem to be morally better than number 4, which we have. But for God to do less than His best is an evil. Therefore, it was evil for God to create (4) a world where sin would occur.

In response to this objection the theist argues that worlds 1 through 3 are not *morally better* than number 4 and, also, that number 4 world *is* the morally best world. First, no world (1) and no free world (2) cannot be said to be *morally* better than this one (4). Worlds 1 and 2 are not even moral worlds, since neither of them has free moral creatures. Since they are not even moral worlds, then surely they cannot be *morally* better. A moral judgment can be made only where a moral standard applies. But a moral standard cannot be applied to no world (1) or to no moral (free) world (2). Number 2 world may in some sense be *physically* better, since, presumably, it could be free of all sickness, pain, and death. But it is a confusion of categories to say that what is physically better is thereby morally better. It is akin to arguing that a physically healthy Hitler is morally better than a sick apostle Paul.

Second, number 3 world—where sin never occurs—does appear to be more desirable than the one we have, where sin does occur. The fact that it seems *logically possible* or conceivable and even *morally desirable,* however, in no way means it is *actually achievable*. It is logically possible that you could have robbed a bank instead of reading this book. But is is *actually unachievable* because you chose not to rob the bank, even though you would have gotten much more money! In short, in a free world not everything logically possible is actually achievable. It all depends on what persons do with their freedom. In other words, the question is not a logical question; it is a factual question, depending on whether men choose to sin. And, so it may be argued, it is impossible for God to actually create a world that in fact would guarantee sin would never happen. And since the very nature of God as absolutely perfect insures that He will do the best that is possible, then we can be certain that either (a) a world in which sin never occurs would not be better than one in which it does, or (b) no sinless world would ever have occurred.

The second point the theist can make is to ask, Would a world where sin was never permitted be the *best* world or only a good one? Or would it not be *better* to permit evil in order to defeat it? Is it not better to permit some evil for achieving the greater good? Certain levels of virtue and pleasure cannot be attained without permitting some pain and evil. It may be that God permitted this evil world as a means of producing the greatest good.

This is not the best of all possible worlds. The answer to the previous question seems to assume that this is the best possible world. But it seems obvious, as Voltaire showed in *Candide,* that this present world is *not* the best possible world. Just one less murder or one less rape, to say nothing of war and cruelty, would improve the world. But if this is not the best possible world, then God has done an evil in creating and/or permitting it. The argument may be formulated this way:

(1) If there is a morally perfect God, then He must always do His best, morally speaking.
(2) But this world is not the morally best world possible.
(3) Therefore, there is no morally perfect God.

The problem with this argument from a theistic standpoint is premise 2. First, it may be that this world is not the best world but only the *best way* to get to the best world. This world may only be a precondition of perfection, the way tribulation is a precondition to patience, and the like. Second, the argument contains an ambiguity in the word *possible.* Does it mean "best world logically *conceivable*" or "best world actually *achievable*"? It may very well be that in the progress of the world toward its final point of perfection, this world is the best world *presently achievable.* Perhaps God is maximizing good in the world today and at every moment, given the limits of (a) human behavior and (b) the stage of progress toward the final goal. Today's world is certainly not the best world conceivable and (humanly speaking) hopefully is not the best world ultimately achievable, but it could be best world achievable *today.*

Why not save all men? Some atheists object to the above conclusion because it assumes that evil is permitted as a precondition of a future greater good. But Christianity promises that only some, not all, will be saved in the future. Atheists point out that it might be worth it if in the end all were saved, but since the Bible seems to say only "few" will be saved (Matt. 7:13–14), certainly this is not the best world possible.

Theists respond that: (1) "The Lord is not willing that any should perish but that all should come to repentance" (II Peter 3:9). God desires all men to be saved but they must come freely; He will not force them against their will. No one can be *forced* to love God. Forced love is not love; it is rape. (2) No human knows for sure what percentage of people will eventually be saved, but the biblical theist knows for sure—as sure as he knows the nature of God—that whatever the percentage, the final result will be the best world *achievable* within the limits of freedom and dignity. That is, an all-loving God will not save persons ''at all cost''—not, at least, at the cost of their freedom and dignity. The Christian God is not a Cosmic Manipulator who behaviorally determines everyone and ''programs'' them into the Kingdom. Jesus said, ''O, Jerusalem! O, Jerusalem, how often I would have gathered you as a hen gathers her chicks, *but you would not*'' (Matt. 23:37). In a free world, God has limited Himself to work within (not contrary to) human freedom. And whatever is the highest number of persons who will freely respond, it may be assumed that God will save that number. Thus, the final world will be ''the best world achievable.''

In summation, the atheist has not shown that God and evil are incompatible. It may very well be that God has some good purposes for evil not fully known to us. Indeed, if an all-perfect, all-powerful God does exist, then this fact is in itself the guarantee that there is a good purpose for evil and that the greatest good will ultimately be achieved.

Views Affirming Both God and Evil

As we have observed, pantheism affirms God and denies evil. Atheism affirms evil and denies God. Now we turn our attention to views that affirm both God and evil.

Dualism: good and evil in eternal opposition.   The first view affirming both good and evil is an ancient one, commonly held by the Greeks. Perhaps the best example, however, is the third-century Persian prophet, Mani, the founder of Manichaeism. There are two basic philosophical arguments that may be extracted from the dualistic position that good and evil are coeternal opposites.

a. the first argument for dualism
Good and evil are opposites. But the dualist claims that nothing can be the source of its opposite; for example, evil cannot come from good.

It follows, then, that both good and evil must have existed eternally. That is, there is an eternal first principle (some say substance) at the basis of all good, and another first principle at the root of all evil.

There are two reactions to this argument from a theistic perspective. First, good *can* give rise to evil, not essentially but incidentally. For instance, a hunter can accidentally kill another hunter in the pursuit of food for his family. Likewise, a good God can will that men be free to enjoy life and thereby incidentally give them the power to bring misery on themselves (through the God-given power of free choice).

Second, not all opposites have first principles, especially not eternal first principles (or substances). Short and tall are opposites, but this does not mean that there is an eternal (and infinitely) tall being versus an eternal (and infinitely) short one.

b. the second argument for dualism

The second argument for dualism is more of an argument *against* non-dualism (especially theism). The dualist says that the theist cannot escape the following conclusion:

(1) God is the author of everything that exists.
(2) Evil is something that exists.
(3) Therefore, God is the author of evil.

Since theists affirm God's sovereignty and creative power over all that exists, they cannot deny premise 1. Likewise, since theists do not, like pantheists, deny the reality of evil, they cannot deny premise 2. But this means theists seem stuck with an unwanted conclusion, since it makes God directly responsible for creating evil.

Theists respond to both premises. First, God is the author of some things only indirectly. For example, God created freedom, but He does not perform acts of evil Himself or through man's free choice. To state it another way, God does not create evil directly or essentially but only *incidentally*. God is directly responsible only for the *fact* of freedom, not for all the *acts* of freedom. Of course, God did create the *possibility* of evil when He made men free. But it is free creatures who bring about the *actuality* of evil. God is indirectly responsible for evil in that He made evil possible. But the possibility of evil is actually a good—it is necessary for human freedom. The power of free choice is a good power; the fact that men abuse freedom does not make freedom bad. Men abuse everything, including the water and air in their environment. But this obviously does not mean that water and air are bad.

Many theists also object to the second premise. Evil is not a "thing" (or substance). Evil is a *privation,* or absence of good. Evil exists in another entity (as rust exists in a car or rot exists in a tree), but does not exist in itself. Nothing can be totally evil (in a metaphysical sense). One cannot have a *totally* rusted car or a *totally* moth-eaten garment. For if it were completely destroyed, then it would not exist at all. The Christian points to Scripture which says everything God made was "good" (Gen. 1:31); even today "every creature of God is good" (I Tim. 4:11), and "nothing is unclean in itself" (Rom. 14:14). To be sure, the Bible teaches that men are totally depraved in a moral sense, since sin has extended to the whole man, including his mind and will (Rom. 3; Eph. 2). But total depravity is to be taken in an *extensive* sense (affecting the whole man), not in an *intensive* sense (destroying the very essence of man).

When the theist says that evil is no "thing" (substance) he is not saying evil is "nothing" (that is, unreal). Evil is a *real* privation. Blindness is real—it is the real privation of sight. Likewise it is *real* to be maimed—it is a genuine lack of limb or sense organ.

Evil is not a mere absence, however. Arms and eyes are absent in stones, but we would not say that stones are *deprived* of arms and eyes. A privation is more than an absence; it is an absence of some form or perfection that *should be there* (by its very nature).

One further point should be made about dualism. It faces the following dilemma, both alternatives of which lead to theism.
(1) Good and evil are either judged by a standard beyond themselves or they are judged by each other.
(2) But if they are judged by a standard beyond themselves, then that is the one and only ultimate by which all is judged (which is actually the theistic definition of "God").
(3) If good is judged by evil, then evil is the single ultimate by which all else is measured.
(4) If evil is judged by good, then good is the single ultimate by which all else is measured.
(5) In both cases there is one, not two, ultimate standard (contrary to dualism).

Further, as Augustine pointed out in reply to the Manichaeans, evil is measured by good and not the reverse. For when we take all that we call *evil* away from something, then what is left is better (for example, remove all rust from a car and one has a better car). But when we take all that is called *good* from something, then nothing is left. *Good,* therefore, is the positive and *evil* is the privation, or lack of good.

Finitism: good lacks infinite power in its struggle with evil. Since we have previously spoken of finite godism (see chap. 18), we will only note its relation to evil here. Basically, finite godism, while not denying either evil or the reality of God, denies the *infinity* of God. God is either not infinite in love and does not care to overcome evil (called *sadism*), or else He is not infinite in power and cannot overcome evil. Few stress the former but many philosophers (including Plato, Mill, Whitehead, and Brightman) have held the latter.

The basic argument for finitism is as follows:
(1) God exists.
(2) If God were all-powerful, He would destroy evil.
(3) Evil is not destroyed.
(4) Therefore, God (even if He desires to destroy evil—and most assume He does) is not all-powerful.

There are several problems in finite godism's response to evil. First, it is not really a solution to evil. It leaves evil undefeated and the situation in perpetual conflict. The only real *guarantee* that evil will be defeated is if there is an infinitely loving and powerful God—the very premise finite godism has given up.[2] Second, there is no need to despair about the power of God and give up His infinity simply because evil has not *yet* been destroyed. If there is an infinitely good and powerful God (as the theist claims), then He is the proof that evil will one day be destroyed just as the Bible predicts (Rev. 21–22). Further, according to many theists, a finite god is not God at all. For if every finite being needs a cause, then there is a Cause of all finite beings which cannot itself be caused, that is, God. No finite, changing being can be uncaused, since as finite or limited it is dependent on something else for its existence (it is caused).

Necessitarianism: it was impossible for God to avoid creating an evil world. Necessitarians are generally pantheists, although some theists have adopted this pantheistic premise in order to explain evil.

---

2. The response of the finite godist, that the undefeated condition of evil is a good motivating factor to enlist men in the struggle against evil, can be countered by pointing out that the sword swings both ways. It can be very discouraging to fight when there is no real basis for hope in an ultimate victory.

Theists traditionally hold that God was free to create or not to create the world. Necessitarians argue that God was not free; it was necessary for God to create this kind of world and evil is a necessary result.

The argument takes many forms, but can be basically stated as follows:

(1) Creation flows necessarily from God.
(2) Creation necessarily involves imperfections.
(3) Therefore, evil is necessary.

There are, needless to say, some serious problems with necessitarianism. First, why is it necessary for God to create? Simply because He is a Necessary Being? But this only explains why He cannot be created or destroyed—because by nature He cannot *not* exist. A Necessary Being does not by nature have to *do* anything; He simply has to *be* the Necessary Being He is. Further, all other beings are contingent beings, and the contingent can place no necessity on the Necessary. Second, even if God had to create (which He did not), there is no reason why He had to create an evil world. It makes no sense to claim that a Perfect Being necessarily had to create an *imperfect* world. Certainly there is no *metaphysical* necessity that God create an evil world. A strong case could be made for just the opposite. Neither is there any *moral* necessity that God create an evil world. It is nonsense to say God is morally obligated to produce evil.

Impossibilism: God could not foresee evil.   This position is held by some theists. They claim that God is all-powerful and all-knowing but deny that He could foresee evil would occur when He made the world. Hence, God is exonerated from the charge of evil because He did not know what free creatures would do when He created them. The reasoning for impossibilism is as follows:

(1) God can know anything that is possible.
(2) God cannot know the impossible.
(3) It is impossible to know in advance what free creatures will do.
(4) Therefore, God did not know that free creatures would sin when He made them.

There are at least two serious flaws in this view. First, even if God did not know what free creatures would do, surely He knew what they *could* do when He made them free. Second, if God is a non-temporal (eternal) Being as theists have traditionally maintained, then it is incorrect to speak of Him as knowing "in advance." If God is above time, then He knows everything in one eternal *now*. That is, He does not really *fore*-know; He simply *knows*. And if God knows in the eternal present what flows from creation, then He knows the evil that flows therefrom. Further, impossibilists have difficulty justifying the contention that God cannot know future free acts. Often their argument is as follows:

(1) If God knows the future infallibly, then what He knows *must* come to pass.
(2) God knew Judas would betray Christ.
(3) Therefore, Judas *must* betray Christ.
(4) What one *must* do he is not free *not* to do.
(5) But Judas was free not to betray Christ.
(6) Therefore, God did not infallibly know that Judas would betray Christ.

In short, says the impossibilist, either we are free or we are not. If we are, then God cannot know for certain what we will do with our freedom. And, if God did not know that evil would come about, then He cannot be blamed for creating this world.

One objection to impossibilism has already been mentioned, namely, that God is non-temporal. He does not *fore*-see what evil will be done but, rather, He *sees* what evil is being done. It does not contradict free choice to know what free choice is doing, nor is it contrary to free choice to know for certain what it will do. It *is* contradictory to say God knows for certain what Judas must do *whether he wills or not*. For in this case Judas is not free. All the theist need insist is that God necessarily knows what Judas will contingently do. That is, the event is *necessary* with regard to the ultimate cause (God's knowing) but *contingent* with regard to its immediate cause (Judas's free choice).

Theism: God uses evil for good ends.   Implied throughout the discussion has been the adequacy of the theistic explanation of evil, namely, that God *permits* evil in order to produce a greater good. There are several elements of this theodicy. First, God freely created the world, not because He had to, but because He wanted to do so. Second, God created creatures like Himself who could freely love Him. But such creatures could also hate Him. Third, God desires all men to love Him, but will not force any against their will to love Him. Forced love is not love. Fourth, God will persuade as many to love

Him as He can (II Peter 3:9). God will grant those who will not love Him their free choice—forever (that is, hell). Finally, God's love is magnified when we return His love (since He first loved us) as well as when we do not. It shows how great He is that He will love even those who hate Him. (Jesus said of those crucifying Him: "Father, forgive them; for they know not what they do" [Luke 23:34]).

Thus, in the end the greatest good will be achieved in several ways. First, God will have shared His love with all men ("For God so loved the world . . ." [John 3:16]). Second, God will have saved as many as He could without violating their free choice (I Tim. 2:1; II Peter 3:9). Those not saved will be given their own freely-chosen destiny; thus the good of their freedom will be respected. Finally, throughout all God will be glorified in that (a) His sovereign will had prevailed; (b) His love is magnified whether it is accepted or rejected; (c) He has defeated evil by forgiving sin (through the cross) and by separating good from evil forever (through the final judgment); and (d) He has produced the best world achievable (where the most men possible are saved and secured from evil forever).

There are two very important aspects of this theodicy that should be stressed. First, it is a "best-way" (versus a "best-world") theodicy. That is, this present evil world is not the best world possible, but it is the best *way* to achieve the best world. Permitting evil is a precondition of producing the best world. As Paul said, "Where sin increased, grace abounded all the more" (Rom. 5:20). Or, as Joseph said to his brothers who had sold him into slavery, "You meant evil against me; but God meant it for good" (Gen. 50:20).

Second, this solution is not a soul-*making* but a soul-*deciding* theodicy. God is not conceived as a cosmic behavioral manipulator who is programming people into heaven against their will. God operates with men only with their "informed consent." God never goes beyond freedom and dignity to save men *at any cost*—not at the cost of their freedom or dignity. Whosoever *will* may come, but whoever *won't* will not be forced to come. In a truly free world, God cannot make souls act against their will. He can only lovingly persuade them and then respect their decision—whatever it may be.

Conclusion

There are three basic ways to relate God and evil. Some affirm evil and deny God's reality (*atheism*). Others affirm God and deny the reality of evil (*pantheism*). Finally, many attempt to affirm both. *Dualism* affirms both good and evil in eternal opposition, which is a denial of God's supremacy. *Finitism* claims God cannot overpower evil, which denies His infinity. Still others deny God's freedom to create (*necessitarianism*) or His omniscience in knowing evil would occur (*impossibilism*). None of these positions is without serious difficulties. Theism holds the most adequate explanation of evil, namely, that an infinitely good and powerful God permitted evil in order to produce the greater good. This free world is the best way to produce the best world. God will do His best.

Suggested Readings

Aquinas, Thomas. *Summa Theologica,* I
Augustine, St. *On the Nature of the Good*
Camus, Albert. *The Plague*
Flew, Antony. *New Essays in Philosophical Theology*
Geisler, N. L. *The Roots of Evil*
Leibniz, Gottfried. *Theodicy*
Voltaire. *Candide*

22 Can We Experience God?

Religious experience is universal to the human race. In fact, it is extremely doubtful that there have ever been any purely secular cultures. Man is incurably religious. Manifestations of this character trait have differed widely from place to place and from time to time, but most people have claimed to have some religious experience. Since we have already discussed the various ways to conceive of "God" (chap. 18), we will concentrate here simply on the nature and justification of religious experience.

What Is a Religious Experience?

Both religion and experience are notoriously difficult to define. It is necessary, however, to have some understanding of the terms before we proceed.

What Is Meant by "Experience"?

Experience may be viewed in two ways—generally and specifically. General experience includes a wide range of consciousness, such as the awareness of being alive. It is an awareness subjects have of other subjects or objects. Specific experience focuses on a given aspect or moment within the whole of one's consciousness. General experience is more like an awareness of *being* married, whereas special experience is more like *getting* married.

Religious experience can also be both general and specific, but since we are more concerned here with what is readily available to the philosopher, we will focus on religious experience in general rather than on specific visions, dreams, or revelations.

There is another distinction important to our discussion. Experience may be either primary or secondary. Primary experience is an original, unreflective awareness of something. Secondary experience is the consciousness of being aware of something. It is a reflection on one's primary experience. Secondary experience includes what we often call "reason." Reasoning, then, is an experience and, as such, will play an essential part in our discussion of religious experience.

What Is Meant by "Religious"?

Religion involves an awareness of the Transcendent, or what in the Western world is commonly called *God*. There are two senses of the word *transcendent*. One refers to the process of self-transcendence, or man's attempts to go beyond the limits of his finite condition. The other refers to the object of this process, which we will call the Transcendent (or God).

Considered as the object of religious experience, the Transcendent implies two things. First, it is believed to go *beyond* or to be *more* than the world of one's experience (the empirical world). It is more than the empirical world the way the meaning of a sentence is more than letters in the sentence, or as the whole is more than the mere parts. Second, the Transcendent is in some sense ultimate or final. It is the More beyond which there is no more. It is that to which one gives an ultimate commitment. The patriot's "my country right or wrong" or the moralist's "duty for duty's sake" function as examples of this kind of ultimate devotion. This leads to a third characteristic of the Transcendent as object of religious experience—it has ultimate *value*. One gives it final devotion because it has intrinsic worth. Since it is intrinsically and ultimately worthy, it is the object of worship.

What Are the Dimensions of Transcendence?

One of the reasons it seems as though some cultures or groups of people do not believe in God or the Transcendent is that there are different ways transcendence can be viewed. Those who look for the transcendent in one direction tend to think that those who look in another direction are denying God altogether. When we examine a complete typology of the Transcendent, it is doubtful that anyone is genuinely atheistic. It would seem that those who claim to be "anti"-Transcendent are against (or without) a certain kind of Transcendent (or God), but they replace this traditional way of viewing God with another form of the Transcendent. A brief examination of seven kinds of transcendence will illustrate the point.

Transcending Backward

According to Professor Mircea Eliade, it is common to primitive religions to transcend "backward." That is, they look to the "Beginning" or "Origin" as the point at which God broke through. Their myths and rituals dramatize or recite the mystery of man's origin. God reveals Himself in the repetition of the original revelation of creation.

Transcending Upward

The neo-Platonic thinker Plotinus thought of God as "up there," as the Highest. The world flows "down" from God and man moves (by asceticism and mysticism) back "up" toward God. Since God is Absolutely One, the movement upward is toward greater unity. Finally, by mystical union, one is alone with the Alone and becomes one with the One. This is the Highest point of all.

Transcending Outward

Others prefer to describe God as "out there," beyond our limits. The German mystic, Meister Eckhart (c. 1260–1328), spoke of God as "an infinite sphere whose center is everywhere and whose circumference is nowhere." God is the boundary-less Beyond, a limitless Sphere toward which man can move in any direction.

Transcending Downward

Many contemporary thinkers, such as Rudolph Bultmann, have insisted that modern science has made it impossible to think of God as "up there" or "out there." These ancient mythological structures must be "demythologized."

In place of the myth of God "up there" or "out there," Bishop John A. T. Robinson suggests God as "downward," in the depth of our being. In this respect there is a similarity with Paul Tillich's description of God as the "ground of our being." These thinkers claim that persons cannot transcend or go "beyond" by going "above," but perhaps they can go "below" or, better, "beneath," to the depth.

Transcending Within

Akin to the previous form of transcendence is the desire to find God at the "center" of life. The French Catholic, Teilhard de Chardin, spoke of God as a "universal milieu" or the "ultimate point upon which all realities converge." This Focus or Source, he says, is everywhere, "precisely because He is the center that fills the whole sphere." One finds the Transcendent, then, not by ascending a mystical ladder but by plunging within the depths of one's being and beyond.

Transcending Forward

One of the ironies of this issue is that even the recent "God is dead" movement was not a negation of all Transcendence. The God "up there," "back there," and so on, is dead, but, according to Thomas Altizer, we must transcend "forward." Thus for Altizer only traditional views of the Transcendent are "dead." That is, when the God "up there" came "down here" in the incarnation of Christ, then God was no longer "up there." The God "up there" actually died. However, we must rejoice in this and move forward toward the "End." In short, Altizer negated vertical transcendence and replaced it with horizontal transcendence. He traded theological transcendence for eschatological transcendence. God is not the Origin, Height, Depth, or Center; He is the End. One goes "beyond" not by going backward, upward, downward, or inward, but by going forward.

As secular and atheistic as Marxism professes to be, nevertheless it too is a form of forward transcendence. It looks to the inevitable End of history, the predestined goal or communistic Utopia to come. Into this general category can be placed thinkers such as Jürgen Moltmann, and others, whose position emphasizing eschatology has been called the *theology of hope*.

Transcending in a Circle

If anyone qualifies as an atheist, one would certainly think Nietzsche does. However, even Nietzsche posited a form of transcendence. His concept of the superman or *over*man indicates a person who transcends the common "herd morality" and lives in the overflow of his will-to-power. But even more important, Nietzsche held that in the face of the meaninglessness of life, one should courageously will the eternal recurrence of the same state of affairs. Herein is a kind of cyclical transcendence—overcoming by coming over, and over, and over again—eternally.

Perhaps there are some purely non-transcendent lifestyles. If so, even those who profess to be atheists have not attained them. Man seems to be by his very nature inclined toward transcendence. There are many ways to transcend—at least seven—but there is apparently no way to avoid transcendence.

How Does Religious Experience Differ from Other Experiences?

There is a close association, and sometimes an overlap, between a religious experience and a moral experience, as well as between religious and aesthetic experiences. It will be helpful, nonetheless, to try to distinguish them.

Religious Experience in Contrast to Moral Experience

Some thinkers (such as the empiricist R. B. Braithwaite) have suggested that morality supplies an intention to behave in a certain way, whereas religion adds certain beliefs to those intentions. William James distinguished between the two by saying that morality *accepts* the yoke of the universe, but religion *welcomes* it. Schleiermacher added that morality is man's *duty* to the universe, but religion is man's absolute *dependence* on it.

Perhaps no one distinguished between morality and religion more sharply than Sören Kierkegaard. The ethical, he said, is a response to the moral law, but the religious is a response to the moral Lawgiver. The law indicates man's responsibility *in* the world; religion points to his responsibility *beyond* the world (that is, to God). The former is universal; the latter is individual. Morality is centered in lifetime duty; religion is centered in eternity.

Although not all agree with Kierkegaard's distinctions, there are a few general characteristics that differentiate religion from morality. A religious commitment is: (1) broader in scope (a commitment of the whole man to the Whole); (2) different in kind (what one *wills* to do rather than what one *ought* to do); (3) having a higher object (morality covers man's duty to man, but religion, his devotion to God); and (4) motivating power (morality points to our shortcomings, but religion provides a way of overcoming them).

Religious Experience as Different from Aesthetic Experience

There is also a close connection between religion and art. Some contend that recreation and religion often have the same origin in ritual (the kinship between a holiday and a holy day is used to support this). And, often an aesthetic experience (beautiful music or mountaintop scenery) can be used to evoke a religious experience.

There are some differences, however, between a religious and an aesthetic experience. First of all, as Schleiermacher pointed out, science is speculative, art is practical, and religion is intuitive. Art reflects the existence of man in things, but religion points to the existence of all things in God.

Again, Sören Kierkegaard made the most radical distinctions between the aesthetic and the religious. The former deals only with *feeling,* the latter with *existing.* The aesthetic deals with the routines of life, but the religious with God's revelation about eternal life. In brief, the aesthetic life is what one *has* with other men, but the religious is what one *is* before God. Perhaps the simplest way to explain the difference between the aesthetic and the religious is that the former deals with our sense of the sublime and the latter with our sense of the sacred or holy. One deals with beauty and the other with ultimate worth. The aesthetic brings pleasure, but the religious occasions worship. The former involves a sense of amazement, but the latter a sense of adoration. These feelings are sometimes overlapping and concurrent, but they are nontheless distinguishable.

Some Attacks on the Reality of Religious Experience

Few philosophers, whether religious or non-religious, dispute that most men have a religious experience as defined above. Often atheists admit to a feeling of absolute dependence or a sense of devotion to the All. But they claim that there may be no basis in reality for these feelings. In other words, persons often have a real commitment to the Ultimate, but this does not necessarily mean the "Ultimate" is real. The object of religious devotion may be purely imaginary or illusory.

Attacks on the Reality of the Transcendent

Some philosophers have raised serious questions about the reality of the Transcendent. We will examine several of the more important ones.

Is it a mere projection of human imagination? The German atheist, Ludwig Feuerbach, argued that God is nothing but a projection of human imagination. He wrote: "The nature of God is *nothing else* than the subject's own nature taken objectively." Thus what man thinks of God is simply a subconscious projection of his own nature. Heaven is a cosmic mirror by which one sees himself.

There is, no doubt, a good deal of truth to this in much of religious experience. However, it is less than adequate as a comprehensive explanation of *all* experience of God for several reasons. That is, some may be worshiping a mere projection of their own imagination, but it is not necessarily true that all are. First, such an analysis only fits well with some religious experience, not with all. Second, just the opposite may well be true, that man is made in God's image (as Gen. 1:26 says), rather than God being made in man's image. Third, Feuerbach has made a serious, even self-defeating, overstatement. How can one know that God is *nothing but* a projection of his own imagination unless he knows *more than* his own imagination? The only way to place absolute limits on thought is to be able to transcend those limits.

Is belief in God merely wish-fulfillment?   Sigmund Freud, in *The Future of an Illusion,* insisted that religion is based on mere wish-fulfillment, which in turn is the basis of illusion. In view of the crushing realities of life, men desire a kind of heavenly "Linus blanket" or a "Cosmic Comforter." It would be nice if there were a God, forgiveness, and heaven (and a pot of gold at the end of the rainbow), but the very fact that we *wish* it to be so makes it highly suspect.

Freud no doubt speaks the truth about some of religious experience. Many probably do construct a God to their own liking. This does not mean, however, that all persons do so. There are several objections to this Freudian explanation of God. First, there is a difference between wish (want) and need. Perhaps man's desire for God is more than a wish; maybe it is a genuine need. Maybe man cannot live "by bread alone," as Jesus said. If men really need God, then it is possible that a God really exists to fill that need. Further, perhaps *disbelief* in God is an illusion. It would be nice if there were no God to whom we must give account some day, but the very fact that many free-living persons *wish* it that way makes their belief (that there is no God) suspect. Finally, illusory (wish-based) beliefs do not prove that the object of belief does not exist; at best they simply indicate that the basis for those beliefs is not well-founded, or that we should be more critical in evaluating such claims. (As argued in chap. 19, there are good reasons, not just fond dreams, to believe God exists.)

Is God only the subconscious?   William James suggested that only one side of religious experience is subject to scientific analysis—the psychologically describable side. It is, in fact, identical to "the subconscious continuation of our conscious life." This he called the "hither" side of God. The "thither" or "farther" side is simply a matter of "over-belief." Others have denied there is any "farther" side at all. Perhaps God is nothing but the subconscious—either one's individual subconscious or the collective subconsciousness of the human race, as Carl Jung suggested.

In its most extreme form, the subconscious view is subject to some of the same criticisms as Feuerbach's view. First, it is another form of "nothing-but-ery." However, as we have noted (p. 344), "nothing but" statements imply "more than" knowledge. Second, it is possible that God is more than the subconscious. Rather than the unbeliever having "more than" knowledge that eliminates God, perhaps it is true that God is more than the unbeliever's consciousness. Finally, believers confess that God is essential to their consciousness, not their subconsciousness. That is, most men, even some unbelievers, confess to a conscious dependence on the All (which believers call "God").

The Need for Examination of Religious Experience

It is important to note that the views that challenge the reality of religious experience do point back to the Socratic dictum: The unexamined life (or experience) is not worth living. One must not accept uncritically the "God" of religious experience.

First, illusion and even delusion are possible, even if they are not probable. Many people have been seriously fooled about many things. One must not fool himself about something of utmost importance, namely the existence of God.

Second, the object of religious experience is conceived very differently by different persons. Some think of God pantheistically and others theistically. Some claim to experience many gods and others only one God. Some insist God is finite and others that He is infinite. It seems clear, then, that something more than pure (primary) experience is necessary. One must critically reflect on these experiences (by reason) in order to establish their consistency.

Third, experience *as such* does not establish anything except that one has had that experience. Experiences of God are not self-interpreting. Even in the Bible there were three different interpretations of one event (John 12). Some called the sound "the voice of God." Others claimed it was "angels." Still others insisted it was only "thunder." Presumably the same objective event (sound) was available to all. But "hearing" is more than mere objective sound waves; it involves a subjective response as well. This subjective element "colors" what we understand the experience to mean. This is where philosophy enters. We must use the objective categories of reason to interpret our experiences. At least two functions must be performed on experience by reason: reason must make sure the experience is *consistent* with itself and with other known facts, and reason must make sure the experience is *authentic*. That is, reason must clarify and justify the belief generated by experience. Experience *as such*, without reason, is neither self-interpreting nor a safe guide for life.

How Can One Know Religious Experience Is Real?

There are several ways to show the reality of religious experience. We will examine two of them.

Argument from Religious Encounter

The argument from religious encounter is a much stronger one than is often thought. In essence it argues:
(1) Many intelligent, self-critical persons testify to an encounter with God.
(2) If even one of them is correct, then God exists.
(3) It is highly unlikely that all of them are totally deceived.
(4) Therefore, God exists.

The crucial premise is the third one. While it is logically *possible* that everyone in the whole history of mankind, including Abraham, Moses, Isaiah, and even Jesus Himself, was totally deceived about the object of his religious encounter, it does not seem probable. But if even one of these on one occasion when he believed himself to be encountering God was not deceived, then God does exist. It is incredible that some of the most brilliant, scientific, and philosophical minds that have ever lived, including Augustine, Aquinas, Pascal, and Kierkegaard, were totally misled about their encounter with God.

Argument from Religious Need

One form of the argument from need is obviously weak. It can be summarized as follows:
(1) Men have a basic need for God.
(2) All basic needs of men are fulfilled.
(3) Therefore, there is a God.
The second premise is obviously false. Humans have a basic need for

food and water, but people die of hunger and thirst nevertheless. The fact that someone is lost in a desert and needs an oasis is no guarantee he will find one.

The argument from religious need, however, is much stronger than the above "straw man" form of it would indicate, and cannot be so easily dismissed. The stronger form can be stated this way:

(1) Men have a fundamental need for God.
(2) What men fundamentally need is fulfillable.
(3) Therefore, there is a God who can fulfill man's fundamental spiritual need.

The key word in this statement of the argument is *fulfillable*. Not everyone who needs water or food will have this need fulfilled, but this does not mean that food and water do not exist. Likewise, not everyone will find God, but from this it does not follow that there is no God to be found. Perhaps those who do not find God are moving in the wrong direction, in the same way that those traveling away from an oasis in the desert will not find it.

A major objection to this argument, which centers around the first premise, can be stated this way:

(1) Many (even all) men may desire God.
(2) But not all that men want is fulfillable, let alone fulfilled.
(3) Therefore, the desire for God may be unfulfillable (there may be no God).

The problem with this objection is that it confuses *want* and *need*. It is obviously true that not all human wishes are fulfilled or even fulfillable. One may wish for a pot of gold at the end of the rainbow, but this wish is in no way a guarantee that there is any reality to the object wished. However, it may be an entirely different matter with real human needs. Persons may *wish* for fortunes, but they *need* food and water. It is not illogical that there are not great fortunes for all, but it would be incredible if there were no food anywhere for anyone. Likewise, if men really need God, then it would be incredible if there were no God anywhere to fill that need.

Ironically, both believers and unbelievers have confessed a need for God. Augustine's famous statement summarizes the believer's need for God: "The heart is restless until it finds its rest in Thee, O God!" As for unbelievers, Nietzsche once confessed of his atheistic life, "My life now consists in the wish that it might be otherwise than I comprehend, and that somebody might make *my* 'truths' appear incredible to me."[1] The French existentialist Jean-Paul Sartre said in his auto-biography, "I needed God . . . I reached out for religion, I longed for it, it was the remedy."[2] Walter Kaufman admits that "religion is rooted in man's aspiration to transcend himself. . . . Whether he worships idols or strives to perfect himself, man is the God-intoxicated ape."[3]

Conclusion

The essence of a religious experience rests in man's desire—even need—to transcend. There are many "directions" to transcend, but all men (even confessed atheists) seem to experience this same inclination toward Transcendence. Of course the mere fact that men *want* God (the Transcendent) is no proof He is there. But man is incurably religious; he does *need* God. If this is the case, however, man's need is a much better indicator of whether God exists than man's desire that God is. In fact, it is plausible to argue that if men actually need an Ultimate, then the Ultimate is real. It is in accord with human expectation that needs are fulfillable.

Further, if man's need for God is so great, then one is cruelly unjust to himself to give up the search for God in despair. Simply because a wanderer in the desert has not yet found an oasis does not mean there are none to be found. On the other hand, one cannot simply accept all alleged experiences of God as authentic. One must exercise critical judgment about such matters. In this sense religious experience cannot be isolated from philosophical reasoning.

Suggested Readings

Buber, Martin. *I and Thou*
Feuerbach, Ludwig. *The Essence of Christianity*

---

1. *Portable Nietzsche,* ed. W. Kaufman (Princeton, N.J.: Princeton University Press, 1968), p. 441.
2. Jean-Paul Sartre, *The Words,* trans. B. Frechtman (New York: George Braziller, 1964), pp. 102, 97.
3. Walter Kaufman, *Critique of Religion and Philosophy* (New York: Doubleday, 1961), pp. 354, 355, 359.

Freud, Sigmund. *The Future of an Illusion*
Otto, Rudolf. *The Idea of the Holy*
Plotinus *Enneads*
Schleiermacher, F. *On Religion: Speeches to Its Cultural Despisers*
Trueblood, D. Elton. *Philosophy of Religion*

PART FIVE

What Is Good or Right?

23 What Is the Right?

Ethics is the study of what is right and what is wrong. Epistemology is concerned with the *true*, and ontology with the *real*, but ethics with the *good*. In this first chapter our primary concern will be defining just what is meant by the right or the good.

Different Theories of the Meaning of Right

A brief survey of the way various philosophers have conceived of the right will set the stage of the discussion of the meaning of right and wrong.

Might Is Right

The ancient Greek philosopher, Thrasymachus, is supposed to have held that "justice is the interest of the stronger party," stated more simply as "might is right." That is to say, right is defined in terms of power. Presumably this would mean political power (cf. Machiavelli), although it could mean physical, psychological, or any other kind of power.

Thankfully, this is not a widely-held ethical view, even though it seems too often to be a human practice. First, most men see a difference between *power* and *goodness*. It is possible to be good without power and powerful without goodness. An evil tyrant is sufficient practical disproof of Thrasymachus's "theory" of right. Second, some have insisted that almost the opposite is the case, arguing that power corrupts and absolute power corrupts absolutely. There is much evidence in human experience for rejecting the view that right is might.

Morals Are Mores

Some hold that right is determined by the group to which one belongs. Ethics is identified with the ethnic; moral commands are considered community demands. This, of course, implies a cultural relativity of morality. Any overlapping of ethical principles between cultures and societies that would seem to give the appearance of universality is accidental. The most one can say for apparently universal ethical norms is that all groups "happen" to come up with similar codes (probably because of common aspirations or situations).

This view has several problems. First, it is based on what Hume called the "is-ought" fallacy. Just because something *is* the practice does not mean it *ought* to be. It *is* the case that people are cruel at times; they hate and kill. This in no way means that *ought* to be the case. Second, if each community is right, then there is no way to solve conflicts *between* communities and nations. Whatever each one believes is right—even if it means the annihilation of the other—is right.

Man Is the Measure

The Greek philosopher Protagoras said, "Man is the measure of all things." If this is taken in an individual sense, then right is measured by an individual's will. The right is what is right to me. What is right for one may be wrong for another and vice versa.

The most common criticism of this is that it would lead to chaos. If everyone literally "did his own thing," then there would be no community, that is, no unity in society. Further, what particular aspect of man should be taken as the "measure"? One cannot answer, "the 'good' aspects." For in that case it presupposes that "good" apart from man is really the measure of man, and not man the measure of good.

The Race Is Right

One way to avoid the individualism and ethical solipsism of the former two views is to insist that neither individuals nor individual communities are the ultimate arbiters of what is right but, rather, the whole human race is the final court of appeals. In this way the part does not determine the whole; the whole race determines what is right for the individual members. In short, mankind rather than man is the measure of all things.

The first objection to this view is that just as groups are often wrong, so the whole race could be wrong. Communities have committed mass suicide. What if the race decided suicide was right, and all dissenters were forced to do likewise? Second, the race is in a state of flux. If the race were the ultimate norm, then how could one make judgments such as, "Mankind is not perfect," or, "The world needs improvement"? These statements are meaningless unless there is some standard outside the race by which its degree of goodness can be measured.

Right Is Moderation

According to the ancient Greek view, especially exemplified in Aristotle, the meaning of right is found in the path of moderation. The "golden mean," or moderate course between extremes, was considered to be the right course of action. For instance, temperance is the mean between indulgence and insensibility. Pride is the mean between vanity and humility. And courage is the mean between fear and aggression.

There is, of course, much wisdom in taking the path of moderation. The question is, however, whether the middle course should be seen as a *definition* of what is right. First of all, the right sometimes seems to call for extreme action, as in emergencies, self-defense, war, and so on. Even some virtues, such as love, seem best expressed not moderately but liberally. Second, the "middle of the road" is not always the wisest (or safest) place to be. It all depends on how extreme the situation is. One extreme sometimes calls for another. For instance, extreme sickness (cancer) often calls for an extreme operation (removing the diseased tissue). Finally, moderation seems to be at best only a *general* guide for practice, not a universal definition of right.

There Is No Right

Some philosophers simply deny that anything is right or wrong. They are called "antinomian" (against-law). Few actually claim to be complete antinomians, but many views can be reduced to this. A. J. Ayer insisted that all "ought" sentences actually translate to "I feel" sentences. Hence, *"You ought not* to be cruel" means *"I do not like* cruelty."* Ethics is not prescriptive; it is simply emotive. There are no commands; there are only ejaculations of one's personal feelings.

The first objection to this view is its radical solipsism. The right is reduced to what "I like," which reduces truth to mere taste. The ethical content of "Hitler should not kill Jews" is considered no different in kind from "I do not like chocolate." Second, the view does not *listen* to the meaning of "ought" statements; rather, it *legislates* what they must mean. In other words, on what basis is "ought" reduced to "I feel"? There are things I *ought* to do (such as be loving and just) whether I feel like it or not.

Right Is What Brings Pleasure

The Epicureans (fourth century, B.C.) are credited with the original philosophy of hedonism. Simply put, hedonism claims that what brings pleasure is right and what brings pain is wrong. Actually, the formula for right is a little more complicated. It is this: What brings the maximal pleasure and the minimal pain is the right thing to do.

There are obvious difficulties with this theory. First, not all pleasures are good and not all pain is bad. Sadistic pleasure gotten from torturing people is bad. The pain of study or hard work can be good. Second, one may ask—pleasure for whom and for how long? Pleasure for the individual and for the moment? What about for all men and for all time?

Right Is the Greatest Good for the Race

Utilitarians answer the last problem of the hedonistic view by claiming the right is what brings "the greatest good to the greatest number of persons (in the long run)." Jeremy Bentham (1748–1832) suggested that good should be understood in a *quantitative* sense. That is, it depended on how much pleasure was gotten for how long for how many. John Stuart Mill accepted utilitarianism, but insisted that good be understood in a *qualitative* sense as well. Some goods are higher than physical (and other) goods. An unhappy man is better than a happy pig, said Mill.

Clearly Mill's view is an improvement over both hedonism and Bentham's quantitative utilitarianism. There are, however, other difficulties. First of all, how does a human being—who can only rarely predict short-run consequences—determine what will result from his actions in the long run? Many evil actions (lying and cheating, for example) seem to "work" for people for long periods of time. Does this make them right? Second, how long is the long run? If it means the remote future or end of the world, then it is too out of reach to be of any help in making decisions today. But if it means the near future, then that would justify obviously evil things which work well for a short time (corrupt governments, cruelty, and deception). Finally, even when the results are obvious, how does one know they are "good" results unless he has some standard of good beyond the results? But if there is a norm for rightness or wrongness *beyond* the results, then the results as such do not determine rightness.

Good Is What Is Desired for Its Own Sake

The difficulty that has emerged from the above criticism is this: no matter how one defines right or good in terms of something else, one can still ask, "But is *that* right?" If good is defined as pleasure one can ask, "But is the pleasure good or bad?" If right is defined in terms of results, then one can still ask, "Are the results good or bad?" Perhaps the solution to this is to follow Aristotle and define the right or good in terms of itself. Maybe the good is that which is desirable for its own sake, namely, that which has intrinsic value in and of itself. In other words, good should never be desired as a means but only as an end.

Critics of this view have pointed out several problems. First, men seem to desire some evil ends for their own sake. How can the desire to annihilate a race be called a good desire? Aristotle would answer that every evil action is performed for a good end. Even the suicide victim acts for the alleged "good" it will bring to himself by eliminating all his problems. However, this answer leads to another criticism, namely, some "goods" are only apparent goods and not real ones. If we define good simply in terms of the end, then what we call "good" is often not really good at all but is evil.

Finally, there is a problem with providing *content* for the meaning of good. If good were simply the object of what is *desired,* then logically one should be able to examine the object(s) of his desires and discover the content of the meaning of good. But this will not do, since, as has already been noted, what we desire is not always genuinely good; sometimes it is only apparently good but actually evil. Thus we are faced with the dilemma that good cannot be defined in terms of anything else, and yet it seems to have no content when understood in terms of itself. Is there any way out?

Good Is Indefinable

G. E. Moore (1873–1958) insisted that the good is an unanalyzable and indefinable concept. Every attempt to define good in terms of something else commits what he called the "naturalistic fallacy." This fallacy results from assuming that because, for example, pleasure can be attributed to good then it is of the nature of Good, that is, identical with it. All that we can say is that "the Good is good," nothing more. The Good is known, then, only intuitively.

There are grounds for what Moore says, but there are also dangers. The first problem is that apparently not all people "intuit" the same content in the good or right. Further, many argue that intuitions are vague. They lack clarity, which is one of the things a philosopher pursues. Further, there is the problem of how to avoid the charge of tautology when all one can say is, "Good is good."

There is, however, some truth to Moore's position, especially since he recognized that ultimacy of "good" makes it resistant to definition in terms of something else. For eventually, every discipline and point of view must acknowledge *something* as its ground or source, in terms of which everything else is understood. To the Christian, who thinks of God in terms of the ultimate Good, this is very appealing.

Good Is What God Wills

One solution to the problem of defining good or right is to proclaim that something is right if God wills it right, and wrong if He wills it wrong. This would solve the problem of determining content in the meaning of good, as well as the difficulty involved in defining good in terms of something not ultimate. Christians claim God's sovereign will is ultimate and the Bible spells out the content of that will to us.

Although this does solve the problems above, it creates a few new ones. First, is something right because God wills it, or does He will it because it is right? If one takes the former (voluntaristic) alternative, then it seems to make God arbitrary. Could God actually will hate, instead of love, to be the right thing to do? Could He change His will and make cruelty right and kindness wrong? But if one takes the latter alternative, then God is acting according to a standard beyond Himself (goodness). This would contradict the Christian definition of God as the Ultimate. Many Christian ethicists (essentialists) have insisted that God can only will in accordance with His unchangingly good nature, which is not beyond Himself. Something is good because ultimately it is in accord with God's immutably good nature.

Further, if good is defined as what God wills, then we must first ask, Which god? Which revelation? There are many contenders for the title "God." We have, however, already given our reasons for believing that there is only one God, the theistic God (see chaps. 18, 19). Does this mean that there are no ethical norms for those who do not believe in God or in the Christian God? If ethics are to be normative for all men, then would not limiting the meaning of right and wrong to a particular religious revelation of right and wrong deny ethical norms for those who do not have any revelation from God?

A Christian View of Right and Wrong

The above discussion points out the difficulties in the various approaches to what is right. In view of these problems several conclusions emerge, all of which are accounted for by the Christian view of right and wrong.

The Synthesis of the Other Views

Even though the various non-Christian views of ethics were found unable to provide an adequate ethical system as such, there is an element of truth within each view.

First, it was discovered that "right" cannot be defined in terms of something else. The good is a basic category of its own. Feeling, pleasure, communal code, the consensus of the race, or the results— have all been found to be unreliable at times. Good is what has intrinsic value and should be desired for its own sake.

Second, we found that when good is so defined, it has ultimacy but it lacks content. One cannot supply the content by simply studying the object of his desires, since not everything desired is genuinely good. Some things which are desired for the good one sees in them are only apparently good but actually evil.

Third, it is inadequate to claim that the ultimate content of good can be defined by claiming that whatever God wills is good. This assumes an arbitrariness in a Being considered to be ultimately and essentially good. Something is not good simply because God wills it; rather, God wills it because it is good. And it is good because it is in accordance with His unchangeably good nature.

Fourth, there is, however, some truth in relating good to long-range results. If there is an absolutely good God, then surely He is interested in bringing about the greatest good for the greatest number in the long run. However, the results (in the long run) do not determine right; rather, what is right according to God will determine what the results will be. Further, since only an omniscient God can know what will bring the greatest good to the greatest number in the long run, then only God is in a position to determine the right way to bring about these best results.

Fifth, the same kind of argument applies to pleasure. Surely a good God is interested in maximizing pleasure and minimizing pain. But only God really knows what will bring "fulness of joy . . . [and] pleasures for evermore" (Ps. 16:11). What we think is good is often no more than the "fleeting pleasures of sin" (Heb. 12:25).

Sixth, there is a good deal of truth to the emotive theory of ethics.

Much of what is passed off as universal ethical "oughts" is no more than personal feelings. Not everything claimed to be prescriptive is actually more than emotive. We often strengthen our personal preferences by putting them in a divine imperative form.

Finally, not all aspects of ethical codes have universal applicability. Some rules are local and communal, such as speed laws. The mores of cultures do vary from place to place and from group to group; what is wrong in one place is right in another. Ethnocentricity is, however, a fact of life. We tend to judge other groups in terms of our own less-than-universal standards.

Christian ethics recognizes these cultural differences and does not demand that one give up his own culture in order to keep God's commands. Christianity asks only that one implement God's commands within that culture. For example, early Christians kissed one another in greeting. American Christians, however, usually shake hands as a greeting. Others embrace. All of this is culturally relative. We cannot conclude that there is nothing ethically binding on all Christians. In fact, within this cultural relativity there is a universally binding imperative: greet one another in love.

Elaboration of a Christian View of Right

The origin of the right. The Christian ethic is anchored ultimately and firmly in the unchanging nature of a God of perfect love and justice. The Christian avoids the false dichotomy that says either ethics is based on God's arbitrary will, or else God is subject to something beyond Himself. The Christian notes that there is a third alternative: God's will is subject to His own unchanging nature. "I the Lord do not change" (Mal. 3:6). "The Glory of Israel will not lie or repent" (I Sam. 15:29). Indeed, Hebrews tells us that "it is impossible that God should prove false" (Heb. 6:18).

Not only is the Christian God immutable, but He is omnibenevolent. The Scriptures declare: "God *is* love" (I John 4:16). That is, love is of the very essence of God. Indeed, "God so loved the world that he gave his only Son, that whoever believes in him should not perish but have eternal life" (John 3:16). In short, morality is based not in the arbitrary will of a supreme power, but in the unchanging nature of a loving Father. The Christian God has other attributes as well. He is just (Deut. 32:4); hence, we are assured that His love will be impartial (Rom.

2:11). Indeed, it is for this reason that "God so loved the *world* ..."
and that He is "longsuffering ... , not willing that any should perish,
but that all should come to repentance" (II Peter 3:9).

We cannot here give an exhaustive treatment of the attributes of
God, but we simply note that Christian ethics is based in the will of
God, who acts in accord with His unchanging character, loving justice,
and just love. God is neither arbitrary in His will nor is He subjected,
like Plato's Demiurge, to something beyond Himself (the Good),
something more ultimate. God's will is subjected only to what is
essentially Himself, that is, His unchanging loving and holy character.

First sphere of God's revelation of right.   The Christian believes
that God has revealed Himself in two spheres available to men: in His
world (including mankind), and in His Word (the Scriptures).
The former is called "natural revelation," and the latter is "supernatural revelation." Sometimes these revelations of God are called,
respectively, "general" (since it is available to all men), and "special" (since it is available only to those who have access to a Bible or
its truths).

In His providence, God knew that not all men would have access to
the truths of Scripture at all times, so He inscribed a law upon their
hearts. Paul wrote, "When Gentiles who have not the law do by nature
what the law requires, they are a law to themselves, even though they
do not have the [written] law. They show that what the law requires is
written on their hearts, while their conscience also bears witness ..."
(Rom. 2:14–15). Some Christian thinkers have described this knowledge of the law as "innate" or as "a natural inclination."[1] Even some
non-Christians admit to the universality of ethical principles.

The great moral creeds of mankind's civilizations have given testimony to the general revelation of God in the striking resemblance of
their basic ethical principles. C. S. Lewis has assembled many of these
creeds in the excellent appendix to his book, *The Abolition of Man.*[2]
Further evidence of the universal availability of God's "natural revelation" comes to light when one asks the following questions: What
person does not expect to be treated as a person? Who ever actually

---

1. Thomas Aquinas. *Summa Theologica* I.103.8.
2. C. S. Lewis, *The Abolition of Man* (New York: Macmillan, 1947), pp. 95–121.

believed that it was right to take what belonged to anyone at any time? Who ever truly believed that murder, rape, or cruelty to children was morally right?

To be sure, mankind has not always lived up to its moral ideals—this is an indication of our depravity and need for Christ's redemption. One's true moral principles cannot always be discovered from what one *does;* one does sometimes break his own moral principles. A Christian believes in the Golden Rule (Matt. 7:12), but what Christian (or non-Christian) perfectly practices it? It is what men *believe ought to be done* that is a closer clue to the natural law within them. Hence, it is in the great moral creeds of mankind, and perhaps even more so in their deep-seated beliefs, that we may discover God's general revelation.

Of course, even in moral creeds we may expect some divergence. Man's finitude alone, to say nothing of his sinfulness, can account for much diversity of interpretation. After all, scientists have been studying the same objective world for centuries and often have come to very different interpretations of it. It should not be surprising, then, that the objective and universal moral world (God's natural revelation) should be viewed somewhat differently by different men at different times. There is, nonetheless, a surprising unanimity of understanding of "natural revelation" as is indicated by the great moral creeds of mankind.

There is an even deeper indication of the universality of the moral law of God than human creeds; it is the *expectations* of human hearts. We see this not in what people *do* or even in what they *say* ought to be done; rather, we see it in what they *expect* others to do to them. In order to discover whether or not a man really believes one has a right to take anyone's property (or mate) at any time, do not ask him what he wishes to *do,* nor what he *says* one has the right to do. Just watch carefully how he reacts when someone attempts to seize what he dearly loves. In this sense the moral law can be discovered more by one's *reactions* than by his actions.

Surely it is fallacious to argue, as many humanists do, that what people *do* is what they *ought* to do. One can no more legitimately move from "do" to "ought" than he can from "is" to "ought," as Hume and others have pointed out. God's voice speaks to the hearts of all men, even those who do not have the written law of God. Paul wrote,

"All who have sinned without the [written] law will also perish with-out the law, and all who have sinned under the [written] law will be judged by the law" (Rom. 2:12).

Before we leave God's revelation in nature it is worth noting that it is this common revelation that makes dialogue and common social action possible. If there was nothing but a special revelation (such as Scripture), as regrettably some theologians have claimed (Karl Barth, for example), then there would be no meeting place possible between Christians and non-Christians. All one could do would be to shout his view at his opponents from the pinnacle of his own revelational pre-supposition. But thanks to God's general revelation, this is not neces-sary. Even non-Christian humanists, who explicitly reject God's reve-lation in Scripture, operate nonetheless in the sphere of God's natural revelation. Hence, both common light and common morals are avail-able for cooperative efforts between Christians and non-believers.

Another important aspect of God's general revelation is that it en-ables us to explain how non-Christians can sense a duty to perform moral acts without accepting the Bible. Indeed, since the moral law is available to men without any explicit theistic connections, one can even believe in an absolute moral law, as some humanists do, without believing in God. This being the case, no humanist can justifiably charge that adopting the Christian point of view entails rejecting the possibility of any ethical standard for non-Christians. This is by no means the case. The moral law is available to the non-Christian whether or not he wants to confess there is a moral Lawgiver. In like manner creation is available to all men, even those who will not explicitly admit there is a Creator.

Second sphere of God's revelation of right.   In addition to general revelation, the Christian has a special revelation in Scripture. The Bible claims to be the divinely inscripturated truth of God (II Tim. 3:16, 17). It is a special revelation of the same moral character of God that is revealed in nature and the hearts of men.

This immediately raises the question why God has two revelations. Is the first one insufficient? If so, why? If not, then is the second revelation redundant? The Christian responds that there are two rea-sons God adds His supernatural revelation to the natural one. First, the supernatural revelation is necessary to overcome the effects of sin on the minds of fallen men; and second, it provides more information about God than natural revelation.

Since these two are related, we will treat them together. "Sin came into the world through one man and death through sin, and so death spread to all men because all men sinned" (Rom. 5:12). Through sin the minds of men are darkened (Eph. 4:18) and, therefore, special light is needed to illuminate man's mind. Only then can he see the truth that is revealed to him in the natural world which his sin has obscured. Hence, sin occasions the need for both supernatural revelation and redemption through Christ.

Further, God's special revelation is more clear and explicit than general revelation. Indeed, special revelation is not only higher in kind but it is greater in extent. One can know more truths through special revelation than through general revelation. Most evangelical Christians, for example, believe that the so-called "mysteries" of the faith, such as the Trinity and the two natures of Christ, are not known by natural revelation.

Likewise, most evangelicals hold that natural revelation is sufficient only to reveal the moral standard to man; it is not sufficient for man's salvation (cf. Rom. 1:19, 20, and 2:12). It is generally agreed, however, that if one seeks to follow the light he has from natural revelation, God will give him the added (supernatural) light he needs to be saved. As Peter put it, "in every nation any one who fears him [God] and does what is right is acceptable to him" (Acts 10:35). The context of this verse is the story of Cornelius, a Gentile, who was seeking God and to whom God sent Peter with the gospel. In this regard the Book of Hebrews informs us that "whoever would draw near to God must believe that he exists and that he rewards those who seek him" (Heb. 11:6).

Those who do not seek God's light find themselves in darkness, for "men [love] darkness rather than light, because their deeds [are] evil" (John 3:19). But if anyone anywhere chooses to know and to do the will of God, God will reveal Himself, whether through a preacher of the gospel (Rom. 10:14), through a dream or vision (Dan. 2), through an angel (Rev. 14), or through the Scriptures themselves (Heb. 4:12).

Thus God has revealed Himself to all men through natural creation, "for what can be known about God is plain to them, because God has shown it to them" (Rom. 1:19). The problem is man's sin, and for this reason "the wrath of God is revealed from heaven against all ungodliness and wickedness of men who by their wickedness suppress the truth" (v. 18). Man's sin has darkened his mind and obscured the light of God's natural revelation which would shine through the windows of his soul. For this reason God has given a special revelation to aid in overcoming the noetic (intellectual) effects of sin. The natural revelation to a fallen man is like the occasional lightning that illuminates the landscape under the storm of sin—it momentarily but clearly reveals what is there. However, these flashes of light are not as great as the sustained noonday sun of special revelation.

In short, the Scriptures provide specific information and instruction for those who freely choose to know more about the Light. Those who prefer to stay bound in the darkness of their own decisions are left with the darkened world of flickering natural light and of shadows which become ever dimmer as they move farther away from the entrance of the light of Scripture.

The Scriptures are definitive and specific in the declaration of God's moral will for the lives of men. Special revelation is more clear, more precise, more easily promulgated without distortion, and less subject to misunderstanding and misrepresentation than is the more intuitively known revelation in the hearts of men. The Bible provides an objectively knowable reference point for discovering the will of the immutably loving and just God. To be sure, Scripture can be misunderstood, misapplied, and even twisted. But abuse does not bar use.

The absolute nature of the right. Absoluteness is a distinctive characteristic of evangelical ethics. This absolute basis for morality is grounded on the belief in an infinitely perfect God who wills men to be good in accordance with the unchanging perfection of His own nature. "You, therefore, must be perfect, as your heavenly Father is perfect" (Matt. 5:48).

One of the incongruities of the contemporary taste for relativism is that it holds to the absolute certainty of the truth of relativism. Humanism has often championed relativism, but has seldom appreciated the absolutes it harbors in its own bosom: the belief in the absolute character of its own humanistic presuppositions. Ironically, the absolutes that many non-Christian forms of humanism store in their own cellars have often been borrowed from the Judeo-Christian tradition. In essence, much (if not all) of the value of humanism is derived from the Christian character of its premises or presuppositions. In this moral sense, Western humanisms are often in effect non-theistic Christian cults.

But can the humanist logically borrow an ethic based in Christian theism without buying into Christian theism? It would seem that the dilemma of humanism is this: either admit relativism, or acknowledge the absolutes embodied in the Christian ethic.

Christian ethic is discovered, not created by men. One marked difference between the Christian ethic and non-Christian ethics is that for the Christian, values on which moral principles are based are not the result of mere human *decision*. Values, for the Christian, are determined by God and disclosed by revelation to man. Men do, of course, decide whether they will accept the values they discovered. Free creatures are free to reject any value (except the value to exercise their freedom).

This does not negate the fact that men come to the recognition of values in a normal psychological and sociological way. Non-Christian humanists usually confuse the *psychological* process by which one comes to adopt a value and the *epistemological* (and ontological) basis for believing it. However, simply because one came to know mathematical truths through a sociological process does not mean math has only a sociological basis. One plus three equals four regardless of the social flux. So it is with absolute moral values.

If God is all-good and all-knowing as the Christian believes, then He and He alone is in the best position to declare what is valuable and what is not valuable for finite creatures. Of course, there are rebellious souls who do not wish to accept any authority in their lives. This explains why many non-theists declare God out of bounds in their life. Sartre, for example, dismissed God from his life when God convicted him of a wrong in his young life.[3] Nietzsche said that hubris, or pride, overcame him when anyone would speak to him about God's claim on his life.

The superiority of the Christian view of right. From the foregoing discussion it is clear that a number of values of the Christian ethic show it to be superior to the humanistic ethic.

First, the Christian view of right has a superior *source*—God. The

---

3. Jean-Paul Sartre, *Words,* (New York: George Braziller, 1964), p. 102.

Christian claims God is an infinitely loving, personal Being whose perfections are absolute. Even the most optimistic non-Christian humanist can at best offer a human species which is hopefully and emergently being perfected by trial and error. If the Christian claim is correct, then the ultimate source of its morality (the character of God) is infinitely superior to any mere humanistic ethic.

There is a consequence here that humanists have not fully faced. If an infinite value is of greater value than a finite value, then the only successful way for a humanist to argue that his ethic based in man is superior, is to demonstrate that the Christian God does not exist. But all such attempts to disprove God have been notoriously unsuccessful. Indeed, many such attempts boomerang, for they are inconsistent (see chap. 18).

Second, the Christian ethic has a superior personal *manifestation*— Jesus Christ. The Bible teaches that Christ is God incarnate, that is, in human flesh (John 1:1; Heb. 1:8; Col. 1:16–17; and so on). The New Testament proclaims Him to be the Jehovah of the Old Testament on numerous occasions (cf. Rev. 11:17 with Isa. 41:4; Phil. 2:10 with Isa. 45:23). Jesus Himself claimed to be the "I Am" of Exodus 3:14 (John 8:58) and to be the eternal partner of God's glory (John 17:5), which Isaiah 42:8 says Jehovah will never give to another. Jesus claimed to be able to forgive sins and raise the dead, which elicited outcries of blasphemy from the monotheistic Jews to whom He spoke (Mark 2:7; John 5:25f., cf. 8:59). Jesus accepted worship on numerous occasions (cf. Matt. 28:17; John 9:38). When He made these claims the Jews picked up stones to kill Him, saying, "We stone you for no good work but for blasphemy; because you, being a man, make yourself God" (John 10:33).

In view of the unique, miraculous fulfillment of dozens of prophecies uttered hundreds of years before His birth, many of which Jesus could not possibly have manipulated (such as the time and place of His birth, Dan. 9 and Mic. 5), and in view of His sinless, miraculous life and His supernatural resurrection from the grave—which is historically verifiable—the most reasonable conclusion is to accept Christ's claim about Himself to be God. Numerous skeptics have examined these claims in the light of historical and legal evidence and have been converted to Christianity.[4] The claims are still open for examination today.

---

4. See Frank Morison, *Who Moved the Stone?* (Grand Rapids, Mich.: Zondervan, 1977).

In the light of Christ's deity and His incarnation, the Christian possesses an ethical manifestation superior to any mere humanism. He who was God Himself was one of us and lived among us, showing us how to live with ourselves. Humanism as such has never produced a perfect man, let alone the God-man. Christianity presents the second person of the Godhead who became man and dwelt among us (John 1:14). Jesus is the One "who in every respect has been tempted as we are, yet without sinning" (Heb. 4:15). Jesus was truly human in every sense of the word. He ate and slept, He became tired, He cried, He experienced hunger and anger, He knew loneliness and suffering.

Because of all this, we have a personal and human referent—a perfect one—for our morality. Christ is our complete moral example. In view of Him, morality is not a mere legalistic assent to a written code; it is a dynamic relation to a living Person. The essence of morality is not the love of abstract laws; it is the love of a person, Jesus Christ, and through Him and by Him the love of all persons (Matt. 22:36, 37). The Christian ethic, then, is eminently human and personal in its manifestation.

Further, Christianity has a superior ethical *declaration*—the Bible. God is love, and Christ is God's love manifest in personal form. The law, or written Word of God, is love manifest in propositional form. Moral laws are God's way of putting love into words. Indeed, Jesus said that all of the moral laws of the Old Testament are really expressions of two loves, one for God and one for man (Matt. 22:36, 37). Law, then, for the Christian is a propositional statement of personal concern that calls for personal, loving response.

This love cannot be forced; love can be commanded but it cannot be demanded. That is, moral laws can tell us what is best for us and exhort us to do it (and surely an infinitely wise and loving God knows this better than we do), but moral laws cannot force us to conform. Love always leaves space to say no. Thus while moral laws have a positive force they cannot in this sense have a positive enforcement. Laws indicate the direction that is best for the true happiness of the individual, but they do not dictate.

Further, the Christian view of right entails a superior *motivation*—the love of Christ. Non-Christian humanists can give very little motivation to perform what humanism holds to be moral rules or goals. Indeed, it might be said that they are often correct in stating the general moral laws (or at least the goals) but they cannot generate the motivation from within their humanism to encourage men to obey those laws.

Christianity also provides a superior *justification* for ethics. A non-Christian can believe in good ethical principles, but he lacks the rationale for belief that the Christian God provides. When the egoist says, "Why should I love others?" the Christian can answer, "Because God says so, and He will judge us someday." The Christian remembers the words of Paul, "For God has done what the law, weakened by the flesh, could not do: sending his own Son in the likeness of sinful flesh and for sin, he condemned sin in the flesh, in order that the just requirement of the law might be fulfilled in us, who walk not according to the flesh but according to the Spirit" (Rom. 8:3, 4).

The moral law was never intended to give man the *ability* to live up to it, any more than yardsticks are made to make people grow taller or plumblines are made to straighten buildings. The law was given to *show* us the standard; when we fall short of it we do not use the standard to correct the situation. A mirror will show a man the dirt on his face, but it will not wash the dirt away.

The law reveals man's guilt before a Holy God in the light of His moral standards, but the law cannot save. In this sense, the law brings condemnation but not salvation. Only Christ can save. But here is precisely the superiority of the Christian system. Where does one get the motivation to love others in accordance with God's love? What motivated the great social movements that started hospitals, launched the Red Cross, established rescue missions, improved working conditions, and sent thousands to the underdeveloped nations with strategic help? In all of these cases and numerous other social efforts Christians motivated by the love of Christ provided the needed energy to accomplish these tasks. Christian men and women said in essence, "The love of Christ controls us, because we are convinced that one has died for all; therefore . . . those who live might live no longer for themselves but for him who for their sake died and was raised" (II Cor. 5:14, 15).

Conclusion

There is, of course, the crucial question of how one can justify the Christian claim of what is right. That is the subject of the next chapter. Here we are concerned only with the *nature* of right. Several views of what is meant by "right" have been examined and found wanting. It has been suggested, however, that these deficiencies are not found in the Christian view of right. Furthermore, the values present in these views are also found in the Christian view. The Christian view of ethics has a superior source (God), a superior manifestation (Jesus Christ), as well as superior declaration (the Bible), and superior motivation (love of Christ).

Suggested Readings

James, William. *Pragmatism*
Kant, Immanuel. *Critique of Practical Religion*
Lewis, C. S. *Mere Christianity,* part one
Moore, G. E. *Principia Ethica*
Nietzsche, Friedrich. *Beyond Good and Evil*
Owen, Joseph. *The Moral Argument*
Stevenson, C. L. *Ethics and Language*

24 How Do We Know What Is Right?

There have been various attempts to justify ethical principles, most of which depend on particular definitions of the right. We will first examine inadequacies in the prominent views and then offer a more adequate justification from a Christian point of view.

Justifying What Is Meant by Right

The differences in what is meant by *right* (see chap. 23) will of course affect the justifications of ethical points of view.

Justification by Results

William James unabashedly suggested that something was right if it "worked." The good is the expedient, he claimed; acts or intentions are not good as such, but they become good if they bring good results. The rightness or wrongness of actions is judged not by their roots, but by their fruits. To use James's term, the "cash-value" of the term *right* is its results. What brings desirable consequences is good and what does not is bad.

One of the most pointed criticisms of James's pragmatism was given by Josiah Royce, a colleague at Harvard, who wondered whether James would be satisfied "to put a witness on the stand in court and have him swear to tell 'the expedient, the whole expedient, and nothing but the expedient, so help him future experience.'" Furthermore, one could ask, "Results desired by whom?" For obviously, results desirable to some are undesirable to others. In addition, even desired consequences do not prove something right. Lying, cheating, and even killing sometimes bring desired consequences, but this does not make them right. Finally, even when the consequences are clear, one can still ask, "Are they good or bad?" If the question of right or wrong is not answered by results, then results cannot be the sole justification for what is meant by right actions. Bad motives (for example, being generous to be praised by men, not out of concern for the poor) can bring good results, and vice versa.

Justification by the Self-Destructive Nature of the Contrary

Immanuel Kant insisted that there is a universal "categorical imperative" binding on all men. Duty demands that we treat others always as ends and never as a means to an end. They should be treated as persons, never as things. This categorical imperative demands that we never lie to another or murder another person. In short, one should never do anything that he cannot will as a universal law for all men. The justification of this position, Kant argued, is that it is self-destructive to will the opposite of what duty demands. That is, the opposite of a categorical duty cannot be universally applied. For instance, if one were to will lying (the opposite of truth-telling) as a universal law, then there would be no more truth to lie about, since all would be false. Likewise, if one were to will killing universally, then there would be no more people to kill. In short, the self-destructive nature of the opposite is a kind of justification for right actions.

There are several lines of attack on Kant's position. First of all, it is not self-destructive to will lying in some cases, or even killing in some cases. One could will as a universal law, for example, that one never kill, except in self-defense. Second, some existentialists ask why the criterion for what is right be universalizable (rather than particularizable). They believe Kant begs the question to insist that the rule must be universal before it can qualify as an ethical duty. Third, some say Kant's justification is really only pragmatic.

Justification by Intuition

Many ethicists have insisted that what is good is known only by intuition. G. E. Moore argued that since the good is not definable in terms of anything other than itself, it follows that one must know it intuitionally. Good is good, and we know that only as a whole. It cannot be analyzed, or broken down into parts.

There have been many others who have argued for an intuitive *source* for knowing the good, but not all would use intuition as a *justification* for knowing what is right. It is this latter sense which involves serious problems.

First, not everyone intuits the same meaning of the term *right*. Intuitions are often quite different and obviously colored by culture and environment. Second, using intuition as a grounds for ethical belief confuses the *source* of belief and *substantiation* of that belief. One may derive beliefs—ethical or otherwise—from any source he wishes (dreams, intuitions, and so on), but the question here is how one *justifies* holding one belief over opposing beliefs. Finally, at best the justification would not be the intuition itself, but the self-evidence of the principle being intuited (such as, good = good).

Justification by Self-Evidence

Some ethicists argue that basic ethical norms are self-evident. Thomas Aquinas contended that there are *first principles* for all knowledge, such as the law of non-contradiction in epistemology, and the law of benevolence in ethics. All first principles, he insisted, are self-evident. However, not all principles are immediately self-evident. Some are only self-evident upon *inspection*. Take the principle of benevolence as an example: "Be good to every person." This is not immediately self-evident, but is clear on inspection of the terms. For "person" is one who has intrinsic worth or good, and "good" is what should be desired for its own sake (what has intrinsic worth). Therefore, the benevolence principle simply means, "treat persons as persons," or "do good to that which deserves good."

There are two basic problems with this view. First, not everyone defines the terms of statements in the same way, in which case they would not be self-evident, even on inspection. Second, to some, self-evident principles are void of content, or at least are so general as to be unhelpful for practical application. Some would ask, What is the value of telling someone to be "good" if we cannot spell out precisely what is meant by "good"?

Justification by Appeal to Human Authority

The question, "How do we know what is right?" could be answered, as Thomas Hobbes did, "The King said so!" That is, one can appeal to some sovereign authority, whether it be some government or other leader. This authority could be an individual or a group, either present or past. Since many things cannot be *directly* known, either epistemologically or ethically, much of our belief and action must be based on the testimony of others. So, it is argued, what is right and wrong should be accepted on the authority of another.

This view has numerous problems. First, what evidence is there that the authority is worthy? If there is none, the authority should not be accepted. If there is evidence that the authority is worthy, then this *evidence* becomes the justification for what is "right," rather than the fact that an authority said it is. Second, authorities have often been wrong. And any authority that can be wrong is obviously not the final authority for what is right, since it too must be judged by a norm beyond itself for what is right. Further, even if the authority is right, it would not be final, since it would always be possible to ask why one should accept it. Finally, if we answer, "How do we know this is right?" by, "The authority told us so," then one can still ask, "Who told him?" Until one finally reaches the "Ultimate Authority" who nobody told what is right but who simply "knows," he has not reached the real ground for what is right. But once one reaches this "Ultimate Authority" who just "knows," then he has arrived at God. This leads to the next justification.

Justification by Appeal to Divine Authority

Christianity, Judaism, Islam, and other religions often answer the question, "How do I know this is right?" by affirming, "God said so!" This position avoids some obvious difficulties. First, it is a final appeal to the Ultimate beyond which there is no appeal. Also, it avoids the problem of defining the good in terms of something else. God is good, and that settles that. What He says is final.

The problems with the appeal to divine authority are these. First, is the authority based simply in God's will (voluntarism)? If so, how do we know it is a "good" will? Unless the authority for good is based in God's goodness, that is, His nature (essentialism), then this authority cannot be an authority for what is good. Simply because God is powerful would not make Him an authority for good—might does not make right. It is goodness in God that makes Him an Ultimate Authority on what is good. Second, even if goodness is based in God's good nature, the question still remains concerning how we can know the nature of God. It will not suffice to reply: "He has revealed it in His Word," because one can still ask, "Which Word is that? The Koran, the Bible, or the Book of Mormon?" All these, and others, claim to be God's Word. The thinking believer is still faced with the Socratic dictum (restated): "The unexamined revelation is not worth believing." Further, if what is meant by "good" depends on belief in God and the Bible, then is there any basis for good conduct available to an atheist or one that does not believe the Bible is God's Word?

A Christian Justification of the Right

Not all Christians go about justifying what is right in the same way. We will describe briefly several different Christian approaches and then try to spell out what seems to be an adequate method of justification of the Christian belief in what is right or good.

Most Christians fall into two general classes on this issue: (1) those who attempt to justify both a supernatural and a natural revelation, and (2) those who give justification only for a supernatural revelation. (In addition, there are some who call themselves Christians who deny all supernatural revelation, but their view is not distinctively Christian.) First, let us turn our attention to the supernatural revelation.

Appeal to Faith Alone

Some Christians have been content to give no justification whatsoever for their belief in the Bible. They simply believe the Bible is God's Word, and that is final. This view is called *fideism*.

Fideism. The heart of fideism is that no evidence or argumentation can bear upon a religious belief in God or in His Word. If God's Word is Ultimate, then there is nothing more ultimate in terms of which it can be justified. For since God "had no one greater by whom to swear, He swore by Himself" (Heb. 6:13). That is, if God is Ultimate, then the only criteria to which we can appeal to discover whether He is God is Himself. For if appeal is made to a rational argument, then the argument is considered more ultimate than God. "Lions do not need to be defended; they need only to be let loose," such Christians say. Likewise, the fideist believes that God does not need to be defended; we need only to listen to His authoritative Word, the Bible. Does not the Bible say, "Without faith it is impossible to please him [God]" (Heb. 11:6)? Some fideists would say that doubting Thomas was rebuked for demanding empirical evidence of the resurrected Christ—for Jesus replied, "Have you believed because you have seen me? Blessed are those who have not seen and yet believe" (John 20:29).

In short, for a fideist the only grounds for believing in God is God Himself. Anyone who believes in God *because* of any evidence or reasoning process has exalted human reason above God. Christian fideists object that others make God subject to rules of reason such as the law of non-contradiction. Should we not rather do as the apostle Paul exhorted us, and "take every thought captive to obey Christ" (II Cor. 10:5)? Did not God say through the prophet, "for my thoughts are not your thoughts . . . says the Lord" (Isa. 55:8)?

Evaluation of fideism. Since fideism has already been evaluated (see chap. 17), we will only discuss it briefly here.

First of all, Christian fideists seem to be correct *ontologically*. That is, if there is a God, and if He has spoken in the Bible (as Christians believe), then whatever the Bible says should be accepted, no questions asked. For God is Ultimate and His Word is final. As Paul said, "Who are you, a man, to answer back to God?" (Rom. 9:20). God should be believed for no other reason than that He is God. Any grounds for belief in God other than the fact that He is the ultimate, good Authority, are less than the most worthy grounds. We should not believe in God because of rational arguments, but because He is God. For "it is impossible that God should prove false" (Heb. 6:18). We trust in "God who never lies" (Titus 1:2). Therefore, "let God be true though every man be false" (Rom. 3:4). In this Christian fideists seem to be correct.

Second, however, fideists are incorrect *epistemologically*. To be sure, *if* there is a God, and *if* He has spoken in the Bible, then all of the above follows. But those are big "ifs"! The real question is, how do we know God has spoken infallibly in the Bible? This is the epistemological question, and it cannot be answered by a simple appeal to faith, for the following reasons. (1) An appeal to whose faith? Persons of different religions have different faiths. How do we know which is right? (2) Faith in which Book? The Koran, the Bible, the Book of Mormon? Which one? They all claim to be God's Word and yet their claims contradict one another. (3) Belief statements are not a *justification;* they are simply an affirmation. Beliefs are not knowledge; they must be justified before they can be known to be true.

Third, there is a difference between "belief *that*" and "belief *in*." The fideists appear correct in what they say about "belief *in*"; it requires no evidence but is simply an act of faith. For instance, one does not love his wife because of any evidence, but because of who she is—a person worthy of love. This is like "belief in." On the other hand, suppose one's wife has been dead for years, but one continues to talk to her as though she were alive. One would be considered insane if he continued to believe *in* someone if he had no evidence *that* she was alive. In short, "belief *that*" demands evidence, and it is prior to "belief *in*" someone. The fideist fails to appreciate that it is necessary for us to have good evidence or reason to believe *that* God is, and *that* the Bible is His Word before we place unconditional faith in God and in His Word.

Fourth, is not the fideist inconsistent when he offers any reason for his position? For if reason does not bear on the question of God—only faith is valid—then how can one offer reasons for accepting fideism as true? The dilemma is this: either a fideist offers some justification for fideism or else he does not. If he does offer justification for his position, then he is no longer a fideist. He should simply believe it. If he does not offer any justification for his position, then it is an unjustified belief which cannot claim to be true. All truth claims must be justified, or else anything and everything *claimed* to be true, is true.

Finally, non-fideists are not necessarily exalting reason above God when they insist on testing truth claims. Even the Bible that Christian fideists accept commands: "Do not believe every spirit, but test the spirits to see whether they are of God" (I John 4:1). And concerning the laws of reason, such as the principles of non-contradiction, the apostle Paul exhorted: "Avoid . . . contradictions of what is falsely called knowledge" (I Tim. 6:20). Peter also commanded that believers give "a reason of the hope that is in [them]" (I Peter 3:15, KJV). God Himself bids us, "Come now, let us reason together, says the Lord" (Isa. 1:18). God is reasonable and He demands that we use our reason, for we are made in His image and likeness (Gen. 1:26). Thus when a Christian tests alleged revelations, avoids contradictions, or thinks reasonably, he is not exalting himself above God; rather, he is obeying the God who is reasonable and who demands that we use our reason.

Appeal to Reason

If faith alone applies to "belief *in*" but is insufficient as a basis for "belief *that*," then the Christian must appeal to some kind of justification for his belief that the Bible is God's Word, the final authority for what is right and wrong. The intellectual discipline that deals with this is called "Christian Apologetics" or "Christian Evidences." Since it is beyond the scope of the book to state the case in detail, we will summarize the basic type of argument that can be used.

The theistic God exists. The reasons for this have already been given in chapter 18.

If God exists then miracles are possible. A miracle is an act of God in the natural world that confirms the message of God through His prophet or apostle (Heb. 2:3–4). Miracles are automatically possible in a theistic world where there is a sovereign God beyond the world in control of its processes and laws. Miracles are not contrary to nature; rather, they go beyond natural events. Natural law is the way God regularly operates in His world; miracles are the way He acts occasionally. Since God is all-powerful, He can do anything that is not a contradiction. Therefore, miracles are possible.

Jesus claimed to be God in human form.   There is more than
sufficient historical evidence that Jesus lived and that the New Testament documents are a reliable record of what He actually taught.[1] But
the New Testament tells us that Jesus claimed to be God (John 5:23f.;
8:58; 10:30f.; Mark 2:7f.; 14:61f.). Furthermore, Jesus miraculously
fulfilled dozens of prophecies about the coming Messiah-God (Ps.
45:7; 110:1; Isa. 9:6), including where He would be born (Mic. 5:2),
when He would die (Dan. 9:24f.), how He would suffer (Isa. 53), how
He would die (Ps. 22:15), and even how He would rise from the dead
(Pss. 2, 16). In addition to this, Jesus lived a sinless life (Heb. 4:15;
I Peter 1:19; I John 3:4) filled with miraculous confirmations of who He
was, including a virgin birth (Matt. 1; Luke 2), and a confirming voice
from heaven three times (Matt. 3, 17; John 12). He performed numerous miracles (John 20:30) including raising the dead (John 11), and
died a unique death (John 19). Finally, Jesus predicted (John 2; Matt.
12, 17) and accomplished His resurrection from the dead (John
10:10f.; Matt. 28). Hence, there was miraculous confirmation from
birth to resurrection of who Jesus claimed to be. But a miracle is an act
of God confirming the Word of God through the mouthpiece of God
(that is, a prophet). Jesus' claim to be God was divinely confirmed to
be true: Jesus is God!

Whatever God says is true.   The fact that all of God's statements
are true follows from His very nature as an absolutely perfect and
omniscient being. If He knows all, then He cannot make a mistake.
And if He is morally perfect, then He will not deceive. In the words of
Scripture, "It [is] impossible for God to lie" (Heb. 6:18, KJV).

Jesus taught that the Bible is the Word of God.   Jesus affirmed
that the Old Testament was God's unbreakable truth (John 10:34–35),
even in the tenses of verbs (Matt. 22:32) and the smallest parts of
letters (Matt. 5:17, 18). He proclaimed both its inspiration (Matt.
22:43) and final authority, over Satan (Matt. 4:4, 7, 10) and over all
human teaching (Matt. 15:1f.). Jesus declared the unity of the Old
Testament (Luke 24:27, 44) as well as its inerrancy (John 17:17; Matt.
22:29). He affirmed the truth of the creation story (Matt. 19:35), the

---

1. See F. F. Bruce, *The New Testament Documents: Are They Reliable?* (Grand
Rapids: Eerdmans, 1943).

world-wide flood in Noah's day (Matt. 24:38-39), and that Jonah was in a great fish for three days (Matt. 12:40-42). In short, Jesus affirmed the divine authority, authenticity, and historicity of the Old Testament. He called it "the Word of God" (John 10:34).

Furthermore, Jesus placed His own words on par with the Old Testament (Matt. 5:18, cf. Matt. 24:35), and said that the apostles would be guided in remembering (John 14:26; 16:13) and teaching everything He had taught them (Matt. 28:18-20, cf. Acts 1:1; 2:42; Eph. 2:20). Hence, the Gospels and Epistles of the New Testament are on the same level as the Old Testament, as was recognized by Paul (I Tim. 5:18) and Peter (II Peter 3:15-16).

Therefore, the Bible is the Word of God.　The whole Bible is the Word of God, in accordance with the teaching of Jesus. Jesus is God, and cannot lie or teach what is false. Jesus taught that the Bible is the Word of God. Therefore, it is true that the Bible is the Word of God.

This, in brief, is an argument that Christians can and have used to justify their claim that the Bible is God's Word, the final authority on what is right and wrong.

The Nature of General Revelation

If Christians have their own "special" revelation from God on which to base their conduct, what about non-Christians who do not accept Scripture? The answer to this is that there is a "general" revelation which is available to all men.

According to Romans 2:12-16, there is a law written on the hearts of unbelievers (v. 15), so that they know "by nature what the law requires" (v. 14). In the first chapter of Romans, pagan sins (including homosexual practices) are said to be "against nature" (v. 26, KJV). This revelation of God in human nature is usually called "the natural law." Natural revelation has been available to all men "since the creation of the world," and so men are "without excuse" (v. 20) for not following it. Since this revelation is universal, it serves as a basis for cooperative ethical action with those who do not accept the Christian God or Scriptures. It means that the Christian's "special" law does not prevent contact, communication, and even cooperation with non-Christians on common social or human goods. Since all men (even fallen man) are made in God's image (Gen. 1:27; 9:6; James 3:9), and since God "did not leave himself without witness" to any people (Acts 14:17), then there is every reason that Christians and non-Christians can act together on the basis of this general revelation and "do good to all men" (Gal. 6:10).

There are definite advantages in having a written revelation concerning right and wrong. First, it is not so easily distorted. Consciences can be distorted by sin (Rom. 2:15) and even "seared" (I Tim. 4:2) or deadened by constant rejection of the truth. Further, written revelation is more specific. It spells out in more detail the meaning of right thoughts and actions. Finally, a written code is more easily preserved and more accurately transmitted from generation to generation. But, of course, with greater light (from the special revelation in Scriptures) comes greater responsibility.

The Justification of General Revelation

The problems in justifying a natural ethic have already been discussed. If the Christian wishes to maintain that there are grounds for right conduct apart from the Scriptures, then he must offer some justification for his belief in right and wrong. We will not repeat here the reasons for the inadequacies in some attempted justifications (stated in the first part of this chapter). We will simply mention the basic elements in what seems to be an adequate justification of a Christian concept of right.

Intuitional basis. In the final analysis it seems necessary to accept some kind of intuitional *source* for natural "right." For if what is right cannot be understood or defined in terms of something else, then it must be understood intuitionally. This should not seem strange. Bertrand Russell believed that the principle of induction was intuitionally derived. Further, if "ought" is a basic category that cannot be reduced to "is" or anything else, then one must understand it intuitionally, since there is no way to break it down further. As Aristotle said, all reasoning is based on first principles and these cannot be proven. Whatever cannot be known in terms of something else, must be understood in terms of itself. This is what is meant by "intuition."

Self-evidence. Of course, intuitions are not justifications, but only a *source* of what Christians believe about right and wrong. But if there is no way to further break down or reduce what we intuit as right, then perhaps right and wrong are in some sense either self-evident or necessary. Not all Christians agree with Aquinas that one must be able to state the basic good intuited in such a way that the predicate is reducible to the subject. Many do agree, however, that what is known cannot be broken down any further. Its truth is evident in itself. The problem is, however, that if this is correct, then all we know is that "good = good" and "right = right." How can we put *content* into the intuited, self-evident principles of good?

Human expectation.   One suggestion of the way particular ethical principles can be discovered is by an examination of human expectations. That is, perhaps what is right is not determined by what is *done* (for the wrong is often done by men), nor by what is *believed* ought to be done (for there are incorrect beliefs about right). Rather, perhaps right is discovered by what persons expect should be done to them. A man's true ethic is discovered not by what he does but by what he expects others to do to him. (This may be why Jesus said in Matthew 7:12, the "Golden Rule," "Whatever you *wish* [desire, expect] that men would do to you, do so to them.") In brief, it may not be a man's actions (in doing to others) but his *reactions* (when others do to him) that reveal his true ethics.

Let us illustrate the point. An ethics professor once received a brilliant, scholarly paper written by a student who defended antinomianism, claiming that there are no moral principles. The professor wrote on the paper, "F. I do not like the blue folder you used for your paper." The student protested vociferously, "That's not fair! That's not just! I should have been given the grade I deserved and not an 'F' simply because the folder was blue!" "Oh," replied the professor, "you *do* believe in moral principles after all, such as 'justice' and 'fairness.' In that case I will give you the grade you 'deserve.' Here is an 'A' for a well-written paper." From this illustration it is apparent that what the student *said* he believed, he did not *really* believe. His *reaction* to an injustice done to him proved what he *expected* to be done to him.

Perhaps, then, by an examination of the way humans desire (expect) to be treated, we can put content into what is meant by "do good to all men." Surely, all men, for example, do expect to be treated as an end and not as a means, as a person and not a thing. Surely, all persons feel they have intrinsic value and not merely extrinsic value. If so, then one can begin to provide some content from human experience to disclose the meaning of the moral law.

Conclusion

There have been numerous attempts to justify the concept of *right*. All of those who attempt to justify the right pragmatically, socially, or politically fail because these grounds are often evil. Neither can right be justified by intuition, for intuition is only a source, not a justification, of knowledge. An appeal to authority to justify right will eventually end in the Ultimate Authority (God) beyond which there is no court of appeal. But even here one must have some justification for believing in God. The Christian provides reason both for his belief in God and in the Bible as an authoritative rule for conduct. Christians believe in both a "special" revelation (in the Bible) and a "general" revelation (in human nature) which is available to all men. The latter is known by intuition and justified by human expectation.

Suggested Readings

Aquinas, Thomas. *Summa Theologica,* vol. 28
Austin, John. *The Province of Jurisprudence Determined*
Brandt, R. "Toward a Credible Form of Utilitarianism," in *Morality and the Language of Conduct,* ed. H. Castenada and George Nikhnikian
Donagan, A. "Is There a Credible Form of Utilitarianism?" in *Contemporary Utilitarianism,* ed. Michael Bayles
Ross, David. *The Right and the Good*

The Relationship Between Rules and Results

Basically there are two approaches to ethics. One centers in rules and the other in results. The former is duty-centered and is called *deontological*. The latter is end-centered and is called *teleological*.

The Right Is Right Regardless of the Result

The deontological view has been held by many great philosophers, including Plato and Immanuel Kant. It can be understood by contrast with the teleological view.

Contrast of Command and Consequence

According to deontological ethics, keeping the rule will determine the right results; right results do not determine the rule. What is intrinsically right determines the best results; one cannot determine what is right by the results. Keeping the ethical commands will bring the best consequence.

According to deontological ethics, the right is *principial,* not pragmatic. That is, right is discovered to be based in some intrinsic good; it is not determined by the alleged extrinsic goods it may bring. What is right, therefore, is found in norms, not in ends. It is determined by the demands of duty, not by the destiny of the human race. In brief, the deontologist insists that ethics be normative, not utilitarian.

Source of Deontological Ethics

Deontologists are generally intuitional in their approach to what is right. The right is either discovered by human intuition or else it is determined by divine command (see chap. 24). If by divine command, ethics is theological (about God), not eschatological (about the End). If by intuition, values are not determined by human intentions or actions; rather, values are *discovered* by human intuition. But in both cases, duty is centered in rule (or command), not in result (or consequence).

Justification of Deontological Ethics

We have already surveyed the various attempts to justify theories of right (see chap. 24). It is sufficient to note here that deontological ethics is usually justified by an appeal to intuition (self-evident values) or else by an appeal to a command of God. This, too, has been discussed in the previous chapter. There are two basic ways proponents have defended deontological ethics.

The indirect defense of duty.   If duty is based on an intuition of some first principle, then there is nothing beyond the principle (since it is *first*) in terms of which it can be defended. The principle must in some sense be self-evident. That is, once the terms are understood, the truth is clearly seen. For example, "Do good to all persons" means, on analysis, "Treat the intrinsic good in persons as an intrinsic good." The principle, then, is self-evident.

Defense by self-destruction of the opposite.   Immanuel Kant defended his duty-ethic by contending that any denial of a duty-principle (which he called the "categorical imperative") will be self-destructive. For example, by willing the opposite of one's duty not to kill, one is willing that *all* be killed.

Right Is Determined by Results

In contrast to duty-centered ethics, the utilitarian position argues that long-range consequences determine what is right and what is wrong. Since the teleological position involves a criticism of the deontological view, we will turn our attention immediately to that.

Background of Utilitarianism

The Epicureans had insisted that pleasure is good and pain is evil. Hence, if one can maximize pleasure and minimize pain, he has done the good thing. However, taken in an individual sense this can be a very selfish endeavor. One could maximize pleasure for himself while making pain for others.

The modern utilitarians offer a solution to this problem. Jeremy Bentham (1748–1832) developed a "hedonistic calculus." The right action, said he, is the one which brings the greatest pleasure to the greatest number of people. This is called *quantitative* utilitarianism, because it stresses the amount of pleasure experienced, as well as the amount of people who experience it. No one kind of pleasure is better than another. As it has been said, "Pleasure being equal, pushpin is as good as poetry."

John Stuart Mill (1806–1873) gave a further sophistication to this view by interpreting pleasure *qualitatively*. He was more concerned with the *kind* of pleasure gained, for he held that some pleasures are base compared to others. The intellectual and cultured pleasures are to be preferred to simple bodily gratification. In this regard Mill believed that "it is better to be a man dissatisfied than a pig satisfied."

In both kinds of utilitarianism, however, the rightness or wrongness of an action is determined by what brings "the greatest good to the greatest number of people." In no case is something good *simply* because someone (even God) says it is good.

The Essence of Utilitarianism

At the very heart of utilitarian or result-centered ethics is the belief that the *rightness or wrongness of actions are determined by their results*. The typical example is this: The attempt to save a drowning man is not *in itself* a good act. For the extreme utilitarian, the act is not good unless it brings good results. If the man is rescued, then the act is a good act; if he drowns, it is not.

Of course, some sophisticated utilitarian might argue that good results do come from even an unsuccessful attempt to rescue a drowning man (the appreciation of the victim's family, one's own personal satisfaction for trying, and the effect on society of the news of a courageous man). All of this notwithstanding, according to utilitarianism, the mere act of attempting to rescue a drowning man is good *if and only if* it brings some good results; the act is not good in itself.

Strictly speaking, for the utilitarian, results and results alone—whether physical or otherwise—determine whether an act is good. There are, of course, some who call themselves utilitarian who believe that societies which have ethical rules are better than those which do not, even apart from the results. Here the distinctions begin to blur and some non-utilitarians insist that this is no longer a utilitarian view.

Two Kinds of Utilitarianism

All utilitarians believe that actions are judged by results. But actions may be understood either individually or as a group. If one judges each individual act in terms of its anticipated results, he is called an *act*-utilitarian. If, on the other hand, one judges a certain kind or class of actions (prescribed by the rule) by their results, then he is called a *rule*-utilitarian. The former tries to discover whether performing a given *act* brings good consequences, and the latter whether keeping a given *rule* will eventuate in the greatest good.

Act-utilitarians. The act-utilitarian is not concerned with finding rules that he believes should always be kept (that is, universal rules). He is content to know that there are general rules which have been discovered by trial and error over long periods of time. These constitute for him a "fund of experience" on which he draws for guidance when trying to determine which course of action will bring the best results. The utilitarian recognizes that he cannot personally predict the distant future, so he must trust the past as a guide to the future. What men have learned from past consequences is the guide for what *generally* will be best in the present. Of course, this is not always the case.

There will be special *exceptions* to these general rules. Murder, for example, is generally wrong based on past experience. However, in some instances (say, killing a tyrant) it might bring the greatest good to kill.

Rule-utilitarians. For a rule-utilitarian there are no justifiable exceptions to a good rule. If the keeping of the rule generally brings good results, then that is sufficient grounds for *always* keeping the rule. The anticipated results of an action are used to justify the rule. Hence, the rule as such must always be followed, even if in specific cases it may seem to be good to break it. For instance, the rule that the governed must pay taxes is a good one. Breaking it would bring bad results to most, since there would be no way to support the government. Without government, chaos would result for all. Hence, according to rule-utilitarians, even if the government is using part of our tax money for a bad purpose (say, to support an unjust war), it is still best to pay taxes. For tax paying *as a rule* brings good results, and failure to support the rule would bring bad results.

In short, since keeping of certain rules brings good results and breaking of these rules brings bad results, one should *always* keep these good rules. Of course, if a rule brings bad results, then one is justified in discarding the rule. But one is never justified in making exceptions to rules that bring good results.

The Justification of Utilitarianism

Although it is obviously not self-evident to many, some believe that utilitarianism is a self-evident position. Others attempt to justify the view by saying that the utilitarian approach brings good results; but this begs the question in favor of utilitarianism (judging truth by results). Still others believe that utilitarianism is simply putting "meat" on what is meant by *justice*. Justice, they say, is simply the proper distribution of good due to others.

In other words, the utilitarians sometimes claim to be fulfilling the Golden Rule, but modify "love your neighbor" to "love your neighbor*s*." For unless one uses the plural, he may be both provincial and selfish in the exercise of love. He may conclude what the Pharisees had come to believe, namely, that if one only love his neighbor, then he need not love those who are not his neighbors. In fact, some carried this one (illogical) step further and concluded that since they did not have to love those who were not their neighbors, then they could hate them. This is why Jesus said, "You have heard that it was said, 'You shall love your neighbor and hate your enemy.' But I say to you, Love your enemies . . ." (Matt. 5:43, 44). A proper concept of justice would overcome the Pharisees' kind of fallacious reasoning. It would, the utilitarian claims, involve bringing the greatest good to the greatest number of people.

Criticism of Deontological Ethics

One reason given for accepting a utilitarian ethic is the perceived inadequacies of the deontological approach. Several criticisms have been offered against the simple duty ethic.

First, it may be argued that the failure to consider the results of our decisions is unloving, if not at times inhumane. The Pharisees felt they were doing their duty by not helping people in need on the Sabbath, but Jesus criticized them for this (Mark 3:1f.). Further, blind duty can be worse than no sense of duty. Because of blind duty men have committed horrible crimes—even suicide—at their cult leader's command.

Second, the deontological ethic is often nearsighted. At best it appears to be concerned only about immediate consequences of actions, not long-range results. If one is not concerned with long-range results, then why buy life insurance or submit to polio inoculation? However, wisdom dictates that one must be concerned about the future (Prov. 30:24, 25).

Third, a simple duty ethic as such is often too individualistic and often fails in its concern for the wider community of mankind. In its preoccupation with the neighbor nearby, it often forgets about the needy far away.

Fourth, the duty ethic has been charged with inconsistency, for it too is concerned with results of actions—immediate results. Indeed, there seems to be no way to separate an action from its immediate results. For instance, the *act* of killing is inseparable from the *result* of someone being killed. Likewise, the *act* of stealing is inseparable from the *result* that something is stolen. Hence, even deontological ethics is concerned about results of actions—immediate ones. The problem is, where do immediate consequences end and long-range ones begin?

The Relation of Right and Result

An examination of these views seems to show that both rules and results play an important part in a comprehensive ethical scheme. It is neither rules nor results; rather, it is both.

Critique of Purely Utilitarian Ethics

Although the utilitarians surely score points in their critique of the deontological view, nonetheless, their position is not without some serious drawbacks of its own. Several of them are noted below.

First of all, strictly speaking, only God can be a utilitarian, since only an omniscient Being can possibly know the long-range results of human actions. No mere mortal can predict the distant future with sufficient accuracy to form the basis for determining what the right rules are. But if only God can be a utilitarian, then it is a defunct ethic for us.

Second, what if the utilitarian claims that God bases the ethical rules on what He perceives to be the greatest good in the long run? Would this not still be a utilitarian ethic, albeit a theistic kind, where the rules were determined (by God) on the basis of the foreseen results? The answer would, of course, be yes. But an opponent could simply respond by claiming that this then is actually a deontological kind of ethic after all because God commands it. For in this case, as far as man is concerned, man's duty is simply to obey the rule; it is God's obligation to foresee that keeping these rules will bring the best results. So in this event, men are not making up the rules on the basis of calculating results. This ethic would be a rule-centered duty ethic of divine command.

A third problem emerges from the foregoing point. No matter who—man or God—determines what rule is right (based on the foreseen results), there must be some concept of what is intrinsically right apart from the results. Otherwise, there would be no way to know whether the results are good or bad. Obtaining *desired* results is not sufficient, for what is desired may in fact be evil. One might, for instance, by genetic engineering produce a superman. But simply because a superman is a desired result does not make either the process or the product morally good. The product could be good and the process evil, as in the case of a baby born as a result of rape. Or, both process and product could be evil, as many believe an artificially engineered "human" being would be. Perhaps man should not play God and attempt to control the creative process to produce his own product. Even if the product were genetically superior, it might be morally inferior. The "super human" may turn out to be the "super anti-human." Whatever the case, there may be, as many Christians claim, a good ethical reason (God's sovereign control over creation) not to tamper with the creative process. Simply because something *can* be done does not mean it *ought* to be done. The U.S.S.R. and the U.S.A. have enough nuclear weapons to completely obliterate mankind. This does not mean they ought to do so.

The point, then, is this—even desired results must be measured by what is good. But if the results are not themselves good but are measured by it, then results as such cannot be used to determine what is right. And even in the case of theistic utilitarianism (where God determines the rules by the results), God, also, must know some intrinsic or ultimate value by which He determines that the results are good rather than bad. This intrinsic value must be inside His own nature rather than outside; otherwise there would be some ultimate beyond God. In brief, even the theistic version of utilitarianism reduces to a deontological duty to be God-like. It is, in the final analysis, a rule-centered duty geared toward emulating the ultimate good (God).

Relating Rule and Result

From the discussion thus far we can see that there is a need for both deontology and teleology, both rule and result, in a comprehensive ethical position. But just how do the two relate? What is the distinctive role of each? Or, to put the question differently, if there must be an ultimate intrinsic value (rule) in the universe upon which moral duty is based, then how does the concern for results—short-range or long-range—relate to this rule?

The wrong use of results. The teleological system of ethics, as such, misuses results. The proper use of results will be discussed below, but first we must point out the misuse of results in an ethical system.

First, and foremost, the anticipated results should not be used to *determine* what is right. For the Christian, the character of God determines what is right. It is our obligation to keep the rules about right; it is God's task to assure that our obedience brings about the best results. God provides the principles and we trust His providence to bring about the final product.

Second, anticipated results should not be the *basis* of an ethical action. The basis should be what is known to be intrinsically good. For the Christian, this basis is the character of God as revealed in Scripture. One may act *with a view* to bringing about the greatest good for the greatest number, but should not act simply *because* these results will probably follow from this activity.

Third, the results do not *make* an act good. Goodness is not conferred by consequence, but is inherent in the value represented by the command. An act of well-intended bravery or benevolence is good in and of itself, whether or not it brings desired results. At best the consequences only manifest the good of an act; they do not make the act good.

Fourth, the consideration of long-range results is not helpful for most ethical acts. Since we cannot really know what the long-range results will be, we must content ourselves with the short-range results. That is, the most that can be gained from contemplating results would be from results that can be *foreseen*. There is no immediate value whatsoever to results that cannot be predicted with some measure of success.

Fifth, results ought never lead us to formulate, change, or break rules known to be based on intrinsic value. For instance, the long-range genetic results of mercy-killing deformed persons may be very good in some respects. However, in this sense the end (a genetically more perfect world) does not thereby justify the means (violating human right to life). It is never right to break a good rule simply to obtain a good result.

Sixth, there is also the issue of *justice* in the distribution of goods. If we are concerned simply with the maximal increase of goods, then we could easily distribute them unfairly by taking away from the deserving and giving to the undeserving.

The right use of results.   Despite the misuse of results by complete utilitarians, there is a proper use of results in connection with a Christian (deontological) ethic. The following suggestions will serve to illustrate the right use of results.

First of all, simply because results do not determine what is right does not mean they should be ignored in *considering* what is the right thing to do. If neither of two courses of action violate any moral duty, and if one of them is reasonably calculated to bring about a greater good, then at least it is not wrong to do the latter. Indeed, doing one's best or maximizing the good at hand may itself be viewed as a moral obligation. In this case, then, *not* to facilitate the achievement of the greatest anticipated future good would be a violation of one's present duty.

Second, action directed toward achieving the greatest good must always be *within* the bounds of intrinsic ethical norms, but never beyond them or against them. For example, most would agree that it is right to inoculate the masses in order to bring about the greatest good of better health; for inoculation as such (at least with informed consent) does not break any moral law. However, forced sterilization for the purpose of population control would seem to go beyond and against the moral principles of freedom and dignity.

Third, as has been already pointed out, in one sense all ethical decisions are made, or ought to be made, with *immediate* results in view. Doctors make such decisions regularly. "What will the probable prognosis be, and what should I do to prevent further harm to this body?" is the continual question before the physician, and rightly so. Indeed, anticipated results are a part of everyday life. "Shall I go to this school? Shall I take that job? Shall I go outside with a sore throat?" and the like, are questions continually before us. Virtually everything we do should be done with a view to bringing the best results possible (within the bounds of our ethical duties). The Christian, however, should by and large be content with acting for short-range results. Since we do not know the future, we should leave the long range to God who does.

Fourth, anticipated results should sometimes be used in a Christian ethic to help determine *which* ethical norm to apply. That is, God determines *what* is right, but circumstances (both present and anticipated) play a role in helping us to discover *which* of God's rules should be applied. For example, whether one has the right to kill in self-defense (see Exod. 22) will be discovered by anticipating whether his life is actually being threatened or not. The anticipated results, however, do not determine the rule regarding self-defense; they simply help one to discover whether that rule applies to the situation at hand or whether another rule does. If the person breaking into one's house, for example, is an unarmed thief not threatening anyone's life, then the killing-in-self-defense rule does *not* apply. But this can only be known by anticipating results, by asking, "Is this thief a danger to my life or not?"

Fifth, results do not make a thing right, but they do often *manifest* what is right. Jesus did say, "You will know them by their fruits" (Matt. 7:20). In other words, good results do not prove the action good, but we may reasonably presume as Christians that following good rules will bring good results. Indeed, the Scriptures say that the command to honor one's parents is accompanied with the promise of good results, "that it may be well with you and that you may live long on the earth" (Eph. 6:3). So right action will bring right results, at least in the long run. But good results are no assurance that the action was right, since God sometimes blesses us in spite of ourselves and He is able to bring good out of evil (Gen. 50:20; Rom. 8:28).

Conclusion

There are two basic approaches to ethics. Deontological ethics is duty-centered in rules. Teleological ethics is end-centered in results. These two aspects are not mutually exclusive; a comprehensive ethic will include both. The rules are not determined by the results, but one should have results in view when decisions are made. Indeed, one of the rules of a duty ethic is to try to maximize the good or bring about the greatest good. The Christian should be concerned with both. He believes that if we keep the rules God has given as our duty, then God will bring about the greatest good in the long run. And in the short run, whenever we can produce a greater good without violating an ethical norm, we should act accordingly.

Suggested Readings

Aristotle. *Nicomachean Ethics*
Fletcher, Joseph. *Situation Ethics: The New Morality*
Kant, Immanuel. *The Critique of Pure Reason*
Lewis, C. S. *The Abolition of Man*
Sartre, Jean-Paul. *Existentialism and Humanism*

26   Is the Right Universal?

One of the persistent problems in ethical theory is the question of the universality of ethical principles. Many people hold that all ethical principles have only a local or general application. Some argue for total relativity. Traditionally, the Judeo-Christian tradition has insisted that the basic moral law of God is universally binding on all men. Our approach in this chapter will be to examine first the two opposing views and then to discuss a unified and comprehensive alternative.

Is the Right Relative?

Since ancient times there have been astute observers of the world who have noted the constant change in things. Some have gone so far as to say that "nothing is constant but change" or "the only thing that

does not change is change itself.'' If this concept were applied to
ethics, it would mean ethical relativism. Many philosophers have contributed to this belief, although not all of them were total relativists
themselves. Nevertheless, these men did lay down principles which
have been used by some to defend ethical relativism.

Relativism in the Ancient World

Three movements in the ancient world may each be singled out for
their influence on ethical relativism: processism, hedonism, and skepticism.

Processism. "No man steps into the same river twice,'' said
Heraclitus, "for fresh waters are ever upon him.'' Everything in the
world is in a continual state of flux. Later, Cratylus carried this flux
philosophy so far that he believed no one could step into the same river
even once. The river—and everything else—has no "sameness" or
unchanging essence to it. So completely did Cratylus believe that all is
flux that he was not even sure of his own existence. Needless to say, if
this process philosophy is correct, then there are no unchanging absolutes, ethical or otherwise.

There are two points that should be made in evaluation of this
position. First, it is important to note that Heraclitus was not a total
relativist. He believed that there is an unchanging *logos* beneath all
change and by which the change itself is measured. Heraclitus believed
that all men should live by this absolute law in the midst of the flux of
life. Second, Cratylus carried change so far that he destroyed the idea
of change itself. When *everything* is changing and nothing is constant,
then there is no way to measure the change. But when change is
destroyed, one returns to the unchanging. Total change is an inconsistent, self-destructive concept.

Hedonism. The Epicureans gave impetus to a relativistic ethic by
making pleasure the essence of good and pain the essence of evil.
Pleasures are relative to individuals and their taste. A roller coaster ride
is pleasure for some and sheer agony for others. If, then, the good is
the pleasurable and pleasure is relative, then what is good is relative to
the time, place, and tastes of particular persons. What is morally good
for one may be evil for another, and vice versa.

The objections to hedonism fall into several categories. First, not all pleasures are good. Sadistic pleasure gotten from cruelty is evil. Second, not all pain is bad. The pain in one's side that warns of an infected appendix is, in the long run, a good pain. Further, it is a category mistake to confuse tastes and values. Tastes may be largely (or even entirely) relative, but basic values are not. Tastes are things persons *have,* and these vary depending on the circumstances. But values are something that persons *are,* and persons are still persons no matter what the circumstances. Thus, all values are not totally relative.

Skepticism. The central dictum of skepticism is, "Suspend judgment on everything." The skeptic argues that all issues have two sides, and they can be argued to a stalemate. Since we cannot come to any firm and final conclusions on anything, the wise man simply doubts all things. He refuses to come to any definite conclusions. Applied to ethics, this would mean one must not accept anything as absolutely or universally right or wrong.

The problems with skepticism are numerous. First of all, the skeptic is in fact dogmatic. He is not willing to suspend judgment on his skepticism. Why not doubt whether one should be doubting some values (such as justice for all)? Second, some things ought not be doubted. Why should someone doubt something he has good reason to believe? And if ethical principles are in some sense intuited or self-evident (see chap. 24), then why should we doubt what seems obviously true unless there is some good reason to do so? Further, ethics has to do with the way we live, and the skeptic cannot live skepticism. He cannot suspend all judgment on whether he should eat. And if he is married, he dare not suspend judgment on whether he should love his wife. In short, there is no reason that one should allow skepticism to lead him to total relativism.

Relativism in the Middle Ages

Since the medieval period was dominated by a Christian point of view, one would not expect to see much relativism. There were, however, Christian writers whose philosophy contributed to ethical relativism.

Intentionalism. Peter Abelard (1079–1142) argued that an act is right if it is done with good intentions and wrong if done with evil intentions. Thus some acts that seem wrong are not. We would not say, for example, that someone who accidentally kills a man is morally culpable. Nor would we morally credit someone who gives money to the poor if we know his motive is to be praised of men. If this is the case, then it would seem that rightness or wrongness is determined solely by the *intention* of the person performing the action. Everything is relative to a person's intentions.

One objection to intentionalism is stated in the truism that "the road to hell is paved with good intentions." Even Hitler had "good" motives for killing the Jews; he wanted to rid the world of what he considered the problem that plagued it (the Jews). Clearly, bad intentions will make an act wrong, but good intentions will not necessarily make an act right. Intention is only one aspect of an ethical action. Another essential aspect is whether the intentions are in accord with what is intrinsically right (namely, a law or divine command).

Voluntarism.   William of Ockham (1300?–1349) insisted that all moral principles are traceable to *God's will,* and that God could have decided otherwise about what is right and what is wrong. If this is so, then whether or not one should love or hate is subject to change. Love could be right today and wrong tomorrow. Everything is relative to God's will, which can change. Many voluntarists take comfort in the fact that they believe God *will not* change His mind on essential ethical norms.

The first difficulty with voluntarism is that it makes God arbitrary and not essentially good. Further, it exalts God's will above His nature and allows it to operate independently of His nature. This is questionable theology at best. Also, voluntarism provides no security that God will not change essential ethical norms. Indeed, it does not even make sense to speak of God not changing "essential" ethical norms, since if they are not based on God's essence or nature, then they are not essential. Finally, an act is not good simply because a sovereign power wills it; it is good only if this power is a *good* power. Hence, tracing what is meant by right to God's will alone is not sufficient; it must be traced to His *good* will, that is, to His will acting in accordance with His good nature.

Nominalism.   Ockham perhaps contributed more to ethical relativism than any other Christian thinker in the Middle Ages. Ockham was a nominalist, and denied that there are universals. Universals, essences, or forms exist only conceptually, but not actually. All reality is radically particular. "Man-ness," for example, is only an abstract concept in our minds. Individual men exist outside our minds, but one will not find man-ness existing anywhere outside a concept in one's mind. It is not difficult to see that if the same reasoning applies to ethical concepts such as goodness or justice, then they, too, exist only in a radically individual instance, but not in any universal way. Thus nominalism entails a radical ethical relativism.

By way of criticism some have argued first that unless there were universal forms of meaning, common to all languages, then one could not translate meaning from one language to another. But universal communication does occur. Hence, there must be some "universals," or a universal basis for meaning. Second, others insist that these universals must apply to *all* the particulars in their respective classes, or they would not be truly universal. In ethical terms this would mean that all individually good acts must somehow partake of goodness, and that goodness is universal or common to all particular goods. Finally, for the Christian the real basis for what is universally right is the nature of God. God is the Absolute Ideal after which we should pattern our lives. Hence, it was doubly inappropriate for Ockham, who was a Christian, to claim there is no universal or essential good.

Relativism in the Modern World

Three relativistic ethical strains will be selected from the modern world to illustrate the growing trend toward relativism.

Utilitarianism. As we discussed in chapter 25, Jeremy Bentham laid down the principle that we should act to bring about the greatest good to the greatest number of people. Of course, the actions that may at the moment bring the greatest good to the most people are not necessarily actions that will be best for all persons at all times. In this sense utilitarianism is relativistic. Some utilitarians frankly admit that there may come a time when it would no longer be best to preserve life. That is, conditions may be such for some (or all) that it would be better not to live. In this case the greatest good would be to promote death.

The first problem with strict utilitarianism as a justification for relativism is that even utilitarianism holds some principles as universally true (for example, one should *always* act to maximize good). Further, utilitarianism implies that the end can justify any means. What if the good end (of genetically purifying the race) demanded that we sterilize (or even kill) all "impure" genetic stock? Would this end justify the means of mercy-killing or forced sterilization? Obviously not. Finally, results alone—even desired results—do not make something good.

Existentialism.   Sören Kierkegaard, the father of existentialism, opened the door to relativism by claiming that a man's highest duty (to God) sometimes transcends all ethical bounds. Kierkegaard believed the moral law which says "thou shalt not kill." However, he also held that when God instructed Abraham to take his son, Isaac, and sacrifice him on the mountain that Abraham had to go beyond the ethical command, in order to obey God's command to sacrifice. There is no reason or justification for such an act, said Kierkegaard. One must simply perform this transcendent duty by "a leap of faith." Other existentialists since Kierkegaard have been even more bold, proclaiming that each man has a right to "do his own thing."

Many criticisms are leveled at existential relativism. First, if everyone literally did "his own thing" it would lead to chaos, which would hinder everyone from doing anything. Second, even freedom needs a context or structure. Absolute freedom (of two or more persons) is impossible. If one man freely chooses to do to another man what that man freely rejects, there will be conflict. Law is intended to structure freedom to maximize one individual's rights without minimizing the rights of another. Third, unless there is some moral justification for an act, one is morally unjustified in performing it. No action escapes the ethical first principle of justice, just as no thought escapes the law of non-contradiction. Both thoughts and actions are governed by first principles. And he who breaks first principles will in the end be broken by them.

Evolutionism.   In the wake of Darwin, men like Herbert Spencer (1820–1903) extended evolution into a theory of cosmic development. Others, such as Thomas Huxley (1825–1895) and his grandson, Julian Huxley (1887–1975), worked out an evolutionary ethic. It is ancient processism viewed in evolutionary terms. The central tenet of evolutionary ethics is that right is what aids the evolutionary development of mankind; wrong is what hinders it.

Julian Huxley laid down three principles of evolutionary ethics: (1)

it is right to realize ever new possibilities in evolution; (2) it is right to respect human individuality and to encourage its fullest development; and (3) it is right to construct a mechanism for further social evolution. (Huxley does not say what to do when 1 or 3 conflicts with 2.) Such an ethic is obviously relativistic, since different mechanisms will aid or hinder the evolutionary process at different times. Hence, right or wrong will be relative to man's stage of development.

The objections to this follow the same lines as objections to process and utilitarian views. First, who decides what the ultimate goal is? "Development" in which direction and in what way—biologically, culturally, or politically? Further, how do we know that desired "development" is actually *good* development? Indeed, one can also develop or progress in evil. Finally, who decides what will "help or hinder" the progress and on what grounds? One must assume some standard outside the evolutionary process by which to judge, otherwise there is no way to know whether the project as a whole is getting *better* or is simply different from a previous stage. Since no one "stage" in the process is considered final, there must be a standard beyond it by which the stages are judged to be relatively good or bad.

Relativism in the Contemporary World

Several movements stand out in contemporary ethical relativism: emotivism, subjectivism, and situationism. In their extreme forms, all of these are antinomian.

Emotivism. A. J. Ayer argued that all ethical statements are emotive. "Thou shalt not . . . " really means "I *feel* it is wrong" or "I dislike it." Ethics is not prescriptive; it is simply *emotive*. Ethical pronouncements are simply an ejaculation of our subjective feelings and not divine imperatives about moral duty. Clearly this is a radical relativism, since on this basis everything would be relative to the vastly different feelings of different individuals.

The first difficulty with this view against moral prescriptions is that it is itself prescriptive. It *legislates* what must be meant by "ought not" statements and insists they must be reduced to "I dislike" statements. Rather than legislate what sentences must mean, it should *listen* to what they do mean. Would it not be better to admit that when one says, "Men ought not to be racists," he really means that men *ought not* be racists? Second, it has been observed that even emotivists do not actually believe all is relative; emotivists assume Hitler *ought not* have attempted genocide. They are not content to say "I feel Hitler was wrong, but you may feel that he was right." Finally, a man who says he believes all is relative to feelings does not react that way, at least not when he is the victim of an injustice. If an emotivist were cheated, robbed, or assaulted, his *reaction* would indicate what he really believed about these activities.

Subjectivism.   Jean-Paul Sartre's atheistic existentialism involves a form of radical subjectivism in ethics. He believes that there is no objective meaning or value to life: "Man is a useless passion," he says. He also writes, "There was nothing left in heaven, no right or wrong, nor anyone to give me orders. . . . I am doomed to have no other law but mine. . . . For I . . . am a man, and every man must find his own way."[1] Man is absolutely free and everything is relative to what the individual wills to do. We create our own values. There are no objective values to be discovered; all values are made subjectively by those who will them. Instead of a divine voluntarism (as in William of Ockham), Sartre has asserted a radically individual and human voluntarism.

It is important to observe, first, that Sartre begins with a radical dichotomy of the subject and object. The basic reason that value cannot be objective is that a subject is not an object, and vice versa. According to Sartre, subject is subject, object is object, and never the twain shall meet. But this dichotomy is highly questionable at best. The Christian view of man declares that man is the subject who has objective value. Second, Sartre would be inconsistent if he did not recognize that human freedom has objective value. For it is not only Sartre who is free, but all other persons are free, too. But if *all* are free—not only one man himself, but also all who exist *outside* him—then this would mean that freedom is an *objective* reality. For that is what is meant by "objective," namely, a reality independent of and outside of one's self (a subject). Finally, Sartre's position is actually antinomian, and as such is subject to the criticism of that position to be given below.

---

1. Jean-Paul Sartre, "The Flies," in *No Exit and Three Other Plays* (New York: Collier-Macmillan, 1966), pp. 121–23.

Situationism. Joseph Fletcher's situation ethics exemplifies the relativistic position. Everything is relative to the situation, says Fletcher. We should avoid "like the plague" absolute words such as *never, always, no,* and *only.* Even the Ten Commandments are only generally true, for there are exceptions to each command. In certain situations it is right to lie, steal, commit adultery, kill, and even blaspheme God. The only thing that is absolute is love—but one cannot know what love means in advance of the situation. Love's decisions are made situationally, not prescriptively. Fletcher boldly proclaims that the end justifies the means. Hence, the end of getting out of prison to be with one's family, says Fletcher, would justify committing adultery with the guard, if pregnancy were the only way to be released. Likewise, the end of saving one's wife's life would justify the means of blaspheming God, and so on. In short, the situation determines what is right and what is wrong.

Perhaps the first and foremost criticism of situationism is that it reduces to antinomianism, for one contentless absolute (love) is the same as no absolute at all. Commanding "love" in every situation without being able to define what love means is like considering *any* answer a student feels is "best in the situation" to be the right answer on the exam. Further, Fletcher's view is plainly inconsistent when spelled out in straightforward English. To "avoid words such as 'never' and 'always' like the plague" really translates as, "One should never use the word 'never.'" Or worse yet, it implies that "it is absolutely necessary to avoid all absolutes." But if one does not avoid universal statements in warning about universal statements, then he has defeated his own project. Finally, Fletcher does not heed his own warning, for even in specific matters Fletcher uses universal language. On abortion he wrote, "*No* unwanted baby should *ever* be born" (emphasis added). Absolutes seem to be unavoidable.

Total Relativism Is Antinomian

Few persons claim to be antinomian, but many actually are. As we discussed earlier, an antinomian is one who does not believe there are any ethical laws (and/or who is actually against them). A. J. Ayer's and Jean-Paul Sartre's views are at root antinomian. Fletcher listed the early Christian gnostics as antinomian, since they believed they had some intuitive insight into reality that went beyond all law.

Friedrich Nietzsche (1844-1900) is a good example of an anti-nomian thinker because he said, "God is dead," and claimed that all objective value died with Him. He asserted that we must go "beyond good and evil" (the title of one of his books). He called himself "the first immoralist" who questioned even the most general of moral principles, such as, "injure no man." Most emphatically did Nietzsche reject the traditional "soft" Christian virtues. He would replace them with the "hard" virtues of the "superman." But these virtues, he said, are not discovered; they are *created* by men with their "will-to-power."

There are several points of criticism to be made about complete relativity in ethics. First, one cannot absolutely deny all absolutes without having an absolute of his own. It is inconsistent to claim that it is absolutely true that there are no absolutes. Second, not everything can be in a state of constant and complete change. Change must be measured by what is not part of the change, otherwise one would not know any change occurred. But what is not part of the changing world must be unchanging. Hence, change entails an absolute. Third, everyone seems to have an "absolute" or "ultimate" in his system. As Paul Tillich observed, everyone has an ultimate commitment, an unconditional center of his life. Without this center he would not be a person. Sartre's absolute was "freedom." Nietzsche's was "will-to-power," or later, willing "eternal recurrence" of the same state of affairs. John Dewey denied all absolutes, but made "progress" his absolute.

All one needs to do is discover what a man is unconditionally committed to, or passionately interested in—that is his ultimate or absolute. However, it is *his* ultimate, and he treats it as such. Finally, every person expects to be treated as a person. The proof that he really believes there are some unconditional values is that he *expects* his freedom and dignity to be respected. In his actions he may not always respect others, but in his *reactions* he proves that he always expects others to respect his freedom and dignity.

Is the Right Universal?

If the right is not always relative and individual, then it must sometimes be universal. Our question here, then, is not whether there is universal right, but rather *what* is universally right or wrong.

Meaning of Right

We have already discussed what is meant by right (chap. 24). It is an intuited value not definable in terms of something else. It is something that "ought" to be followed in one's intentions and actions. For the Christian, the content of right comes both in the natural law (known by examining human expectations) and in supernatural law (known by divine revelation in Scripture). For example, persons have a right to be loved, to be treated justly, to be told the truth, and so on.

What Is the Meaning of Universal?

By a *universal* right is meant a duty that is binding on *all men at all times and in all places*. There are two main ways of grounding universal obligations. One is the rule-utilitarian approach (see chap. 25) and the other the deontological approach.

Rule-utilitarian universal rights. According to the rule-utilitarian view, the *obligation* is universal but the act is not necessarily an intrinsic and universal value. For example, one should always pay taxes, since paying taxes *as a rule* brings better results or brings a better society than not paying taxes. The results justify keeping the rule. However, this in no way means that there is some intrinsic and absolute value in paying taxes. Indeed, there may come a day when tax paying will no longer bring better results, in which case the rule must be discarded. So, technically speaking, rule-utilitarianism rules are not representative of acts that have intrinsic and universal value. They simply represent what seems to be the kind of rules that would be productive of better societies.

Deontological universal rights. According to the deontological view, duty is based on intrinsic value. *Universal* duty, then, would mean an intrinsic value that is binding on all men everywhere and always. This would mean that only those ethical norms that are based on a never-changing good could be considered universal in the ultimate sense. For the Christian this means a universal right is one that is based on the essence or character of God. The Bible declares that among other things God is truth (Heb. 6:18), love (I John 4:16), holy (Lev. 11:45), and just (Zeph. 3:5). Hence, these are universally binding on us. There are no exceptions to these. They are always our ethical duty.

There are other things that are binding in a more limited sense. These are based on the will of God for a particular people and/or time. The ceremonial laws of the Old Testament (such as offering sacrifices or undergoing circumcision) fit into this category. These were universal in the sense that they were binding on all Israelites in all places, but only for the period of time designated by God. There are other biblical examples. Men were not under obligation to obey civil governments until after the flood (Gen. 9:6). And if "all time" is taken to include heaven, then perhaps the vows of marriage will not be binding in eternity (Matt. 22:30).

Some Qualifications of Universal Right

There are some qualifications on the concept of "universal" as applied to ethics. These will help explain some difficulties that arise in conflict situations (to be discussed in chap. 27).

Universal duty and a particular course of action.   A truly universal *duty* does not always imply that a specific course of action should follow from it. There is a universal *duty* not to intentionally kill another human, but sometimes it may be necessary to do so in order to save one's own life (Exod. 22:2f.). There is also a universal duty not to mutilate a human body and yet it is sometimes necessary to amputate in order to save the person's life.

Universal duty and a fallen world.   *Ideally* God designed one husband for one wife, but because this is a fallen world, He allowed polygamy on a limited basis for a certain time (Matt. 19:3f.). *Ideally* God desired the Israelites to keep the Passover on the same day and month they were delivered from Egypt, but because some were ceremonially unclean on this day (due to conditions of this fallen world), God prescribed another day, a month later (Num. 9:10–11). Also, *ideally,* one should always return his neighbor's property on demand, but when the neighbor is asking for his gun back so that he can kill his wife, then this is another matter.

Universal "what" and situational "which."   The situation never determines *what* is right for the Christian; God determines what is right. However, the situation often helps us discover *which* of God's laws should be applied. For example, the facts of the situation are necessary for a jury to discover which ethical law to follow: the one that says release the innocent, or the one that says punish the guilty. The jury does not determine *what* is morally right, but it does decide *which* moral law applies.

Conflict of moral duties. The most pressing problem is that of conflict of moral duties. What should one do when two or more moral principles come into unavoidable conflict? This will be the subject of the next chapter. We note here that some sort of qualification of what is meant by a universal duty would be necessary if two moral principles come into conflict; it goes without saying that something has to "give." One cannot *do* opposites simultaneously. For example, suppose one has a choice between lying to protect a life, and telling the truth to show a murderer where his victim is hiding. One cannot lie to save a life and at the same time not lie. But if one does not lie, then he does not do all he can to protect the innocent life. And if he does lie, then he has not kept the command to be truthful at all times. In view of these kinds of conflict some have suggested that the view be called "contextual absolutism." That is, each principle is absolute in its context. The next chapter will discuss this problem in more detail.

Conclusion

We have discussed the question of the relative versus the universal, and have found that the denial of all absolute value is unsuccessful and even inconsistent. For the Christian the universal ethical norms are anchored in the unchanging character of God. By that it is meant that all men are under certain moral obligations, for example, to love and be just, at all times and in all places. Differing situations, however, do help one discover *which* of God's absolutes applies. But the situation as such does not determine *what* our duty is. Furthermore, absolute duty does not always have a one-to-one correspondence with actual courses of action. There are less than ideal circumstances in this fallen world that call for a corresponding adjustment in action aimed at fulfilling universal obligations.

Suggested Readings

Augustine, St. *On Lying*
Fletcher, Joseph. *Situation Ethics: The New Morality*
Geisler, N. L. *Ethics: Alternatives and Issues*
Lewis, C. S. *The Abolition of Man*, appendix
Murray, John. *Principles of Conduct*
Ramsey, Paul. *Deeds and Rules in Christian Ethics*
Thielicke, Helmut. *Theological Ethics*

27   Do Moral Duties Ever Conflict?

Perhaps the most pressing problem in ethics is what to do when moral duties conflict. Among those who believe there are universal moral duties this problem is particularly acute. Basically, there are three positions taken on this issue. The first position denies that the conflicts are real, and the last two claim that the dilemma is solvable. The three views may be labeled: third-alternative, lesser-evil, and greater-good.

The Third-Alternative View

According to the third-alternative position there is always a moral way out of every ethical dilemma. Conflicts are never really unavoidable. They may be painful and apparently real, but never genuinely so.

There is always a "third alternative," or, better, at least one good alternative to the dilemma. Often the good way out will be to choose one of the two alternatives and not the other. On an examination of the alternatives one may find, it is argued, that only one course of action is really his moral duty. The other course of action may be someone else's obligation.

Basic Elements of the View

The third-alternative view is widely held among Christians. The basic tenets of the position will first be discussed and then criticisms will be offered.

Conflicts are only apparent.   There are no conflicts in God nor in His laws, it is insisted. God cannot contradict Himself. God cannot simultaneously command opposite duties. Hence, whatever conflict may appear to be is due to our misunderstanding of what our duty really is. Christians often quote I Corinthians 10:13 in support of this position: "God . . . will not let you be tempted beyond your strength, but with the temptation will also provide the way of escape. . . ." In short, there is always a way out. All alternatives are not evil.

Never lie to save a life.   The paradigm question used to illustrate all these views is, "Should one lie to save a life?" The third-alternative view gives an emphatic, "No, never," to this question. First, there is only *one* duty in the situation, namely truth-telling. Second, the choice is *not* between lying and killing, in this case. Rather, the choice is between lying and allowing *someone else* to kill. But the individual's duty is only to the truth. It is the would-be murderer's problem what he does with that truth.

Never sin to avoid sinning.   Implied in the above answer is the belief that one should never sin (in this case, lie) in order to prevent a sin (murder). Other illustrations are given. For example, a person should never commit suicide in order to avoid being tortured. Neither should a woman lie to or harm (let alone kill) an assailant in order to avoid being raped. This view would, therefore, reject the idea of a so-called preventive attack on a threatening person or country.

Trust the providence of God. Another element in the Christian defense of the third-alternative view is a strong trust in God to deliver one from the moral dilemma. The story of Daniel in the Old Testament is often used as an example. The king of Babylon ordered Daniel and his colleagues to eat and drink food God had forbidden. Daniel asked for a "third alternative," that is, to be fed a different diet. God blessed Daniel and his friends and helped them avoid disobedience to God's laws.

Many Christians claim that if one prays fervently, God will intervene and keep the murderer from finding or killing the victim, even when we tell the truth about his or her whereabouts. These Christians insist God will always (even miraculously) provide a good way out of every situation if we are faithful.

Real dilemmas are of our own making. Sometimes proponents of the third-alternative view will admit that some real moral conflicts exist. For example, a man may be caught in a traffic situation where he must either hit a loaded school bus head-on or a person walking along the road. But the reason for this real dilemma will *always* be that he was not driving carefully. That is, there is always some prior sin that gets one into the real conflict. If we "make our bed, then we must lie in it." But for the faithful—for those who do not sin themselves into difficulties—there is always a sin-free way out. Prior to our sin there was no moral dilemma. For example, the man was not *forced* to drive so fast; he freely chose to drive recklessly and, hence, placed himself in the dilemma.

Evaluation of the Third-Alternative View

Opponents of the third-alternative position point to the following problems.

Naivety toward real conflicts. While it is true that often third alternatives exist that we should explore (Dan. 1), it is also true that sometimes such alternatives do not exist (as in Dan. 3 and 6). We are commanded to obey human government (Titus 3:1), even every human institution (I Peter 2:13), because they are "instituted of God" (Rom. 13:1). However, the government commanded the three Hebrew children to worship an idol (Dan. 3) and required Daniel to pray to the king (Dan. 6). In both cases there was *no* third alternative. The same was true of Pharaoh's command to kill all male babies (Exod. 1). Real conflicts do occur. Jesus even seemed to generate real conflicts by healing on the Sabbath or allowing His disciples to pluck grain on the Sabbath. On one occasion Jesus justified their action by pointing out that David and his men took (stole?) the forbidden bread from the temple to satisfy their hunger (Matt. 12:3, 4).

It does not suffice to say, as some Christians do, that the commands God "approved" of disobeying were only ceremonial or civil, and therefore unimportant, for several reasons. First, they were still divine commands and there is indeed, then, a real conflict between divine commands. Second, if one says it is the greater good to keep the higher command (say, the moral over the civil), then he is admitting to a form of the "greater-good" view (see below). Third, it is questionable whether the so-called ceremonial and civil can be completely divorced from the moral. Surely one would not say there is no moral intent or implication in the command to obey government. Even the Jerusalem Council in the New Testament placed as morally binding on the Christian some commands considered to be "ceremonial" in the Old Testament (Acts 15:6f.). Finally, not all real conflicts are between ceremonial (or civil) and moral laws. Vows are morally binding (Eccles. 5:4, 5). Yet what about Jephthah's vows to sacrifice his daughter (Judg. 11)? Abraham's conflict was between two moral commands ("Thou shalt not kill," versus, "Sacrifice your son"). The fact that Abraham did not kill Isaac does not matter; he *intended* to do so (cf. Heb. 11:19); and intent to sin would be a sin (cf. Matt. 5:28). Also, the dilemma, "Should a doctor save the mother or baby?" is a moral one, as is, "Should one kill in self-defense?"

A tendency to legalism. There is a kind of moral hardening of the arteries in this position. The attitude behind it and the application of it are often reminiscent of the Pharisees in the New Testament. They insisted that the law of the Sabbath be kept at all cost, even if it meant ignoring a person in need. Jesus' response to the Pharisees' legalism may be applied here: "The sabbath was made for man, not man for the sabbath" (Mark 2:27). In like manner, man was not made for moral laws; moral laws were made by God to help man. But the failure of the legalist to transcend the lower laws in order to be merciful and helpful to persons is evident in his doggedness to keep a law at all cost, even at the cost of a human life.

Placing lower over the higher. Jesus spoke of the "weightier matters of the law" (Matt. 23:23) and of "greater love" (John 15:13), and even "greater sin" (John 19:11). It appears that the third-alternative approach neglects this aspect of Christian ethics. For instance, on the question of lying to save a life, the real conflict is not between murder and lying. Rather, it is between showing mercy to the innocent on the one hand, and telling a falsehood to the guilty. In this case, the failure to falsify is thereby a merciless act. Hence, the third-alternative view, by not falsifying, takes the lesser good over the higher. The parallel dilemma described above, where one's neighbor demands his rightful property (a gun) so that he can kill his wife, is really a conflict between higher and lesser good. Mercy to the innocent is a higher law than property rights of the murderer. Likewise, mercy would seem to take precedence over truth. In I Corinthians 8, mercy to the "weak brother" took precedence over the truth, as the "strong brother" understood it, that meat offered to idols was simply an economical meal.

Divine approval of falsification for life-saving. There are numerous cases in Scripture where God (implicitly or explicitly) commended the faith of those involved in intentional deception in order to save lives. Obadiah hid one hundred prophets to save their lives (I Kings 18). Elisha deceived his would-be captors in order to save his life (II Kings 6:18–20). Rahab hid the spies "by faith" (Heb. 11:31) to save their lives. Indeed, the key to the spies' safety was Rahab's outright lie to the men at her door (Josh. 2:5). Finally, the Hebrew midwives both disobeyed government and lied to the king (Exod. 1:19) in order to save the male babies. And in this case, the text says clearly and unequivocally that "God blessed them and gave them families" as a result of what they did. Since all things in the Old Testament are "for us" (Rom. 15:4) and happened "for our example" (I Cor. 10:11), it seems difficult to avoid the conclusion that these were God-approved examples of how He wants us to behave in similar moral conflicts.

Inconsistency in the position. Certain inconsistent practices are often approved by those who hold the third-alternative position. For example, most people leave their lights on when they are away from home for a few days. Some even buy a device to turn the lights (and radio) on and off at certain times, to make it appear as if they are home. But why this intentional deception? The answer: to protect one's property from thieves. Why, then, is intentional deception (lying) wrong to protect innocent persons from murderers? Surely one does not think more of possessions than of persons!

Second, some of those holding this view also approve of abortion in order to save the life of the mother. Others approve of killing in self-defense. In either case, one is actively taking a life in order to save a life. But according to the third-alternative position, "one should never sin (for instance, take a life) in order to avoid sin." In order to be consistent with this premise of the third-alternative position, one must be a total pacifist, and never allow abortion, even to save a mother. But since the Bible permits killing in self-defense (Exod. 22:2), for capital punishment (Gen. 9:6), and in a just war against aggression (Gen. 14), then the third-alternative view must be rejected at this point. In brief, either the major premise of third-alternativism is wrong, or else it is never right to actively take a life (or falsify) for any reasons. But the Bible does sometimes approve of such activities. Therefore, the third-alternative view is incorrect.

Lesser-Evil View

The second view held by those who believe in universal ethical norms is popularly described as the lesser-evil view. According to this position, there are some genuine moral dilemmas in which both alternatives are wrong. One is obligated simply to do the lesser of the two evils, and then confess his sin.

Basic Elements of the View

The essence of this view is to maintain the absolute nature of moral demands even when they conflict, but to "resolve" the problem by choosing the lesser evil.

The reality of moral conflicts.   Not only does the lesser-evil view admit the possibility of moral conflicts, but it generally holds their *unavoidability*. Contrary to the third-alternative view which stresses the *ideal* relationship between ethical obligations (as God designed them), this view is fully aware of the *real* world. This world is not ideal. It is fallen and, as such, men are faced with tragic moral choices.

"Ought" does not imply "can." A premise often held by duty-centered (deontological) ethics is that "ought" implies "can." That is, responsibility implies the ability to respond. The lesser-evil view is the antithesis of this position. As a matter of fact, this is precisely why one can be confronted with a double duty where both alternatives are evil. That is, one ought not lie *and* one ought not allow cruelty to the innocent. Both are moral obligations, and not to do either is wrong.

Absolute nature of universal norms. No one can fault this position for doggedly clinging to the absolute nature of moral absolutes. A "universal" norm means literally and unequivocally that which should always be followed by all persons at all times and in all places. There are no qualifications, exceptions, exemptions, or modifications allowed. In short, a universal norm is not only binding on all, it can never be broken by any without incurring moral guilt.

One's moral duty in conflicts is to choose the lesser evil. There is a way "out" of moral dilemmas. It is to break the law that prohibits the *lesser* evil. This does not mean that there are any moral grounds for breaking a command of God; there are none. The lesser evil is never justifiable as such; it is simply *forgivable*. One's duty, of course, is to do the *lesser* evil, not the greater. And upon doing the least evil possible, one must confess his sin, ask for forgiveness, and place himself at the mercy of a gracious God.

Two ways to understand the lesser evil. There are two basic ways proponents of this view judge what is the lesser evil. Some take a utilitarian approach. That is, they simply ask which course of action will bring about the greatest good to the greatest number. Others see a kind of hierarchy of ethical norms and believe that one should always keep the higher law and break the lower one. For instance, if mercy is a higher moral law than truth, then one should break the law of truth-telling (that is, one should lie) in order to keep the law of mercy (that is, lifesaving). Christians who hold this view appeal to Scripture for a knowledge of what is higher. For example, Peter said one's duty to God is higher than his duty to man (Acts 5:29).

Evaluation of the Lesser-Evil View

There are four criticisms that can be offered of the lesser-evil view as presented above. The first critique has to do with the two different ways of determining what is the lesser evil.

It reduces either to utilitarianism or a greater-good view.   If the lesser evil is determined by what will bring the greater good in the long run, then at this point the position collapses into utilitarianism and is subject to all the criticisms of that position (see chap. 25). Further, if it is utilitarian, then strictly speaking it is no longer a deontological view, which Christian ethics claims to be. In short, it would seem that the lesser-evil view admits that there are not Christian rules to cover *all* ethical situations, for it appeals to long-range results in order to explain conflict situations. If so, then the Christian ethic is not comprehensive; it needs utilitarianism to save it.

If, on the other hand, those who hold the lesser-evil view appeal to the rule to maximize good, then their position reduces to the greater-good view. For if they insist that the obligation to maximize good in every situation is an intrinsic (deontological) duty, then the position ceases to be a lesser-*evil* view. If one is really doing the maximal or greater *good,* then why call it evil and blame him for it? He is doing a good, indeed, the *greatest* good possible in that situation.

This criticism applies to the second position taken by lesser-evil proponents, namely, that one should keep the higher law at hand and not appeal to any anticipated long-range results to justify his actions. But in this case the lesser-evil view clearly becomes a greater-good position; for if the highest ethical good is performed, then why consider one morally *evil* for doing it? The lesser-evil proponent could answer, "Because he has not *also* done the lesser good as well." But in this case he encounters the following problem.

Attributing moral guilt for the personally unavoidable.   In essence, the lesser-evil view blames one for what is unavoidable. It cannot hold that all moral dilemmas are avoidable, for this is the third-alternative view. Thus the lesser-evil view leads to the morally absurd conclusion that God holds a man personally and morally responsible (and guilty) for what he could not avoid. This is far more than saying that "ought" does not imply "can"; it is saying that at times "ought" implies "can*not*"! To be sure, the Christian doctrine of total depravity means that "ought" does not imply a sinner can on his own do what is pleasing to God for his salvation (Eph. 2:8–9; Rom. 4:5; Titus 3:5–7). However, total depravity is compatible with the view that "ought" implies one can, by the grace of God, do what is pleasing to God. And surely total depravity does not mean what seems to be implied in the lesser-evil view that the sin is unavoidable. In fact, I Corinthians 10:13 promises the Christian that sin is always avoidable by God's grace. If this is the case, then to hold that sin is unavoidable is both contrary to Scripture and to reason (for it demands what is *impossible,* namely, performing *both* the higher and lower good where only one can be performed).

Another way to view this same objection is in respect to amputation or killing in self-defense. It would seem that a Christian holding the lesser-evil view would believe: (1) It is wrong to cut a limb off a human body, and (2) it is wrong not to save a human life if possible. But if *both* are wrong, then we are faced with the seemingly absurd conclusion that a Christian doctor sins every time he amputates to save a life. The same logic applies to killing in self-defense, and to abortion performed to save the life of the mother. These, too, would be unavoidable, but wrong nonetheless. This leads to another criticism.

It involves a duty to sin.   Strange as it may seem, the lesser-evil view results in the absurd conclusion that in conflict situations one has a moral duty to sin. But it makes no sense to say one has a *moral* duty to do what is *immoral.* "Moral duty" for a Christian means, "God commands it." If so, then the lesser-evil view reduces to the contradiction, "God commands that one sin in conflict situations." Surely no Christian can actually hold that, for God cannot sin nor can He command others to sin (James 1:13). But what other option is there? The lesser-evil proponent could hold that there is *no moral duty* at all in conflict situations. One can simply decide what to do on social or personal grounds. But this way out of the difficulty causes other grave problems: (1) It would mean that a Christian is left without any guidance in life's most difficult moral situations. The Christian ethic, then, would be incomplete and inadequate to handle *all* of life's situations.

Surely the Christian who believes that the Bible is sufficient for faith and practice, or that Scripture is God-breathed and authoritative for every good work (II Tim. 3:16, 17) should not be content with this conclusion. (2) To say there is no moral duty would mean that the conflicting commands are not actually commands. It would mean that there are no two unavoidable duties, or that unavoidable duties cancel each other and one is left with *no* duty. (3) If there is no moral duty, then there can be no moral wrong done. But if this is the case, then the lesser-evil view is wrong; conflicts do not demand a lesser evil be performed. We have come full circle, and the lesser-evil view falls short no matter which way we go.

A christological problem. For the Christian there is another problem. The Bible says Christ was without sin, and yet He "in every respect has been tempted as we are" (Heb. 4:15). But according to the lesser-evil view one of these must be untrue, for in lesser-evil situations both alternatives involve sin. Since the sinlessness of Christ is clearly and repeatedly taught in the Bible (I John 3:4; II Cor. 5:21; I Peter 1:19), we may assume that the lesser-evil proponent would want to find another explanation for this apparent conflict. Perhaps Christ never faced lesser-evil situations. Beside the fact that this seems contrary to Hebrew 4:15, there are several other problems. First, it throws doubt on the *completeness* of Christ's example; it seems to admit that Christ is not our model in everything. In effect it says that Christ is only our moral example in the "ordinary" situations; in the really difficult ones we must find some other guide. This, of course, is unbiblical. How can Christ be our redeemer unless He faced all our moral situations squarely and victoriously?

Second, there are two explanations given why Christ did not face lesser-evil conflicts. (1) All lesser-evil situations are brought on oneself by prior sins. But, since Jesus never sinned, He never created any dilemma situations for Himself. Or, (2) God providentially spared Christ from these situations in order not to disrupt the redemptive plan which demanded Christ's sinlessness. But if this is the case, then why does not God also providentially spare us, if He wants us to be perfect also? Did God providentially (even miraculously) spare Christ because He was faithful to God, while we are not always spared because we are not always faithful? But if faithfulness to God will bring deliverance from *all* moral dilemmas, then the lesser-evil view collapses into the third-alternative view, which claims that ultimately (for the faithful) there are no real conflicts.

On the other hand, if we assume that all lesser-evil situations are brought on by prior sin, then we must ask, "Whose sin?" But if it is someone else's sin that forced a lesser-evil situation on us, then others' sin could have forced the same situation on Christ, and we are right back where we started, namely, why did not Jesus face such situations? Further, why should we be held guilty for someone else's misdeeds? Do not the Scriptures declare that one person does not bear the guilt for the sin of another, but only for his own sin (Ezek. 18:20)?

This leaves us with one remaining alternative. Perhaps moral conflicts are *always* created by one's own sin; we bring conflicts on ourselves by prior sins. But Jesus never committed prior sins (or any sins), and therefore He never faced any conflicts. The problem with this alternative is that not all conflicts are brought about because of one's own sin. Indeed, sometimes it is just the opposite, namely, it is one's faithfulness to God that precipitates a moral dilemma. This was certainly true of Abraham (Gen. 22), of the Hebrew midwives (Exod. 1), of Rahab (Josh. 2), and of Daniel (Dan. 6). In each case it was their great *faith* in God that got them into trouble.

The christological refutation. One way to refute the Christian lesser-evil view is to give at least one example of a real moral conflict that Christ faced. If Christ faced any real conflicts, then we know they can be faced without sinning. But if one can face real moral conflicts without sinning, then the lesser-evil view is wrong. For according to the lesser-evil view one cannot avoid sinning in conflict situations. Just one example of a real conflict in Christ's life will suffice, then, to refute the lesser-evil view. The following seem to qualify.

First, the law enjoins obedience to parents and yet when Jesus was twelve He intentionally left them and went to the temple (Luke 2:44–45). When His parents found Him, He replied to His mother's worried questions by asking, "Did you not know that I must be in my Father's house?" (v. 49). Second, Jesus and His disciples "broke" the Sabbath on several occasions by plucking grain (Matt. 12:1–8) and healing persons (Matt. 12:9–14), although there may be elements of human tradition here as well as divine command. Third, it is a moral duty at a trial to defend the innocent (Lev. 5:1), yet Jesus did not defend Himself at His trial (Matt. 27:12–14; see Isa. 53:7) when He was inno-

cently condemned. Indeed, the whole question of the cross raises a
serious crisis for the lesser-evil view. How can God be just if He
sacrifices His sinless Son for sinful man?

The Greater-Good View

There are two basic ways to understand "greater good." It could
mean greater good in the future, or greater good right now. It could
mean greater good judged by results, or "greater good" judged by the
higher rule. Since Christian ethics rejects the former (see chap. 25),
this chapter will discuss the latter. "Greater good," then, means obeying the higher law (as revealed by God in Scripture) whenever there is
an unavoidable conflict between two or more divine commands.

The Basic Elements of the Greater-Good View

There are three basic elements to the greater-good position. Taken
together they yield the conclusion that in real moral conflicts no personal guilt is incurred, providing one keeps the highest command of
God.

There are real conflicts.   As has been defended above, real and
personally unavoidable conflicts *do* occur. Both the Bible and human
experience are replete with examples.

One is not culpable for unavoidable moral conflicts.   There is
always a way of escape (I Cor. 10:13). Another way of stating this is
that "ought" does imply that one "can" by the grace of God always
avoid sinning. Jesus did not sin, and we are commanded to do
likewise; we are enabled to do so by God's grace.

There are higher and lower moral laws.   Jesus spoke of "greater
sin" (John 19:11), "greater love" (John 15:13), "greatest commandment" (Matt. 5:19), and "weightier matters" of the law (Matt. 23:23).
Our duty to God is greater than our duty to our neighbor. It is our
God-given duty to obey government (Titus 3:1; Rom. 13:1), and yet
when this conflicts with the command to worship God, we should
"obey God rather than men" (Acts 5:29).

It is always our obligation to do the greatest good. To do less than one's best is sin. We are commanded to be "perfect" (Matt. 5:48). Further, not to do a good we know we can and should do is sin (James 4:17). We are to give of our best to the Master. For the Christian this means following the greatest (highest) command in every situation.

God does not hold us guilty in unavoidable conflict situations. In the real conflict situations recorded in Scripture there is no condemnation of those who did the greater good. In fact, there is either implicit or explicit commendation. Abraham was rewarded for his willingness to sacrifice his son (Heb. 11:17). The Hebrew midwives who lied and disobeyed the king were blessed by God and given families as a reward (Exod. 1:20–21). Likewise, Daniel and the three Hebrew children were commended for their faithfulness to God when they refused to follow the command of government (Dan. 3, 6). Neither does the Scripture hold guilty those who kill in self-defense (Exod. 22:2).

It is true that unavoidable moral conflicts often involve unpleasant activities. But while one may surely *regret* what is necessary to do in order to obey the higher command, surely he need not repent of it. Keeping the higher law is not an evil; it is the greatest *good*. And as such it involves no guilt.

Problems with the Greater-Good View

Although the greater-good view is more adequate than the other two positions, it is not without some problems of its own.

It is really a kind of situationism. Some object that the greater-good view is really a kind of situation ethic, since *depending on the situation* it, too, holds that it is sometimes right to break moral commands. But this is not an accurate appraisal; the situation is not used to *determine* what is right, but only to *discover* which of God's absolute rules applies. Second, the greater-good view does not actually believe in *breaking* any command. Those who hold this view believe that in keeping the higher command God *exempts* them from obedience to the lower, since they cannot do both. In other words, the lower commands are not destroyed, but only overruled by the higher. In view of the unavoidability of the conflict, one gets a sort of ethical "right-of-way" signal from God.

It is actually a form of relativism. In the same line with the above criticism, it is insisted by some that if exceptions can be made to commandments, then they are no longer universals. Once even one exception is admitted, then the absolute nature of the ethic is forsaken.

Two things may be pointed out in response to this. First of all, the greater-good view does not lessen the absoluteness of the duties; moral obligations are *binding* whether one fulfills them or not. Indeed, the very fact that one finds himself in a real ethical *bind* proves that both norms are still *binding*. The difference between the greater-good and lesser-evil views is that the former holds that God releases one from the necessity of fulfilling this lower obligation in view of the un-avoidability of the conflict. The duty still exists; but God does not require it to be performed in this case. In this way there is no exception to the duty made; there is simply an exemption from fulfilling the lower law. Second, there is a sense, then, in which this view is a *qualified absolutism* (which is not really a relativism). As far as the performance of the universal duty is concerned, there are some instances where God does not require it.

How can there be conflicts in God's commands? Some have objected that if there are real conflicts in God's commands, then He is commanding opposites. But unless God is inconsistent, this cannot be so. Therefore, there must be something wrong with the greater-good view.

This difficulty is easily explained by pointing out that *ideally* there is no conflict in God, nor in His character which the commands reflect. It is only because of this finite, sinful world that such conflicts occur. Without sin (not necessarily one's own sin) there would be no real moral conflicts. In view of the finitude and fallenness of this world, God could not achieve the greatest good *desirable;* therefore, it is our divine duty to do the greatest good *possible.*

Who decides what is higher and what is lower? In the greater-good view it would seem that the higher or lower is decided by the individual on very subjective grounds. How do we know what is the higher law and what is the lower? Who decides?

In response to this the Christian simply answers that God decided, and He has revealed it in His Word. The Christian believes that in principle and/or practice there are biblical precedents for every moral conflict we will face. The basic priority of values is as follows: (1) God comes before persons (Matt. 10:37); (2) one's family comes before others (I Tim. 5:8); (3) persons come before things (Mark 8:36). Not all Christians agree on the details of these priorities, but all must seek the Scriptures to discover in every situation what is the "greatest commandment" and which is the "least."

Conclusion

There are three basic positions on the question of the conflicts of rights. The third-alternative view insists that there are no real conflicts. This view we found to be unrealistic, unbiblical, and inconsistent. The lesser-evil view contends that there are some real dilemmas, but in each case both alternatives are evil. This position was found to be incompatible with the life of Christ, and the fact of the cross. It also involved moral absurdities. The only adequate view is some form of greater-good view, according to which God exempts men from obedience to lower commands in view of their overriding duty to the higher one. For the Christian, the Bible reveals which are the higher commands.

Suggested Readings

Augustine, St. *On Lying*
Fletcher, Joseph. *Situation Ethics: The New Morality*
Geisler, N. L. *Ethics: Alternatives and Issues*
Kant, Immanuel. "On the Supposed Right to Tell Lies from Benevolent Motives," in *Critique of Practical Reason*
McCormick, Richard A., and Ramsey, Paul. *Doing Evil to Achieve Good: Moral Choice in Conflict Situations*
Murray, John. *Principles of Conduct*
Thielicke, Helmut. *Theological Ethics*

Glossary

Abstract. That which exists in the mind rather than the external world; the conceptual as opposed to the objective; the general as opposed to the particular.

Absurd. In logic, a contradiction, as in "round square." In existentialism, the impossibility of objective or ultimate meaning.

Accident. A property or quality not essential to a thing.

Ad hoc. Literally, "to this"; pertaining to one case alone.

Ad hominem. Literally, "to the man"; in logic, an attack on or appeal to the personal rather than to reason.

Ad infinitum. Carried on without end; forever.

Aesthetics. The study of beauty.

A fortiori. Literally, "with greater force"; in logic, the argument with the form, "If this is true, then how much more is that true."

Agnosticism. The belief that one cannot, or at least does not, know reality, or especially, God.

Analytic judgment. According to Kant, a proposition whose predicate is deducible from the subject, as in, "All husbands are married men."

Analytic philosophy. A movement in philosophy, primarily in England and North America, which advocates the analysis of language as the heart of philosophy.

Antinomy. A contradiction comprised of a thesis and antithesis.

Apologetics. Literally, "defense"; in philosophy, the discipline of rationally justifying one's beliefs.

A posteriori. From experience, as opposed to a priori.

A priori. Prior to or independent of experience.

Atheism. The world view which claims that no God exists; the universe is all there is.

Atomism. The ancient belief that the universe consists of innumerable tiny, indivisible pellets of realtiy.

Axiology. The study of values, as in ethics, aesthetics, and religion.

Being. That which is or exists; the real.

Cause. The necessary and sufficient condition for an effect.

Coherence theory of justification. In epistemology, the theory that there are no immediately justified beliefs; justification is a relationship among beliefs, none of which is epistemologically prior.

Coherence theory of truth. A test for truth which considers self-consistency determinative.

Contingent. Dependent on another for its existence or function.

Correspondence theory of truth. Definition of truth as that which corresponds to reality.

Cosmological argument. The argument from the contingent, changing world (cosmos) to the existence of God.

Deduction. Arguing from the general to the particular; also a logical argument whose conclusion follows necessarily from one or more premises.

De facto. Actually; as a matter of fact.

Deism. The belief that God created the world and is transcendent; denies that God is immanent in the world, especially in any supernatural way.

Deontology. The ethical view that stresses duty rather than consequences (see *teleology*).

Demiurge. Plato's concept of a creator or god who formed the world (cosmos) out of the chaos.

Determinism. The belief that all events in the universe (including man's actions) are controlled by previous conditions.

Dialectic. Drawing out truth through dialogue that leads to logical conclusions.

Dialectical. A process of thought or of history which by the tension between thesis and antithesis leads to a synthesis.

Dualism. The world view which teaches the existence of two ultimate realities (such as God and evil, or Spirit and matter).

Efficient cause. The agent by which an effect is produced.

Emanation. In pantheism (Plotinus), the flowing of the universe necessarily from God, as rays flow from the sun or radii flow from the center of a circle.

Empirical verifiability principle. In logical positivism, the belief that only those propositions which are verifiable through sense experience are meaningful.

Empiricism. The theory of knowledge which holds that all knowledge begins in sense experience.

Epistemology. Theory of knowledge or how we know.

Equivocation. Use of the same term with two different meanings.

Eschatology. Study of last things (the future).

Essence. Qualities or attributes of a thing which are necessary; its nature.

Essentialism, ethical. The ethical view that God wills moral rules because they are right, and flow from His essence or character (see *voluntarism*).

Ethics. The study of right and wrong, of what one ought to do.

Exemplar cause. The pattern or blueprint after which something is made.

Existentialism. A philosophical movement which stresses that existence is prior to essence; the concrete and individual is over the abstract and universal.

Ex nihilo. The Christian belief that God created the world "out of nothing."

Fallacy. A logical error of inference, relationship, or conclusion.

Fideism. The view that there are no rational ways to justify one's beliefs; faith alone is necessary.

Final cause. The end or goal for which an agent acts; the ultimate.

Finite. Having specific boundaries or limits.

Finite godism. The world view that affirms there is a god but that he is limited in power and/or love (see *theism*).

First principle. Basic axiom or proposition; self-evident assumption.

Formal cause. The structure or form of which something consists.

Foundationalism. In epistemology, the belief that knowledge is based on first principles or immediately justified beliefs.

Gnosticism. Early religious cult which held God is good, matter is evil, and man is saved by knowledge (*gnosis*) of special hidden truths.

Hedonism. The ethical view which claims that pleasure is the greatest good.

Humanism. The belief that man is the highest value in the universe.

Idealism. The philosophy which holds that reality consists of minds and ideas rather than matter.

Identity, principle of. The law of logic which says a thing is identical to itself, that is, A is A.

Identity theory. The belief that mind and matter are manifestations of one reality, matter. This is a sophisticated form of materialism.

Immanent. Indwelling. God's immanence is His presence within the universe (see *transcendent*).

Immortality. The doctrine that man will live forever.

Indeterminism. The belief that at least some events, especially human behavior, are uncaused.

Induction. Arguing from the particular to the general.

Infinite. Without limits or boundaries.

Infinite regress. The belief that causes are infinitely dependent on dependent causes; it is impossible to arrive at a first principle (see).

Instrumental cause. The means or tools through which an agent acts.

Intuitionism. In ethics, the view that in every situation the right action is self-evident.

Logic. The study of valid thinking and argument.

Logical positivism. The philosophy which holds that metaphysical and theological propositions are meaningless unless they are empirically verifiable.

Material cause. The stuff or matter out of which something is made.

Materialism. The belief that all of reality is material, that no spiritual entities such as the soul or God exist.

Metaphysics. The study of being or reality.

Monism. The metaphysical view that all reality is one (see *pluralism*).

Mysticism. The belief that there are states of mind or reality beyond sensation and reason.

Natural law. In ethics, the view that there are innate or natural moral laws known by all men.

Naturalism. The belief that the universe is all there is; everything operates by natural law (without miracles).

Necessary Being. A Being who cannot not exist, whose very essence is existence.

Necessity. That which must be or cannot be other than it is.

Nihilism. The view that there is no value or being in the universe.

Nominalism. The belief that universal forms or ideas exist only conceptually; all that exist in the real world are particulars.

Non-contradiction, law of. A proposition cannot be both true and false at the same time and in the same sense.

Non sequitur. A conclusion that does not follow from the premises.

Noumena. According to Kant, the "thing-in-itself" or real world, as opposed to the world of appearance (see *phenomena*).

Objectivism. The belief that there

are external objects outside mere states of consciousness.

"Ockham's razor." See *parsimony, principle of.*

Ontological argument. The argument devised by Anselm for God's existence which claims that from our idea of God's essence we can conclude God must exist.

Ontology. The study of being; generally synonymous with *metaphysics.*

Panentheism. The world view which holds that "all is in God"; God is to the world as a soul is to a body.

Pantheism. The world view which denies God's transcendence and identifies God with His immanence in the universe.

Parsimony, principle of. The principle of simplicity; one ought not multiply explanations or causes unnecessarily. Also called "Ockham's razor."

Petitio principii. Begging the question or arguing in a circle.

Phenomena. According to Kant, the world of appearance, as opposed to reality (see *noumena*).

Phenomenology. A philosophical movement which attempts to avoid all presuppositions and begin with the pure data of human consciousness.

Pluralism. The metaphysical view that reality is many (see *monism*).

Polytheism. The belief in many gods.

Positivism. The philosophy which repudiates metaphysics and attempts

only a scientific understanding of the world.

Pragmatism. The philosophy which makes practical consequences the criterion for truth.

Proposition. The meaning conveyed by a sentence. Some philosophers claim that a proposition is identical with a sentence.

Rationalism. The epistemological view that stresses reason or rational explanations.

Realism. The philosophy which holds that there is a real external world which can be known.

Relativism. The belief that there are no absolutes.

Skepticism. The belief that one should doubt or suspend judgment on philosophical questions.

Solipsism. Metaphysically, the doctrine that "I alone exist." Epistemologically, the view that one knows only himself, nothing more.

Subjectivism. In ethics, the belief that there are no objective, universal principles of conduct.

Substance. According to Aristotle, the underlying essence; that in which all qualities of a thing inhere.

Sufficient reason. The principle (from Leibniz) that everything must have a rational explanation or cause.

Syllogism. A concise deductive argument, usually consisting of two premises and a conclusion.

Syncretism. The reconciliation or union of conflicting beliefs.

Tabula rasa. Literally, "blank slate." The empirical belief that man is born with no innate or inborn ideas.

Tautology. In logic, a statement that is true by definition, such as, "All triangles have three sides." Hence, an empty statement which affirms nothing about the real world.

Teleological argument. The argument from the design or purposiveness of the world to the existence of a Designer (God).

Teleology. In ethics, the view which stresses the end, result, or consequences of our actions (see *deontology*).

Theism. The world view that affirms the existence of a personal, infinite Creator of the world, who is immanent in the world, unlimited in power and in love.

Transcendent. That which is more than our experience or goes beyond the world. Theists say God is transcendent because He is outside of or beyond nature (see *immanent*).

Universal. The general concept or idea of a thing, as opposed to a particular instance or example.

Univocal. Literally, "of the same voice," or with the same meaning, as opposed to *equivocal*.

Utilitarianism. In ethics, the view that one should act to bring about the greatest good for the greatest number of people.

Veridical. True or accurate.

Voluntarism, ethical. The ethical view that traces moral principles to God's will; something is right because God wills it (see *essentialism*).

Index

435